Understanding the Global Community

Understanding the Global Community

Edited by

ZACH P. MESSITTE and SUZETTE R. GRILLOT

UNIVERSITY OF OKLAHOMA PRESS : NORMAN

Library of Congress Cataloging-in-Publication Data

Understanding the global community / edited by Zach P. Messitte and
Suzette R. Grillot.
   p. cm.
  Includes index.
  ISBN 978-0-8061-4338-5 (hardcover : alk. paper) 1. Economic history—20th
century. 2. Globalization. 3. International relations. I. Messitte, Zach P., 1968–
II. Grillot, Suzette.
  HC59.3.U53 2013
  327—dc23

2012028657

Chapter 3 is reproduced with permission of Oxford University Press from David
Forsythe, *Encyclopedia of Human Rights,* vol. 2 (New York: Oxford University Press,
2009), 443–55.

The paper in this book meets the guidelines for permanence and durability of the
Committee on Production Guidelines for Book Longevity of the Council on Library
Resources, Inc. ∞

1 2 3 4 5 6 7 8 9 10

Contents

Preface   vii
    Zach P. Messitte and Suzette R. Grillot
Acknowledgments   xi

Introduction: Why We Should Understand the Global Community   3
    Zach P. Messitte and Suzette R. Grillot

PART I: GLOBAL ISSUES

1. American Foreign Policy   11
    Zach P. Messitte

2. International Security   39
    Suzette R. Grillot

3. Humanitarian Intervention   66
    Eric A. Heinze

4. The Global Economy   100
    Mark W. Frazier

PART II: REGIONAL PERSPECTIVES

5. China   127
    Peter Hays Gries

6. The European Union   152
    Mitchell P. Smith and Robert Henry Cox

7. Latin America   173
    Alan McPherson

8. The Middle East   196
    Yaron Ayalon

Conclusion   225
    Zach P. Messitte

Glossary   235
List of Contributors   269
Index   273

Preface

ZACH P. MESSITTE and SUZETTE R. GRILLOT

The introductory class that most undergraduates take in the field of international and area studies can be an unwieldy one for both the professor and the student. Given a semester to span the globe and cover history, politics, economics, and culture, a gateway course has the potential to devolve into a global bus tour of sorts: "If today is Tuesday then we must cover the problems of the Middle East in the next seventy-five minutes before we move on to the international phenomenon of Lady Gaga on Thursday." Even the choice of topics in a fifteen-week course is difficult. Critical or strategic areas of the world get the short end of the stick, and a professor must make decisions such as, "Should we cover global health or global environmental issues in the syllabus?"

Despite the challenges of planning and delivering a course on the global community, it can be one of the most important courses in a student's college career and may even have an impact on his or her choice of major or professional development. For many students, the class is the entry point into a college or university's international curriculum. It may be the gateway course a first- or second-year student takes before embarking on an internationally oriented major. For other students, perhaps seeking to fulfill a general education requirement, this introductory course may be the only international class a student will ever take. We would hope that such an experience would be a positive one for the journalism or business student, for example, who is interested in the important global issues of the twenty-first century. There is also a third group of students: those who use an introductory international and area studies course as a test of their interest in the field. Unsure or disappointed with their current majors, some students may come away from a course on the global community turned on to the subject and impressed by the faculty. Often times these students end up taking more courses and find themselves, somewhat unexpectedly, majoring or minoring in international and area studies.

Because international and area studies is a multidisciplinary subject, faculty members are typically historians, political scientists, international legal scholars, economists, anthropologists, linguists, experts on world literature, or foreign language specialists. Given their diversity of training, a faculty member with a background in international human rights might approach the design of a class on the global community very differently than another who has credentials in Chinese politics. There is no specific or mandated way to teach a course on international studies. Instead, professors often capitalize on their own academic strengths. This book, therefore, is also designed to knit together different academic experiences so that the reader can glimpse not only the specialties of our authors, but also their different disciplinary approaches.

However, no matter what the approach to an international and area studies course, the ultimate lesson is that **globalization** has brought about significant changes in our basic way of life and has influenced our daily experiences when we are not even fully aware of it. For example, take the various items that we eat on a daily basis. College students can easily dismiss middle-age college professors who marvel that local grocery stores in the heartland carry hummus, feta cheese, sushi, and enchiladas, but these are recent developments in our globalized world. Thanks to Starbucks Coffee, many Americans can now visit Rome armed with a coffee vocabulary that would have seemed exotic in 1985: *cappuccino, latte, espresso, Americano, venti,* and *macchiato* belong to the world's vocabulary now.

Naturally, the biggest global change for today's college students is in the area of communication. Most of the professors contributing to this book went off to college in the 1980s equipped with typewriters at a time when it was not unheard of for students to turn in term papers written in longhand. There were pay phones in the dorms, and if you wanted to find out whether your favorite basketball team won a late game on the West Coast, you had to wait until the morning newspaper came to your door. Bootlegged cassettes of Bruce Springsteen or the Grateful Dead were how music spread virally. If you were lucky there might be someone who had a VHS player down the hall for occasional movie nights. Using the library for research meant tackling the card catalog or going back through periodicals on microfilm. The fax machine, not long ago a revolutionary method of international communication, now gathers dust in our offices. Of course, all of this has changed in the span of a very short time.

Today's college students are also more internationally mobile than ever. The ability to go online and book a flight is so easy, and comparatively more affordable than in the 1980s, that students spending the semester at a study abroad program in Italy frequently find a $50 fare on Ryan Air and—like that—they can be in Amsterdam for the weekend. The easy access to global travel has made it possible for many international and area studies programs to require that students have a credit-bearing overseas experience in order to graduate.

What do all these political, economic, and social changes mean in a global context? This question lies at the heart of any course on the global community and is the rationale for this book. By making use of international and area studies faculty expertise, we hope to illuminate key international issues for students and people with a general interest in world affairs.

Understanding the Global Community has two primary audiences. First, for college students, this book is a chance for them to go beyond their primary textbooks. We hope that this book will serve as a companion to a more theoretically oriented text. Beyond the classroom, we hope that this book will be of interest to students around the country who are thinking about pursuing a course of study or a career in international affairs and are looking to get a smart, concise handle on broad international topics and regions. The second audience for this book consists of people who have a keen interest in the world and who want a clearer picture of today's key global issues. We challenged our contributing authors to write chapters that speak to a general intellectual audience. In other words, we told them, you have 10,000 words to tell someone about what issue you study and why it is important to a greater understanding of the global community. That said, however, each chapter is certainly not the definitive study on its respective topic, but they each offer students of international studies insight into some of the most pressing global and regional issues on the world stage today.

Acknowledgments

Any project of this undertaking is a team effort. We owe much gratitude to the University of Oklahoma Press—especially Byron Price and Jay Dew—for their willingness to take on this project and their efforts to shepherd the manuscript through the production process. We thank all of our colleagues who have generously contributed their work to this volume. We are exceptionally proud of the top-notch faculty working in the College of International Studies and are privileged to work with them. We simply cannot thank the staff of the College of International Studies enough for their constant support and assistance. We are also very grateful to the many students who provided research assistance for this project. Specifically, we thank Derek King, Matthew Miller, Holly Presnell, Austin Slaymaker, and Olivia Strong.

Understanding the Global Community

Introduction

Why We Should Understand
the Global Community

ZACH P. MESSITTE and SUZETTE R. GRILLOT

Since the end of the Cold War more than two decades ago, the importance of interconnectivity in the world has grown by leaps and bounds. Whether we like it or not, we live in a fast-moving global community that regularly impacts our daily lives and binds us to people living in different hemispheres. The fact is there are fewer and fewer issues that can be addressed solely at the local, state, or national level. Many policy questions, ranging from law enforcement to the environment to **human trafficking**, are inherently global in nature. The former United Nations secretary general Kofi Annan referred to these complex issues as "problems without passports" (Annan 2002). They are transnational issues that touch our societies and our individual lives as global citizens.

It is difficult, for example, to consider a state or national drug control strategy without taking into account that most opium poppy (used in the production of heroin) and coca leaves (needed in the manufacture of cocaine) are grown in the Andean region of South America, in Central Asia, and in the Golden Triangle region of Southeast Asia. These illegal drugs then transit the Caribbean, Central America, and Europe (places as diverse as Mexico, Pakistan, and Jamaica) on their way to the United States—a country that makes up 6 percent of the world's population but consumes about 50 percent of world's illegal drugs. Drug control, therefore, is a classic example of a "problem without a passport," meaning it does not belong to any one nation or territory. Illegal drug producers in one part of the world, transit countries in a second, and the consumer nations in a third all have a role to play in this global problem. Policy makers around the world trying to solve the drug-trafficking problem must, therefore, work together across borders in an effort to develop and implement effective solutions. Similarly, global health pandemics such as **AIDS, H1N1 (swine) flu**, or **tuberculosis** are illnesses that are impossible to contain and, therefore, cross from one continent to another. Without international cooperation, epidemics quickly become pandemics and lives around the world are lost.

Until recently, too many Americans were unaware of the importance of the emerging global community. Protected by the Atlantic and Pacific Oceans, nuclear weapons, and the predominance of English as the common international language of choice, Americans could blissfully (and somewhat naively) weigh whether it was in their best interest to participate in collective security regimes, multilateral actions, and international organizations. Even as recently as the 1990s, there were members of Congress who openly boasted that they did not need a passport because there was not much to learn from other countries. Nor, for example, did the United States need to pay its regular dues to the **United Nations** (UN) if it suited political purposes because foreign affairs consistently ranked near the bottom of the average American voter's priorities, behind jobs, health care, and welfare reforms. Lack of support for UN funding also reflected U.S. Congressional concerns with the UN bureaucracy and the perceived need for the organization to undergo drastic reform (Lewis 1990; Hirschkorn 2005; Lynch 2009).

The events of September 11, 2001, served as a generational wake-up call for many Americans. Not unlike the fall of Saigon to the Communist North Vietnamese on April 30, 1975, and the Japanese bombing of Pearl Harbor on December 7, 1941, September 11 is a defining moment for many in terms of the need for international awareness. This is certainly the case for today's generation of college students as well as for those entering the work force in the past decade. What happened in New York, Washington, D.C., and Pennsylvania on that fateful day left a lasting imprint on the hearts and minds of most Americans. The terrorists who flew the planes into the **World Trade Center** and the **Pentagon** came from Egypt, Saudi Arabia, Lebanon, and the United Arab Emirates. Some of the hijackers, like Mohammad Atta, the ringleader of the group that flew American Airlines Flight 11 into the North Tower of the World Trade Center, were educated in Europe but were later trained at **al-Qaeda** camps in Afghanistan. Other hijackers participated as holy warriors in the Balkan Wars of the 1990s. Americans quickly realized that combating terrorism was a global problem and that it was going to take more than just American military might and the intelligence work of the Federal Bureau of Investigations (FBI) and the Central Intelligence Agency (CIA) to keep the country safe. There was a realization that the country needed more scholars of the Middle East who understood the history, politics, and culture of the region and spoke fluent Arabic, Pashto, and other Middle Eastern languages if they were to stop future attacks. The United States needed help from other countries to seize bank accounts that had helped fund al-Qaeda's network. It also needed information from other diplomats and intelligence officials to preempt whatever al-Qaeda had in mind to do next.

While September 11 may have brought the reality of the global community into American living rooms, others parts of the world had been on the rise for decades. The **BRICS countries** (Brazil, Russia, India, China, and South Africa) emerged in the first part of the twenty-first century as aspiring world powers with geo-economic and political concerns. Beyond even the tectonic shifts of states and global power, there had already been a profound but sometimes more gradual shift that globalization had brought to the United States and many other corners of the planet over the past half century. For example, the parents and grandparents of today's college students did not dress, eat, or communicate anything like your average sophomore in 2011. Most of today's college students are far more global than even their older brothers and sisters. Odds are that today's students do not own a single piece of clothing made within the borders of United States. This situation marks a huge change from the not-so-distant past when Americans manufactured their own shoes, shirts, and pants. Such specialization once again offers evidence in support of Adam Smith's claim in *The Wealth of Nations* that "The tailor does not attempt to make his own shoes but buys them from the shoemaker. The shoemaker does not attempt to make his own clothes but employs the tailor" (Smith 1902, 161–62). In the era of globalization, Americans may import shoes and underwear, but they export airplanes, movies, and financial services. The globalization locomotive has left the proverbial station, and there is no telling where it will eventually end up.

From the spread of instantaneous global communications, the growth in international travel, and the blurring of national borders to the events of 9/11 and the ever-increasing transnational flow of goods, services, money, and labor, there has been growing interest in and concern about international relations and global security. The pivotal role of Facebook and Twitter in bringing people together across North Africa and the Middle East to create the **Arab Spring** uprisings in 2011 is easily understood by the hundreds of millions of people around the world who turn on a computer every day. If these social network tools can be used to organize parties, blood drives, and fundraisers, couldn't they also be used to organize mass protests that might topple autocratic governments? Similarly, it was unremarkable to most young Americans that a Pakistani blogger posted real-time tweets on the Internet as U.S. Navy Seals invaded the secret compound of 9/11 mastermind Osama bin Laden in Abbottabad, Pakistan, in May 2011. Nor was it shocking that within hours of bin Laden's death, people all over the world turned to Google Earth and viewed satellite pictures of his hideout thousands of miles away.

In response to the growing connectivity, governments, international organizations, businesses, **nongovernmental organizations**, world leaders, students, and individuals are engaging with counterparts at home and abroad to better understand the global community in which we all live. This volume is a collection of chapters designed to enhance understanding about the twenty-first-century global community in which we live.

OVERVIEW OF THE BOOK

Following this introduction and prior to the conclusion are eight chapters organized into two parts. Part I focuses on topical issues, such as American foreign policy, international security, humanitarian intervention, and global economics. In chapter 1, Zach Messitte offers a historical view of U.S. foreign relations in light of **idealist** and **realist** perspectives in international relations. The chapter discusses the importance of presidential leadership in world affairs while assessing the impact of September 11, 2001, on U.S. foreign policy. Messitte concludes with a discussion of President Barack Obama's worldview as well as the foreign policy challenges he faces during his time in office.

In chapter 2, Suzette Grillot focuses specifically on the issue of international security relations. The chapter begins with the history of international security as a concern for decision makers and scholars. After reviewing several theories of international security affairs, Grillot discusses contemporary global security issues such as **terrorism**, the spread of weapons of mass destruction, poverty, **development**, **health epidemics**, and **environmental degradation**. The chapter concludes with a range of solutions to global security problems, from international law and organizations to regime change and the promotion of democracy.

Eric Heinze centers on the issue of **humanitarian intervention** in chapter 3 by looking at how the international community understands its role during **genocides**, civil wars, and other conflicts where civilians bear the brunt of the casualties. The chapter discusses the significance of protecting **human rights** and distinguishes it from **human security**. Heinze outlines criteria for intervening in humanitarian cases and concludes with an analysis of the different types of legal foundations for outside intervention, with a specific evaluation of the United States' **Global War on Terror**.

Mark Frazier offers the final chapter in part I, chapter 4, with a focus on the **global financial crisis**. The chapter reviews the history of global financial institutions, such as the **International Monetary Fund** and the **World Bank**, as well as international economic regulatory arrangements, such as the **World Trade Organization**. Frazier also examines the future of these institutions and how they interact with major economic players, such as the United States, the European Union, and China. Ultimately, Frazier argues that economic cooperation and competition go hand in hand.

Part II of this volume focuses on key geographic regions of the world, such as China, the European Union, Latin America, and the Middle East. In chapter 5, Peter Gries covers China's five-thousand-year journey to near-superpower status in the twenty-first century. The chapter begins by outlining the nature of Chinese nationalism in an effort to explain what it means to be Chinese today. Gries concentrates on China's rise as an economic and political power and the reforms the country is undertaking today. China's position as both a regional and a global player is reviewed, and the chapter concludes with a discussion of U.S.-China relations.

Chapter 6 focuses on the **European Union** (EU), with Mitchell Smith and Robert Cox considering the issue of regional integration in light of the EU's experience. Smith and Cox highlight how the EU developed from humble beginnings after World War II by acting as a transcendent organization, leading Europeans to overcome historical, cultural, and political challenges to work together to address common concerns as a model regional organization.

Alan McPherson focuses in chapter 7 on Latin America—a large geographical area that rarely speaks with one voice. The chapter reviews key issues relevant in the region, such as inequality, poverty, immigration, **remittances**, crime, and violence. It also outlines the anti-neoliberal economics movements and discusses the region's relations with the United States from the **Monroe Doctrine** of 1823 to the present. The global impact of large countries, such as Brazil, and smaller but uniquely important countries, such as Cuba and Haiti, are also discussed. In the end, McPherson emphasizes the duality of Latin American interdependence and division as a significant theme.

The last regional chapter, chapter 8, concentrates on the Middle East. In this chapter Yaron Ayalon covers the turmoil and change of the region. His chapter focuses on four important issues: (1) the Arab-Israeli conflict, (2) relations between Iran and Iraq, (3) the role of Turkey, and (3) the significance of **radical Islam**. The historical treatment of the Middle Eastern region offers a rich perspective for understanding the contemporary conflicts and transformations.

The conclusion draws collective lessons from the substantive chapters, including the continued role of states, the power of nationalism, and the importance of history. It also examines what is missing from the book and might be included in a future edition. In the end, the hope is that students will come away with knowledge on four topical issues and four geographic regions that will lead to critical thinking and exploration about the international issues. Along with reference lists for further reading and a glossary of key terms, this volume is meant to contribute to an understanding of the global community, provide the impetus to learn more, and encourage the reader to become an active global citizen.

REFERENCES

Annan, Kofi A. 2005. "Problems without Passports." *Foreign Policy Magazine*, September 1. www.foreignpolicy.com/articles/2002/09/01/problems_with out_pass ports.

Hirschkorn, Phil. 2005. "House Threatens to Withhold U.N. Dues." *CNN.com*,

June 20. http://articles.cnn.com/2005-06-18/us/un.reform_1_withholding
-dues-reform-bill-final-bill?_s=PM:US.

Lewis, Paul. 1990. "Congress to Hold up Part of U.N. Dues." *New York Times,*
April 8. www.nytimes.com/1990/04/08/world/congress-holds-up-part-of
-un-dues.html?src=pm.

Lynch, Mark. 2009. "Pew: American Views on Foreign Policy 2009." *Foreign Policy
Magazine,* December 4. http://lynch.foreignpolicy.com/posts/2009/12/04/
pew_american_views_on_foreign_policy_2009.

Smith, Adam. 1902. *The Wealth of Nations.* New York: P.F. Collier & Son.

Part I
Global Issues

1

American Foreign Policy

ZACH P. MESSITTE

Much ink has been spilled in recent years about whether or not the United States will remain the world's sole **superpower**. The rise of the **BRICS countries** (Brazil, Russia, India, China, and South Africa), American imperial overstretch in the Middle East, and economic and political problems at home have led many observers to question whether or not America's "**unipolar moment**" that began with the fall of the Soviet Union in 1991 is now coming to an end. This chapter examines the broad trends in American foreign policy and looks at the challenges facing President **Barack Obama** and his team of foreign policy advisers. Beginning with an overview of the theoretical currents that underpin American foreign policy, the chapter proceeds to a short history of presidential leadership in shaping America's role in the world. It concludes with a review of the Obama administration's foreign policy and poses some questions about the global challenges facing the United States in the next decade.

IDEALISM AND REALISM IN AMERICAN FOREIGN POLICY

There is a general misperception that the United States had little in the way of foreign policy design before the end of the nineteenth century. Many introductory classes spend very little time examining the country's relations with the world prior to the **Spanish-American War of 1898**. Branding the Republic isolationist, or focusing instead on **manifest destiny** and the rush to populate the continent from coast to coast, simplifies an analysis of the first 125 years of America's relations with the rest of the world. George Washington's famous farewell address that warned his countrymen to stay away from the intrigue of European politics and "avoid **entangling alliances**" is part of a trinity of pre–Civil War pronouncements that guide most students of the discipline. The big questions Washington asked are as relevant today as they were when he was leaving the presidency in 1796. "Why forego the advantages of so peculiar a situation? Why quit our own to stand upon foreign ground? Why, by interweaving our destiny with that of any part of Europe, entangle our peace and prosperity in the toils of European ambition, rivalship, interest, humor or caprice?" (Washington 1796). When Washington's admonitions are matched up with John Quincy Adams's statement in 1821 that America "goes not abroad, in search of monsters to destroy" and the **Monroe Doctrine** of 1823 that warned Europeans from messing around with the Americas, a very real perception emerges that the new nation had bigger issues than foreign policy (i.e., slavery, states' rights, immigration, and industrial expansion) to deal with during the 1800s. There is some truth in this straightforward analysis of American foreign policy; the pre-1945 global reach of America pales by comparison to the past sixty-five years. The American foreign policy tradition, however, and the basic theory that provides its foundations, stretches back much further than the World War II era.

Idealism and **realism** were at the core of the emerging discipline of international relations that came out of the political failure to stop World War I. The two schools of thought have a long tradition in the conduct of American foreign policy that predates the twentieth century and colors the nation's thinking about the world from the beginning of U.S. history (Mead 2002). Idealism and realism helped shape the three great eras that marked American foreign policy prior to the Second World War: **expansionism, imperialism,** and **isolationism.** They also guided the two major periods that followed 1945: **containment** and the still undefined post–Cold War decades of the 1990s and 2000s. For most of the nineteenth century, however, American foreign policy focused on expansionism (the **Louisiana Purchase of 1803,** the **Mexican Cession of 1848,** and the purchase of Alaska following the Civil War). By the later stages of the 1800s, and into the twentieth century, American imperial adventures dominated foreign policy in places as diverse as Cuba, China, and Honduras and on the battlefields of Belgium and France during World War I. Following the **Treaty of Versailles,** the United States, while still professing a more idealist response to world problems, ultimately cocooned itself from Europe's growing political and economic woes. The U.S. Senate never ratified the League of Nations and later made the **Great Depression** even worse by enacting the protectionist **Smoot-Hawley tariff** that led to a severe reduction of U.S. exports and imports and largely ignored the rise of Nazi Germany.

Historically the American foreign policy realists were fundamentally concerned with the power of the United States and how best to advance the security and economic well-being of the country. Leaders such as **Alexander Hamilton** and **Theodore Roosevelt** fall into this category. Financial stability, credit-worthiness, and the health of defense-related industry preoccupied Hamilton from the birth of the Republic (Harper 2004). Teddy Roosevelt's muscular foreign policy ushered in a twentieth century of occasionally brilliant diplomacy, frequent American military involvement, and protection of business interests abroad. The (Theodore) **Roosevelt Corollary** to the

Monroe Doctrine called for American intervention in any Latin American country that had economic troubles in order to preempt European meddling. Theodore Roosevelt also supported the creation of the **great white fleet**, making the U.S. Navy one of the largest and most mobile in the world.

The idealists, on the other hand, emphasized the legal and moral aspects of the world order. They also made an impact on the scope of American foreign policy prior to World War II by calling on the United States "to help make the world safe for democracy" and, by proxy, to buttress **free trade** and **capitalism**. Most famously embodied by **Woodrow Wilson**, the idealists saw the lessons of World War I as a way to "vindicate the principles of peace and justice in the life of the world as against selfish and autocratic power" (Wilson 1917). The idealists initially took the lead after World War I with the creation of the **League of Nations** and put forth impossibly utopian ideas like the **Kellogg-Briand Pact** outlawing war and the **Washington Conference on Disarmament** in the 1920s. These lofty goals testified to an idyllic vision of American foreign policy that had its roots in the nation's missionary spirit to conquer and civilize North America (Turner 1920). By the 1930s, however, the League of Nations had failed, unable to slow global economic depression and the rise of fascist excesses. The idea that pure aspiration could be the basis of American foreign policy was untenable. It gave rise to realism in the way the nation conducted itself abroad. The idea that power was at the center of the international political order was ascendant (Carr 1939).

Following the Allied victory in World War II and the onset of the **Cold War**, the idealists and realists continued to battle each other for supremacy in the push and pull of the second part of the twentieth century. American foreign policy makers faced the conundrum of having to face down the Soviets by containing them, militarily, economically, and culturally, by using both **hard power** (military and economic supremacy) and **soft power** (cultural and ideological influence) (Nye 2004). American foreign policy during the Cold War became ideologically centered. Soviet and Chinese communism were viewed as threatening and expansionist, intent on converting the world to its beliefs. American political leaders preached that foreign policy was part of a fight for the survival of the United States, democracy, and the American way of life (Commager 1983; Almond 1960).

Since the collapse of the **bipolar world** in the early 1990s and the rise of stateless **terrorism**, the realists and idealists in American foreign policy have redrawn the battle lines about how best to ensure the rise of a stable **new world order** (Lake 2000; Krauthammer 1990–1991). Four presidents (George H. W. Bush, Bill Clinton, George W. Bush, and Barack Obama) have grappled with a world in which the ideological threat of the Soviet Union is no longer the North Star of American foreign policy. Realists and idealists, and their **neoconservative** ("neo-cons") and **neo-Wilsonian** offspring, have each laid claim to theoretical supremacy by varying claims to democracy promotion, the preservation of the **liberal economic order,** and the use of the U.S. military to ensure national security by deploying troops to Somalia, Haiti, Bosnia, Kosovo, Iraq, and Afghanistan.

The neo-cons who directed the foreign policy of the Bush administration in the post-9/11 world believed that universal ideals such as human rights and democracy were worthwhile but only if they helped spread American power (Beinart 2010). Following 9/11, the logic of the neo-cons helped to theoretically justify the Iraq War. The Bush-era neo-cons, however, perverted the original intent of the "new" conservatives in foreign policy. While the movement had been building during the 1950s and 60s, neoconservatism gained strength as a reaction to the Vietnam War by emphasizing the need for renewed toughness in American foreign policy. The neo-cons looked at President Jimmy Carter's desire to put human rights at the center of American foreign policy in the 1970s as hopelessly naïve. **Jeane Kirkpatrick,** one of the godmothers of the neo-con movement, wrote in her famous article "Dictatorships and Double Standards" that it was better to collaborate with repressive autocrats like the **shah** of Iran and Nicaragua's **Anastasio Somoza** because they were "friendly to American interests." In other words, better to have the shah and Somoza than to have an Islamic Iran or a Nicaragua ruled by the Soviet-leaning **Sandinistas**. Kirkpatrick, however, also believed that "democratic governments come into being slowly, after extended prior experience with more limited forms of participation during which leaders have reluctantly grown accustomed to tolerating dissent and opposition" (Kirkpatrick 1979). In the hindsight of the Iraq and Afghanistan Wars of the past decade, Kirkpatrick's caveat shows that the original neo-cons weren't so quick to have America in the nation-building game.

The Vietnam War also jolted the neo-Wilsonians, but instead of putting toughness at the center of their thinking they looked toward the concept of **interdependence** as a new guiding force in American foreign policy. No one exemplified this new Wilsonian ideal better than President Jimmy Carter. In his speech at Notre Dame University in 1977, he said that the United States "can no longer separate the traditional issues of war and peace from the new global questions of justice, equity, and human rights." President Carter argued instead for "constructive global involvement" based on human rights, bonds among democracies, arms control, and peace through diplomacy in the Middle East (Carter 1977). Events in Iran, Nicaragua, and Afghanistan in the second part of Carter's presidential term conspired to make his foreign policy ideas look weak and hopelessly idealistic, but the post–Cold War political world order of the 1990s brought back the "new great debate" between the school of thought that advocated exercising caution overseas—which traced its roots back to George Washington—and the globalism school of thought that had been promoted by Woodrow Wilson (Muravchik 1996).

With the fall of the Soviet Union, a small but vocal group of American political leaders called on the United States to return to its pre–World War II posture, draw down U.S. soldiers serving overseas, and return a **peace dividend** to the American taxpayers as payback for the trillions of dollars it had cost to contain the Soviets for four decades. By the middle part of the 1990s the isolationist argument had retreated to the fringes, with globalization and the great leap forward in communications helping to knit the world together. President Clinton's national security adviser **Anthony Lake** announced in 1993 that "The successor to a doctrine of containment must be a strategy of enlargement—enlargement of the world's free community of market democracies." He defined America's role in the post–Cold War era as one that must be guided by strengthening current market democracies, bolstering fledgling ones, countering states opposed to market democracy, and supporting humanitarian concerns (Lake 1993).

Putting American foreign policy into a theoretical box can sometimes be difficult and contradictory. The Democratic and Republican parties are not necessarily the best guideposts to figure out foreign policy philosophies. Isolationists and realists may both trace their roots to Washington's farewell address, but they don't always see eye to eye. Similarly, neoconservatives may share much in common with Wilsonians, but there are some fundamental differences, particularly about the use of military force to achieve aims. The broad sweep of American foreign policy has veered between the poles of idealism and realism.

According to **Fareed Zakaria**, President Barack Obama falls into a middle ground as a "practical idealist" heavily influenced by his personal experience.

[Obama's] fundamental view of the world was rooted as much in the struggle for development and economic growth as it was in missiles and the Cold War. I think this came first from his mother and Indonesia. His memory of a foreign policy event was not of Vietnam or of the Soviet Union but of life on the ground in Jakarta [Indonesia]. The struggle for survival and development—that's the prism through which he sees the world. (Remnick 2010, 430)

As we will examine later in this chapter, some of Obama's rhetoric and action has put him in the realist camp (his Nobel Prize speech and his response to the **Green Revolution in Iran** and the **Arab Spring**). On the other side of the coin, the U.S.-backed NATO (**North Atlantic Treaty Organization**) intervention that resulted in the toppling and death of Libyan leader **Muammar Gaddafi** might qualify him more as a pragmatic liberal. Complicating matters of how to classify Obama further on the realism/idealism continuum, his administration presided over the extra-territorial killing of **Osama bin Laden** in Pakistan, wound down wars in Iraq and Afghanistan, but stepped up remote drone attacks on **Taliban** leaders.

The ability of the American president to shape world affairs remains unparalleled. While the reach of a global presidency may have dimmed since its zenith in the post–World War II 1940s, no other single leader has the ability to exert as much influence worldwide. For many people around the world, the president embodies the very image of the United States. Upon election the president automatically achieves a political global superstardom reserved for a select few individuals. Taxicab drivers in faraway capitals may know little about the current leaders of China or India, but they do have an opinion about the job performance of the American president—and perhaps his predecessor's performance as well. Since World War II U.S. presidents have become global leaders whose decisions impact distant corners of the world. As one Greek citizen told the *New York Times* during President Bill Clinton's visit to Athens in November 1999, "He is the *planatarchis* [ruler of the planet] so of course he should visit Greece. It is a province of his empire" (Stanley 1999).

The U.S. president also has the ability to try to dictate a set of global ideals. This awesome combination of hard and soft power—to simultaneously serve as the commander-in-chief of the world's military and economic superpower but also as the leader of a country that is the world's media and cultural juggernaut—gives the American president the unique ability to help define an era. While President Barack Obama's foreign policy legacy is far from established, by virtue of his own personal international story and the stark contrast in his worldview from his predecessors, he has already started to make a mark. **Zbigniew Brzezinski**, President Jimmy Carter's national security adviser, characterized Obama's first year in office as "a truly ambitious effort to redefine the United States' view of the world and to reconnect the United States with the emerging historical context of the twenty-first century" (Brzezinski 2010, 16). Obama has the potential to join a select number of presidents who have significantly repositioned American prestige and power in the world.

AMERICAN LEGACY OF PRESIDENTIAL LEADERSHIP IN WORLD AFFAIRS

Since the beginning of the twentieth century, a dozen American presidents have made a significant impact on American foreign policy. Theodore Roosevelt, the first American to win the Nobel Peace Prize for his brokering the end of the **Russo-Japanese War**, helped establish the United States as a global power. Woodrow Wilson, the idealistic former political science professor-turned-president, plunged America into World War I and then tried to realign the international relations through his fourteen points, which included the creation of the League of Nations. **Franklin Roosevelt**, a charter member of the **"Big Three,"** stood beside **Winston Churchill** and **Joseph Stalin** at the spheres-of-influence conferences at **Yalta** and **Casablanca** and faced down **fascism** during World War II. Roosevelt's successor, **Harry Truman,** was in Dean Acheson's words "present at the creation" of the modern American foreign policy order and the nuclear age, developing American-led international organizations (NATO, the **United Nations** [UN], the **International**

Monetary Fund [IMF], and the **World Bank**) as well as a philosophy for dealing with the Soviets (containment) that would dominate much of the rest of the century. **Dwight Eisenhower**, who had already been supreme Allied commander in Europe during World War II before he became president in 1953, went toe-to-toe with the Soviets and left office warning about a military-industrial complex that had come to dominate American life.

The modern era of the global American presidency began with the election of **John F. Kennedy** (JFK) to the White House.[1] The Kennedy administration understood the growing cultural interconnectedness and the power of the presidency to transform the image of the country abroad. Some of this power had to do with the rise of television, but the world also saw Kennedy's youthfulness, his wife's ability to address foreign audiences in fluent French and Spanish, and initiatives such as the **Peace Corps**, the **Alliance for Progress,** and the space program as part of what made America unique among modern nations. While JFK's strategic errors and successes in Cuba and Vietnam and with the Soviets were critically important in defining his foreign policy, they also went hand-in-hand with his cultivated personal aura. A country that could elect a handsome, thoughtful, and worldly forty-three-year old (not to mention Roman Catholic, during an era when that mattered to some people) to its most powerful position said something larger about America's place in the world.[2]

After Kennedy's assassination in 1963, his successor **Lyndon Johnson** inherited the impossible challenge of maintaining JFK's global image as well as an ill-defined and steadily growing mission in Vietnam. Johnson never stood much of a chance. The counterculture 1960s and early 70s—from **Woodstock** to the May 1968 protests in Paris to the **Prague spring**—can be viewed through the prism of Johnson's (and later Nixon's) choices about the U.S. war in Vietnam. The post–World War II high of American prestige abroad had begun to ebb. Vietnam took its toll, but so did the protracted nature of the Cold War and mixed American messages about the importance of democracy and **human rights.** In a host of countries (Guatemala, Iran, Greece, Dominican Republic, Chile, Italy) the United States covertly influenced elections or tacitly approved of "friendly" military coups. President **Richard Nixon**, who was schooled (given his years in Congress and as Eisenhower's vice president) and interested in foreign policy, was able to secretly go to Beijing and begin the process of normalization with the Chinese, but he also dragged out the **Vietnam War** even though he had campaigned on quickly ending the conflict. **President Jimmy Carter** set about trying to rectify America's image abroad by making human rights the center of his foreign policy agenda. Overtaken by the **Iranian hostage crisis** and a lack of response to the Soviet invasion of Afghanistan, Carter was perceived as weak with foreign policy and was punished by the voters for that perceived flaw when he sought reelection in 1980.

President Obama has openly praised **Ronald Reagan**'s eight years in the White House, for having "changed the trajectory of American politics" (Alter

2010, 6). For Obama, a life-long Democrat who came of age politically during the Reagan years, this kind of public admiration (said during the 2008 campaign, no less) speaks volumes about Reagan's impact. His legacy in international affairs, although clouded by the **Iran-Contra affair** and a notable peacekeeping failure in Lebanon where 241 U.S. servicemen were killed by a suicide truck bomb in Beirut, was nonetheless significant. Reagan's singular obsession with communism and his ability to push the Soviets to the brink with the **Strategic Defense Initiative** ("**Star Wars**"), offensive U.S. missiles in Europe, and support for counterinsurgencies in Latin America and Africa helped to hasten the end of the Cold War. By the end of his presidency, Reagan was working with the Soviets to make significant reductions in nuclear weapons stockpiles.

When Reagan's vice president, **George H. W. Bush**, succeeded him in 1989, he came to the office with the world on the brink of a cyclical realignment (Schlesinger 1999). In his first year in office, the Soviet Union collapsed and the Cold War that had defined American foreign policy for more than four decades effectively ended when the **Berlin Wall** came down. The year 1989—with the upheavals in Eastern Europe and Russia and the democratic protests in Beijing—were a pivot point in world history and international relations. President Bush possessed an unmatched foreign policy résumé that included eight years as Reagan's vice president and service in the 1970s as the U.S. ambassador to China, the U.S. ambassador to the UN, and the director of Central Intelligence. President Bush spent much of his single term in office dealing with international crises of epochal proportions. Consider briefly: China (Tiananmen Square protests and massacre), Panama (and the ouster of president/CIA-informant/drug dealer **Manuel Noriega**), the fall of the Berlin Wall and the dissolution of the Soviet Union, the reunification of Germany, and the first Gulf War in Iraq and Kuwait. While Bush's background may have uniquely prepared him for the international challenges of the time, by 1992 the country favored **Bill Clinton,** who had little to no foreign policy experience during his years serving as the attorney general and governor of Arkansas. International events of the 1990s (in Somalia, Bosnia, Rwanda, Haiti, and the Middle East) forced Clinton to learn on the job. He was unable to focus on domestic economic issues to the exclusion of American foreign policy. The Clinton team was stung by criticism during its first term that it viewed foreign policy through the prism of social work and that it was preoccupied with suffering, starvation, and oppression as opposed to the national interest (Mandlebaum 1996). This attitude changed during President Clinton's second term in office, and there were more positive results both in Kosovo and, by the sheer force of his own personality, in the Middle East, where President Clinton came as close as anyone to negotiating a real peace between the Israelis and the Palestinians in the waning weeks of his presidency.

The disputed election of **President George W. Bush** was not lost on the rest of the world. The heated vote counts in Florida and the controversial intervention of the Supreme Court called into question America's role as a paragon of democracy. During the presidential campaign, Bush, then the governor of Texas, showed little interest in foreign policy. He had surprisingly little experience (even his travel as a tourist abroad was limited, and Mexican president **Vicente Fox** mocked the president's Spanish as "grade school level") given his father's impressive foreign policy credentials (Fox 2007, 140). During the second presidential debate, then-governor Bush made a statement that would seem ironic only months later:

> I'm not so sure the role of the United States is to go around the world and say, "This is the way it gotta be." We can help. And maybe it's just our difference in government—the way we view government. I mean, I want to empower people. I don't—you know, I want to help people help themselves, not have government tell people what to do. I just don't think it's the role of the United States to walk into a country, say, "We do it this way; so should you." (Commission on Presidential Debates 2000)

Events would soon conspire to test Bush's emerging worldview and push him down a neoconservative road that saw democracy and nation building in the Middle East as a way to secure American national security.

THE SEPTEMBER 11TH ATTACKS

The events of **September 11, 2001,** changed the international equation for President Bush and American foreign policy makers. It suddenly became imperative for the Bush administration to "walk into a country" and say, "We do it this way; so should you." In the immediate aftermath of the attacks on the **World Trade Center** and the **Pentagon,** there was an outpouring of sympathy with the United States around the world. The famous headline and article in the French daily *Le Monde* on September 12, 2001, "We Are All Americans," summed up the sentiments of even the notoriously cynical French. NATO invoked Article V for the first time in its fifty-plus-year history following 9/11, declaring the attacks on New York and Washington as an attack on every member of the alliance. The decision to pursue Osama bin Laden into Afghanistan and the border regions near Pakistan was supported from the outset by America's traditional allies. NATO established an **International Security Assistance Force** in Afghanistan that once numbered more than 50,000 troops.

Polling data from the Pew Global Research Center's Global Attitudes Project in the aftermath of 9/11 highlighted a mix of international sympathy mixed with finger-pointing blame back at the United States for misguided foreign policies that led to Osama bin Laden's rise. Ordinary people and opinion makers in every region of the world (save the Middle East, where it was just below 50 percent) still held positive views of the United States. These positive views were attributed to the image of America as a land of opportunity and beacon of ideas. These same respondents, however (with the exception of Western Europeans), found great fault with U.S. foreign policy and what the French foreign minister Hubert Vedriné called America's "hyper-power" (Pew Global Attitudes Project 2001; Vedriné 2000).

World opinion about American foreign policy changed rapidly as U.S. forces moved from chasing al-Qaeda and the Taliban in Afghanistan to eighteen months later sending troops into Iraq as well. In both cases, nation building was part of the master American plan to restore Iraq and Afghanistan. On paper, President Bush defended American involvement by defining the policy of preemption. Outlined in a speech at West Point and in the 2002 **National Security Strategy** of the United States, the new doctrine was a significant departure from a long-standing tradition in American foreign policy of using diplomacy and persuasion first and only turning to force as a final resort. Bush put the world on notice that 9/11 had altered a traditional tenet of American conduct in world affairs:

> For much of the last century, America's defense relied on the Cold War doctrines of deterrence and containment. In some cases, those strategies still apply. But new threats also require new thinking. Deterrence, the promise of massive retaliation against nations, means nothing against shadowy terrorist networks with no nation or citizens to defend. Containment is not possible when unbalanced dictators with weapons of mass destruction can deliver those weapons on missiles or secretly provide them to terrorist allies. We cannot defend America and our friends by hoping for the best. We cannot put our faith in the word of tyrants, who solemnly sign non-proliferation treaties, and then systemically break them. If we wait for threats to fully materialize, we will have waited too long. (Bush 2002)

While America's allies initially supported aggressive collective action in Afghanistan to try and disrupt the terror networks of the Taliban and al-Qaeda, there was much less support for the overall thrust of the Bush administration's plans for Iraq. Even prior to the decision to begin planning for war, which was telegraphed far in advance of the actual March 2003 start of the conflict, allies chafed at the worldview the Bush administration took regarding cooperation, diplomacy, and the value of international organizations and treaties. The **Kyoto Accord** on global warming was quickly dismissed, despite being signed by 141 nations, including all European and developed industrial nations except Australia. As for the role of international organizations, President Bush appointed John Bolton as his ambassador to the UN, who once said, "The [UN] Secretariat building in New York has 38 stories. If it lost ten stories, it would not make a bit of difference" (Applebaum 2005, A21).

Massive street demonstrations against the coming U.S. action in Iraq took place in major cities all over the world. The governments of France, Germany, and Russia took an openly hostile position against the Bush administration's plans to invade Iraq.[3] Even in the United States there were calls for a more tempered response to Saddam Hussein. General **Brent Scowcroft**, who had been the national security adviser in President Bush's father's administration, advocated against an invasion. He opined in the *Wall Street Journal* in August 2002 that Iraq would not be "a cakewalk" for the United States and that it would "divert us for some indefinite period from our war on terrorism." Despite General Scowcroft's warnings, and the advice of other foreign policy "wise men" who advocated a containment-style strategy in Iraq, it was harder to ignore Secretary of State **Colin Powell**'s opinion about Iraq's **weapons of mass destruction** (WMD) programs (Ricks 2002).

Secretary Powell's presentation to the **UN Security Council** in February 2003 was stage crafted to be reminiscent of **Adlai Stevenson**'s famous appearance in the same room more than forty years before when the United States offered evidence to the world that the Soviets had placed missiles ninety miles off the coast of Florida in Castro's Cuba. Secretary Powell—with the director of Central Intelligence, **George Tenet,** and the ambassador to the UN, **John Negroponte**, seated directly behind him—laid out a persuasive case, complete with satellite photos and recordings of private phone conversations, to show that Iraq was developing chemical, biological, and quite possibly nuclear weapons. He also laid claim to the possibility that Saddam Hussein had links to al-Qaeda, concluding that the world must act immediately:

> When we confront a regime that harbors ambitions for regional domination, hides weapons of mass destruction and provides haven and active support for terrorists, we are not confronting the past, we are confronting the present. And unless we act, we are confronting an even more frightening future. (Powell 2003)

Secretary of State Powell's address was particularly important for many Americans who were on the fence about whether U.S. forces should invade Iraq. September 11 had raised the specter that a domestic attack was possible at anytime and in any place. For months news reports had detailed the split within the Bush administration between neoconservatives, led by Vice President **Richard (Dick) Cheney** and Secretary of Defense **Donald Rumsfeld** who advocated an invasion of Iraq, and the more cautious and realistic State Department, led by Powell and his deputy **Richard Armitage**. Furthermore, Secretary Powell had been one of the key architects of **Desert Storm** in 1991 when American troops pushed Iraqi forces from Kuwait but, decidedly, did not proceed into Iraq. According to the journalist Bob Woodward, Powell had warned President Bush about an all-out invasion in the summer of 2002:

"You are going to be the proud owner of 25 million people. You will own all their hopes, aspirations, and problems. You'll own it all." In Powell's State Department this concept became known as the "the Pottery Barn Rule," because if "you break it; you own it" (Woodward 2004; Isikoff and Corn 2006). It is important to note this significant difference between the neoconservatives and foreign policy realists. Many realists either opposed the Iraq War or, like Powell, were deeply skeptical about sending in troops. Even though realists are known to be somewhat cynical about improvement in the conduct of international politics and maintain that war is always a possibility to ensure power and national security, they also are extremely vigilant about the introduction of military force. For Colin Powell, who did two tours of duty as a young soldier in Vietnam and was seared by the experience of fighting an unwinnable war, there were doubts that the situation in 2003 warranted the introduction of U.S. troops into Iraq (Schmidt and Williams 2008). Powell, however, played the good soldier and publically backed his commander in chief's position (Beinart 2010).

In the rear-view mirror it is important to remember that the Iraq War was initially hailed by many as a resounding success; the Iraqi Army was cowed by the **"shock and awe"** of American military might, and Saddam quickly went into hiding and was eventually captured. It was originally thought that it would only be a matter of time until the inspectors would uncover WMD. In May 2003 President Bush delivered a speech aboard the USS Abraham Lincoln announcing the end of major combat in Iraq. The setting and the visuals were carefully orchestrated. President Bush, a pilot himself in the Air National Guard during the Vietnam era, sat in the co-pilot's seat of a Navy S-3B Viking and became the first president to land a plane on an aircraft carrier. He then delivered a speech in front of members from the different branches of the U.S. armed services, with a prominent banner behind him that read "Mission Accomplished." While noting the road ahead in Iraq might be difficult, he also tied it to the United States' **Global War on Terror** (GWOT):

> We are helping to rebuild Iraq where the dictator built palaces for himself instead of hospitals and schools. And we will stand with the new leaders of Iraq as they establish a government of, by and for the Iraqi people. The transition from dictatorship to democracy will take time, but it is worth every effort. Our coalition will stay until our work is done and then we will leave and we will leave behind a free Iraq. The battle of Iraq is one victory in a war on terror that began on September the 11th, 2001, and still goes on. (Bush 2003)

While Bush's speech was correct in that there was still "difficult work to do in Iraq," the mission was not nearly "accomplished" and the link to September 11 was tenuous at best. The visuals of the president in a flight suit trumpeting

U.S. military power in defense of democracy rubbed many people the wrong way. The exercise of nation building in Iraq soon proved problematic. Factional fighting between Sunnis and Shia quickly flared into civil-war-like conflict with the Americans caught in the crossfire. U.S. soldiers who had been killed or badly wounded by **improvised explosive devices (IEDs)** began to return to the United States in ever-increasing numbers. A car bomb exploded at the UN compound in Baghdad, killing the Brazilian diplomat who headed the mission and ending the UN's involvement in the reconstruction efforts. Reports about the ineptitude and the extraordinary costs of **Coalition Provisional Authority (CPA)**, an American-led pseudo government that was running and trying to rebuild Iraq, surfaced in major news outlets (Chandrasekaran 2006). Perhaps most damning of all, photos of American soldiers torturing Iraqi prisoners at the **Abu Ghraib** prison in the most graphic and demeaning terms appeared for the whole world to see. There was a palpable sense by the end of 2004 that not only was the war in Iraq going badly for the United States, it was eroding American prestige and power around the world.

President Bush, nevertheless, easily won reelection in 2004. The defeated Democratic nominee Senator John Kerry frequently cited Bush's poor handling of Iraq and Afghanistan and the unsuccessful ongoing hunt for Osama bin Laden as reasons to vote the incumbent president out of office. The Bush administration rightfully saw their re-election as a referendum on their conduct since 9/11 and pressed ahead.[4] By the midterm elections of 2006, with things going badly in Iraq and Osama bin Laden still at large, the American voters repudiated the Bush administration by turning the Republicans out of Congress. Issues such as the war in Iraq and the handling of terrorism ranked high on the list of voter concerns.[5] Barack Obama made his decision to run for president soon after the 2006 midterms, with foreign policy issues looming very large in the mind of the electorate.

America's standing in the world had significantly diminished by the end of the Bush administration. Fending off a global economic crisis and fighting two protracted wars, Bush became the first sitting president not to address his own party's national convention. The rest of the world was rising while America seemed mired in the Middle East and was struggling economically. Brazil and Turkey flexed their muscles as foreign policy powers, China emerged as an economic power in Africa and Latin America, Russia reasserted its autocratic ways, and Iran continued to develop its nuclear capabilities. There was a sense among the electorate that the foreign policy of the Bush administration had contributed to the erosion of American power around the world.

BARACK OBAMA'S WORLDVIEW

When Barack Obama announced that he was running for president, he quickly became a preferred choice in foreign capitals, "to do the right thing in world affairs" (Bortin 2008). Obama's political rise during the Democratic primaries in the spring of 2008 coincided with the first positive signs in a decade that America's global image was improving (Pew Global Attitudes Project 2008). In the heart of the general election campaign, during the summer of 2008 while his opponent was campaigning battleground states like Ohio, Obama took an unconventional week-long trip to the Middle East and Europe, meeting with key leaders and **expatriate** voters at each stop. The trip culminated with a speech at the Victory Column in Berlin. Before an estimated crowd of 200,000 people (many waving American flags), candidate Obama highlighted his own international story and drew a bright line by condemning torture and committing to a set of ideals that "drew my father to American shores" (Obama 2008). The outpouring of enthusiasm for Obama spoke volumes about the failures of the Bush presidency to connect with the rest of the world.

Barack Obama's own international story prior to becoming president couldn't have been more different than George W. Bush's limited scope. In the traditional sense, Obama's foreign policy resume seemed thin. He had been in the U.S. Senate for less than a full term, although he did serve on the U.S. Senate Foreign Relations Committee. Obama's two main rivals for the White House in 2008, Senators Hillary Clinton and **John McCain**, had far more experience.[6] Obama, by contrast, had a much richer personal international experience than both political rivals and, arguably, more than any previous occupant of the White House. Obama's father, a Kenyan of the **Luo ethnic group**, met his mother when he was an international exchange student at the University of Hawaii. Much has been written about Obama's distant relationship with his father, including his own memoir, *Dreams from My Father*. In his book, Obama chronicled his formative childhood years living and going to school in Jakarta, Indonesia, during his mother's second marriage. Obama's mother, Ann Dunham, would turn their years in Asia into a career in international economic development. She would eventually write her doctoral dissertation on the topic, "Peasant Blacksmithing in Indonesia: Surviving and Thriving Against All Odds." Obama's chapter in *Dreams from My Father* on his years living in Indonesia, where he attended school until the fourth grade and learned some of the local dialect, focused on the anthropological differences between the United States and his temporary foreign home:

> I stuck my head out the back seat window and stared at the passing landscape, brown and green uninterrupted, villages falling back into forest, the smell of diesel and wood smoke. Men and women stepped like cranes through the rice paddies, their faces hidden by their wide straw hats. A boy, wet and slick as an otter, sat on the back of a dumb faced water buffalo, whipping its haunch with a stick of bamboo. The streets became more congested, small stores and markets and men

pulling carts loaded with gravel and timber, then the buildings grew taller, like buildings in Hawaii. (Obama 2004, 32)

As a young man Obama enjoyed traveling internationally and was close to foreign students during college, rooming with a Pakistani during his undergraduate years at Columbia University and visiting him for three weeks in Islamabad on a holiday trip. During his undergraduate years, and later while at Harvard Law School, he took courses in international relations and relished discussing world events. He visited his half-sister living in Germany and explored Europe with a backpack. His return visit to Kenya to meet his father's family helped define him. While Obama may have lacked the foreign policy résumé, he had travelled and thought about America's place in the world before he ever reached Washington (Remnick 2010). First elected to the Illinois State Senate in 1996, he had few opportunities from the state capitol in Springfield to weigh in on the key foreign policy issues of the day. When given the chance, however, to take a stand on the Iraq War during the run up to the invasion, Obama showed his realist tendencies. Although little noticed at the time, his 2002 speech against the war in Iraq would eventually have a impact on his political fortunes. Overshadowed by bigger political names at a Chicago rally against the war, the video of Obama's anti-Iraq War speech was used as proof during his 2008 presidential run that he might represent something different in American foreign policy.

I know that even a successful war against Iraq will require U.S. occupation of undetermined length, at undetermined cost, with undetermined consequences. I know that an invasion of Iraq without a clear rationale without strong international support will only fan the flames of the Middle East, and encourage the worst, rather than the best, impulses of the Arab world, and strengthen the recruitment arm of Al Qaeda. I am not opposed to all wars. I'm opposed to dumb wars. (Remnick 2010, 347)

After easily winning the U.S. Senate seat, he lobbied the Democratic leadership to become a member of the Foreign Relations Committee, where one of his first votes was to confirm **Condoleezza Rice**, one of the Iraq War architects, as secretary of state. He forged an alliance with a powerful Republican senator, Richard Lugar of Indiana, and traveled with him to Russia, Ukraine, and Azerbaijan to inspect weapons storage facilities. Upon their return, Obama and Lugar introduced bipartisan legislation, modeled after the **Nunn-Lugar legislation** that helped contain loose nukes from the former Soviet Union, to do the same with conventional weapons. They even published a joint op-ed together in the *Washington Post* that warned of the spread of "shoulder-fired antiaircraft missiles that can hit civilian airliners" (Lugar and Obama

2005). It was hard to determine how to classify Obama's foreign policy outlook from his short stint in the Senate. Neither a dreamy idealist nor a hard-hearted realist, his initial foreign policy actions and statements suggested a pragmatic grounding—someone willing to try anything that works to get the desired result.

Foreign policy was supposed to be the strong suit of Obama's Republican opponent, Senator John McCain, whose Vietnam heroism and command of defense policy was formidable. McCain, however, was stuck with the unenviable task of defending the Iraq and Afghanistan wars. He tried to exploit Obama's vote in the Senate against "the surge" of American troops into Iraq that led to positive results and a decrease in sectarian violence. McCain (like Hillary Clinton) also went after Obama for his comments during the Democratic primaries in which he stated that he would pursue "aggressive personal diplomacy" with Iran, a regime with which the United States had broken relations in 1979 over the taking of hostages at the American embassy in Tehran (Gordon and Zeleny 2007). Hillary Clinton even ran a television ad that emphasized Obama's lack of experience by asking voters to choose what they would do in a dangerous world when "It's 3 a.m., and your children are safe and asleep. But there's a phone in the White House, and it's ringing. Who do you want answering the phone?" (Alexovich, 2008). The issues of Obama's foreign policy experience, his votes on Iraq, and his pronouncements on Iran gained little traction with the voters. In the first presidential debate the financial crisis ended up overwhelming everything else. Foreign policy, ironically, played a much larger role in defining the selection of the 2008 vice presidential nominees. Obama's selection of Senator **Joseph Biden** of Delaware, the long-time chairman of the Senate Foreign Relations Committee, signaled a commitment to foreign policy that contrasted sharply with McCain's selection of Alaska governor **Sarah Palin**. Biden had travelled the world, met with international leaders, and sat through thousands of arcane committee hearings in his nearly four decades in the Senate. Governor Palin, by contrast, gave a series of perplexing interviews that highlighted her lack of knowledge about the world, most famously to Katie Couric of CBS News, where she touted her home state's proximity to Russia as foreign policy experience and noted, "As [Russian Prime Minister] Putin rears his head and comes into the air space of the United States of America, where do they go? It's Alaska" (Palin 2008).

THE OBAMA ADMINISTRATION'S FOREIGN POLICY CHALLENGES

President Obama's election in November 2008, along with the Democratic Party's consolidation of power in Congress, set in place the possibility that there could be a sea change in U.S. foreign policy. Changing course, however, would prove to be a daunting task. In addition to winding down the Iraq War and putting in place a long-term strategy in Afghanistan, the new administration faced a full international agenda. Among the most pressing questions: How to avoid a global economic meltdown? Could relationships with old allies, stung by the unilateralism of the Bush years, be restored? Should the United States be talking to "enemies" like Iran and North Korea? Could American leadership in areas such as international treaty making (global warming) be reestablished? What should be done about China's economic aspirations in Africa and Latin America? How would Obama manage relations with the once and future Russian president and autocrat **Vladimir Putin**? Would the Bush administration's policy of preemption be continued, and did it extend to humanitarian interventions? Was the "war on terrorism" really a "war"? Could the Obama administration step up the pressure on Pakistan to oust **al-Qaeda** and capture Osama bin Laden? Could President Obama use his personal popularity to bring about a lasting peace between the Israelis and Palestinians?

Even prior to his inauguration Obama promised to close the Guantanamo (Gitmo) Bay facility in Cuba that was being used to hold suspected terrorists for undetermined periods of time. The Bush administration had claimed that these prisoners were not subject to the **Geneva Convention** and the standard rules of war because al-Qaeda was not a state and, therefore, not a signatory to any treaty. For many, Gitmo had come to symbolize everything that was wrong with American unilateralism under the Bush administration. In one of his first acts as president, Obama signed executive orders to close the prison by January 2010. This timetable proved too optimistic, and the new president was forced to backtrack. The White House encountered political and legal difficulties in making good on their seemingly simple promise. Members of Congress opposed moving prisoners to their home state correctional facilities. Foreign countries balked when asked to take detainees for trial. The suspected terrorists, some of whom had likely been tortured in prison, now had a case that the integrity of the evidence collected against them would not be admissible in a U.S. court of law. By November 2009 Obama admitted that there was no way Gitmo would close on time, nor could he even give a definite date for closure (Kornblut 2009). Obama's inability to make good on his promise to close **Guantanamo Bay** became symbolic for some critics in the Wilsonian camp. Could he move beyond the good intentions and the soaring speeches to fundamentally move American foreign policy in a new direction?

The historian Walter Russell Mead concluded that Obama struggled between his inner Thomas Jefferson and his inner Woodrow Wilson and that if he did not soon reconcile his worldview it would tear his presidency apart and "turn him into a new Jimmy Carter." Mead argued that like Jefferson, Obama's primary instinct was to rebuild American democracy at home (Mead 2010). The administration's obsessive focus on health care and the shoring up the domestic financial system starved the president's foreign policy agenda from his full attention during his first year in office. Nevertheless, Obama also kept up his profile as an idealist in favor of human rights and dignity for all, particularly as reflected in a high-profile speech in Cairo, Egypt, and by his winning the Nobel Peace Prize award.

The Cairo speech, delivered at a university in front of a largely student audience, had a big objective. It would try to open a new dialogue with the Muslim world and call for an end to "this cycle of suspicion and discord." He opened his speech with the traditional greeting of peace in Arabic, "assalaamu alaykum," and drew upon his personal story of coming from "a Kenyan family that includes generations of Muslims." Gone was the moralizing about freedom and President Bush's division of the world into being "with us or against us." In its place was "mutual interest and mutual respect," where "we must say openly the things we hold in our hearts, and that are too often said behind closed doors" (Obama 2009c). President Obama enumerated these behind-closed-doors issues to include frank discussions about violent extremism, Israel, nuclear weapons, democracy, religious freedom, women's rights, and economic development. The speech caught the attention of opinion makers in the Muslim world and was praised as "the speech no other president could make" (Freedland 2009). Even some conservative commentators in the United States found something to like in his message (Boot 2009). Wilsonian at its core, the speech was also pragmatic. It admitted that there had to be a more innovative way for the United States to view the Middle East than it had in recent years.

Events in Afghanistan, however, forced President Obama to make a decision between his rhetorical idealism and the realism on the ground. He acknowledged this tension in his stunningly realistic Nobel laureate address that he was the "Commander-in-Chief of the military of a nation in the midst of two wars." While he paid homage to two former leaders who adhered to a guiding principle of non-violence, Dr. Martin Luther King and Mohandas Gandhi (both prior Nobel Peace Prize winners), at the same time he dismissed them as incomplete examples for someone in his position.

> But as a head of state sworn to protect and defend my nation, I cannot be guided by [King and Gandhi] alone. I face the world as it is, and cannot stand idle in the face of threats to the American people. For make no mistake: evil does exist in the world. A non-violent movement could not have halted Hitler's armies. Negotiations cannot convince al Qaeda's leaders to lay down their arms. To say that force may sometimes be necessary is not a call to cynicism—it is recognition of history; the imperfections of man and the limits of reason. (Obama 2009b)

The **Nobel Prize** came as a surprise to Obama and his political advisers, who saw the award as potentially a political negative (Alter 2010). President Obama's foreign policy advisers had spent the fall of 2009 trying to devise a long-term Afghanistan strategy. U.S. involvement in the mountainous country was already approaching (it has since passed) the length of the Vietnam War, and there was a lack of a clear objective and a real exit strategy. Secretary of Defense **Robert Gates** fired General David McKiernan, the top U.S. commander in Afghanistan, in May 2009 after less than a year in the job, calling for "fresh thinking" and "fresh eyes" (Tyson 2009). To a certain extent Obama had boxed himself into a corner. He had campaigned on a platform of stepping up U.S. efforts in Afghanistan and had made a public pronouncement that September 11 made Afghanistan "a war of necessity" (Obama 2009d). His closest advisers were split about how best to proceed. Vice President Biden wanted a lighter military footprint and greater use of remote drones. Biden argued that fewer troops on the ground would deprive the Taliban of targets and a way to rally new recruits. It would also force the Afghan government to take a larger responsibility for fighting the Taliban. The U.S. ambassador to Afghanistan, Karl Eikenberry, warned that the Afghan population perceived the U.S. military presence as too heavy-handed. Secretary of State Clinton and the military countered that there was no political future in Afghanistan until the Taliban had been neutralized and that having U.S. boots on ground was imperative to any success (Alter 2010). The president worried that he was at the same decision juncture that President Johnson faced in 1965 when trying to figure out whether to escalate American involvement in Vietnam. He invited six historians of the Vietnam conflict to the White House to get their opinions about the parallels between the two wars.

In his first major foreign policy decision as president, Obama decided to split the difference between his advisers and the military. He would immediately call for an additional 30,000 U.S. troops (less than the military had requested), bringing the total American presence in the country to 100,000 soldiers. The switch back was that these forces would begin to depart Afghanistan by July 2011 (Sanger 2009). The president's compromise satisfied no one. Those who wanted a clear exit strategy and reduced U.S. presence thought it was a piecemeal response. Many in the military believed that setting an artificial date for withdrawal was a guarantee of failure. They argued that all the Taliban had to do was wait the Americans out. The military grumbling got so loud that it ended up costing **General Stanley McCrystal**, the U.S. commander in Afghanistan, his job. In an interview with *Rolling Stone* magazine, General McCrystal and his senior aides made fun of Vice President Biden and the national security team at the White House and talked down about the president, calling him "uncomfortable and intimidated" in front of military leaders (Hastings 2010). President Obama fired General McCrystal and replaced him with the architect of "the surge" in Iraq, General **David Petraeus,** who would later become Obama's second director of Central Intelligence.

If there were doubts about Obama's ability to make a hard military choice, the decision to act upon intelligence and assassinate Osama bin Laden on

May 1, 2011, put that talk to rest, at least temporarily. The raid that killed bin Laden was led by a U.S. Joint Special Operations Command that involved the U.S. Navy SEALs and the CIA. Obama's determination to order the attack won plaudits from political friends and foes alike. The events signified a milestone for both the Obama administration and American foreign policy. Osama bin Laden was the face of terror on 9/11, and his death brought both a sense of justice and closure—for many—to the destruction of the World Trade Center and the Pentagon. Bin Laden may have been wanted "dead or alive" in President Bush's words, but for almost a decade the inability to locate him was a source of impotence and embarrassment to the U.S. military and intelligence communities. Bin Laden would periodically issue statements on grainy audio- or videotape that had an unnerving effect on national security and allies in Europe, who notably dealt with al-Qaeda attacks after 9/11 in Madrid and London. The raid that led to bin Laden's killing was dangerous and politically risky for Obama. It involved ordering helicopters into an urban setting deep inside another sovereign country (Pakistan) without their prior knowledge. The potential for failure and embarrassment was high, but the raid and its aftermath—which included ascertaining bin Laden's identity, photographing him, and burying his body (with traditional Islamic rights, including the washing of the body) at sea—was handled with thoughtfulness (Wilson, Whitlock, and Branigan 2011).

Bin Laden's killing came in the midst of an eventful season that was reshaping the Middle East. No one had predicted that a series of uprisings against some of the worst autocrats in the region was even possible until the **Arab Spring** began to unfold in early 2011. It is true that the **Green Revolution**, a pro-democracy movement in Iran in 2009–2010 that had gained worldwide attention for its protests against Mahmoud Ahmadinejad's blatant maneuver to fix elections, could have been a harbinger of things to come. The steam, however, soon came out of the protests as Ahmadinejad consolidated power. The Obama administration had been cautious in the case of Iran, not wanting to be "seen as meddling." Although he expressed concerns over the Iranian elections, Obama quickly ruled out any direct U.S. involvement while his Republican opponents criticized him for passivity (Zeleny and Cooper 2009). The Obama administration may have been working the levers of international power quietly and covertly against Iran, but there would be no boots on the ground or showy displays of anger. President Obama preferred instead, in the words of one adviser, to "lead from behind" (Lizza 2011). This policy guided the Obama administration through the Arab Spring as Syria, Tunisia, Egypt, Yemen, and Libya saw protests (in some cases violent) that seemed like they might engulf the entire region. In the case of Libya it seemed initially as if the better organized and armed forces of Libyan strongman Muammar Gadaffi would overrun the ragtag group of rebels swept up in the romance of the Arab Spring. Leading from behind, the United States worked through the UN

Security Council to authorize NATO to intervene militarily to help the rebels with missile strikes on Gadaffi's forces. Cell phone video captured Gadaffi's violent death in October 2011, and a month later Libyan leaders had formed a provisional government. The United States had achieved its goals in Libya by leading a multilateral coalition of allies with minimal loss of U.S. blood and treasure.

While "leading from behind" has been praised by some for its pragmatism, other international activists with Wilsonian tendencies—such as Bono, the lead singer of U2, who applauded Obama's quick selection as a Nobel Peace Prize winner because "The world wants to believe in America again because the world needs to believe in America again"—have since become disenchanted (Bono 2009). Obama is clearly not going to be a radical change agent in foreign policy as some may have hoped. There has been muted action on human rights in areas where taking too strong a stand might cause problems. In China, Secretary of State Clinton signaled early on that **Tibet**, religious and press freedoms, and internal judicial questions would not get in the way of core economic and strategic concerns (CNN 2009). The Obama administration's risky strategy of dealing directly with Sudanese president Omar al-Bashir, who was indicted for war crimes by the **International Criminal Court**, has raised eyebrows of those who thought Obama would lean toward his idealist tendencies, especially when it came to Africa. Similarly, the president attended the **Copenhagen summit** on global warming but left with little to show for his personal involvement. Peace between Israel and its neighbors appears as distant as ever, and President Obama's special envoy to the region, **George Mitchell**, a former Senate majority leader from Maine who helped resolve the long-running Northern Ireland conflict in the late 1990s, resigned in disgust at the lack of progress in 2011.

Some of the disconnect between expectations of Obama and the reality of his first term in office lies in the rise of competing poles of power in global business, culture, and communication. Obama does not have the same kind of ability to make quick and fundamental changes to the world order the way that Franklin D. Roosevelt or Harry Truman did at the end of World War II. However, that said, some of the items projected by Obama's supporters on to his foreign policy agenda, such as democracy promotion and human rights, were never at the center of his foreign policy vision. There were three basic goals that Obama talked about during the campaign. The first was to wind down the conflict in Iraq. The Obama administration quietly reduced the number of troops in Iraq to 50,000 in August 2010, down from the high of nearly 160,000 in 2005 and 2006. The last combat troops left Iraq at the end of 2011, as the Obama administration successfully disengaged the military and foreign policy establishment's attention away from Iraq and toward Afghanistan. This change of focus to Afghanistan was the second of Obama's objectives. Even defining what determines American success in Afghanistan remains problematic. The stability and reliability of the government of Afghan leader **Hamid Karzai** is cause of great concern (Sanger 2009). The third Obama goal was to reduce the omnipresent threat of terrorism that loomed over the United States in the first years after September 11, 2001. The killing of Osama bin Laden has hastened a sense that it may be time to wind down America's post-9/11 obsession with al-Qaeda and perhaps with the Middle East as well.

If there is a short-term political question for Obama, it is the following: in his rush to deflate the perceived cowboy diplomacy of the Bush administration, did he go too far by demeaning American exceptionalism in foreign policy? The 2012 Republican presidential candidates seem to think so and often cite a statement made during Obama's first trip abroad as president in April 2009 as an example that his worldview is out of the mainstream. Speaking to a reporter, Obama said

> I believe in American exceptionalism, just as I suspect the Brits believe in British exceptionalism and the Greeks believe in Greek exceptionalism . . . the fact that I am very proud of my country and I think we've got a whole lot to offer the world does not lessen my interest in recognizing that we're not always going to be right, or that other people have good ideas, or that in order for us to work collectively, all parties have to compromise and that includes us. (Obama 2009a; Page 2010)

Republican presidential candidate **Mitt Romney**, for example, took issue with Obama on the question of American exceptionalism as "a profoundly mistaken view" that "there is nothing unique about the United States" (Romney 2011). While this may just be a partisan reading of a rather benign viewpoint, it calls into question America's role in the world order.

CHALLENGES FOR AMERICAN FOREIGN POLICY

Romney's critique of Obama plays into a nagging longer term, and perhaps more significant question: are we at the beginning of the end of what *Time* magazine editor Henry Luce famously called "the American Century"? There has been no shortage of work on the coming American decline. Fareed Zakaria's "rise of the rest," Parag Khanna's *Second World* (including Europe and other second-tier powers such as Turkey), and Niall Ferguson's argument that "most imperial falls are associated with fiscal crises" all herald the collapse of American power in the twenty-first century (Zakaria 2008; Khanna 2008; Ferguson 2010). This kind of rush to decline has plenty of recent historical company. Depending on your perspective (and age), the international challenges facing the United States are no greater than the period right after World War II or following the **Korean War**, or countering the supposed missile and space race gaps. The aftermath of the Vietnam War and the response to the Soviet offensive in the third world seemed daunting too. It is easy to forget that it has been less than a generation since the demise of Soviet communism. American foreign policy's cyclical nature has led some to compare it to Icarus's hubris of flying with wax wings too close to the sun. Periods of strength and confidence are often followed by eras of introspection and recrimination. America's foreign policy makers continue to relearn the lessons of previous generations (Beinart 2010).

The unforeseen foreign policy challenges for the United States in the coming years are just that—impossible to predict. It would be hopelessly Wilsonian for the American foreign policy establishment to simply embrace the UN and adopt multilateral action to try to achieve success in bringing peace and democracy to the Middle East. Multilateral action has limitations in containing the spread of nuclear weapons in rogue states like Iran or North Korea. On the flip side, it would be despairingly realistic for the United States to confront issues like **climate change** through the self-interested economic prism of the United States alone. What is needed is that elusive perfect mix: a reconciliation of just enough realism and just enough idealism.

NOTES

1. President Obama was born in 1961, the same year John Kennedy became president.

2. Political commentators often drew parallels between Barack Obama and John Kennedy. Both men were elected to the presidency in their forties, both were Ivy-League-educated, and both were quite telegenic. Prior to Obama's election to the White House in 2008, John Kennedy was also the last candidate to come directly from the U.S. Senate.

3. In Germany, the sitting chancellor Gerhard Schroeder, a Social Democrat, used his opposition to the Iraq War as a successful electoral issue against the Christian Democratic candidate Edmund Stoiber. French opposition to the U.S. effort in Iraq led to the renaming of "French fries" to "freedom fries" in some American restaurants. Russia, also an ally since the end of the Cold War, opposed the invasion as well. The British and the Italians were supportive of the Iraq invasion, sending significant numbers of troops and assistance.

4. Senator John Kerry, the Democratic candidate who lost to President Bush in 2004, highlighted differences on foreign policy issues during the campaign. In his acceptance speech at the Democratic National Convention in Boston, Kerry said, "I know what we have to do in Iraq. We need a president who has the credibility to bring our allies to our side and share the burden, reduce the cost to American taxpayers, reduce the risk to American soldiers. That's the right way to get the job done and bring our troops home" (www.guardian.co.uk/world/2004/jul/30/uselections2004.usa5).

5. See CNN exit polling for the 2006 midterm elections (www.cnn.com/ELEC TION/2006/pages/results/states/US/H/00/epolls.0.html, accessed July 20, 2010).

6. Hillary Clinton had been a member of the Senate since 2000, serving on the Armed Services Committee. As the wife of President Bill Clinton, she visited numerous foreign countries as First Lady from 1993 to 2000, showing a particular interest in international development and women's issues. John McCain was born in Panama to an American military father and spent significant time on military bases abroad. A Vietnam veteran and a prisoner of war for almost six years, McCain had been outspoken on foreign policy issues in both the U.S. House and the Senate since 1982. He was a longtime member of the Senate Armed Services Committee.

REFERENCES

Alexovich, Ariel. 2008. "Clinton's National Security Ad." *New York Times*, February 29. Accessed January 16, 2012. http://thecaucus.blogs.nytimes.com/2008/02/29/clintons-national-security-ad/.

Almond, Gabriel. 1960. *The American People and Foreign Policy*. New York: Praeger.

Alter, Jonathan. 2010. *The Promise: President Obama, Year One*. New York: Simon and Schuster.

Applebaum, Anne. 2005. "Defending Bolton." *Washington Post*, March 9. Accessed July 23, 2010. www.washingtonpost.com/wp-dyn/articles/A18706-2005Mar8.html.

Beinart, Peter 2010. *The Icarus Syndrome: A History of American Hubris*. New York: Harper Perennial.

Bono. 2009. "Rebranding America." *New York Times*, October 17. Accessed July 23, 2010. www.nytimes.com/2009/10/18/opinion/18bono.html.

Boot, Max. 2009. "Obama in Cairo." *Commentary Online*, June 4. Accessed July 25, 2010. www.commentarymagazine.com/blogs/index.php/boot/68462. (Now available at http://mediamatters.org/research/200906050031.)

Bortin, Meg. 2008. "Bush's Exit Helps U.S. Restore Its Image Abroad, Survey Shows." *Global Edition of the New York Times*, June 13.

Brzezinski, Zbigniew. 2010. "From Hope to Audacity: Appraising Obama's Foreign Policy." *Foreign Affairs* 89, no. 1: 16–30.

Bush, George W. 2002. "Text of Bush's Speech at West Point." *New York Times*, June 1. Accessed July 23, 2010. www.nytimes.com/2002/06/01/international/02PTEX-WEB.html.

———. 2003. "Text of President George W. Bush's Speech Aboard the U.S.S. Abraham Lincoln." *Washington Post*, May 1. Accessed July 23, 2010. www.washingtonpost.com/ac2/wp-dyn/A2627-2003May1.

Carr, E. H. 1939. *The Twenty Years Crisis: An Introduction to the Study of International Relations*. London: Macmillan and Co.

Carter, Jimmy. 1977. "University of Notre Dame, Address at Commencement Exercises at the University." May 22. Accessed January 15, 2012. www.presi dency.ucsb.edu/ws/index.php?pid=7552#axzz1jamRTUlQ.

Chandrasekaran, Rajiv. 2006. *Imperial Life in the Emerald City.* New York: Vintage.

CNN. 2009. "Clinton: Chinese Human Rights Can't Interfere with Other Concerns." February 21. Accessed July 25, 2010. www.cnn.com/2009/POLITICS/02/21/clinton.china.asia/.

Commager, Henry Steele. 1983. "Misconceptions Governing American Foreign Policy." In *Perspectives on American Foreign Policy*, edited by Charles W. Kegley, Jr., and Eugene R. Wittkopf, 510–17. New York: St. Martin's Press.

Commission on Presidential Debates. 2000. "October 11, 2000 Debate Transcript." Transcript from debate held in Winston-Salem, N.C., October 11. Accessed July 23, 2010. www.debates.org/index.php? page=october-11-2000 -debate-transcript.

Ferguson, Niall. 2010. "Complexity and Collapse: Empires on the Edge of Chaos." *Foreign Affairs* 89, no. 2 (March–April): 18–32.

Fox, Vicente. 2007. *Revolution of Hope.* New York: Penguin.

Freedland, Jonathan. 2009. "Barack Obama in Cairo: The Speech No Other President Could Make." *Guardian* (UK), June 4. Accessed July 25, 2010. www .guardian.co.uk/world/2009/jun/04/barack-obama-speech-islam-west.

Gordon, Michael R., and Jeff Zeleny. 2007. "Obama Would Engage Iran If Elected, He Says." *New York Times,* November 1. Accessed July 23, 2010. www.ny times.com/2007/11/01/world/americas/01iht-obama.5.8154185.html.

Harper, John. 2004. *American Machiavelli: Alexander Hamilton and the Origins of U.S. Foreign Policy.* Cambridge: Cambridge University Press.

Hastings, Michael. 2010. "The Runaway General." *Rolling Stone*, June 22. Accessed July 24, 2010. www.rollingstone.com/politics/news/the-runaway-general -20100622.

Isikoff, Michael, and David Corn. 2006. *Hubris: The Inside Story of Spin, Scandal and the Selling of the Iraq War.* New York: Crown Publishers.

Khanna, Parag. 2008. *The Second World: Empires and Influence in the New Global Order.* New York: Random House.

Kirkpatrick, Jeane. 1979. "Dictatorships and Double Standards." *Commentary*, November. Accessed May 13, 2012. www.commentarymagazine.com/article/dictatorships-double-standards.

Kornblut, Anne E. 2009 "Obama Admits Guantanamo Won't Close by Jan. Deadline." *Washington Post,* November 18. Accessed July 23, 2010. www.washing tonpost.com/wp-dyn/content/article/2009/11/18/AR2009111800571.html.

Krauthammer, Charles. 1990–1991. "The Unipolar Moment." *Foreign Affairs* 70, no. 1 (America and the World 1990–1991): 23–33.

Lake, Anthony. 1993. "From Containment to Enlargement." Speech given at Johns Hopkins University, School of Advanced International Studies, September

21. Accessed May 13, 2012. http://www.fas.org/news/usa/1993/usa-930921
.htm.

———. 2000. *Six Nightmares: Real Threats in a Dangerous World and How America Can Meet Them.* Boston: Little, Brown.

Lizza, Ryan. 2011. "The Consequentialist." *New Yorker,* May 2. Accessed January
18, 2012. //www.newyorker.com/reporting/2011/05/02/110502fa_fact_lizza?
currentPage=1.

Lugar, Richard G., and Barack Obama. 2005. "The Junkyard Dogs of War." *Washington Post,* December 3. Accessed July 23, 2010. www.washingtonpost
.com/wp-dyn/content/article/2005/12/02/AR2005120201509.html.

Mandlebaum, Michael. 1996. "Foreign Policy as Social Work." *Foreign Affairs* 75,
no. 1 (January–February): 16–32.

Mead, Walter Russell. 2002. *Special Providence: American Foreign Policy and How
It Changed the World.* New York: Routledge.

———. 2010. "The Carter Syndrome." *Foreign Policy* 177 (January–February):
58–64.

Muravchik, Joshua. 1996. *The Imperative of American Leadership.* Washington,
D.C.: AEI Press.

Nye, Joseph. 2004. *Soft Power: The Means to Success in World Politics.* New York:
Public Affairs.

Obama, Barack. 2004. *Dreams from My Father.* New York: Three Rivers Press.

———. 2008. Transcript of speech in Berlin, Germany. *New York Times,* July 24.
Accessed July 23, 2010. www.nytimes.com/2008/07/24/us/politics/24text-
obama.html.

———. 2009a. "News Conference by President Obama." News conference held in
Strasbourg, France, April 4. Accessed January 15, 2011. www.whitehouse.
gov/the-press-office/news-conference-president-obama-4042009.

———. 2009b. "Remarks by the President Accepting the Nobel Peace Prize."
Speech given in Oslo, Norway, December 10. Accessed January 16, 2011.
www.whitehouse.gov/the-press-office/remarks-president-acceptance-nobel
-peace-prize.

———. 2009c. "Remarks by the President on a New Beginning." Speech given
in Cairo, Egypt, June 4. Accessed July 23, 2010. www.whitehouse.gov/the
-press-office/remarks-president-cairo-university-6-04-09.

———. 2009d. "Remarks at the VFW National Convention." Speech given in
Phoenix, Arizona, August 17. Accessed May 13, 2012. www.washingtonpost.
com/wp-dyn/content/article/2009/08/17/AR2009081701657.html.

Page, Susan. 2010. "Obama and America's Place in the World." *USA Today,* December 21.

Palin, Sarah. 2008. "Exclusive: Palin on Foreign Policy" (interview by Katie Couric. *CBS Evening News,* September 25. Accessed July 23, 2010. www.cbsnews.
com/stories/2008/09/25/eveningnews/main4479062.shtml.

Pew Global Attitudes Project. 2001. "America Admired, Yet Its New Vulnerability
Seen As Good Thing, Say Opinion Leaders." December 19. Accessed July 18,

2010. http://pewglobal.org/2001/12/19/america -admired-yet-its-new-vulner ability-seen-as-good-thing-say-opinion-leaders/.

———. 2008. "Global Economic Gloom—China and India Notable Exceptions." June 12. Accessed July 22, 2010. http://pewglobal.org/2008/06/12/global -economic-gloom-china-and-india-notable-exceptions/.

Powell, Colin. 2003. "Transcript of Powell's UN Presentation." New York, , February 6. Accessed July 18, 2010. http://edition.cnn.com/2003/US/02/05/sprj .irq.powell.transcript/.

Remnick, David. 2010. *The Bridge.* New York: Knopf, 2010.

Ricks, Thomas E. 2002. "Some Top Military Brass Favor the Status Quo in Iraq." *Washington Post,* July 28. Accessed July 23, 2010. www.washingtonpost. com/wp-dyn/articles/A10749-2002Jul27.html.

Romney, Mitt. 2011. "Mitt Romney Delivers Remarks on U.S. Foreign Policy." October 7. Accessed January 18, 2012. www.mittromney.com/blogs/mitts -view/2011/10/mitt-romney-delivers-remarks-us-foreign-policy.

Sanger, David E. 2009. *The Inheritance: The World Obama Confronts and the Challenges to American Power.* New York: Harmony Books.

Schlesinger, Arthur M., Jr. 1999. *The Cycles of American History.* New York: Mariner Books.

Schmidt, Brian C., and Michael C. Williams. 2008. "The Bush Doctrine and the Iraq War: Neoconservatives Versus Realists." *Security Studies* 17, no. 2. Accessed January 18, 2012. www.tandfonline.com/doi/full/10.1080/096364108 02098990.

Scowcroft, Brent. 2002. "Don't Attack Saddam." *Wall Street Journal,* August 15. Reprinted in *The Iraq War Reader,* edited by Michael L. Sifry and Christopher Cerf, 295–97. New York: Simon and Schuster, 2003. Page references are to the 2003 edition.

Stanley, Alessandra. 1999. "Huge March in Athens Protests Visit by President Clinton." *New York Times,* November 18. Accessed January 16, 2011. www .nytimes.com/1999/11/18/world/huge-march-in-athens-protests-visit-by-clinton.html.

Turner, Frederick Jackson. 1920. *The Frontier in American History.* New York: Henry Holt and Co.

Tyson, Ann Scott. 2009. "Top U.S. Commander in Afghanistan is Fired." *Washington Post,* May 12. Accessed July 22, 2010. www.washingtonpost.com/ wp-dyn/content/article/2009/05/11/AR2009051101864.html.

Vedriné, Hubert. 2000. *France in the Age of Globalization.* Washington, D.C.: Brookings Institution Press.

Washington, George. 1796. "Washington's Farewell Address." September 19. Accessed January 12, 2012. http://avalon.law.yale.edu/18th_century/washing.asp.

Wilson, Scott, Craig Whitlock, and William Branigin. 2011. "Osama Bin Laden Killed in U.S. Raid, Buried at Sea." *Washington Post,* May 2. Accessed January 18, 2012. www.washingtonpost.com/national/osama-bin-laden-killed -in-us-raid-buried-at-sea/2011/05/02/AFx0yAZF_story.html.

Wilson, Woodrow. 1917. "Joint Address to Congress Leading to a Declaration of War Against Germany." President's address, April 2. Accessed January 9, 2012. www.firstworldwar.com/source/usawardeclaration.htm.

Woodward, Bob. 2004. *Plan of Attack*. New York: Simon and Schuster.

Zakaria, Fareed. 2008. *The Post-American World*. New York: W.W. Norton and Co.

Zeleny, Jeff, and Helene Cooper. 2009. "Obama Warns Against Direct Involvement by US in Iran." *New York Times,* June 16. Accessed January 18, 2012. www.nytimes.com/2009/06/17/us/politics/17prexy.html.

2

International Security

SUZETTE R. GRILLOT

Images of insecurity around the world are plentiful. On a daily basis, televisions, newspapers, and computer screens display images of war, conflict, violence, and destruction. Throughout history, civilization has grappled with the aftermath of war—in more recent years facing the destruction caused by missiles, bombs, bullets, and other weaponry. Warfare is most often carried out in either a traditional (war between national combatants) or a nontraditional (terrorism, insurgency, and violence directed at civilians) manner. Regional conflicts between adversaries often heat up and cool off and heat up again over time. In addition to dealing with violence and conflict, populations must also sometimes contend with significant environmental devastation leading to health epidemics and widespread disease. Other significant sources of insecurity focus on human migration, the drug trade, and natural disasters. These troubling issues, and numerous more, illustrate why we must study, learn, contemplate, and ultimately develop responses for and solutions to the causes and consequences of international security problems.

This chapter is intended to provide a general overview of the field of international security studies and the relevant concepts important for the study of it. The chapter also offers discussion of several contemporary security problems and concludes by outlining various tools and recommendations for addressing the many security problems causing concern around the world. The hope is that the chapter will not only inform the reader about significant security concerns in existence today, but that it will also motivate the reader to engage on these issues and put knowledge into action.

HISTORY, PRINCIPLES, AND DEFINITIONS OF INTERNATIONAL SECURITY

The academic study of international security issues is a relatively recent undertaking, dating back to the twentieth century and the First and Second World Wars. Because World War I and World War II were extremely destructive, deadly, bloody, and damaging to state governments and their combat troops, as well as large numbers of civilians, scholars began to study the causes of war and violent conflict in an effort to highlight ways in which we might avoid them. Of course, the preoccupation of early security studies was the state and officially recognized governments, rather than the civilian population. The primary question was how governments can and should prevent, manage, and ultimately end major, deadly wars and direct military threats (Nye and Lynn-Jones 1988; Hough 2008; Buzan and Hansen 2009).

This focus on state and government carried over into the post–World War II Cold War period when questions of managing **weapons of mass destruction** and avoiding nuclear war were paramount. More specifically, security studies in this era focused on **nuclear strike capabilities** and the ability to withstand an initial nuclear blow in order to retaliate with a **second strike**, as well as the stabilizing and destabilizing factors of the **nuclear arms race**. Many studies explored limiting the damage of a nuclear attack and discussed the opportunities for limited nuclear conflict. Few, if any, studies took on issues of nuclear disarmament during this time. Nor did many studies address the problems associated with conventional (non-nuclear) weapons and wars, despite the fact that a major **conventional war** in Korea (1950–1953) and French and U.S. wars in Vietnam (1952–1975) were being waged throughout that time (Nye and Lynn-Jones 1988).

Despite the extreme focus on nuclear strategies and tactics, the 1960s and 1970s gave birth to a number of other important concepts and methods in security studies, including processes relevant for the making of foreign policy. Events in the 1960s, such as the **Vietnam War** and the **Cuban Missile Crisis**, provided fertile ground for security studies specialists to analyze how leaders make difficult decisions, such as how and when to go to war or whether to engage in a nuclear exchange. Moreover, the oil crises and resulting economic difficulties of the 1970s led to the inclusion of global economic issues in general understandings of international relations, which up to that point in time had been focused almost exclusively on military security. Because the oil crises had a significant impact on countries around the world, scholars began to develop concepts such as **interdependence** as a way to understand how decisions made in faraway and distant places can affect pocketbooks around the world. Although not traditionally related to international security, issues such as poverty in the developing world and environmental devastation began to emerge as significant problems. The international security focus, however, continued at the level of official government interaction—even within international organizations—rather than at the level of the human population (Nye and Lynn-Jones 1988; Walt 1991).

After this short gap in strict attention to nuclear war and the arms race, there was a return to concerns about the nuclear arms race and the potential for nuclear exchange in the late 1970s and into the 1980s, when **Cold War** tensions between the United States and the Soviet Union heated up yet again. A more traditional focus on military threats, the use of force, **deterrence** of attack, and maintaining a military balance returned and, in fact, lasted until the Cold War ended in the late 1980s and early 1990s (Walt 1991; Baldwin

1995). It was at that time, when nuclear war among heavily armed superpowers seemed far less likely, that a shift toward a more nontraditional, **human security** focus became not only evident, but necessary (Hough 2008).

In the wake of the Cold War, civil, ethnic, and religious conflicts—including incidences of **genocide**—emerged as some of the most visible and concerning aspects of armed violence. The armed conflicts in the **former Yugoslavia** and the various wars in Africa stand out as extremely troubling examples of the post–Cold War international structural shift. This shift occurred simultaneously with the fall of the Soviet Union, the rise of a single superpower (the United States), and the global cascade of weaponry that followed. Ultimately, insurgents, terrorists, **guerrilla** fighters, political opportunists, and corrupt despots were able to gain access to additional weaponry and fill a vacuum in power left in the wake of the international structural shift. Although traditional, conventional wars among states—such as the **Persian Gulf War** (1991) between Iraq and a coalition of states led by the United States—continued in the immediate aftermath of the Cold War, most of the wars and violent conflicts that were waged in the 1990s and 2000s were characterized by violence among armed groups that may or may not have been representing a state government. This violence resulted in significant civilian casualties and cycles of devastation for numerous human populations (Dannreuther 2008; Williams 2008).

Historically speaking, therefore, the field of study of international security has a relatively short past experience and a fairly significant widening in terms of definition and understanding. The field developed initially in light of military concerns and capabilities while economic, human, cultural, and other aspects of security were rarely acknowledged. However, less traditional security matters such as **climate change, health epidemics, ethnic conflict, human trafficking,** and **organized crime** have gained space in the international security discussion. The global security agenda has, in fact, become quite diverse and lengthy. No longer are decision makers singularly focused on the military causes of war and the consequences for governments and their alliances. Examination of the causes of conflict now includes various factors, both military and nonmilitary in nature. Moreover, the *consequences* of violence, disaster, terrorism, and other dangerous and damaging occurrences are equally compelling today. Nonetheless, there remains a debate among international security scholars regarding "traditional" security studies versus "widened" security studies (Hough 2008; Collins 2010).

CONCEPTS, APPROACHES, AND THEORIES OF INTERNATIONAL SECURITY

Given the field's history, it is important to discuss the general theoretical tools and approaches that have emerged to help us understand international security relations. Theories of international relations, which have their roots in efforts to assist states in the avoidance of war, enlighten us regarding the various factors or variables that have an impact on international security concerns and outline the ways in which security actors interact. Attention to theory is important because we may use theoretical concepts, approaches, and tools to understand cause, effect, and correlation in international security studies. Specifically, theoretical approaches such as **realism, liberalism, economic structuralism, social constructivism,** and others guide us in our study of international security matters.

Realist Theory and International Security Relations

Realist theory is perhaps the most dominant approach in international security studies. It focuses exclusively on the state as the primary actor in international relations and assumes that state actors are motivated entirely by the goal of ensuring their security and survival. The most key concept outlined by early realist theorists is the notion of **international anarchy.** Realists characterized the international political environment as anarchical because there is no central authority—or world government—that is the ultimate arbiter, judge, or responsible party to which members of the international community may turn for assistance, accountability, or supportive action. In other words, if any one state in the international system of states has a grievance vis-à-vis another state, or is attacked or wronged in some way, there is no central authority that will necessarily respond or that will oversee a just outcome (Morgenthau, Thompson, and Clinton 2005).

International anarchy means states must help themselves as they interact with other states in the international community. Theoretically speaking, anarchy requires states to develop the relevant capabilities—often military capabilities—that will allow them to fend off potential attackers and ensure their individual security and survival. Realists argue that states, operating within an anarchical environment, must seek military power—and maybe even military dominance—because other states pose potential threats, particularly because they, too, are operating in an anarchical, **self-help** environment where seeking military power in an effort to enhance security is required. Therefore, because states are all operating in the same environment and all are focused on individual security and survival, they find themselves in a security spiral, the dilemma being that any capability achieved by one state to better secure its own survival may inherently threaten another. Ultimately, realists believe the military gains of one state detract from another (Morgenthau, Thompson, and Clinton 2005; Mearsheimer 2001).

Later versions of realism—otherwise known as **neorealism** (or **structural realism**)—maintain many of the major tenets of traditional realism. However, neorealism focuses less on the security fears and motivations of states and more on the distribution of power in the international system as the key factor in determining the constraints on and decisions of states. States are still interested in maintaining their individual security, but concentrations or poles of power tend to characterize the international system and determine the ways in which states interact. For example, **unipolar systems**, where power capability is concentrated in a single actor; **bipolar systems,** where power is more equally distributed between two poles of power; and **multipolar systems,** where power is more widely dispersed among several actors all have an impact on the quality, quantity, and outcomes of state behaviors and relations. One of the key facets of neorealism, therefore, is military power capability and its distribution among important players—primarily great powers—who are the very actors who define and determine the international security environment (Waltz 1979; Mearsheimer 2001).

Liberal Theory, Neoliberal Institutionalism, and International Security Relations

Liberal international relations theory (or **liberalism**) has its roots in the years between World War I and World War II. Shortly after the First World War, scholars and practitioners began to focus on how the spread of democratic forms of government and liberal economic systems could possibly perpetuate common values and facilitate peace and security. Borrowing from **Immanuel Kant'**s *Perpetual Peace* (Kant 1795/1983), liberal theorists emphasized the importance of democratic institutions, international trade relations, and societal interactions beyond borders as a way to mitigate war and perpetuate peace. More modern day **"democratic peace"** theorists demonstrate that democracies rarely, if ever, go to war with one another; therefore, they suggest that a global policy of promoting democracy is a solution to international security problems (Doyle 1986; Russett 1994).

Although tenets of early liberal theory continue to be promoted in international security studies—particularly as they are reflected in the democratic peace literature—another variant of liberalism, known as **neoliberalism** or neoliberal institutionalism, reflects the importance of **international (governmental) organizations, transnational actors,** and interdependence in international relations. Interestingly, however, neoliberals borrow somewhat from realists by arguing that states operating in an anarchical international environment without a central authority and facing the uncertainty of the security dilemma develop international organizations and arrangements in an effort to address common problems. More specifically, because states are motivated to ensure their survival and must provide for their own security, they will work collectively with other states to jointly maximize their self-interest (Keohane and Nye 2000; Keohane 1984).

After all, many of the security problems states face today—such as international terrorism; weapons proliferation; drug, human, and commodities trafficking; global health epidemics; and environmental degradation—are undoubtedly transnational problems that one state cannot address alone. When international organizations develop rules and regulations to prescribe and constrain state actions, it helps establish appropriate standards of state behavior. States comply with the rules and regulations because it is in their interest to do so, but it is particularly in their interest for other states to do so. A common criticism of such an approach, however, is that it is difficult to enforce compliance within international organizations. Moreover, some suggest that international organizations that focus less on security issues and more on economic or other types of issues are more likely to induce cooperation and compliance among states because security matters are too central to state independence, autonomy, and survival (Jervis 1982). Nonetheless, international security organizations, such as the **North Atlantic Treaty Organization** (NATO), do exist and provide evidence that states seek collective action to address common security problems.

Economic Structuralism: Class Conflict and International Security

Economic structuralists begin from a similar position as do realists by suggesting that international anarchy is quite likely to lead to international conflict and violence. However, unlike realists, who argue that it is the self-help environment, resulting security dilemma, and the global distribution of power capabilities that ultimately characterize and determine the international security environment, economic structuralists suggest that it is the distribution of wealth and resources, and therefore power, among countries that "have" or "have not" that best explains global conflict, violence, and international security interactions.

The economic structuralist approach to international relations actually has its roots in the 1960s era of **decolonization** and the ensuing divide between wealthy, developed countries and poor, **lesser-developed countries**. Moreover, economic structuralist theory is often connected to Marxist notions of class conflict and neo-Marxist concerns about inequality (Gibson-Graham, Resnick, and Wolff 2001; Howard and King 1988). Noticing that the newfound period of state independence throughout Africa, Latin America, Asia, and the Middle East did not necessarily lead to economic gains in these regions, scholars began to question whether the capitalist economic systems of the developed world were perhaps taking advantage of and exploiting the resources of the less-developed world. No longer did this arrangement take place through colonial practices, but through free market activities where wealthier countries could pay rock-bottom prices for valuable commodities, such as oil, minerals, timber, and other natural resources. Economic structuralists argue that weaker governments in newly independent countries did not possess the economic, social, or political infrastructures to maintain themselves as truly independent countries but instead were quite dependent on the economic transactions that largely benefited already well-developed and wealthy countries. This system of exploitation, economic structuralists suggest, primarily benefits those who already "have" and impairs those who "have not"; such exploitation results in poor relations and an insecure environment (Wallerstein 1976; Linklater 1996).

A so-called **North-South divide** among the wealthy and poor, therefore, emerges as a result of this process of exploitation—as does a divide between the elite and the masses in the poor countries of the **global South**. In an effort to gain access to desirable resources, rich countries of the **global North** establish close yet corrupt relations with elite decision makers in the South. These relations with key decision makers pave the way for the wealthy government to have access to the poor country's resources, including goods and labor for cheap prices, but the relations also pave the way for decision makers in these poor countries to benefit personally from the transactions. This system of buying-off local leadership establishes local classes of haves and have-nots, which often leads to conflict within the poor country. Therefore, economic structuralists suggest that we may understand violence, conflict, and warfare among countries and within countries based on the consequences of the global capitalist system whereby the rich benefit at the expense of the poor, further perpetuating a class divide around the world (Cardoso 1979; Evans 1979).

Social Constructivism: International Society, International Norms, and Nongovernmental Organizations

A key distinction between the theoretical approaches discussed above and what many have labeled a social constructivist approach to international relations is the focus on material versus nonmaterial factors as explanations for international interactions. Realists, liberals (especially neoliberals), and economic structuralists all emphasize material and measurable variables—such as power capability, international rules and regulations, or differences in wealth and resources—as the primary causes of international relations and the international security environment. Social constructivists, however, highlight the importance of identity and community among states within an international society, the international norms that guide behavior, and the key role of nongovernmental organizations (NGOs) and their transnational networks that push states into behaving in ways they may not otherwise, even with regard to security matters (Wendt 1994; Keck and Sikkink 1998; Onuf 1989; Wendt 1999).

With regard to international anarchy, constructivists argue that "anarchy is what states make of it" (Wendt 1992). In other words, where realists, liberals, and globalists suggest that international anarchy requires or encourages states to behave in certain ways—from seeking power and domination to establishing rules, regulations, or exploitive relations—constructivists contend that the lack of a central authority in the international system does not necessarily "cause" states or international actors to behave one way or another. More specifically, international anarchy could just as easily lead to cooperation among international actors as it could lead to conflict. What matters, constructivists suggest, is a history of interaction—either positive or negative—that influences actor identity and perceptions of self and other, which in turn affects actor interests. Interests are not, therefore, defined and determined by the international anarchical environment. Regarding international security relations, a realist would focus on interests in security and survival vis-à-vis power accumulation, a liberal would focus on interests in democratic regime formation or development of international organizations to jointly maximize self-interest, and a globalist would focus on interests in self-perpetuation at the expense of others, whereas a constructivist would focus on how interests flow from interaction and identity (Wendt 1999).

The result of constructivist attention to interaction and identity is a shift in conception about the international environment. Rather than an international "system" characterized by state units that are equally self-interested and functionally indistinguishable, constructivists emphasize an international "community" characterized by states and various actors who may or may not be self-interested and are certainly distinguishable by function and a whole host of other factors that separate actors into numerous categories. Moreover, like neoliberals, constructivists do believe that norms and standards of behavior affect how states interact and conduct themselves. Unlike neoliberals, however, constructivists argue that states comply with norms and standards not simply because they are rational actors that are jointly maximizing their self-interest, but because they come to identify with certain notions of appropriateness and feel a sense of affinity with others who share these notions (Wendt 1999; Onuf 1998).

Along with an emphasis on nonmaterial factors, such as identity, community, norms, and standards, the constructivist approach also underscores the importance of international actors other than states. Although states do remain the primary actors in international security relations, there is a growing role for nongovernmental actors in influencing security matters (Keck and Sikkink 1998). State decisions regarding the use of landmines and other weapons that are perceived by some activist groups to be unethical and inhumane, for example, have been greatly affected as NGOs have pressured state authorities to undertake changes in the kinds of weapons they develop, export, or deploy (Rutherford, Brem, and Matthew 2003). Similar signs of nongovernmental influence have been documented in the areas of human rights, global health, and the environment. State decisions such as these (e.g., to limit the types of weapons used during war, to change humanitarian practices, or to regulate certain environmental activities) are not likely to have been made without nongovernmental actors raising awareness about and pressuring states to address their concerns. Constructivist approaches capture this kind of activity and highlight its importance.

Theoretical Debates Remain

As with the historical debate between traditional security studies scholars and those advocating a widening of the international security agenda, debates among international relations theorists regarding the appropriate theoretical assumptions, concepts, tools, and approaches continue. The study of international relations in general and international security more specifically is inherently fraught with debate about who are the most important actors, what are the most important questions, what are the most important explanatory variables, and which are the most important security issues worthy of focus. Without a doubt, there are numerous international security problems to study, consider, and solve. No one theoretical approach, however, can help us understand the multitude of global security concerns evident today. Despite the contentious debate about how best to study international security, therefore, there are multiple conceptual tools to help explain, understand, and address significant security problems facing states and peoples today.

CONTEMPORARY INTERNATIONAL SECURITY ISSUES

When asked to develop a list of the various international security concerns evident around the world today, students often produce a rather lengthy inventory that includes both traditional threats to the security of states as well as problems that threaten the security of human populations. To be sure, numerous and varied security issues occupy the time of government officials, **nongovernmental organizations**, **international (governmental) organizations**, and **multinational corporations** on a daily basis. It is impossible to discuss all international security concerns on the global agenda in this limited space or in an introductory course. Instead, this chapter offers a representative sample of some of today's more pressing global issues. This is not to say that these are the only—or the most important—security concerns that require attention. But the five security concerns outlined here—international terrorism, the spread of weapons of mass destruction, poverty and development, global health epidemics, and environmental degradation—have garnered significant official and scholarly consideration in recent years.

International Terrorism

Images of international **terrorism** are everywhere. One only has to recall the images of large airliners flying directly into the two **World Trade Center** towers in New York City and the **Pentagon** in Washington, D.C., on **September**

11, 2001. The aftermath of smoldering and collapsed ruins and nearly 3,000 lives lost has had an indelible effect on the global psyche regarding the vulnerability of society. This insecurity is precisely what terrorists want to achieve: they want to affect our psychological sense of well-being, safety, and security (Richardson 2006). How we respond is key. But what deserves a response and what determines our reaction is difficult to resolve given the sheer complicated nature of terrorism. From definitions of what constitutes terrorism to whether and how you respond to terrorist actions, there is no easy and straightforward formula.

The words "terrorism" and "terrorist" are, indeed, extremely difficult to define. The literature on the subject of terrorism is voluminous, with each published piece typically offering its own nuanced view of what constitutes terrorist activity. In general, however, there are a few key components that distinguish terrorism from other forms of armed violence. First, victims of terrorism are commonly "innocent" civilian populations rather than military combatants. However, regarding the second distinguishing factor, the victims who are directly affected by the terrorist action, either by death or injury, are not necessarily the primary targets. Terrorist attacks are meant to garner attention from and reaction by governments and the general public. A third distinction is that often it is **non-state actors** with political aims who perpetrate terrorist acts. In sum, terrorism generally constitutes the use of violence against a relatively small segment of society to gain attention from a larger audience, both governmental and nongovernmental, in an effort to further political views and ambitions (Hoffman 1999; Cronin 2002–2003).

This type of violence falls outside of acceptable behavior in that it does not conform to international laws and norms regarding which actors have the right to use force as well as which actors are legitimate targets of hostility. Recognized states are believed to hold a monopoly on the use of force. Non-state actors are expected to engage with others in a nonviolent manner. Moreover, civilian populations are not expected to be targets of violence. Although general populations are very often caught in the midst of armed conflict among states, the impact on ordinary people from deliberate and unpredictable attacks creates a level of insecurity that is unacceptable not only for society, but also for governments that are in place to protect them (Cronin 2002–2003).

Despite the improper and deplorable character of terrorist activity, however, the incidence of terrorism has grown significantly since the late nineteenth century, particularly since the end of World War II (de Nevers 2007). In fact, international terrorist attacks skyrocketed between 1968 and 1986, growing from 140 incidents to more than 650 attacks. However, terrorist activities declined throughout the post–Cold War period, despite the major attacks carried out on September 11, 2001 (Wilcox 2002). The types of terrorist actors have also changed in recent years. Prior to the end of the Cold War, terrorist organizations were often characterized by one of four factors: (1) left-wing efforts that were entangled with communist movements throughout the

Cold War era of East-West politics; (2) right-wing groups that were motivated by post-WWII fascist movements in Europe; (3) separatist efforts inspired by ethnic or nationalist tendencies following the process of decolonization after World War II; and (4) organizations motivated by religion attempting to defend or promote their religious zeal (Cronin 2002–2003). By the end of the twentieth century, while there was a demonstrated decrease in the numbers of international terrorist attacks overall, there was an increase in religious motivation behind the violence, an increase in the destructive capacities of terrorist actors, and, specifically, an increase in the number of American targets (ibid.).

Some scholars suggest that **globalization**, in particular, has had a significant impact on international terrorist activities—both as a cause and a facilitator of terrorism (ibid.). Although modern terrorism tends to incorporate religious tenets, it is possible to see terrorist actions "as part of a larger phenomenon of **anti-globalization** and tension between the have and have-not nations, as well as between the elite and underprivileged within those nations" (ibid., 35). The concern that the process of globalization has enriched some but impoverished others may be an underlying cause of violent behavior among non-state actors. Moreover, the spread of technology around the world has certainly facilitated terrorist efforts. Global financial operations have also helped terrorists fund their violent activities; global weapons technologies have allowed terrorists to better arm their violent campaigns; and global information technologies, such as cellular phones and the Internet, have assisted in recruitment, planning, coordination, and communication efforts. Terrorists today are much more efficient in their operations because of globalization.

Ironically, however, another aspect of globalization is that terrorists may also be likely to move their campaigns from violence against people to attacks on information technologies and cyberoperations. It is not clear whether cyberthreats are based on hyperactive imaginations or actual truths in fact, but nonetheless, **cyberwarfare** (or **cyberterrorism**) is a concern in the twenty-first century. As many governments, businesses, and individuals around the world have become more attached to and dependent on information and communications technologies, such technologies have potentially become a target for disruption and damage. Obviously, traditional security policies and conventional warfare methods are not likely to assist with combating cyberattacks. Therefore, cyberterrorism is of great concern should terrorist actors seek to harm the global information systems on which so many have come to rely (Clarke and Knake 2010).

Ultimately, while international terrorism has commanded much attention in recent years, some of this focus may be excessive. Although the unpredictable, deadly, and tragic nature of terrorist violence quite understandably deserves significant attention, some scholars suggest that terrorist actors never will garner the power and capability necessary to alter the world order or affect the global position and influence of powerful states. In fact, some scholars have gone so far as to refer to terrorist actors as annoying ankle biters that must be addressed, managed, and prevented from engaging in destructive activities (Kupchan 2003). The foreign policies of states and interactions of international organizations should not be dominated by terrorist considerations. Anti- and counterterrorist policies are a must, but should they dictate and determine the primary activities of major international actors? Most scholars say no. However, what if terrorist actors manage to acquire destructive capability that rivals that of states? It is to the issue of weapons of mass destruction and their effect on the international security environment that this chapter now turns.

The Spread of Weapons of Mass Destruction

According to many scholars and practitioners, the nuclear age that emerged at the end of World War II has been a source of insecurity in international relations. The Cold War era is most characterized by the nuclear arms race between the United States and the Soviet Union (Siracusa 2008). Worries about nuclear attacks and retaliations throughout the Cold War period were certainly warranted as the world's two superpowers developed ever more powerful nuclear capabilities and seemed willing, although reluctant, to use such weapons. Concerns about nuclear and other (chemical and biological) weapons of mass destruction, however, were heightened in the post–Cold War era. After the collapse of the Soviet Union, four newly independent former Soviet states inherited nuclear arsenals. Once part of a tightly controlled territory, the new states of the former Soviet region suffered from porous borders, insecure nuclear facilities, and nuclear scientists looking for their next paycheck. The threat of "**loose nukes**" falling into the hands of undesirable groups was, therefore, amplified. Moreover, other countries of concern, such as North Korea and Iran, began to express nuclear ambitions. As a result of these developments, the spread of weapons of mass destruction has climbed the agenda as a pressing international security issue (Allison et al. 1996; Allison et al. 2007; Sagan and Waltz 2002).

In general, there are at least five reasons why weapons proliferation is an international security concern. First, the spread of mass destructive weapons complicates the foreign policy of most states. Possession of the world's deadliest weapons poses challenges for the diplomatic missions of most governments as nuclear weapons states tend to fall in a category that often requires higher levels of attention and respect. Such complications are particularly true for the United States, which often serves as the "guarantor" of global nonproliferation activities. Second, instability during crisis may likely be more challenging and difficult to address and resolve when weapons of mass destruction are involved. Third, the spread of these weapons increases the probability that they will be used unintentionally. There is also an enhanced possibility of nuclear accidents—either accidental launches or nuclear incidents that result in irradiated areas. Fourth, as weapons of mass destruction become more widespread, they are more likely to be transferred—either purposefully or inadvertently—to terrorist groups or other non-state actors. Finally, the spread of these weapons, if allowed to proliferate unchecked, will undoubtedly be acquired by some state actors that "are likely to be politically unstable, aggressive, and difficult to deter" (Fetter 1991, 28; Sagan and Waltz 2002).

In reality, weapons of mass destruction have spread relatively little since the Cold War ended. Few states beyond the five "legitimate" nuclear power states (China, France, Russia, United Kingdom, and United States) and two additional self-declared nuclear states (India and Pakistan) have actually expressed nuclear ambitions. Those who have articulated or are suspected of such aspirations include North Korea and perhaps Iran, with Israel being somewhat silent on the matter despite evidence that Israel does indeed possess nuclear arms. Some nuclear inheritors—Belarus, Kazakhstan, and Ukraine, for example, who inherited nuclear weapons when the Soviet Union collapsed—have in fact relinquished their nuclear arsenals. Other states that once articulated interests in developing nuclear weapons programs—such as Libya, South Africa, Argentina, and Brazil—have since rolled back such aspirations (Reiss 1995; Paul 2000; Rublee 2009). There remain, however, both state and non-state actors that desire to develop or acquire nuclear programs and other weapons of mass destruction. For as long as nuclear weapons remain the currency of power in the international system, there will be interested parties ready to develop, deploy, and ultimately use such weaponry. Moreover, for as long as select nuclear facilities—particularly in the former Soviet Union—remain unsecured and vulnerable to breach, and as long as certain state actors remain willing to share nuclear secrets, the threat of weapons proliferation will continue (Allison et al. 1996; Allison et al. 2007).

Nuclear Weapons Possession in the Global Community

Nuclear Weapon States
China, France, Russia, United Kingdom, United States

Non-NPT (Nuclear Nonproliferation Treaty) States That Possess Nuclear Weapons
India, Israel, Pakistan

States of Immediate Proliferation Concern
Iran, North Korea, Syria

States That Have Relinquished Nuclear Weapons or Programs
Argentina, Belarus, Brazil, Iraq, Kazakhstan, Libya, South Africa, South Korea, Taiwan, Ukraine

Source: www.armscontrol.org/factsheets/Nuclearweaponswhohaswhat.

To combat the spread of nuclear and other weapons of mass destruction, global efforts have been made to develop international norms, standards, and procedures regarding who may possess what kinds of weaponry. International rules also govern whether and how nuclear and other important components of weapons programs can be shared and with whom. One of the most important of these efforts is the **Nuclear Nonproliferation Treaty** (NPT). The NPT was signed in 1968 and came into force in 1970 in an effort to prevent the proliferation of nuclear weapons, materials, technologies, and know-how. Nearly all states in the United Nations system have signed and ratified the NPT, and there has been near-universal compliance. Only four states—India, Pakistan, North Korea, and Israel (all of which have declared or are suspected of possessing nuclear weapons)—have refrained from joining the NPT. Perhaps the most important element of the NPT is the creation of the **International Atomic Energy Agency** (IAEA), which is tasked with monitoring and verifying the nuclear activities of member states.

A number of other global efforts have also emerged to combat the spread of weapons of mass destruction, such as the **Chemical Weapons Convention** (CWC), **Biological Weapons Convention** (BWC), **Global Partnership Against the Spread of Weapons and Materials of Mass Destruction**, **Fissile Material Cut-off Treaty** (FMCT), and **Comprehensive Test Ban Treaty** (CTBT). These add to a whole host of other bilateral arrangements between states and multilateral activities in regional settings. Some of these efforts have been successful (CWC and BWC, for example), but many others suffer from a lack of acceptance and compliance. Clearly, governments often struggle to accept and adhere to nonproliferation treaties and agreements. Moreover, non-state actors, who are not legitimate international players involved in the negotiation and signing of international treaties and agreements, are left outside the purview of nonproliferation activity and are not, therefore, included in nonproliferation efforts. Thus, the overall prospects for successfully preventing the spread of weapons of mass destruction remain good but not perfect. Since the advent of nuclear technology and the beginning of mass destructive weaponry, the global community has faced potential threats in this area. For example, confrontation between the United States and the Soviet Union in 1962 over missiles in Cuba nearly ended in the launch of nuclear warheads. More recent concerns with nuclear capabilities in Iran have garnered much attention in Israel, the United States, and elsewhere. Nonetheless, the probability of widespread devastation and destruction from nuclear weapons remains somewhat small and limited. However, the possibility of a mass destructive event is real.

Poverty, Development, and Global Economics

While international terrorism and weapons proliferation are more reminiscent of traditional security concerns in the international community, concerns about poverty, economic **development**, and global economic relations are less traditional. International security topics such as terrorism and weapons of mass destruction continue to evoke concerns about death, damage, and destruction. Economic security concerns are perhaps less conventional in that they do not immediately call to mind death and devastation. However, by extension there is a significant connection between insecurity and the economic well-being of states, governments and humans around the world.

A few scholars have focused on economic factors that have an impact on national power capability, although this field was not particularly mainstream in early security studies. In particular, some scholars have argued that variables such as industrial capacity, technological capabilities, and access to key resources such as steel, coal, and oil are key components of national power (Klare 2002; Morgenthau, Thompson, and Clinton 2005). Military capability, in fact, is derived from economic capacity, stability, and growth. Financial crises, a lack of or interrupted access to natural resources, and stagnant economic growth may actually contribute to national instability and, therefore, vulnerability. For **nation-states** to be secure in a rather traditional sense, governments must ensure their economic capacities in order to guarantee their power capabilities.

More recent conceptions of economic security and notions of the relevance of economic factors in international security tend to focus on several contemporary issues, such as (1) the impact of globalization on war and conflict (Stiglitz 2003); (2) the relationship between economic development and poverty and instability and violence (Harris 1999; Bardhan 2004); (3) how scarce resources are a source of violence and conflict (Klare 2002); and (4) the extent to which illicit economic activities, such as the illicit trafficking of valuable commodities, contributes to armed violence, instability, war, and conflict (Benedek et al. 2010). There is awareness that national economic systems are interconnected around the world and that disruptions in economic activity in one location, particularly when disruptions are due to conflict or violence, have an effect on another location. War and conflict, therefore, may have an impact on the economic capacity and well-being of not only those involved in the violence, but also those who are economically connected via resources, supply chains, or global business. Moreover, some argue that globalization itself creates a system of **dependency** and exploitation between rich and poor countries as **multinational corporations** situated in wealthy regions take advantage of cheap resources and labor in less privileged regions. This process, they argue, creates dissatisfaction, discontent, and frustration in poor areas, which may lead to violence and conflict (Schneider, Barbieri, and Gleditsch 2003; Barkani 2005).

Much has been written about the relationship between poverty and a lack of economic development and armed violence, tension, and disputes. Such violence in poverty-ridden settings is often internal and localized. In fact, research has shown that areas that experience higher levels of economic growth are less prone to internal violence and conflict. The link between economic growth and domestic tranquility is most visible in the human security literature, where scholars focus on key indicators of development, such as access to education and employment, to demonstrate that fewer economic and social opportunities contribute to lower levels of economic growth, lower levels of hope, and higher levels of organized frustration, violence, conflict, and crime. Arguments of causation between poverty and war, however, are difficult to make. Anecdotal evidence suggests that poverty and a lack of development are found in areas where war, conflict, and insecurity are taking place. It is not clear, however, whether poverty causes war or war causes poverty (Ballentine and Sherman 2003).

Just as there is a great deal of scholarship about traditional understandings of national power and how certain natural resources are key to national power capabilities, much has also been written about how competition over scarce natural resources may contribute to violence and conflict. Access to energy resources, such as oil and coal, or life-sustaining resources, such as water, contributes to development and human well-being. These resources, however, are limited in their availability, which contributes to competition for and potential conflict over access to them. There is evidence of such competition and its impact on violence and conflict in terms of how powerful countries such as the United States and some of its European allies have been willing to go to war in the Middle East to protect access to oil fields (Klare 2005). Access to water underlies part of the conflict between Israelis and Palestinians (Klare 2002), just as access to diamond mines in African countries such as Sierra Leone has funded destruction and death (Campbell 2004).

Finally, the illicit trafficking of economic commodities is related to insecurity, war, conflict, and violent crime. Certain goods—such as diamonds, timber, and strategic rare earth minerals that may be used in batteries, computers, and other important products—have been exploited for sale in illicit markets and are often illicitly traded across borders. The value of such commodities lies in the basic concept of limited supply and great demand, which contributes to the development of a global **black market** that operates outside the law and often adds an element of violence. Moreover, terrorists, organized criminals, and paramilitary or insurgent forces often rely on the illicit trafficking of goods, resources, and even people to support their violent campaigns. Ultimately, researchers suggest that the illicit trafficking of economically desirable materials perpetuates systems of violence (Benedek et al. 2010; Eichstaedt 2011).

In numerous ways, therefore, economic factors have an impact on power, security, violence, and conflict. Global economic matters cannot be ignored in the analysis of international security issues. It is not entirely clear how, when, and where economic issues cause international security problems— or whether and to what extent international security concerns contribute to economic problems. However, it is clear that, at a minimum, economic considerations are important aspects of international security and insecurity.

Global Health Epidemics

One of the key human security concerns on the international radar today relates to human health. Since 1945, there have been 150 million deaths worldwide attributed to three infectious diseases: **AIDS, tuberculosis,** and **malaria**. The number of deaths from disease dwarfs the approximately 23 million killed by war and violent conflict during the same period. In fact, six different infectious diseases—AIDS, pneumonia, tuberculosis, diarrheal diseases, malaria, and measles—account for about 90 percent of all disease-related deaths around the world (Peterson 2002–2003). AIDS alone has claimed 25 million lives worldwide, with another 33 million living with AIDS today (UNAIDS 2008). In terms of human security, therefore, health epidemics are clearly of significant concern.

Regional HIV and AIDS Statistics

Region	Adults and Children Living with HIV	Adults and Children Newly Infected with HIV
Sub-Saharan Africa	22,500,000	1,800,000
Middle East and North Africa	460,000	75,000
South and South-East Asia	4,100,000	270,000
East Asia	770,000	82,000
Central and South America	1,400,000	92,000
Caribbean	240,000	17,000
Eastern Europe and Central Asia	1,400,000	130,000
Western and Central Europe	820,000	31,000
North America	1,500,000	70,000
Oceania	57,000	4,500
Total	33,300,000	2,600,000

Source: www.unaids.org/en/media/unaids/contentassets/dataimport/pub/factsheet/2009/20091124_fs_global_en.pdf

The consequences of health epidemics are considerable and reach well beyond local communities. First, widespread illness and disease has an impact on economic development. A sick population that has been deprived of its working-age inhabitants will be less likely to make economic progress. Widespread health epidemics overburden health care facilities, which are often unable to treat not only those suffering from the epidemic, but those requiring other health assistance. Epidemics also negatively affect education institutions. When teachers, administrators, and students are victims of an epidemic, schools systems and educational programs shut down. Given the significant connections between economic well-being, public health treatment, and institutions of learning, pervasive communicable disease not only kills people, but prevents development and facilitates poverty (Elbe 2010).

A second factor is the effect of health epidemics on governance and military security. Governments struggling to facilitate development and growth may become overloaded with public health crises resulting from widespread epidemics. Scarce funds in government coffers committed to treat a sick population are funds that cannot be spent on education, economic development, or national defense. Governments are then faced with a confusing spiral of where to commit their efforts. Moreover, government leaders and decision makers have also become victims of health epidemics, further weakening institutions of governance and contributing to vulnerable and **failed states**. Military personnel, in particular, may be most likely to suffer from or spread infectious diseases. Given the military's likelihood to travel and interact with a broader population, they are perhaps at greater risk of exposure to communicable illnesses. Widespread illness among military troops and personnel also contributes further to weakened institutions of national security. With a sick military, governments are much less effective in responding to threats to national well-being (Chen, Leaning, and Narasimhan 2004).

Although health epidemics and their security consequences are, at least initially, local in nature, there are significant international security concerns that result from health crises as well. Disease and illness are not elements that can be contained within national or other boundaries. Disease, by nature, is transnational and can spill over to neighboring populations. Governments and national authorities that are weakened by rampant illness and disease are, therefore, less able to contain them (Price-Smith 2009). Moreover, diseases can also travel long distances as people board various transportation sources all around the world. There have been, for example, global concerns about **Severe Acute Respiratory Syndrome** (SARS) and the **H1N1 (swine flu)** virus (Drexler 2009; Abraham 2007). Additional overflow effects of disease include the spreading of instability, violence, and conflict that may extend well beyond local and national boundaries as refugees flee their local circumstances and, in some cases, turn to crime in an effort to ensure their survival (Price-Smith 2001 and 2009).

Finally, health security is also relevant to national and international security in a more traditional sense. The possibility of weaponizing disease and using biological agents in an act of war or terrorism is a real threat. Purposefully causing illness and death may certainly serve the purpose of an enemy in conflict, or a terrorist seeking to cause widespread panic. Spreading disease via local water supplies or by means of some airborne release in congested areas of human population may be a highly effective way to render a target helpless and create mass hysteria. Fortunately, it is still very difficult to develop, deploy, and deliver biological weapons, but with dangerous germs and biological agents readily available around the world, the use of such weapons is undoubtedly possible (Johnstone 2008).

Environmental Degradation

Security concerns stemming from environmental issues have previously been mentioned insofar as they are connected to the security of economic well-being and the facilitation of economic development (see section titled *Poverty, Development, and Global Economics*). Competition over scarce natural resources, such as oil, water, coal, and other minerals, is clearly related to issues of environmental security and the traditional conflicts to which environmental resources may contribute. "Energy stress," for example, certainly can lead to "economic stress" (Mathews 1989). There are, however, other important ways in which environmental issues have an impact on international security and insecurity. Above all, the environmental degradation that is the result of damage to land, water, forests, habitats, and the atmosphere results in significant security concerns.

Such environmental neglect is often the result of ecologically unfriendly practices that reap much from the earth without sowing the seeds of restoration and recovery (Homer-Dixon and Blitt 1998). Unsustainable farming, deforestation, and fishing, as well as rampant polluting, are primary culprits. Farming activities that overuse land and introduce chemical pollutants into the soil, ground water, and surrounding areas of water runoff initiate environmental concerns and threaten supplies of food and water. Indeed, the security of food and water is a significant concern in many areas around the world and is likely to remain so well into the future (Turrel, Burke, and Faures 2011). The destruction of forests around the world for the clearance of farmland and grazing pastures, as well as for the use of timber for energy and other products, has had significant consequences for clean air and the protection of our atmospheric ozone levels. Over-fishing of oceans, seas, lakes, and rivers contributes to depleted resources and threatens the survival of key industries. In addition, an entire spectrum of pollution—from emissions such as greenhouse gases to the disposal of toxic waste—poses additional threats to the land that society needs to live and grow food, the potable water supply for drinking and nourishing food supplies, the availability of clean air to breathe, and the health of the atmosphere that filters the sun's harmful rays.

Of prime environmental concern today is the climate change that may result from environmental degradation. Although some politicians and scholars disagree, most scientists argue that with an altered and damaged environment comes a change in climate that contributes to **desertification**, floods, droughts, melting glaciers, and rising sea levels (Mazo 2010). The loss of arable land in Sudan, for example, has contributed significantly to the war and conflict in Darfur as groups fight over land for farming and grazing. Floods in Pakistan and droughts in Ethiopia have led to horrible humanitarian crises leaving death, destruction, famine, and disease in their wake. Rising global temperatures lead to the melting of oceanic ice and continental glaciers and a resulting rise in sea levels, threatening millions of people and thousands of cities that are located very near coastlines all around the world.

Ultimately, such environmental changes have an impact on political, economic, and social stability. **Environmental degradation** causes shifts in demography as populations are displaced, either because of the environmental changes or shifts in climate alone or because of the violence and conflict that may result from such changes or shifts. **Environmental refugees** attempting to escape the conditions of insecurity contribute further to instability and a lack of security, which strains political, economic, and social structures even more. The result is a cycle of insecurity, violence, and conflict that is challenging to manage, minimize, and overcome (Homer-Dixon and Blitt 1998; Homer-Dixon 2001).

As with other security concerns presented in this chapter, the security threats that are a consequence of environmental degradation transcend local and national boundaries. Such threats, therefore, endanger the global community as the effects of environmental damage often spread and affect larger populations (Homer-Dixon 2008). Therefore, solutions to environmental, as well as other security problems discussed here, require collective efforts at a global level in addition to individual efforts at the local level. Such efforts, however, remain challenging. Governments around the world continue to find it difficult to reach collective decisions on greenhouse gasses, levels of emissions, and ways to stop and prevent devastating pollution. Weak agreements such as the **Kyoto Accord** and heightened concerns about industrial pollution in China and India illustrate such difficulties. Nonetheless, despite the challenges, there are few alternatives. Security, after all, is a commodity we all seek, from which we all benefit, and to which we all have no choice but contribute. Consequently, it is to the subject of solutions we now turn.

SOLUTIONS AND CONCLUSIONS

The various security threats outlined and discussed in this chapter have at least one thing in common: they are all characterized by their international or transnational nature. As noted in the introduction to the book, former UN secretary-general, Kofi Annan, often referred to such concerns as "problems without passports." In other words, none of these issues can be addressed or solved by any one government, state, group, or individual. The causes and consequences of today's security concerns transcend traditional national boundaries and must, therefore, be managed, mitigated, and resolved with collective efforts. Such collective, or multilateral, action typically involves (1) international governmental organizations; (2) international treaties, laws, rules and regulations; (3) international norms and standards of behavior; and (4) transnational networks, NGOs, and groups of individuals. Moreover, security solutions may also be found in national domestic political development and changes in internal state governance structures.

International (governmental) organizations, or what we often call IGOs or IOs, are groups of states that have come together, typically by signing a charter or some sort of governing document, in an effort to address common problems (Karns and Mingst 2009; Pease 2009). The **United Nations** (UN), for example, was established after World War II to resolve security threats and prevent another massive global war. Organizations like the **European Union** (EU), **North Atlantic Treaty Organization** (NATO), **Organization of American States** (OAS), and **Organization for Cooperation and Security in Europe** (OSCE) have emerged over the last several decades to jointly discuss, consider, and solve the concerns that member-states raise. Although these organizations do not always prevent violence from occurring—the UN, for example, has not prevented armed conflict—they do serve as a forum for sharing ideas and concerns and developing and promoting solutions in many different ways. The **World Health Organization** (WHO), for instance, has been very successful in its more than sixty years of operations in addressing health problems, such as access to vaccinations, and in fostering the development of public health systems in local communities.

International treaties, laws, rules, and regulations are another way in which national governments address international security concerns (Nelson 2006). Although such international instruments are sometimes the result of activity within international organizations, international treaties, laws, rules, and regulations may sometime emerge out of irregular and informal interaction among states to establish a solution to a recognized common problem. The Convention on the Prohibition of the Development, Production, Stockpiling and Use of Chemical Weapons and on Their Destruction—otherwise known as the **Chemical Weapons Convention,** or CWC—and other similar agreements among states outline international rules regarding a single-issue area. The CWC "governs" in the area of chemical weapons by forbidding states who are signatories of the convention from developing, producing, procuring, stockpiling, transferring, deploying, or using chemical weaponry. Other international treaties that outline particular laws governing certain issue areas include, among others, the NPT, the **Law of the Sea Treaty,** and the **Convention on the Rights of the Child**.

Often, the laws and treaties that emerge among states are the result of **multilateral interaction** within international organizations. International norms and standards of behavior also influence actions not only of states, but of **non-state actors** and individuals. Ideas about how we *should* behave toward one another, for example, may influence how states, groups, and individuals interact, shaping and affecting security-related consequences at multiple levels (Sandholtz and Stiles 2008). Norms about when, why, and how it is appropriate and just to engage in war (*jus ad bellum* and *jus in bello*), for example, provide guidance for states as they consider going to war. Such ethical consideration of when it is just to go to war may also inform states as to when, where, why, and how it is necessary to intervene militarily to prevent or stop human suffering. Humanitarian intervention, in other words, may largely be viewed as a result of normative or ethical deliberations rather than mere state security concerns. International standards regarding health, disease, sanitation, and avoidance of illness also guide states as well as groups and individuals. Those working to spread ideas and information about the causes, consequences, and prevention of disease play a significant role, for instance, in individual activities that may prevent the transmission of communicable illness. Moreover, international norms and standards concerning environmental protection have an impact on what states, groups, and individuals do to safeguard resources and avoid environmental degradation.

Transnational networks, NGOs, and groups of individuals that have an interest in particular international security issues also have a role to play in solving security problems. Particularly with the growth of telecommunications (especially the Internet) and travel opportunities, NGOs have emerged as important players in international relations, coordinating their actions to more effectively address certain security concerns that national governments and IOs fail to address adequately. Most often targeting issues such as the environment, human rights, health, development, and women's/children's rights, NGO networks have also tackled more traditional issues such as national and international security methods that have humanitarian consequences (Keck and Sikkink 1998). For example, the **International Campaign to Ban Landmines** (ICBL) developed in the early 1990s as a collection of more than a thousand NGOs who shared concerns about the negative humanitarian effects and indiscriminate nature of antipersonnel landmines, of which there are millions scattered in various places around the world. The ICBL coordinated a campaign to ban the development, production, acquisition, stockpiling, transfer, sale, deployment, and use of antipersonnel landmines. After a few short years, the ICBL was able to facilitate state action on the issue and pushed governments to sign the **Ottawa Treaty** in 1997 outlawing antipersonnel landmines for any purpose. The treaty came into force in 1999 and has broad international support, with the exception of three important countries: China, Russia, and the United States. Nonetheless, the landmine ban is the result of collective NGO and individual action—groups of people who were particularly concerned about one particular international security problem. Moreover, the ICBL was awarded the Nobel Peace Prize in 1997 for its efforts.

Finally, although today's international security concerns most often require collective or multilateral action, there do remain ways in which individual states may contribute answers to global security problems. Internal political changes such as the development of **democratic institutions, rule of law,** and **transparency,** for example, may ultimately lead to more peaceful relations with other nations—particularly with other democracies (Russett 1994). Democratic institutions such as free and fair elections, separation of powers, and bureaucratic checks and balances have been shown to mitigate easy and quick decisions to go to war or engage in violent conflict. Because democratically elected leaders who do not hold absolute power within their system of governance are likely to be held accountable to the electorate for unreasonable and extreme decisions, war and violent conflict must be carefully managed and implemented. Moreover, the peaceful resolution of conflict within domestic society—supported by stable and fair judicial practices that allow for the resolution of conflict in peaceful ways—also mitigate quick judgments and decisions to go to war and violently resolve international disputes. This is not to suggest that democracies do not go to war when they deem it appropriate and necessary, but that (1) democracies rarely go to war with one another; and (2) when they do go to war, they do so after, typically, long public debate and careful consideration.

With the evolution of national and international security threats and concerns, there has been an evolution in the field of security studies. From more traditional notions of government or state security to a more contemporary focus on human security, there have been significant changes in what constitutes security and insecurity. Within international security studies, theoretical approaches have developed to help understand and explain international security phenomena—and theoretically enlightened research remains important and should be continued. Ultimately, however, the management of and solutions to international security problems require knowledge and awareness as well as collective attempts to address them.

REFERENCES

Abraham, Thomas. 2007. *Twenty-First Century Plague: The Story of SARS.* Baltimore: Johns Hopkins University Press.

Allison, Graham, Owen R. Cote, Jr., Richard A. Falkenrath, and Steven E. Miller. 1996. *Avoiding Nuclear Anarchy: Containing the Threat of Loose Russian Nuclear Weapons and Fissile Material.* Cambridge, Mass.: MIT Press.

Allison, Graham, Herve De Carmany, Therese Delpech, and Chung Min Lee. 2007. *Nuclear Proliferation: Risk and Responsibility.* Washington, D.C.: Trilateral Commission.

Baldwin, David A. 1995. "Security Studies and the End of the Cold War." *World Politics* 48, no. 1 (October): 117–41.

Ballentine, Karen, and Jake Sherman, eds. 2003. *The Political Economy of Armed Conflict: Beyond Greed and Grievance.* Boulder, Colo.: Lynne Rienner.

Bardhan, Pranab. 2004. *Scarcity, Conflicts and Cooperation: Essays in the Political and Institutional Economics of Development.* Cambridge, Mass.: MIT Press.

Barkani, Tarak. 2005. *Globalization and War.* Lanham, Md.: Rowman & Littlefield.

Benedek, Wolfgang, Christopher Daase, Petrus Van Duyne, and Dimitrijevic Vojin, eds. 2010. *Transnational Terrorism, Organized Crime and Peace-Building: Human Security in the Western Balkans.* Hampshire, UK: Palgrave Macmillan.

Buzan, Barry, and Lene Hansen. 2009. *The Evolution of International Security Studies.* Cambridge: Cambridge University Press.

Campbell, Greg. 2004. *Blood Diamonds: Tracing the Deadly Path of the World's Most Precious Stone.* New York: Basic Books.

Cardoso, Fernando Henrique. 1979. *Dependency and Development in Latin America.* Berkeley: University of California Press.

Chen, Lincoln C., Jennifer Leaning, and Vasant Narasimhan, eds. 2004. *Global Health Challenges for Human Security.* Cambridge, Mass.: Harvard University Press.

Clarke, Richard A., and Robert Knake. 2010. *Cyber War: The Next Threat to National Security and What to Do About It.* New York: Ecco.

Collins, Alan, ed. 2010. *Contemporary Security Studies.* 2nd ed. Oxford, UK: Oxford University Press.

Cronin, Audrey Kurth. 2002–2003. "Behind the Curve: Globalization and International Terrorism." *International Security* 27, no. 3 (Winter): 30–58.

Dannreuther, Roland. 2008. *International Security: The Contemporary Agenda.* London: Polity Press.

de Nevers, Renee. 2007. "Imposing International Norms: Great Powers and Norm Enforcement." *International Studies Review* 9:53–80.

Doyle, Michael. 1986. "Liberalism and World Politics." *American Political Science Review* 80, no. 4 (December): 1151–69.

Drexler, Madeline. 2009. *Emerging Epidemics: The Menace of New Infections.* New York: Penguin.

Eichstaedt, Peter. 2011. *Consuming the Congo: War and Conflict Minerals in the World's Deadliest Place.* Brooklyn, N.Y.: Lawrence Hill Books.

Elbe, Stefan. 2010. *Security and Global Health.* London: Polity Press.

Evans, Peter. 1979. *Dependent Development: The Alliance of Multinational, State, and Local Capital in Brazil.* Princeton, N.J.: Princeton University Press.

Fetter, Steve. 1991. "Ballistic Missiles and Weapons of Mass Destruction: What Is the Threat? What Should Be Done?" *International Security* 16, no. 1 (Summer): 5–42.

Gibson-Graham, J. K., Stephen Resnick, and Richard Wolff, eds. 2001. *Re/Presenting Class: Essays in Postmodern Marxism*. Durham, N.C.: Duke University Press.

Harris, Geoff, ed. 1999. *Recovery from Armed Conflict in Developing Countries: An Economic and Political Analysis*. New York: Routledge.

Hoffman, Bruce. 1999. *Inside Terrorism*. New York: Columbia University Press.

Homer-Dixon, Thomas. 2001. *Environment, Scarcity and Violence*. Princeton, N.J.: Princeton University Press.

———. 2008. *The Upside of Down: Catastrophe, Creativity and the Renewal of Civilization*. Washington, D.C.: Island Press.

Homer-Dixon, Thomas, and Jessica Blitt, eds. 1998. *Ecoviolence: Links Among Environment, Population and Security*. Landham, Md.: Rowman & Littlefield.

Hough, Peter. 2008. *Understanding Global Security*. 2nd ed. New York: Routledge.

Howard, M. C., and J. E. King. 1998. *The Political Economy of Marx*. 2nd ed. New York: New York University Press.

Jervis, Robert. 1982. "Security Regimes." *International Organization* 36, no. 2: 357–78.

Johnstone, R. William. 2008. *Bioterror: Anthrax, Influenza and the Future of Public Health Security*. Santa Barbara, Calif.: Praeger.

Kant, Immanuel. 1795/1983. *Perpetual Peace, and Other Essays on Politics, History, and Morals*. Repr. translated by Ted Humphrey. Indianapolis, Ind.: Hackett Publishing.

Karns, Margaret D., and Karen A. Mingst. 2009. *International Organizations: The Politics and Processes of Global Governance*. 2nd ed. Boulder, Colo.: Lynne Rienner.

Keck, Margaret E., and Kathryn Sikkink. 1998. *Activists Beyond Borders: Advocacy Networks in International Politics*. Ithaca, N.Y.: Cornell University Press.

Keohane, Robert O. 1984. *After Hegemony: Cooperation and Discord in the World Political Economy*. Princeton, N.J.: Princeton University Press.

Keohane, Robert O., and Joseph S. Nye. 2000. *Power and Interdependence*. 3rd ed. New York: Longman.

Klare, Michael. 2002. *Resource Wars: The New Landscape of Global Conflict*. New York: Henry Holt.

———. 2005. *Blood and Oil: The Dangers and Consequences of America's Growing Dependency on Imported Petroleum*. New York: Holt Paperbacks.

Kupchan, Charles. 2003. *The End of the American Era: U.S. Foreign Policy and the Geopolitics of the Twenty-first Century*. New York: Vintage.

Linklater, Andrew. 1996. "Marxism." In 3rd ed. of *Theories of International Relations*, edited by Scott Burchill, Andrew Linklater, Richard Devetak, Jack Donnelly, Matthew Paterson, Christian Reus-Smit, and Jacqui True, 110–36. Basingstoke, UK: Palgrave.

Mathews, Jessica Tuchman. 1989. "Redefining Security." *Foreign Affairs* 68, no. 2 (Spring): 162–77.

Mazo, Jeffrey. 2010. *Climate Conflict: How Global Warming Threatens Security and What to Do about It.* New York: Routledge.

Mearsheimer, John. 2001. *The Tragedy of Great Power Politics.* New York: W.W. Norton.

Morgenthau, Hans, Kenneth Thompson, and David Clinton. 2005. *Politics Among Nations: The Struggle for Power and Peace.* 7th ed. Columbus, Ohio: McGraw-Hill.

Nelson, Sheila. 2006. *Pioneering International Law: Conventions, Treaties and Standards.* Broomall, Pa.: Mason Crest.

Nye, Joseph S., and Sean M. Lynn-Jones. 1988. "International Security Studies: A Report of a Conference on the State of the Field." *International Security* 12, no. 4 (Spring): 5–27.

Onuf, Nicholas. 1989. *World of Our Making: Rules and Rule in Social Theory and International Relations.* Columbia: University of South Carolina Press.

———. 1998. "Constructivism: A User's Manual." In *International Relations in a Constructed World,* edited by V. Kublakova, N. Onuf, and P. Kowert, 58–78. New York: M.E. Sharpe.

Paul, T. V. 2000. *Power Versus Prudence: Why Nations Forgo Nuclear Weapons.* Montreal, Quebec: McGill-Queen's University Press.

Pease, Kelly-Kate S. 2009. *International Organizations: Perspectives on Global Governance.* 4th ed. Upper Saddle River, N.J.: Prentice Hall.

Peterson, Susan. 2002–2003. "Epidemic Disease and National Security." *Security Studies* 12, no. 2 (Winter): 43–81.

Price-Smith, Andrew T. 2001. *The Health of Nations: Infectious Disease, Environmental Change and Their Effects on National Security and Development.* Cambridge, Mass.: MIT Press.

———. 2009. *Contagion and Chaos: Disease, Ecology and National Security in the Era of Globalization.* Cambridge, Mass.: MIT Press.

Reiss, Mitchell. 1995. *Bridled Ambition: Why Countries Constrain Their Nuclear Capabilities.* Washington, D.C.: Woodrow Wilson Center Press.

Richardson, Louise. 2006. *What Terrorists Want: Understanding the Enemy, Containing the Threat.* New York: Random House.

Rublee, Maria Rost. 2009. *Nonproliferation Norms: Why States Choose Nuclear Restraint.* Athens: University of Georgia Press.

Russett, Bruce. 1994. *Grasping the Democratic Peace.* Princeton, N.J.: Princeton University Press.

Rutherford, Kenneth, Stefan Brem, and Richard Matthew, eds. 2003. *Reframing the Agenda: The Impact of NGO and Middle Power Cooperation in International Security Policy.* Santa Barbara, Calif.: Praeger.

Sagan, Scott D., and Kenneth N. Waltz. 2002. *The Spread of Nuclear Weapons: A Debate Renewed.* 2nd ed. New York: W.W. Norton.

Sandholtz, Wayne, and Kendall Stiles. 2008. *International Norms and Cycles of Change.* Oxford, UK: Oxford University Press.

Schneider, Gerlad, Katherine Barbieri, and Nils Petter Gleditsch, eds. 2003. *Globalization and Armed Conflict.* Lanham, Md.: Rowman & Littlefield.

Siracusa, Joseph M. 2008. *Nuclear Weapons: A Very Short Introduction.* Oxford, UK: Oxford University Press.

Stiglitz, Joseph. 2003. *Globalization and Its Discontents.* New York: W.W. Norton & Co.

Turrel, Hugh, Jacob Burke, and Jean-Marc Faures. 2011. *Climate Change, Water and Food Security.* Rome, Italy: Food and Agriculture Organization.

UNAIDS. 2008. *2008 Report on the Global AIDS Epidemic.* New York: United Nations. www.unaids.org/en/KnowledgeCentre/HIVData/GlobalReport/2008/.

Wallerstein, Immanuel. 1976. *The Modern World-System: Capitalist Agriculture and the Origins of the European World-Economy in the Sixteenth Century.* New York: Academic Press.

Walt, Stephen M. 1991. "The Renaissance of Security Studies." *International Security Studies* 35, no. 2 (June): 211–39.

Waltz, Kenneth. 1979. *Theory of International Politics.* Columbus, Ohio: McGraw-Hill.

Wendt, Alexander. 1992. "Anarchy Is What States Make of It: The Social Construction of Power Politics." *International Organization* 46, no. 2: 391–425.

———. 1994. "Collective Identity Formation and the International State." *American Political Science Review* 88: 384–96.

———. 1999. *Social Theory of International Politics.* Cambridge: Cambridge University Press.

Wilcox, Phillip C., Jr. 2002. "The Rise and Decline of International Terrorism.," In *Combating Terrorism: Strategies of Ten Countries*, edited by Yonah Alexander, 23–61. Ann Arbor: University of Michigan Press.

Williams, Paul D., ed. 2008. *Security Studies: An Introduction.* London: Routledge.

3
Humanitarian Intervention

ERIC A. HEINZE

In the early spring of 2011, amidst the **Arab Spring** uprisings across the Middle East region, a bloody civil war raged in Libya between forces loyal to Libyan dictator Muammar Gaddafi and opposition rebel forces. Reports coming out of Libya indicated that Gaddafi forces had carried out aerial bombings of unarmed civilian protesters in Tripoli, while the conflict in general entailed the widespread abuse and targeting of civilians by Gaddafi forces, including the use of systematic rape as a weapon of war and threats by Colonel Gaddafi himself that his forces would "show no mercy" to those supporting the uprising in the rebel-held city of Benghazi. In response, the **United Nations (UN) Security Council** on March 17, 2011, adopted Resolution 1973, which authorized member-states to enforce a no-fly zone over Libya and use "all necessary means," including the use of military force, but short of the use of ground troops, to protect Libyan civilians. The result was a lengthy bombing campaign carried out largely by France and the United Kingdom, with substantial assistance from the United States, under the auspices of the **North Atlantic Treaty Organization (NATO)**. The bombing campaign, while justified by reference to a "responsibility to protect" Libyan civilians from massacre by their own government, eventually turned the tide of the war in favor of the rebels, leading to the ouster of Colonel Gaddafi and eventually his death, paving the way for a transitional government to take control over of Libya. (See Appendix A.)

This resort to using military force by NATO and other coalition partners in Libya is an example of what is broadly referred to as **humanitarian intervention**, which has been the subject of a vigorous debate by scholars and analysts in the decades surrounding the beginning of the twenty-first century. The increased attention given to international human rights, particularly since the creation of the **United Nations (UN) Charter** (1945) and the **Universal Declaration of Human Rights** (1948), has led to an international debate about the appropriateness of intervention by international organizations, groups of nations, or single countries under the banner of saving lives. In particular, the idea that state **sovereignty** no longer permits a government to treat its citizens however it pleases has lent itself to the argument that if a state turns viciously against its own population, then outside actors may legitimately (if not legally) intervene to come to their rescue, by using military force if necessary. Although Cold War **geopolitics** provided a disincentive for influential states to take seriously the suffering of human beings living under murderous governments, the lifting of this global political superstructure in the early 1990s created space within which states could act through a reinvigorated UN to come to the aid of people suffering at the hands of their own governments.

As a corollary to the end of the Cold War, ethnic rivalries that were suppressed under the global preoccupation with superpower rivalry boiled over. Particularly in places like the Balkans (i.e., the **former Yugoslavia**) and Africa (e.g., Somalia, Rwanda), a newly liberated UN had ample opportunity to fulfill its promise of dealing with threats to international peace and security, which would come to include gross violations of human rights *within* states. Although the several UN-sanctioned interventions of the 1990s achieved at best mixed results, it was the 1999 NATO intervention over Kosovo—which was *not* authorized by the UN—that provided the most traction for the contemporary debate over humanitarian intervention (see Appendix A).

Humanitarian intervention is generally understood to be an act of military intervention by an actor or actors (usually states) into the jurisdiction of another state for the purpose of halting or averting gross human abuse. The contemporary debate that has emerged in response to the various military interventions that allegedly fall under this classification has indeed been thought-provoking, addressing issues such as what acts are rightly considered "humanitarian interventions," whether and under what conditions such action is morally and politically desirable, and when, if ever, humanitarian intervention is allowable under **international law**. This chapter outlines the contemporary debate over humanitarian intervention by first giving meaning to the concept of "humanitarian intervention" and distinguishing it from other kinds of interventions in international affairs. The chapter then explores the prevailing ethical arguments and political debates, followed by an examination of the extent to which humanitarian intervention is considered permissible under international law. The last section of this chapter briefly reviews the debate over humanitarian intervention in light of the **Global War on Terror**. Two appendices at the end of the chapter briefly outline and summarize several historical and recent cases that have influenced the current humanitarian intervention debate.

THE CONCEPT OF HUMANITARIAN INTERVENTION

Humanitarian intervention, broadly construed, can mean a number of things, including the use of military force, the delivery of **humanitarian aid**, the oversight of democratic elections, or even the imposition of economic sanctions. In the scholarly and legal literature, however, the term more specifically entails the use of military force to halt or avert the grave mistreatment of people in other countries. Among the more commonly employed definitions of humanitarian intervention are the following: "action taken against a state or its leaders, without its or their consent, for purposes which are claimed to be humanitarian or protective" (**International Commission on Intervention and State Sovereignty** [ICISS] 2001, 8); "the threat or use of force across state borders by a state (or group of states) aimed at preventing or ending widespread and grave violations of the fundamental human rights of individuals other than one's own citizens, without the permission of the state in whose territory force is applied" (Keohane 2003, 1); and "the threat or use of armed force by a state, a belligerent community, or an international organization, with the object of protecting human rights" (Brownlie 1974, 217). All these definitions share some general characteristics: they involve the threat or use of military force that violates the territorial integrity (sovereignty) of another state for the purposes of promoting or protecting the human rights of individuals in that state who are ostensibly being abused by their governments.

The Responsibility to Protect

Although these and similar definitions are the most common in the literature, other treatments of the subject encompass important differences. For instance, even the very term "humanitarian intervention" has been contested by the ICISS, which published an authoritative report in 2001 entitled *The Responsibility to Protect*. This important report was published as a result of the controversy surrounding NATO's 1999 intervention over Kosovo and argues that it is unhelpful to frame the debate in terms of a "right of humanitarian intervention," but rather advocates using the language of a "responsibility to protect." The ICISS argues that the language of intervention unnecessarily focuses attention on the "right" of the intervening actors, whereas the language of a "responsibility to protect" implies evaluating the issue from the point of view of the potential beneficiaries of such intervention—that is, those in need of rescuing. Likewise, the language of "intervention" too narrowly focuses on the act of intervention itself, thus neglecting the "responsibility" of outside actors not only to intervene, but also to engage in prior diplomatic efforts to avoid conflict in the first place and provide follow-up assistance in the aftermath of conflict. Most important, the more familiar language of "intervention" serves to trump state sovereignty before the debate even begins, whereas the language of "responsibility" implies that the primary responsibility for the welfare of individuals lies with the state concerned. Therefore, the ICISS proclaims that "it is only if the state is unable or unwilling to fulfill this responsibility, or is itself the perpetrator, that it becomes the responsibility of the international community to act in its place" (ICISS 2001, 17). This semantic move was largely inspired by the idea of **sovereignty as responsibility**, which implies that sovereignty is not a right or a license of a government, but a responsibility that governments have to protect their citizens and provide for their general welfare (Deng, Kimaro, Lyons, Rothchild, and Zartman 1996).

The purpose of changing the terms of the debate, although it does not change the substantive issues, is to facilitate a consensus on how and when the international community should react to grave human suffering and ideally to remove barriers to effective action. Some scholars and governments are increasingly using this broader, more inclusive language in discourse on humanitarian intervention, such as in the debate over potential intervention in Darfur, Sudan, in 2004–2008 (Clough 2005). The prevalent approach in the academic literature, however, has been to use the more familiar and specific term "humanitarian intervention." The reality is that humanitarian intervention is but one aspect of the broader idea of the "responsibility to protect," which entails a responsibility to prevent, react, and rebuild.

The Problem of Motive

Another conceptual issue that been the subject of debate in the humanitarian intervention literature concerns the motives of the intervening parties. Until recently, the prevailing definition of humanitarian intervention emphasized the primacy of humanitarian motives of the interveners, with some writers arguing that the threat or use of force must be for the *sole* purpose of halting or averting human rights violations (Hehir 2010, 149–55; Pattison 2010, 154–67). The implication is that if a military intervention is not motivated by a humanitarian purpose, then it is not rightly a humanitarian intervention. On the other side of this debate is the view that the motive of the intervener matters less than whether or not the intervention achieves a humanitarian outcome. The most well-known proponent of this view is Nicholas Wheeler in his important book *Saving Strangers*. Wheeler argues that preoccupation with the motives of the interveners "takes the intervening state as the referent object for analysis rather than the victims who are rescued as a consequence of the use of force" (Wheeler 2000, 38). According to this thinking, placing the victims at the center of this analysis, as opposed to the interveners, "leads to a different emphasis on the importance of motives in judging the humanitarian credentials of the interveners" (ibid., 38–39). What matters, then, is whether the intervention promotes human rights *in fact*, not whether the resort to force was *motivated* out of a desire to do so.

If the problem with Wheeler's view is that it would possibly provide political and moral cover for self-serving and aggressive war, as long as one could reasonably argue that the target state is better off than before, then the problem with requiring purity of motive is that it is simply unreasonable to expect humanitarian concerns to be the sole purpose of any intervention. Thus, the dominant view in this debate lies somewhere in between these extremes and suggests that humanitarianism should be the *primary*, but not necessarily the *sole*, motive for intervention. This is the position endorsed by the ICISS as well as most scholars (Bellamy 2005).

The issue of motive was present in the 2011 NATO intervention in Libya, whereby NATO's bombing campaign was justified as a humanitarian intervention and in many circles was framed as discharging a "responsibility to protect" Libyan civilians from grave mistreatment by forces loyal to Colonel Gaddafi. Controversy emerged, however, when NATO allies began to undertake more proactive strikes in support of the rebel military effort. These controversial actions led to charges, specifically by Russia, that NATO had exceeded the mandate granted by the UN Security Council, which had authorized force to establish a no-fly zone to protect civilians, not act as the de facto air force for the rebels. This supposed discrepancy between the alleged motives of NATO to protect civilians and its subsequent actions that were seemingly in support of the rebel military effort raises the concern of whether NATO states participating in this intervention were truly motivated out of a desire to protect civilians or out of a perhaps more self-interested desire to remove Gaddafi from power (see Appendix A).

Human Rights vs. Human Security

A final important definitional question is how to conceptualize the human suffering that the intervention aims to halt or avert. The vast majority of the scholarly literature on humanitarian intervention characterizes the nature of such human suffering in terms of **human rights**. That is, humanitarian intervention is military intervention that is undertaken to protect or promote human rights or to halt or avert human rights violations. Consistent with the efforts of the ICISS to broaden the range of responsibilities that potential intervening actors undertake when they seek to alleviate human suffering, a parallel effort is underway that seeks to reconceptualize those conditions that trigger humanitarian intervention. This reconceptualization has taken the form of "**human security**" (Hehir 2010, 109–111). According to this approach, humanitarian intervention is to be undertaken (or not undertaken) in the interests of promoting human security, not just human rights. The **UN Development Programme** (UNDP) generally defines human security in a two-fold manner as (1) "safety from chronic threats as hunger, disease and repression" and (2) "protection from sudden and hurtful disruptions in patterns of everyday life" (UNDP 1994, 23). Although the growing literature on human security is far broader in scope than its relationship to humanitarian intervention, this language has nevertheless started to make its way into the humanitarian intervention discourse, including in a few scholarly treatments (Thomas and Tow 2002; Heinze 2006).

One reason for insisting on using the language of human security as opposed to human rights is that the latter necessarily entails legal processes. That is, human rights are essentially a legal recourse that permits individuals to claim something that they are legally guaranteed by government or society. Humanitarian intervention does not necessarily occur to ensure that individuals have these legal processes or that states enshrine international human rights in their legal systems, but rather to achieve a minimal state of safety among individuals in a society. This conceptual debate has important implications for the conditions under which humanitarian intervention is said to be permissible, for a situation where a government strips individuals of their *rights* can certainly be empirically different from one in which they are actually subject to *insecurity*. In other words, to have a concern for bringing about *human rights* for all—meaning all individuals having legal recourse to claim certain protections or goods against one's government or society—is quite different than an empirical state of *human security* for all—meaning a general state of safety and protection from deprivation and danger (Heinze 2006). Furthermore, whereas the concept of human rights typically involves how governments treat their own people, human security considers not only threats that originate from *within* states, but also outside threats such as external aggression. Thus, if intervening states are acting out of a concern for human security, they are not only concerned about alleviating human suffering caused from within the target state, but must also consider the implications that their use of military force will itself have on the imperiled population. Hence, those who are contemplating intervention must take into consideration that the act of humanitarian intervention itself—which involves the use of deadly force—may actually harm the at-risk population more than if it were left at the mercy of an abusive government. In other words, the best human security strategy in some cases may be to refrain from military intervention.

The problem with using human security as the gauge of well-being in the conduct of humanitarian intervention is that it is an especially broad conception of human welfare that includes virtually every possible threat to individuals (Donnelly 2002). Such threats include, among other things, poverty, pollution, violent crime, infectious disease, and other situations that may not be prudent grounds for using military force. Thus, there seem to be too many and too diverse a range of human security concerns for them all to be addressed through the implementation of a particular macro-strategy. Furthermore, the purpose of anointing these various issues as "security" issues is to change the status of such issues in a government's policy hierarchy, thus making them a "matter of security," worthy of "special attention, better resources, and a higher chance of satisfactory resolution" (Khong 2001, 231–37). So when every conceivable threat to human well-being is made into a security issue, the skeptics argue, we end up prioritizing everything and therefore nothing at all. Although this position does not preclude prioritizing one human security challenge over others in the same way that one might prioritize certain human rights violations as worse or more severe than others, these conceptual challenges have so far precluded widespread incorporation of the human security literature into the debate over humanitarian intervention by scholars.

The humanitarian intervention debate, therefore, remains firmly ensconced in the broader discourse on international human rights.

WHAT HUMANITARIAN INTERVENTION IS *NOT*

International relations scholars have noted that almost all international interactions can be construed as intervention, especially foreign policy acts by stronger states toward weaker ones (Haas 1993, 68). Although definitions vary, we have so far understood humanitarian intervention as entailing the use of military force by a state, group of states, or international organization that takes place in the territory of another state without that state's permission, primarily for the purpose of halting or averting gross human suffering of people in that state. To be perfectly clear, humanitarian intervention as it has been discussed in this chapter means to wage war and therefore must be distinguished from other military acts such as protecting one's own nationals abroad, **peacekeeping**, and other nonmilitary "humanitarian" acts such as providing outside aid or assistance to populations in need.

Rescue of Nationals

First, humanitarian intervention must be distinguished from military interventions by states to rescue their own nationals facing extreme danger in the territory of another state, the government of which is unable or unwilling to protect the endangered nationals. Rescue missions to save one's own nationals have at times been referred to as humanitarian intervention but are more accurately characterized as acts of self-defense or even self-help. Perhaps the best-known example of a rescue of nationals was Israel's military raid of the airport in Entebbe, Uganda, in July 1976 to rescue some one hundred Israeli citizens who were being held hostage on a hijacked airliner (see Appendix B). The legitimacy of such interventions relies on the legally recognized bond between states and their citizens, and when such interventions have taken place, they have tended to rescue *only* that state's nationals. This was the case when French and Belgian military forces evacuated their citizens from Rwanda in 1994 yet left hundreds of thousands of Rwandans to their fate in the ensuing genocide (Kuperman 2001).

Peacekeeping

Arguably the most important distinction to be made is between peacekeeping and humanitarian intervention. Peacekeeping entails the deployment of military and civilian personnel to war-torn states to help them create the conditions for sustainable peace. It requires the consent of the government on whose territory the operation takes place, and it requires neutrality with respect to the (former) warring parties involved. Humanitarian interventions, on the other hand, normally do not obtain the target state's consent, and such interventions do entail partiality, at least at the point of initial engagement (Mayall 2000, 324). Although peacekeeping may involve the limited use of coercion to help alleviate human suffering, it is more appropriately construed as a form of conflict resolution, whereby a nonbelligerent intervening party engages in various confidence-building measures and assists conflicting parties in implementing peace agreements that they have concluded. Peacekeeping also maintains what could be called *deterrent* or *defensive* rules of engagement that aim to enforce stability and order with the minimum use of force. Though usually conducted mainly by military personnel, peacekeeping missions also involve certain nonmilitary functions, such as providing electoral support, promoting the rule of law, aiding with crowd control, disarming civilian agitators, and other quasi-police functions. Humanitarian intervention, by contrast, employs *pro-active* or *offensive* rules of engagement and actively pursues one party militarily in order to disable its capacity to bring about human suffering (Hoffman 1996, 38). In short, actors conducting a humanitarian intervention resemble belligerents in an armed conflict. Peacekeepers are more akin to armed mediators.

Most peacekeeping operations take place under the auspices of the UN, with personnel on loan from UN member-states; such personnel are referred to as UN "blue helmets." Although the term "peacekeeping" does not appear in the UN Charter, former UN Secretary-General Dag Hammarskjöld suggested that the UN's authority to conduct peacekeeping operations comes from "Chapter VI and a half"—somewhere between peaceful settlement of disputes under Chapter VI and coercive enforcement under Chapter VII. An example of a peacekeeping operation would be the UN Assistance Mission for Rwanda (UNAMIR), which was established in 1993 to help implement a peace agreement between parties to a civil war in that state. This was a peacekeeping mission par excellence, as the troops on the ground were operating under strict orders of neutrality and were not authorized to intervene against either party to stop abuses being committed against innocents. Once hostilities resumed and certain identifiable parties began implementing a campaign of genocide, the commander of the peacekeepers, Romeo Dallaire, requested that the UN expand his mandate under Chapter VII to permit his forces to use offensive force to disarm and disable the *génocidaires* (Kuperman 2001). Had Dallaire's request been granted, his peacekeeping mission would have become a *peace-enforcement* operation, which some argue is essentially the same as a humanitarian intervention, as it involves non-self-defensive military force (see Appendix A).

Although some UN peacekeeping missions operate under more robust Chapter VII peace enforcement mandates—such as the former UN Organization Mission to the Democratic Republic of the Congo (MONUC)—these operations are not generally considered to be humanitarian interventions because the peacekeepers are not themselves engaged in armed conflict in the same way the intervening agents of a humanitarian intervention are. As such, when humanitarian interventions take place, they do not normally take the form of peacekeeping operations conducted by UN blue helmets under the direction of the UN Department of Peacekeeping Operations (DPKO). Rather, they are undertaken by states operating outside the command structure of the UN, even if they are "UN sanctioned." What this means is that the UN Security Council has given its blessing for one or more UN member-states to engage in armed humanitarian intervention under Chapter VII, though the states themselves are more or less autonomous in conducting the actual military operations. The subject of UN authorization of humanitarian interventions is discussed in more detail below.

Humanitarian Aid

Other forms of **humanitarian aid** or assistance, such as the delivery of food and medical supplies to civilians and/or refugees, do not themselves entail a coercive aspect but take place in response to human suffering that is an unintended corollary of some other phenomenon, such as a natural disaster, famine, or war. Like peacekeeping, providing humanitarian aid is in theory neutral—meaning that it is not intended only for one group of people, but for all those who are made to suffer in a given humanitarian disaster. Such operations must also obtain the permission of the state on whose territory it will be operating. There have been numerous examples of situations where outside actors—even militaries—have engaged in the provision of this kind of humanitarian relief. Operation Lifeline Sudan (OLS), which was established in 1989, is an example of humanitarian aid. This effort involved a consortium of UN agencies working in tandem with over thirty-five **nongovernmental organizations** (NGOs) to deliver humanitarian assistance to civilians suffering from famine as a result of drought and civil war. The activities of OLS had to be negotiated with both the government of Sudan and the rebel group it was fighting (Heinze 2009, 43).

THE ETHICS AND POLITICS OF HUMANITARIAN INTERVENTION

The literature on humanitarian intervention that goes beyond these conceptual issues tends to deal with legal questions (as discussed below), though the political discourse tends to examine specific cases of humanitarian intervention and the roles played by various actors, such as states, the UN, or other international organizations. As such, the dramatic increase of scholarship in reaction to the 1999 intervention by NATO against Serbia over its policy of **ethnic cleansing** in the province of Kosovo revealed substantial controversy over when (if ever), where, and how humanitarian intervention ought to be undertaken. This disagreement was the catalyst for the ICISS project mentioned above, which aimed at forging a consensus on this controversial and contested subject and making it more workable in practice.

A majority of the scholarship on the subject tends to assume that humanitarian intervention, under certain circumstances, can be desirable. Although some scholars mount ethical objections to humanitarian intervention on pacifistic or other moral grounds (Atack 2002), the tendency in the literature is to argue that humanitarian intervention, in theory, can be a good thing under certain circumstances. The resulting debate has centered on identifying these circumstances and has taken place largely in the form of political and/or ethical theorizing, drawing heavily from **Just War theory** and various strands of **liberalism** (or **liberal international relations theory**; Walzer 2000; Tesón 1997).

The early theoretical literature on the question of humanitarian intervention centers on the moral foundations of the idea of state sovereignty. On one side of the debate are **cosmopolitans**, who argue that states whose institutions fail to conform to appropriate principles of justice—that is, that fail to respect the human rights of their citizens—have no moral claim to the right of nonintervention that is part and parcel of state sovereignty. Such states may be subject to forcible intervention to reform their institutions (Beitz 1979). In opposition to this view is the **communitarian** argument, most famously articulated by Michael Walzer, which suggests that even repressive states must be afforded the right of nonintervention because state sovereignty creates space for a self-determining political community to win its own more durable freedom (Walzer 2000). For Walzer, an oppressed people have the right to rebel, "but this right does not easily transfer to foreign states or armies and become a right of invasion or intervention" (Walzer 1980, 214). So the cosmopolitan view, on one hand, is that states have the right to intervene against states whose governments demonstrate something less than the ideal list of human rights protections. The communitarian tendency, by contrast, is to tolerate such regimes because even though they do not uphold all or most human rights, they are governing in accordance with the traditions of a particular political community, which must decide for itself if it wants to rebel and win a more permanent and meaningful freedom. However, Walzer makes the exception that if a government is engaging in enslavement, massacre, or mass expulsion, then outside intervention is permissible to stop such atrocities. Therefore, the criteria for justifying humanitarian intervention become a matter of degree—that is, the severity and scale of the abuses being perpetrated in a given situation (Heinze 2006).

Threshold Criteria for Humanitarian Intervention

Arguments that attempt to ascertain the severity and scale of abuse that must be present before humanitarian intervention is considered draw heavily from the Just War criterion of **proportionality**. Applied to the conduct of humanitarian intervention, this criterion requires that if actors are going to use force to halt or avert human suffering, they must not bring about more harm than would have otherwise occurred. That is, the use of military force in the conduct of humanitarian intervention will itself bring about harm, so the harm that it seeks to halt or avert must necessarily be greater in scale and severity (Fixdal and Smith 1998, 303). This sort of reasoning corresponds to an approach to moral theorizing called **consequentialism**, which is essentially an ethical approach that appeals to the consequences (expected or actual) of an act as the basis for its evaluation. The problem for consequentialist approaches to humanitarian intervention, however, is that the bases for evaluating the desirability of intervention are not known until after it has taken place. Nevertheless, many of the assumptions and criteria that scholars use to appraise humanitarian intervention involve some form of consequentialist reasoning (Heinze 2009; Pattison 2010). Virtually all serious works thus argue, one way or another, that humanitarian intervention is only permissible under extreme cases, such as massacre, genocide, or ethnic cleansing on a large scale, essentially because intervening for "lesser" abuses would do more harm than good (ICISS 2001, 31). However, a vast majority of the literature takes this to be an assumption, rather than a point for analysis. As such, when scholars and analysts argue for thresholds of "extreme cases," "conscience-shocking crimes," or "supreme humanitarian emergencies," this only gives us a general idea of the humanitarian conditions under which military intervention is thought to be permissible.

Two related concerns that also draw from Just War theory are that the means of the intervention must be proportionate to the humanitarian goal, and that the intervention must have a reasonable prospect for succeeding in actually averting the atrocities that are the basis for the intervention. Concerning the former, most scholars argue that the scale, duration, and intensity of the military operation should be the minimum necessary to achieve the humanitarian objective. Consistent with the consequentialist principle that the intervention should do more good than harm, this criterion would forbid causing unnecessary harm in the conduct of humanitarian intervention, such as using certain unnecessarily destructive weapons (such as nuclear weapons), deliberately targeting civilians or civilian infrastructure, or otherwise engaging in tactics that needlessly put innocent civilians in harm's way. This was a problematic issue in the 1999 Kosovo intervention because NATO bombed several **dual-use targets** such as bridges, used **cluster bombs**, and only bombed from extremely high altitudes in order to minimize risks to its own pilots (see Appendix A). Any humanitarian intervention must, nevertheless, use sufficient military force to have a reasonable prospect for success, which suggests that if the level and duration of violence required to prevail militarily would cause more harm than would have otherwise occurred, then intervention would not be permissible. These criteria would preclude humanitarian intervention against powerful adversaries, such as one of the permanent members of the UN Security Council, which would almost certainly bring about more harm than would have otherwise occurred (Fixdal and Smith 1998).

Much scholarship on humanitarian intervention, borrowing again from Just War theory, suggests that all peaceful options to alleviate suffering must be explored before actors resort to using military force. In other words, force must be used only as a last resort. Peaceful options could involve diplomatic negotiations, the use of economic carrots and sticks, or other measures short of all-out military intervention. This criterion is somewhat controversial in the literature mainly because, in practice, it has not been uncommon for the perpetrators of atrocities to use diplomacy as a stalling tactic while they carry out their crimes. Slobodan Milošević, for example, mastered this tactic during his ethnic cleansing campaigns throughout the 1990s in the former Yugoslavia. Therefore, some have suggested that in emergency situations more lives could be saved if the resort to force were undertaken sooner rather than later (Weiss, Forsythe, and Coate 2004, 60). The ICISS takes the position that every noncoercive option need not literally be attempted and proven unsuccessful before the resort to military intervention is had. Rather, there must be reasonable grounds for believing that these efforts would be unsuccessful (ICISS 2001, 36). Again, however, what constitutes reasonable grounds is subject to interpretation.

The issue of the timing of humanitarian intervention is thus of crucial importance, for if it is undertaken too early, actors might find themselves in a military conflict that could have been avoided had they more vigorously pursued peaceful avenues to resolve the crisis. On the other hand, if actors wait too long, they miss the opportunity to fulfill the purpose for which humanitarian intervention is said to exist: to prevent or stop atrocities. For instance, the French intervention in Rwanda in 1994—Operation Turquoise—took place after most of the victims of the genocide had already perished. In this humanitarian catastrophe, the international community largely missed its opportunity to avert genocide (see Appendix A). As such, most scholars agree that the purpose of humanitarian intervention is to prevent or halt atrocities, not to punish the perpetrators of such atrocities after they have been committed. This view has been eloquently argued by Kenneth Roth, executive director of Human Rights Watch, in response to U.S. claims that the Iraq invasion of 2003 was justified on humanitarian grounds. As Roth argues, there were times in the past when humanitarian intervention would have been justified in Iraq, such as during the atrocities committed against Iraq's Kurdish population in 1988. However, when the United States and United Kingdom invaded in 2003, there was no ongoing or imminent large-scale slaughter that the invasion sought to avert. As such, the extraordinary remedy of military invasion must be countenanced only if there is evidence that a large-scale atrocity is imminent or ongoing and can only be averted militarily (Roth 2004, 18; see also Appendix A).

The Interveners: Selectivity, Political Will, Partisanship, and Efficacy

As the world's inaction over the Rwanda genocide attests, even where there has been genocide and mass murder, humanitarian intervention has not always been forthcoming. The fact that activity that is reasonably characterized as humanitarian intervention occurred in places like Somalia (1992–1993), Haiti (1994), Bosnia (1993–1995), Sierra Leone (1997), Kosovo (1999), East Timor (1999), and Libya (2011) but not places where there have been equally heinous and large-scale atrocities like Rwanda (1994), the Democratic Republic of Congo (1997–2001), Sudan (1998, 2003), Syria (2011), and others has drawn charges of inconsistency and selective indignation. Humanitarian intervention is controversial, so when it does take place, the charge that the interveners are being "selectively humanitarian" comes up frequently. Again, the Kosovo intervention proved to be a magnet for such charges. It is, after all, hard to reconcile NATO's seemingly enthusiastic humanitarian intervention over Kosovo with the world's utter indifference over genocide in Rwanda. If the NATO intervention were a moral imperative, then inaction in Rwanda would cast serious doubt on the morality of a rule that is applied so arbitrarily and selectively. Thus, the argument that humanitarian intervention should be universal and uncompromising has a certain amount of cognitive appeal (Brilmayer 1995; Pattison 2010, 169–72).

Although there are some writers who take this position, as well as some who argue for at least a more consistent approach, most serious scholarship on humanitarian intervention acknowledges the extreme practical difficulties in attempting to right every wrong in the world. Resources are finite, and the world's crisis-response function will remain decentralized for the foreseeable future, with military force provided primarily by states whose motives are almost always self-serving. Though consistency is desirable, the consensus in the literature has been that some level of inconsistency is tolerable, and that an act of commission is not invalidated by several acts of omission. As a result, according to most scholars, the fact that states have failed to stop slaughter in the past is not a morally persuasive reason for them to ignore it in the future.

Of course, the purpose of having principles and criteria for humanitarian intervention is to create a consensus on when and where humanitarian intervention is best undertaken in the hope of at least treating like cases alike, thus aspiring to a more consistent approach. The question arises, however, whether any set of criteria for humanitarian intervention is to represent the conditions under which it is *permissible*, or those under which it is *required*. In other words, can humanitarian intervention be considered a moral *duty* (Pattison 2010, 15–20)? Although some moral philosophers have argued that a moral duty to intervene indeed exists, the political discourse more readily acknowledges the problems posed by a lack of political will on the part of states to do so. As **realist international relations theory** would argue, states will engage in humanitarian intervention only if they perceive that they have a more self-serving interest at stake (Mason and Wheeler 1996). It can be reasonably argued, however, that states *do* have an interest in contributing to the resolution of problems that lead to the types of gross abuses that may require humanitarian intervention, quite apart from the moral imperative to do so.

Furthermore, an increasing number of scholars are using insights from **social constructivism** to suggest that ethical arguments about doing the right thing in particular contexts extend normative beliefs to new areas of practice and eventually change dominant practices (Crawford 2002; Finnemore 2004). In other words, the more that states and other actors engage in an ethical discourse that favors a norm of humanitarian intervention, the more their identity, and thus interests, are constituted by such a norm and the more likely their subsequent behavior will conform to a norm of, for example, a responsibility to protect. To date, however, the emerging norm of humanitarian intervention remains relatively weak and extremely controversial, and those governments that have endorsed it in the abstract have yet to demonstrate a strong determination to fulfill such a commitment.

Aside from the problem of overcoming the lack of will on the part of states to engage in humanitarian intervention, a related concern has to do with who exactly has the right (or duty) to undertake it. In the Just War literature, the question of "right authority" essentially concerns both who has the right to resort to force and how this right can be justified. The latter concern is intertwined with questions of the legitimacy of humanitarian intervention under international law, given that humanitarian intervention involves the violation of a state's sovereignty. This issue will be discussed below. The former concern, however, involves two contested issues. The first is whether humanitarian intervention should be multilateral or unilateral, and the second is whether states that engage in humanitarian intervention must themselves have a sound human rights record or otherwise demonstrate credibility as moral actors.

Arguments in favor of multilateral intervention have been widely made and are straightforward: multilateral action is preferable because it acts as a check on one state pursuing its own interests, which might be contrary to the humanitarian objective of the intervention. Thus, the argument goes, even if the intervention is not conducted by a multinational force under a UN mandate, it is at least preferable that the intervention be conducted through some formal multilateral decision-making institution, such as a regional organization like NATO or the African Union (AU). For example, the 1999 NATO intervention over Kosovo was not authorized by the UN Security Council but still maintained a certain degree of legitimacy as a multilateral intervention conducted by the world's foremost alliance of liberal democracies (Farer 2003, 75–76). On the face of it, then, multilateral intervention is optimal because it reduces the likelihood of partisan abuse. As preferable as it might be for humanitarian intervention to be undertaken multilaterally, in light of the imperfect nature of international organizations and the profound difficulty of getting several states to come to an agreement that military intervention is desirable in a specific situation (such as Rwanda in 1994), proponents of humanitarian intervention have begun to soften this requirement. Multilateral intervention is thus preferred, but unilateral intervention could be tolerated, all other conditions being met (Reisman 2000).

Another problem with multilateral humanitarian intervention is effectiveness. This was another difficulty that came to the fore after the Kosovo intervention when the cumbersome multilateral decision-making process frustrated military commanders who constantly had to obtain approval from the various NATO foreign ministries before they could attack specific targets. Toward the end of this intervention, the United States began circumventing the NATO chain of command because it was perceived as an impediment to the effective projection of U.S. military force—a problem that some U.S. officials argued prolonged the conflict and cost more lives (Heinze 2009, 119–120).

The issue of the efficacy of the intervening agent is particularly important and requires that the intervening agent maintain a significant power advantage over the target state, lest the intervention fail to meet the requirements of proportionality and of having a reasonable prospect of succeeding (Pattison 2010, 69; Heinze 2009, 112–25). The international community, however, is increasingly viewing with suspicion the powerful states that are likely to be the most effective in conducting humanitarian intervention. The actor with the greatest ability to quickly deploy dominant military force to virtually anywhere in the world at the beginning of the twenty-first century is the United States. But as a result of its controversial record of past military interventions, especially the vastly unpopular invasion of Iraq in 2003, some have argued that much of the world views the projection of American military force abroad with profound mistrust, therefore making any U.S.-led humanitarian interventions less desirable.

This problem was raised during the debate over whether to intervene with the state-sponsored atrocities being committed in the Darfur region of western Sudan starting in 2003. The U.S. military could arguably have easily deployed sufficient forces to end what the U.S. government itself has called "genocide." To date, however, it has not done so, perhaps because its credibility as a state that uses its military for the common good has been severely undermined by the unpopular Iraq war, particularly after the revelation of detainee abuse in places like Abu Ghraib and Guantanamo Bay. In other words, the United States' justification of the Iraq invasion on humanitarian grounds after the fact was viewed by much of the rest of the world as an attempt to hide more imperialistic objectives (Williams and Bellamy 2005). One can thus reasonably expect many governments—particularly in the Arab and **Muslim** world—to be especially unenthusiastic about the deployment of U.S. military forces, especially to another predominantly Arab (and oil-rich) country in the heart of the Muslim world. Some also argue that powerful European states such as France and the United Kingdom are viewed with similar (if not equal) suspicion because of their exploitative colonial pasts. Likewise, the humanitarian credentials of any military intervention conducted by either China or Russia would indeed be suspect given China's poor record on human rights and the overtly brutal methods with which Russia has prosecuted its bloody war against the breakaway republic of Chechnya.

A similar logic could be said to have influenced the 2011 NATO intervention in Libya. In this operation, the United States played a supporting role to that of the French and British, as opposed to its usual role as a leader and initiator of such activities. While it may be a stretch to conclude that the French or British have any more credibility as agents for good in this region than the United States, the Obama administration had good reason to believe that domestic public opinion would be skeptical about the United States initiating a third war in that region, while the intervention would perhaps be less likely to be branded internationally as yet another example of "American imperialism" if the U.S. role were minimized to that of supporting a French- and British-led effort.

The literature on humanitarian intervention has not persuasively dealt with the question of who has the right to conduct humanitarian intervention other than to outline which qualities of interveners are morally relevant (e.g., efficacy, legitimacy) and assess the relative importance of these qualities (Pattison 2010). There is agreement that states that egregiously violate the human rights of their own citizens—the North Koreas, Zimbabwes, and Sudans of the world—are in no position to engage in unilateral humanitarian intervention, while even the most free, democratic, and rights-respective states do not have clean hands, particularly the powerful ones. Although some argue that the answer lies in regional organizations, most of these (save for NATO) lack the degree of organization and institutionalization required to enable their member-states to decide upon and authorize something as complicated and demanding as humanitarian intervention (Kurth 2005). This problem, like so many other aspects of the ethics and politics of humanitarian intervention, is one that requires further examination.

HUMANITARIAN INTERVENTION IN INTERNATIONAL LAW

The international legal issues surrounding humanitarian intervention have probably received the most treatment in the scholarly literature, though like those explored above, these issues are also controversial and subject to intense debate. Because humanitarian intervention involves transboundary military intervention, the most relevant body of international law is that pertaining to the use of force. The legal regime relevant to the resort to armed force essentially consists of the charter of the United Nations, as well as evidence of state practice that might constitute **customary international law**. Thus, the legality of humanitarian intervention depends on whether it is in conformity with UN Charter principles or the extent to which it conforms to prior state practice of humanitarian intervention that has crystallized into binding law.

The UN Charter Paradigm

The UN Charter maintains a general presumption against the use of force in international affairs. Specifically, Article 2(4) states that "All Members shall refrain in their international relations from the threat or use of force against the territorial integrity or political independence of any state, or in any other manner inconsistent with the purposes of the United Nations." In addition, Article 2(7) prohibits intervention "in matters which are essentially within the domestic jurisdiction of any state," though such matters may change over time. The charter contains two explicit exceptions to the Article 2(4) prohibition: Article 51 permits states to use force in self-defense, while Articles 39, 42, and 43 permit the UN Security Council to authorize the use of force to maintain and restore international peace and security—the council's so-called Chapter VII powers. Thus, the most obvious situation under which humanitarian intervention is legal is if it is explicitly authorized by a UN Security Council resolution adopted under its Chapter VII authority. In fact, there have been several times the council has authorized other states to intervene militarily into the jurisdiction of another state without that state's permission (see Appendix A).

A landmark event for UN-authorized humanitarian intervention was the humanitarian disaster in Somalia in 1992–1994. Here the UN Security Council for the first time declared a situation of gross human suffering *within* a state as a threat to or breach of international peace and security. This declaration allowed the council to invoke its Chapter VII powers to authorize states to use "any means necessary"—a euphemism for using military force—to restore international peace and security. Since then, the UN has used its Chapter VII powers to authorize humanitarian interventions in Haiti (1994), Rwanda (1994), Bosnia (1992–1995), and East Timor (1999; see Appendix A).

The legal status of humanitarian intervention is thus rarely contested where there is explicit authorization from the UN Security Council. The controversy lies in whether or not humanitarian interventions undertaken in the absence of a clear UN authorization are legal. That's why NATO's 1999 Kosovo intervention triggered so much debate: it was undertaken without authorization from the UN Security Council. Under a textual reading of the charter rules on the use of force, this intervention was technically illegal (Independent International Commission on Kosovo 2000). Although the council did declare the situation a threat to international peace and security, none of its resolutions contained an explicit force authorization.

There are two relatively common arguments for the legality of humanitarian intervention absent UN Security Council authorization. One involves an interpretive reading of Article 2(4), and the other involves a potential customary law exception. Regarding the first, the argument is that Article 2(4) does not forbid *all* uses of force, just that which is directed against the territorial integrity and/or political independence of states, and/or that which is inconsistent with the purposes of the UN Charter. Most scholars, however, do not take this view, as research into the *travaux préparatoires* (the legislative history) of the UN Charter has revealed that such language was intended to reinforce, rather than restrict or create loopholes in, the general prohibition of the use of force (Chesterman 2002, 49).

Customary International Law

The customary law exception for humanitarian intervention is a more complicated and controversial argument. Customary international law is created by the consistent practice over time of states who maintain the view that their behavior is either permitted or required by law at the time the action is undertaken (this latter "mental" element is known as **opinio juris**). The argument is that the prohibition in Article 2(4) of the UN Charter has effectively been modified by humanitarian interventions that ostensibly violated the charter rules but were thought to be legal by states engaging in the act at the time. There would thus be a "customary exception" to Article 2(4) for uses of force aimed at preventing or averting massacres and large-scale atrocities (Chesterman 2002, 45–87).

There are several reasons why this view—though entertained by imaginative international lawyers—is not the prevailing one among legal scholars. First, the modification of treaty rules by custom is itself a contested area of international law, although there have been instances where this can be said to have happened. Second, there are numerous **UN General Assembly** declarations that provide evidence *against* such a legal norm and in favor of the well-established legal principles of state sovereignty and its correlate of non-intervention. For example, General Assembly Resolution 2625 (XXV) states that "no state or group of states has the right to intervene . . . for any reason whatever, in the internal or external affairs of any other state." Although such resolutions do not constitute binding law, they are interpreted by international law scholars as evidence either in favor of or opposed to the existence of a customary legal norm. Thus, there is conflicting evidence concerning whether the UN Charter can be or has been modified to allow an exception for humanitarian intervention.

In any event, even if we accept that treaties can be modified by state practice and ignore the substantial evidence against the existence of a customary norm permitting humanitarian intervention, it is still debatable whether there exists sufficient and consistent enough state practice of humanitarian intervention, accompanied by *opinio juris*, to constitute a modification of the UN Charter's rules on the use of force. State behavior cannot modify existing rules unless the existing rules are broken. As a result, much of the state practice of humanitarian intervention that has potentially contributed to the formation of a new customary rule may not be considered a part of accumulated state practice because it was authorized by the UN Security Council and was thus perfectly legal under charter law.

Of the potential humanitarian interventions prior to Kosovo that might be counted toward a customary rule, legal scholar Simon Chesterman (2002, 65–83) has identified eleven that warrant consideration: Belgium in the Congo (1960), Belgium and the United States in the Congo (1964), the United States in the Dominican Republic (1965), India in East Pakistan (1971), Israel in Uganda (1976), Belgium and France in Zaire (1978), Tanzania in Uganda (1978), Vietnam in Cambodia (1978), France in the Central African Republic (1979), the United States in Grenada (1983), and the United States in Panama (1989). To these one might add West African states' interventions in Liberia (1990–1992) and Sierra Leone (1997–1998; most of these cases are summarized in appendices A and B). Those who object to considering these interventions as constitutive of a customary exception for humanitarian intervention usually argue that most were motivated by factors other than rescuing foreigners from massacre by their government, such as rescuing nationals or protecting other interests abroad. Critics also argue that there is even less evidence that these states believed that what they were doing was permitted or required by an emerging legal doctrine that permits humanitarian intervention. Thus, when the 1999 Kosovo intervention took place, most scholars were of the view that there had not been sufficient prior state practice accompanied by *opinio juris* to "legalize" that intervention as a technical matter of international law. However, several scholars argue that the Kosovo intervention, itself, contributes to the possible future formation of a customary exception for humanitarian intervention (see Merriam 2001, 111). To date, however, the prevalent view is that there is little evidence that a customary legal rule exists that permits humanitarian intervention. Thus, as a technical legal matter, the prevalent, though not uncontested, view is that humanitarian intervention is legal only if the UN Security Council authorizes it. Whether or not humanitarian intervention *should* be legal absent UN authorization is a matter that is currently under debate, with the prevalent view in favor of the status quo that it should *not* be legal unless authorized by the Security Council (see Goodman 2006).

This prevailing view has not prevented scholars from searching for a more abstract legal grounding for humanitarian intervention that treats international law as a **normative system** rather than a **positivist legal system** in the same way we think of national legal systems, in which acts are strictly either legal or illegal. This point of view is most closely associated with the work of the so-called New Haven school, which regards international law not as the mechanical application of previously existing rules, but as authoritative social processes that are shaped by social, moral, and political considerations (Willard and Reisman 1988). Scholars have also espoused related legal defenses of humanitarian intervention based on natural law, which is essentially a conception of international law that considers moral principles in ascertaining the meaning of the law (Tesón 1997). Other arguments in this vein point out that there is noteworthy evidence that states have increasingly come to accept the idea that the legal principle of state sovereignty should not permit governments to massacre their citizens. And, of course, in some cases of massacre and gross human rights violations, states on the UN Security Council have unequivocally declared humanitarian intervention to be a lawful remedy to such intolerable acts. In other words, at times, humanitarian intervention is perfectly legal, but this depends on the arbitrary and capricious determination of the UN Security Council—a political body that lacks the kind of consistency of application that is demanded by law.

If we treat like cases alike, as most systems of law would demand, one can reasonably construe the emergence of a norm of humanitarian intervention. Under these more theoretical and philosophical treatments of the subject, humanitarian intervention is still technically illegal, but to the extent that it is consistent with the overall normative intent of international law that would permit actors to take action to stop such massacres, humanitarian intervention maintains a "legal basis within the normative framework of international law" (Stromseth 2003, 244). Humanitarian intervention remains technically illegal if not authorized by the UN Security Council, but according to this thinking, actions such as NATO's intervention over Kosovo in 1999 could be considered "less illegal" or even "lawful."

HUMANITARIAN INTERVENTION AND
THE GLOBAL WAR ON TERROR

The terrorist attacks of September 11, 2001, and the ensuing **Global War on Terror** spearheaded by the United States have undoubtedly affected the context of ideas, interests, and values in which the debate over humanitarian intervention rose to prominence. With the world's most powerful military now preoccupied with fighting terrorism, there seem to be at least some grounds for anticipating fewer, rather than more, genuine humanitarian interventions in the post-9/11 world. The debate over humanitarian (non)intervention in Darfur, Sudan, mentioned above appears to provide some evidence for this assertion, although the intervention in Libya seems to reaffirm that states are still willing to intervene for ostensibly humanitarian purposes.

On the other hand, some have argued that the use of force in places like Afghanistan and Iraq opens up the possibility that military interventions could be used to promote both counterterrorism and human rights. According to this argument, the menace of global terror and the events of September 11, 2001, may have brought home to Western states the reality that instability and repression within states, or even their collapse, can have effects that reach far beyond particular regions of the world. As such, 9/11 may have inadvertently encouraged a reconceptualization of states' national interest by bringing together humanitarianism and state security more than ever before. There is now, it has been argued, a persuasive reason for states to muster the political will to take repression of the sort perpetrated by the Taliban and **Saddam Hussein** seriously—something notably absent from the oftentimes belated and half-hearted humanitarian interventions that took place (or should have) in the 1990s (Wheeler 2004).

This debate came into full swing after the U.S. invasion of Iraq in 2003. After failing to find **weapons of mass destruction** (WMD) or demonstrate a meaningful link between Saddam Hussein and **al-Qaeda** terrorists, the George W. Bush administration began to emphasize the humanitarian benefits of toppling the Hussein regime, even though humanitarian concerns were clearly secondary at the time when the case for invasion was being made (Roth 2004). With humanitarianism clearly less important, and there being no imminent or ongoing atrocity in Iraq that an intervention sought to avert, most commentators have been skeptical of Iraq as a legitimate humanitarian intervention. Nevertheless, the loose normative consensus regarding the conditions under which humanitarian interventions are considered permissible at least made this argument plausible for the Bush administration. As some commentators have observed, however, it has become virtually impossible for a liberal democracy to wage war without somehow emphasizing its humanitarian aspects (Rieff 2002). The fact that the Iraq War is being conflated with humanitarian intervention has nevertheless raised serious concerns about the subsequent development of interventionist precedents and the continued sanctity of the general presumption against the use of force in international law (Drumbl 2003; Franck 2003). After all, if a state can argue that its military intervention will eventually render the target state better off than before in terms of liberal values such as human rights, then it dramatically weakens the normative constraints on what is considered the legitimate use of force in international affairs.

CONCLUSION

Examining humanitarian intervention in the context of the Global War on Terror has thus injected a certain degree of dynamism into the scholarly debate, even if the prospects for genuine and effective humanitarian interventions remain elusive. Given the apparent inevitability of more humanitarian crises throughout the globe, the challenges posed by the fight against global terrorism, as well as the seemingly insurmountable problems of mounting effective humanitarian interventions, the topics outlined above will no doubt continue to occupy scholars and analysts who study this subject. The age-old theoretical and conceptual concerns about sovereignty and human rights will, of course, continue to be debated by scholars and analysts, while events on the ground will no doubt continue to affect the direction and nature of the debate. Although one can be fairly certain that there will never be a perfect prescription for undertaking humanitarian intervention, the debate continues to make modest progress and incorporate new and challenging realities as the events of the twenty-first century unfold.

APPENDIX A

SELECT CASES RELEVANT TO THE HUMANITARIAN INTERVENTION DEBATE: THE POST-COLD WAR ERA

ECOWAS Intervention in Liberia, 1990; and Sierra Leone, 1997–1998

Civil war broke out in Liberia in 1989 causing thousands of deaths and precipitating a large refugee crisis. In the absence of UN action, the Economic Community of West African States (ECOWAS) negotiated a ceasefire and established a Monitoring Group (ECOMOG) to implement and monitor it. Upon deployment, ECOMOG immediately clashed with the forces of rebel leader (and former prime minister) Charles Taylor. Although technically a peacekeeping force, ECOMOG engaged in extensive bombing raids against the rebel groups to force them to reach a negotiated settlement in 1990. This action was not authorized by the UN Security Council beforehand, though in 1992 the council retroactively approved the operation.

The conflict, however, spilled over into neighboring Sierra Leone, eventually leading to the overthrow of the government there in 1997 and a bloody civil war. ECOWAS already had peacekeeping troops in Sierra Leone and, led by Nigeria, proceeded to undertake major military assaults against the rebels, cutting them off from their military supplies. These actions were once again validated by the UN Security Council after the fact (Levitt 1998).

U.S.-led Enforcement of No-Fly Zones in Iraq
(Operation Provide Comfort), 1991–2003

In the aftermath of the First Gulf War in 1991, the UN condemned Iraq for its brutal treatment of its Kurdish and Shiite populations. As the situation worsened, the United States, the United Kingdom, France, and the Netherlands launched an operation to create safe havens for refugees and established no-fly zones over northern and southern Iraq to protect these vulnerable populations. This operation at one time entailed some 20,000 troops guarding safe areas, while the no-fly zones were patrolled by U.S. and UK fighter jets. While the relevant UN Security Council resolution did not contain language authorizing force, these states nevertheless relied on the resolution as the legal basis for their action (Harrington 1993).

U.S./UN Intervention in Somalia (Operation Restore Hope), 1992–1993

Amidst civil war, anarchy, and mass starvation in Somalia, the UN deployed a peacekeeping force (UNOSOM) in order to protect the delivery of humanitarian aid from marauding bandits and armed groups who had been stealing it for their own use. As the situation deteriorated and as UNOSOM proved ineffectual, the UN Security Council sanctioned the deployment of 28,000 U.S. troops, eventually providing them with a mandate to "use any means necessary" to protect the delivery of humanitarian aid by taking measures against those attacking UN personnel. The U.S. mission eventually led to an operation in October of 1993 intended to arrest one of the leading warlords, Mohamed Aideed, thought to be responsible for attacking UN personnel and frustrating humanitarian delivery. The operation, however, failed when a U.S. Blackhawk helicopter was shot down and U.S. troops were engaged in a day-long firefight. The nineteen U.S. casualties prompted a fierce domestic backlash, causing the United States to withdraw its participation in the mission. This event is important, however, in the sense that it was the first time the UN Security Council characterized an entirely *internal* situation of gross human suffering as a threat to *international* peace and security (Rutherford 2008).

UN-Mandated "Safe Areas" in Bosnia Enforced by NATO (Operation Deny Flight, Operation Deliberate Force), 1993–1995

The break-up of the former Yugoslavia was accompanied by a bloody conflict between Serbs, Croats, and Muslims, with combatants perpetrating gross atrocities against civilians of rival ethnic groups. This "ethnic cleansing," as it came to be called, prompted the UN to deploy a peacekeeping mission to the area: the UN Protection Force (UNPROFOR). As the situation deteriorated, UNPROFOR was charged with protecting UN-designated "safe areas" around five Bosnian towns and the city of Sarajevo, for which NATO was authorized to supply air support as needed (Operation Deny Flight). While this solution served to deter attacks in the short term, NATO was extremely reluctant to undertake anything but pinprick airstrikes, and the Bosnian Serb forces became ever more brazen as they kidnapped UNPROFOR peacekeepers and held them hostage. In July of 1995, Serb forces overran the UN safe area around the city of Srebrenica, resulting in the Serb massacre of over 7,000

Bosnian Muslim men and boys. This massacre prompted a more decisive response by NATO, which subsequently undertook Operation Deliberate Force in 1995, a massive bombing campaign that was instrumental in ending the conflict and forcing the parties to reach the settlement in the Dayton Accords (Wheeler 2000, 242–84)

Rwandan Genocide and Subsequent French Intervention (Operation Turquoise), 1994

After a prolonged civil war in Rwanda fought primarily between armed groups associated with the Hutu and Tutsi ethnic groups, a ceasefire was implemented by the UN in 1993 under the auspices of the Arusha Accords. Under the agreement, the UN was to deploy a peacekeeping contingent known as UNAMIR (UN Assistance Mission for Rwanda) to monitor the former warring parties' observance of the ceasefire. All the while, however, the Rwandan Hutu leadership was planning to eliminate their Tutsi rivals in an elaborate genocidal campaign to be undertaken by the Rwandan government forces, Hutu militias, and everyday Hutu citizens. UNAMIR was not authorized by the UN Security Council to use force to prevent the mass murder of Tutsi civilians, so a hundred-day-long campaign of genocide ensued in which about 800,000 Tutsis and moderate Hutus were murdered. Only after the fact did the UN authorize a French-led force (Operation Turquoise) to establish safe areas for those fleeing the genocide, yet it was the Tutsi rebel group, the Rwandan Patriotic Front (RPF), that ultimately put a stop to the genocide. Most observers now agree that Operation Turquoise did more to shelter Hutu militants who perpetrated the genocide than it did to protect those who were its primary victims. The conflict subsequently spilled over into neighboring Zaire (now the Democratic Republic of the Congo) and precipitated a series of conflicts in that country that have continued well into the 2000s (Kuperman 2001).

U.S. Intervention in Haiti (Operation Uphold Democracy), 1994

In 1991, the democratically elected president of Haiti, Jean-Bertrand Aristide, was overthrown in a coup led by General Raoul Cédras. This coup led to the violent persecution of Aristide supporters, and by 1993, despite the imposition of economic sanctions by the UN, there was a full-blown humanitarian and refugee crisis. In 1994, the UN Security Council convened and authorized the United States to use force to secure Haiti and restore the Aristide government. The mere threat of invasion, however, caused Cédras to agree to allow Aristide to return to power, so over 17,000 U.S. troops were deployed to Haiti without a shot being fired. The U.S. decision to take decisive action to restore democracy to Haiti is widely understood to be motivated by the desire to avoid a flood of Haitian refugees into U.S. territory, though it is frequently characterized as either a pro-democratic or humanitarian intervention (Ballard 1998).

NATO Intervention over Kosovo (Operation Allied Force), 1999

Kosovo was a predominantly Albanian Muslim autonomous republic within Serbia, whose autonomy was revoked by Slobodan Milosevic in 1989 and which subsequently declared independence in 1990. Curiously, Kosovo was left out of the Dayton negotiations so its status had never been resolved. In 1998, however, events escalated when Kosovar separatists, the Kosovo Liberation Army (KLA), clashed with Serb security forces, which began directing their attacks against Kosovar civilians. (It is now widely reported that the KLA leadership deliberately provoked the Serbs into reacting brutally against Kosovar civilians in the hopes of attracting international support for their cause.) The UN Security Council repeatedly condemned the excessive use of force by Serbs against Kosovars, and NATO became involved in the effort to convince Milosevic to withdraw his forces from Kosovo. This effort eventually resulted in U.S. and NATO leaders giving Milosevic an ultimatum: leave Kosovo alone or be bombed. When Milosevic did not relent, NATO undertook a phased bombing campaign against targets in Serbia; it took seventy-eight days to force Milosevic to a negotiated settlement that ultimately ended the conflict. Importantly, the UN Security Council did not authorize this use of force by NATO, which sparked heated debate about the legality of NATO's campaign. The campaign was also controversial because it only used high-altitude bombing raids in an effort to minimize risk to U.S. and NATO pilots (Schnabel and Thakur 2000).

Australian-led Intervention in East Timor, 1999–2000

East Timor had been a de facto part of Indonesia since 1975, when Indonesia invaded and annexed the former Portuguese colony and subsequently used its military to effectively suppress the East Timorese population for the next twenty-four years. In 1999, a referendum was held in East Timor, organized and monitored by the UN, wherein nearly 80 percent voted for East Timorese independence from Indonesia. When the results were announced, pro-Indonesian militias, supported by the Indonesian military, carried out a campaign of violence against the East Timorese population, killing nearly 1,500 people, causing hundreds of thousands of refugees, and devastating much of the country's infrastructure. In September 1999, Australia persuaded the UN Security Council to authorize an Australian-led multinational force (INTERFET) to restore order in East Timor, formally a province of Indonesia that had struggled for independence for decades. While the force was deployed under a Chapter VII mandate, it is also the case that Indonesia consented to the intervention. Furthermore, most observers agree that Australia's interest in acting to stop the violence in East Timor was a result of strong domestic political pressure having to do with concern about Timorese refugees arriving in Australia (Wheeler and Dunne 2001).

U.S. Invasion of Afghanistan (Operation Enduring Freedom), 2001

In October 2001, the United States invaded Afghanistan in response to the September 11 attacks perpetrated by the al-Qaeda terrorist organization, which was operating from within the state of Afghanistan and was tolerated by the ruling regime there, known as the Taliban. Although the United States justified its invasion as an act of self-defense, the fact that the invasion had as one its main goals the removal of the Taliban regime gave it a certain humanitarian appeal. That is, given that the Taliban was one of the most brutal, repressive, and violent regimes, its ouster from Afghanistan would stand to achieve a positive humanitarian outcome. Thus, the invasion was understood by some advocates of humanitarian intervention as serving a dual purpose— that of fighting terrorism as well as enhancing human rights (especially for women) in Afghanistan. The United States, at times, used this humanitarian argument to justify its invasion and continued occupation of Afghanistan, though it is clear that the primary purpose of the invasion was self-defense. Although the Taliban has been removed from governmental power, a nominally democratic government has been installed (though through an arguably flawed election process), and human rights have generally improved, the Taliban and al-Qaeda remain ensconced in the tribal regions along the border between Afghanistan and Pakistan and the United States remains very much engaged in combat with them (Wheeler 2004).

U.S. Invasion of Iraq (Operation Iraqi Freedom), 2003

In March of 2003, the United States, the United Kingdom, and Australia led a coalition of states into Iraq to depose the regime of Saddam Hussein. The invasion was the culmination of a series of accusations by the United States that Iraq had illegally procured WMD, including chemical and biological weapons as well as a nuclear weapons program, and that Saddam Hussein's regime had connections to al-Qaeda. The United States also argued that the invasion would emancipate the Iraqis from the brutal reign of Saddam Hussein, a cruel despot who had turned viciously against his own citizens several times in the past. As the allied occupation of Iraq commenced and the claims regarding Iraqi WMD and ties to al-Qaeda turned out to be highly exaggerated, if not outright false, the United States began to more vocally emphasize the humanitarian aims of the invasion. So while some have argued that the Iraqi invasion could be construed as a humanitarian intervention, given that one of its aims was to remove a brutal tyrant, most observers generally have viewed this argument with deep suspicion and see it as a cynical abuse of humanitarianism as a back-up argument for an invasion whose original justification turned out to be highly misleading (Hehir 2010, 221–40).

Darfur Conflict and Subsequent AU/UN Peacekeeping, 2003–

In February of 2003, rebels from the Darfur region of Sudan rose up against what they perceived as increasingly repressive rule from the Islamic government in Khartoum. In response, the Sudanese government undertook a brutal counterinsurgency, whereby it armed and supported Arab militias, commonly referred to as *Janjaweed,* which were used as proxy forces and whose strategy was essentially to depopulate the countryside of sympathetic Darfurians. This strategy precipitated a humanitarian catastrophe of enormous proportions, as tens of thousands of civilians were killed outright and hundreds of thousands more were displaced and forced to live in refugee camps, where many more died of starvation and disease. By 2004, the U.S. government concluded that this strategy constituted "genocide," thus triggering calls by advocacy groups, and even some governments, for humanitarian intervention. For a variety of reasons related to the ongoing Global War on Terror and especially the United States' lack of credibility owing to the extremely unpopular Iraq War, no intervention was forthcoming and the massacres continued. In 2004, the African Union (AU) obtained permission from the Sudanese government to deploy a peacekeeping force known as the AU Mission in Sudan (AMIS), though the force was not of sufficient size, strength, or mandate to stop the killings and was itself frequently targeted by the *Janjaweed*. In 2007, the AMIS was replaced with a hybrid AU/UN peacekeeping force called UNAMID, though the force does not have a mandate that would allow it to use offensive force to protect civilians. The lack of a decisive military intervention to stop the killings in Darfur has led to the charge that powerful states largely lack the will to stop atrocities in Africa, even after the failure to do so in Rwanda a decade prior (Hehir 2010, 241–57).

NATO/Coalition Intervention in Libyan Civil War
(Operation Unified Protector), 2011

In February of 2011, protests occurred in the Libyan city of Benghazi in opposition to the brutal forty-year rule of Colonel Muammar Gaddafi. When security forces fired on the crowd, the protests escalated into all-out rebellion, spreading rapidly across the country and resulting in an armed conflict between government forces loyal to Colonel Gaddafi and a loosely organized group of rebels seeking to remove him from power. Gaddafi loyalists used a variety of brutal tactics in their effort to suppress the rebellion, including indiscriminate shelling of civilian areas, deliberate targeting of unarmed protesters, and the use of rape as a weapon of war. Gaddafi himself publically urged his supporters to "go out and cleanse the city of Benghazi." On March 17, 2011, the UN Security Council authorized the use of force in order to impose a no-fly zone over parts of Libya and to take "all necessary means" to protect civilians from abuse by Gaddafi's forces. As a result, the United States and the United Kingdom began attacking targets in Libya with cruise missiles, French and British warplanes undertook numerous air sorties against loyalist military targets, and the Royal Navy imposed a blockade. Importantly, the mission of imposing the no-fly zone was handed over to NATO command several days into the operation (Operation Unified Protector), while the mission of attacking Gaddafi's ground forces remained with coalition partners—primarily France and the United Kingdom, with the United States providing intelligence, targeting, and logistical support. As many as nineteen states—including Belgium, Canada, Denmark, France, Italy, Norway, Qatar, and Spain—participated in the military effort. The intervention received broad support among the international community, including from the Arab League and the European Union. Support waned as the operation continued through the summer of 2011, and especially Russia criticized the NATO-led effort for causing civilian casualties and for exceeding the mandate of the Security Council by going beyond protecting civilians and actually siding with the rebels. Either way, the intervention clearly turned the tide of the conflict in favor of the rebels, who eventually prevailed in the conflict once Gaddafi was killed in October of 2011 (Pattison 2011, 251–92).

APPENDIX B

SELECT CASES RELEVANT TO THE HUMANITARIAN INTERVENTION DEBATE: THE COLD WAR ERA

Belgian Intervention in the Congo (Leopoldville), 1960

Shortly after Congo achieved independence from Belgium in 1960, violence broke out involving Congolese militants targeting primarily Belgian and other European nationals residing in Congo. Belgium soon intervened in order to rescue Belgian and other foreign nationals. This case is usually considered an instance of rescue of nationals and received some support at the UN, but it proved quite controversial once it became clear that Belgium was supporting rebels in the breakaway Congolese province of Katanga (Abi-Saab 1978).

Belgian and U.S. Intervention in Congo (Stanleyville Operation), 1964

Amidst continued fighting in the aftermath of Congolese independence from Belgium, rebel forces took thousands of foreign residents hostage in the cities of Stanleyville and Paulis. Belgian forces once again intervened, this time with support of U.S. aircraft, which eventually resulted in the release of most of the hostages. The intervention took place with the consent of the Congolese government (Prime Minister Tshombe), and although at one time it was considered a paradigmatic case of humanitarian intervention, it is now considered a case of rescue of nationals with the consent of the government (Weisberg 1972).

Indian Intervention in East Pakistan/Bangladesh, 1971

This conflict is one of the most widely discussed cases of humanitarian intervention, involving a brutal and indiscriminate military operation by Pakistan against the primarily Bengali population of East Pakistan, which resulted in up to ten million Bengali refugees fleeing to India. As a result of this "refugee aggression," as India called it, as well as a preemptive strike by Pakistan against Indian airfields, India invaded Pakistan on two fronts and effectively ended the massacre of Bengalis and established the independent state of Bangladesh. Although India initially asserted humanitarian motives, it ultimately relied on the more traditional (and more widely accepted) argument of self-defense to justify its actions. International reaction to the intervention was mixed, but India's humanitarian justifications appear to have tempered criticism, though few states accepted this as a legitimate basis for the intervention (Wheeler 2000, 55–77).

Israeli Intervention in Uganda (Entebbe Operation), 1976

Normally classified as a case of rescue of nationals, this operation was launched by Israel after Palestinian militants had hijacked an aircraft on a flight to Paris, diverted it to Uganda, and held over a hundred Israeli passengers hostage. Israeli commandoes successfully rescued all but three hostages, who were killed in the raid along with their captors. The means and methods deployed in the operation were controversial, but it is generally accepted as a justified instance of rescue of nationals (Boyle 1982).

Tanzanian Intervention in Uganda, 1978–1979

After Ugandan forces under the leadership of the brutal dictator Idi Amin invaded, occupied, and attempted to annex part of bordering Tanzania, the Tanzanian army retaliated in self-defense and proceeded to march on to the Ugandan capital city of Kampala to overthrow the regime of Idi Amin. While the ouster of Amin was widely supported as a desirable result—given that Amin presided over one of the most brutal and abusive regimes in Africa—the intervention was clearly precipitated by Uganda's armed attack on Tanzania and thus was justified on grounds of self-defense. The ouster of Amin,

however, although perhaps not necessary for self-defense, was largely tolerated by the international community because of the likely humanitarian outcomes to which it was thought to lead (Wheeler 2000, 111–38).

Vietnamese Intervention in Kampuchea/Cambodia, 1978–1979

Amidst sporadic fighting on the border between Vietnam and Kampuchea
(Cambodia), Vietnamese troops eventually mounted an all-out invasion with
help from a Kampuchean insurgent group, the United Front, which was bent
on overthrowing Pol Pot's Khmer Rouge regime. Vietnam eventually captured
the capital city, causing Pol Pot and his clique to flee, thus ending the murderous reign of his Khmer Rouge, which had killed as many as two million
people. While the international community strongly objected to the human
rights violations in Cambodia, there was little international support for Vietnam's actions. Interestingly, Vietnam took pains to distinguish between the
border war, in which it justified its resort to force as an act of self-defense,
and the "revolutionary war" of the Cambodian people, which had caused
the ouster of Pol Pot. Thus, Vietnam was careful to not assert a right of humanitarian intervention, which would have likely been rejected by most states
(Wheeler 2000, 78–110).

U.S. Intervention in Grenada (Operation Urgent Fury), 1983

In response to a violent coup staged by a radical Marxist group, a coalition
of over 2,000 (mostly U.S.) troops landed in Grenada and quickly ousted the
coup leaders in a matter of days. This case is often referred to as an instance
of pro-democratic intervention, which is a military intervention intended to
restore a democratic regime that has been forcibly overthrown. However, the
United States justified its actions on three bases in which it expressed humanitarian motives: (1) military assistance was requested by the legitimate
(deposed) leadership of Grenada, (2) it was requested to intervene by the Organization of East Caribbean States, and (3) it was protecting U.S. nationals.
The facts supporting all these justifications, however, have been contested,
and a UN Security Council resolution that condemned the invasion as a violation of international law failed only because of a U.S. veto. The intervention
did not receive broad international support, and the United States stopped
short of invoking a right of pro-democratic or humanitarian intervention
(Joyner 1984).

U.S. Intervention in Panama (Operation Just Cause), 1989–1990

In 1980, some 24,000 U.S. troops invaded Panama to overthrow and capture
Manuel Noriega. The United States justified its actions on four grounds: (1)
to protect U.S. nationals, (2) to defend democracy in Panama, (3) to combat

drug trafficking, and (4) to enforce the Panama Canal Treaty. Analyzing the legitimacy of this operation is challenging because of the different justifications put forth. While the strongest legal case can perhaps be made on the basis of protection of nationals, this event is most widely cited by scholars as an example of pro-democratic intervention. However, a UN Security Council resolution condemning the action failed only because of the U.S. veto, and a General Assembly resolution condemning it was adopted by a large majority. The case is, therefore, not indicative of the existence of a widely accepted right to pro-democratic intervention (Nanda 1990).

REFERENCES

Abi-Saab, Georges. 1978. *The United Nations Operation in the Congo, 1960–1964.* Oxford: Oxford University Press.

Atack, Iain. 2002. "Ethical Objections to Humanitarian Intervention." *Security Dialogue* 33, no. 3: 279–92.

Ballard, John R. 1998. *Upholding Democracy: The United States Military Campaign in Haiti, 1994–1997.* Westport, Conn.: Praeger.

Beitz, Charles R. 1979. *Political Theory and International Relations.* Princeton, N.J.: Princeton University Press.

Bellamy, Alex J. 2004. "Motives, Outcomes, Intent and the Legitimacy of Humanitarian Intervention." *Journal of Military Ethics* 3, no. 3: 216–32.

———. 2005. "Responsibility to Protect or Trojan Horse? The Crisis in Darfur and Humanitarian Intervention after Iraq." *Ethics & International Affairs* 19, no. 2: 31–52.

Boyle, Francis A. 1982. "The Entebbe Hostage Crisis." *Netherlands International Law Review* 29, no. 1: 32–71.

Brilmayer, Lea. 1995. "What's the Matter with Selective Intervention?" *Arizona Law Review* 37, no. 4: 955–70.

Brownlie, Ian. 1974. "Humanitarian Intervention." In *Law and Civil War in the Modern World*, edited by John N. Moore, 217–28. Baltimore: Johns Hopkins University Press.

Chesterman, Simon. 2002. *Just War or Just Peace? Humanitarian Intervention and International Law.* Oxford: Oxford University Press.

Clough, Michael. 2005. "Darfur: Whose Responsibility to Protect?" In *Human Rights Watch World Report 2005*, 25–39. New York: Human Rights Watch.

Crawford, Neta. 2002. *Argument and Change in World Politics: Ethics, Decolonization, and Humanitarian Intervention.* Cambridge: Cambridge University Press.

Deng, Francis M., Sadikiel Kimaro, Terrence Lyons, Donald Rothchild, and I. William Zartman. 1996. *Sovereignty as Responsibility: Conflict Management in Africa.* Washington, D.C.: The Brookings Institution.

Donnelly, Jack. 2002. "Genocide and Humanitarian Intervention." *Journal of Human Rights* 1, no. 1: 93–109.

Drumbl, Mark A. 2003. "Self-Defense and the Use of Force: Breaking the Rules, Making the Rules, or Both?" *International Studies Perspectives* 4, no. 4: 409–31.

Farer, Tom J. 2003. "Humanitarian Intervention Before and After 9/11: Legality and Legitimacy." In *Humanitarian Intervention: Ethical, Legal and Political Dilemmas*, edited by J. L. Holzgrefe and Robert O. Keohane, 53–89. Cambridge: Cambridge University Press.

Finnemore, Martha. 2004. *The Purpose of Intervention: Changing Beliefs about the Use of Force*. Ithaca, N.Y.: Cornell University Press.

Fixdal, Mona, and Dan Smith. 1998. "Humanitarian Intervention and Just War." *Mershon International Studies Review* 42, no. 2: 283–312.

Franck, Thomas M. 2003. "Force after Iraq: What Happens Now?" *American Journal of International Law* 97, no. 3: 607–20.

Goodman, Ryan. 2006. "Humanitarian Intervention and Pretexts for War." *American Journal of International Law* 100, no. 1: 107–41.

Grotius, Hugo. 1949. *The Law of War and Peace*. Translated by Louise R Loomis. New York: Walter J. Black.

Harrington, Michael E. 1993. "Operation Provide Comfort: A Perspective in International Law." *Connecticut Journal of International Law* 8, no. 2: 635–56.

Hass, Ernst B. 1993. "Beware the Slippery Slope: Notes Toward the Definition of Justifiable Intervention." In *Emerging Norms of Justified Intervention*, edited by Laura W. Reed and Carl Kaysen, 63–87. Cambridge, Mass.: American Academy of Arts and Sciences..

Hehir, Aidan. 2010. *Humanitarian Intervention: An Introduction*. New York: Palgrave.

Heinze, Eric A. 2006. "Maximizing Human Security: A Utilitarian Argument for Humanitarian Intervention." *Journal of Human Rights* 5, no. 3: 283–302.

———. 2009. *Waging Humanitarian War: The Ethics, Law and Politics of Humanitarian Intervention*. Albany, N.Y.: SUNY Press.

Hoffman, Stanley. 1996. *The Ethics and Politics of Humanitarian Intervention*. South Bend, Ind.: University of Notre Dame Press.

Independent International Commission on Kosovo. 2000. *The Kosovo Report*. Oxford: Oxford University Press.

International Commission on Intervention and State Sovereignty (ICISS). 2001. *The Responsibility to Protect*. Ottawa, ON: International Development Research Centre.

Joyner, Christopher C. 1984. "The United States Action in Grenada: Reflections on the Lawfulness of Invasion." *American Journal of International Law* 78, no. 1: 131–44.

Keohane, Robert O. 2003. "Introduction." In *Humanitarian Intervention: Ethical, Legal and Political Dilemmas*, edited by J. L. Holzgrefe and Robert O. Keohane, 1–12. Cambridge, UK: Cambridge University Press.

Khong, Yuen Foong. 2001. "Human Security: A Shotgun Approach to Alleviating Human Misery?" *Global Governance* 7, no. 3: 231–37.

Kuperman, Alan J. 2001. *The Limits of Humanitarian Intervention: Genocide in Rwanda*. Washington, D.C.: The Brookings Institution.

Kurth, James. 2005. "Humanitarian Intervention after Iraq: Legal Ideals vs. Military Realities." *Orbis* (Winter): 87–101.

Lepard, Brian D. 2002. *Rethinking Humanitarian Intervention: A Fresh Legal Approach Based on Fundamental Ethical Principles in International Law and World Religions*. University Park: Pennsylvania University Press.

Levitt, Jeremy. 1998. "Humanitarian Intervention by Regional Actors in Internal Conflicts: The Cases of ECOWAS in Liberia and Sierra Leone." *Temple International and Comparative Law Journal* 12, no. 2: 333–76.

Mason, Andrew, and Nicholas J. Wheeler. 1996. "Realist Objections to Humanitarian Intervention." In *The Ethical Dimensions of Global Change*, edited by Barry Holden, 94–110. Basingstoke, UK: Macmillan.

Mayall, James. 2000. "The Concept of Humanitarian Intervention Revisited." In *Kosovo and the Challenge of Humanitarian Intervention: Selective Indignation, Collective Action, and International Citizenship*, edited by Albrecht Schnabel and Ramesh Thakur, 319–33. Tokyo: United Nations University Press.

Merriam, John J. 2001. "Kosovo and the Law of Humanitarian Intervention." *Case Western Reserve Journal of International Law* 33, no. 1: 111–54.

Nanda, Ved P. 1990. "The Validity of United States Intervention in Panama under International Law." *American Journal of International Law* 84, no. 2: 494–503.

Pattison, James. 2010. *Humanitarian Intervention and the Responsibility to Protect: Who Should Intervene?* Oxford: Oxford University Press.

———, ed. 2011. "Roundtable: Libya, R2P, and Humanitarian Intervention." *Ethics and International Affairs* 25, no. 3: 251–92.

Reisman, W. Michael. 2000. "Unilateral Action and the Transformation of the World Constitutive Process: The Special Problem of Humanitarian Intervention." *European Journal of International Law* 11, no. 1: 3–18.

Rieff, David. 2002. *A Bed for the Night: Humanitarianism in Crisis*. London: Vintage.

Roth, Kenneth. 2004. "War in Iraq: Not a Humanitarian Intervention." In *Human Rights Watch World Report 2004: Human Rights and Armed Conflict*, 13–33. New York: Human Rights Watch.

Rutherford, Kenneth R. 2008. *Humanitarianism Under Fire: The US and UN Intervention in Somalia*. Hartford, Conn.: Kumarian Press.

Schnabel, Albrecht, and Ramesh Thakur, eds. 2000. *Kosovo and the Challenge of Humanitarian Intervention: Selective Indignation, Collective Action, and International Citizenship*. Tokyo: United Nations University Press.

Stromseth, Jane. 2003. "Rethinking Humanitarian Intervention: The Case for Incremental Change." In *Humanitarian Intervention: Ethical, Legal and*

Political Dilemmas, edited by J. L. Holzgrefe and Robert O. Keohane, 232–72. Cambridge: Cambridge University Press.

Tesón, Fernando. 1997. *Humanitarian Intervention: An Inquiry into Law and Morality*. 2nd ed. Dobbs Ferry, N.Y.: Transnational Publishers.

Thomas, Nicholas, and William T. Tow. 2002. "The Utility of Human Security: Sovereignty and Humanitarian Intervention." *Security Dialogue* 33, no 2: 177–92.

United Nations Development Programme (UNDP). 1994. *Human Development Report 1994*. New York: Oxford University Press.

Walzer, Michael. 1980. "The Moral Standing of States: A Response to Four Critics." *Philosophy and Public Affairs* 9, no. 3: 209–29.

———. 2000. *Just and Unjust Wars: A Moral Argument with Historical Illustrations*. 3rd ed. New York: Basic Books.

Weisberg, Howard L. 1972. "The Congo Crisis 1964: A Case Study in Humanitarian Intervention." *Virginia Journal of International Law* 12, no. 2: 261–76.

Weiss, Thomas G., David P. Forsythe, and Roger A. Coate. 2004. *The United Nations and Changing World Politics*. 4th ed. Boulder, Colo.: Westview.

Wheeler, Nicholas J. 2000. *Saving Strangers: Humanitarian Intervention in International Society*. Oxford: Oxford University Press.

———. 2004. "Humanitarian Intervention after September 11." In *Just Intervention*, edited by Anthony F. Lang, Jr., 192–216. Washington, D.C.: Georgetown University Press.

Wheeler, Nicholas J., and Timothy Dunne. 2001. "East Timor and the New Humanitarian Interventionism." *International Affairs* 77, no. 4: 805–27.

Willard, Andrew R., and W. Michael Reisman. 1988. *International Incidents: The Law the Counts in World Politics*. Princeton, N.J.: Princeton University Press.

Williams, Paul D., and Alex J. Bellamy. 2005. "The Responsibility to Protect and the Crisis in Darfur." *Security Dialogue* 36, no. 1: 27–47.

4

The Global Economy

MARK W. FRAZIER

What do we mean by the term "the global economy," and who are its most important actors and organizations? Why is the global economy, whose annual output of goods and services is an estimated $60 trillion,[1] so unevenly distributed? This chapter addresses these and related questions by providing an overview of the global economy and its primary actors. Growing the global economy in a sustainable manner—to reduce poverty, increase human security, conserve natural resources, among much else—remains the elusive goal of states and leaders who make up the global economic community. These goals have proven difficult to achieve in part because of the fragmented and highly uneven distribution of wealth and power among the national economies that make up the global economy community.

We almost always hear the global economy discussed in terms of the **gross domestic product** (GDP) of goods and services produced and sold among individual states and regions, and not in aggregate terms such as the annual growth in "gross world product." For all the talk about globalization and the rapid flow of goods, services, money, people, ideas, and much else across national boundaries, the global economy remains compartmentalized into nearly two hundred states and territories. Only a portion of the $60 trillion in annual global output of goods and services is sold across state boundaries. International **trade** amounts to about $12.5 trillion per year (on an exchange rate basis), meaning that just over one-fifth of the global economy consists of cross-border exchanges of goods and services. For reasons soon to be explained, states have a strong tendency to create a vast array of barriers to prevent foreign firms, workers, investors, and countless other entities from selling goods and services within the domestic economy.

The problem with any state that pursues restrictive trade policies is that consumers, as well as companies, have to pay higher prices for generally substandard goods under these so-called **protectionist policies**. Reaching comprehensive, global agreements on how to avoid the protectionist tendencies of states and how to induce cooperation to lower trade barriers is the essence of politics in the global economic community. As the discussion in this chapter shows, it turns out that the most important of these comprehensive agreements have come in the middle of global economic crises. The global economic community, which was struck with its most serious crisis in eight decades in 2008, has yet to come up with an adequate response in the form of new agreements or institutions.

The **Global Financial Crisis** (GFC) began in the United States first as a credit contraction by banks in 2007 and then spread globally in 2008, causing a loss of an estimated $30 trillion in stock market share prices and $11 trillion in home values between fall 2008 and spring 2009 (*Economist* 2009, 4). Unemployment was equally staggering: twenty-five million people lost jobs in the richest thirty countries, and another twenty-three million migrant workers in China were said to have lost their jobs in early 2009. The causes of the crisis lay with a comprehensive failure of domestic financial regulatory policies, especially those of the United States. This disastrous blow to the global economy beginning in 2008 was not the result of states engaging in overly restrictive policies to curb flows of goods, capital, and people. How states respond to the GFC will be crucial in whether the global **recession** that it spawned becomes a decade-long affliction or a serious but relatively short downturn of a few years. In the fall of 2008, governments of the world's major economies launched massive spending programs, often known as **stimulus packages**, aimed at replacing the capital **investment** that the private sector could no longer provide. By 2010, the political momentum for such government spending had been reversed, and governments began to engage in the potentially dangerous practice of prematurely cutting spending by wrongly concluding that the recession had ended. At the same time, these states adopted equally perilous nationalist policies that threatened to restrict foreign imports and investment, much to the detriment of developing countries that so desperately depended for their growth on **export** markets in the advanced economies.

In addition to being compartmentalized, the global economy is also highly uneven in terms of the distribution of the world's GDP. The United States (with about 5 percent of the world's population), accounts for nearly 19 percent of the global economy. The wealthiest other twenty-five economies take up nearly two-thirds of global wealth, leaving the rest of the world with just under 17 percent of global GDP.[2] No one expects for the global economy to be evenly distributed, but even the most self-interested American analysts make the argument that American prosperity lies to a certain extent with the ability of U.S. producers to sell their goods to foreign consumers.[3] Thus, wealthy states have an interest in growing the size of the global economy, even if poorer countries grow faster and gain a larger share of global GDP.

This brings us to a point of longstanding controversy in the global economic community: the sources of **global economic inequality**. To oversimplify, some analysts argue that the best way to remedy this inequality is to create a much more open global economy so that poor countries can sell more

Table 4.1 Largest GDP in Terms of PPP

	2010 GDP–PPP ($ trillion)[a]	2010 Share of Global Economy (%)[b]	2008 Share of World Trade (%)[c]
United States	14.60	19.73	10.87
China	10.08	13.62	8.03
Japan	4.31	5.82	4.84
India	4.00	5.41	1.48
Germany	2.93	3.96	8.37
Russia	2.22	3.00	2.40
Brazil	2.18	2.95	0.62
United Kingdom	2.18	2.95	3.42
France	2.14	2.89	4.13
Italy	1.77	2.39	3.44
Global Economy	74.00		

Note: GDP = gross domestic product; PPP = purchasing power parity.
[a]*Source*: International Monetary Fund, World Economic Outlook Database, www.imf.org/external/pubs/ft/weo/2010/02/weodata/index.aspx.
[b]*Source*: World Trade Organization, Trade Profiles Database, http://stat.wto.org/CountryProfile/WSDBCountryPFHome.aspx?Language=E.
[c]*Source*: *World Trade Report 2009* (Geneva: World Trade Organization, 2010), p. 13.

of their goods in rich country markets. To the contrary, say others, the very cause of impoverishment in poor countries is the operation of market forces in the global economy, because markets by their very nature only exacerbate inequalities between rich and poor. Instead, these analysts say, states need to cooperate on curbing the excesses of the global capitalism, which generates its own cycle of crises that hurt the poor more than the rich. Also, argue these analysts, rich countries should provide a more just and equitable share of global wealth through various means, including aid and preferential access to their markets.[4]

Regardless of which of these or other positions a student of the global economy might hold, the crucial point in this chapter is that states will remain the most important actors in determining whether the global economy is relatively open or closed, whether the GFC is short or long in duration, and whether global income gaps can ever be narrowed. **Multinational corporations** and other transnational actors such as **nongovernmental organizations** (NGOs) have considerable but limited powers to influence events in the global economy. Global financial institutions can move markets instantaneously and can

Table 4.2   Largest GDP Nominally

	2010 GDP ($ trillion)[a]	2010 Share of Global Economy (%)[b]	2008 Share of World Trade (%)[c]
United States	14.62	23.60	10.87
China	5.75	9.28	8.03
Japan	5.39	8.70	4.84
Germany	3.31	5.34	8.37
France	2.56	4.13	4.13
United Kingdom	2.26	3.65	3.42
Italy	2.04	3.29	3.44
Brazil	2.02	3.26	1.19
Canada	1.56	2.52	2.74
Russia	1.48	2.39	2.40
Global Economy	61.96		

Note: GDP = gross domestic product.
[a]*Source*: IMF, World Economic Outlook Database, www.imf.org/external/pubs/ft/weo/2010/02/weodata/index.aspx.
[b]*Source*: World Trade Organization, Trade Profiles Database, http://stat.wto.org/CountryProfile/WSDBCountryPFHome.aspx?Language=E
[c]*Source*: *World Trade Report 2009* (Geneva: World Trade Organization, 2010), p. 13.

compel governments to make policy responses. Mega-foundations such as the **Bill and Melinda Gates Foundation** provide more in aid to poor countries than do most of the wealthiest countries in the world. Despite the powers of these and many other non-state actors, and the ease with which information flows, it is states that possess the ultimate and decisive influence over the most important questions facing the global economic community: whether global income inequality can be reduced, poverty can be alleviated, natural resources can be protected, and climate change can be mitigated, among many other vital goals. The central questions for the economic well-being of the global community are the same ones that have always faced states: how can their collective interest in expanding global economic welfare supersede national interests in gaining economic supremacy at the expense of rival states? Put another way, how can states curb their tendency to view the global economy in competitive terms?

This chapter addresses these questions and offers a skeptical assessment regarding cooperation in the global economic community. It does so by examining the ways in which states in the global economy—most centrally the

United States, China, and the European Union (EU) member states—have over the past decade abandoned serious efforts toward strengthening multilateral institutions to govern the global economy and have turned to unilateral, nationalist policies. Such policies now threaten not only to forestall recovery from the GFC, but also to abandon prospects for achieving policies that could create a more equitable and prosperous global economic community.

The discussion that follows first outlines the general problem that states face in terms of economic cooperation. The second section describes the most successful resolution of that problem to date, known as the **Bretton Woods system**. After the Second World War, the United States and other major economic powers created a set of institutions that they hoped would help overcome obstacles to economic cooperation. The goal was to encourage an open, or liberal, economic order in which states abided by a set of principles and rules that were intended to apply broadly to all participants. In the third section of this chapter, the future of the global economic community is addressed through an assessment of the recent international economic policies of its most influential participants: the United States, the EU, and China. A concluding section raises concerns about the future of multilateral cooperation within the global economic community.

THE BASIC PROBLEM

States in the global economy face the same dilemmas that they encounter in the security realm: doing what is seemingly in one's national interest ends up posing threats to other states, who in turn respond in ways that reduce one's economic well-being (and security). Restricting imports, putting controls on inflows of foreign capital, curbing immigration, and other protectionist measures can at times make good political sense from a domestic standpoint. Powerful firms and sectors, trade unions, political parties, and other influential actors in domestic politics may form coalitions at different times to block flows of goods, capital, or labor into the national economy. However, such policies can have utterly disastrous consequences if all states, especially the world's major economic powers, decide to do so in an extended retaliatory spiral. This is precisely what occurred in the early 1930s after a global financial collapse in stock prices created political currents and reactions against global flows of goods and money. World trade plummeted, capital flows halted, and a serious recession became what we now know as the **Great Depression**.

The roots of this behavior by states to try to make economic gains at the expense of others can be explained with some background first on how international trade operates in terms of accounting. When a firm in a given country exports goods or services to a customer in another country, the money paid by the customer to the exporter shows up in international accounts (also known as **balance of payments**) as a credit or monetary inflow for the country whose firm exported the goods or services. The same transaction shows up as a debit or monetary outflow in the international accounts of the country whose customer purchased the goods or services. Because of the way such international flows of goods and services are accounted for, the global economy is always "in balance"—that is, the value of exports and imports when totaled as credits and debits adds up to exactly zero. Thus, until the unlikely era of interplanetary trade of goods and services arrives, the global economy will never run a **trade deficit** or a **trade surplus**. If the balance of world economic transactions is always zero, some states will have to run trade surpluses and some states will have to run trade deficits. China, Germany, and Japan are the world's leading exporters, with the United States, Spain, and Great Britain its leading importers. Since the balance of transactions in the global community is always zero, if every state tries to pursue surpluses, trade and other international exchanges will quickly collapse. Through most of the modern economic history of the world, trade and other transactions are made possible because some states agree to run deficits while others pursue surpluses. These highly misleading terms of "deficit" and "surplus" imply very different things for ordinary consumers in these countries. Consumers in deficit countries, as any American knows well, enjoy the practice of consuming more than they produce, which means among other things the benefit of low-priced goods from all over the world. Conversely, consumers in so-called surplus countries have to live with the fact that they produce more than they consume, which means fewer choices in goods and a lower standard of living relative to economies with the same levels of national income—a paradox that any Japanese citizen can readily understand.

States in the global economy not only have to avoid policies that damage the global economy. The wealthiest economies also need to coordinate their domestic policies—such as measures to curb inflation or to stimulate their economies—in such a way that those measures are not undermined by offsetting domestic policies of their trading partners. If one state decides to stimulate its economy with increased government spending and lower interest rates, it might find that it can never bring its economy out of stagnation if that state's major trading partners are engaging in the opposite type of policies by cutting spending and raising interest rates. No better real-world example of this problem can be seen than in the heated debate among American, European, and Chinese leaders over how to pull the global economy out of stagnation and spark a sustained recovery from the GFC.

At the 2010 Toronto summit of the Group of 20 (**G-20**; a larger coordinating body that includes so-called emerging economies such as China, India, and Brazil), leaders disagreed sharply over how to cope with mounting **debt** without choking off the apparent recovery from the global recession. U.S. officials cautioned against German and British measures to reduce the risks of their public debt burdens because this would reduce the ability of their citizens to purchase American exports. The Chinese government, holding an unknown but very large share of its $2.5 trillion in foreign exchange reserves as U.S. government bonds, was equally nervous about the lack of commitment to debt reduction by the American government. This squabbling over domestic policies took place amid growing concern that the recovery had stalled, with signs of persistently high unemployment in the world's major economies. At subsequent meetings, some called for revisiting and reforming the global institutions that had been in place for over half a century.

THE BRETTON WOODS SOLUTION

The Bretton Woods institutions (the **General Agreement on Tariffs and Trade**—later to become the **World Trade Organization**, the **International Monetary Fund**, and the **World Bank**) were created after World War II to address many of the same problems in cooperation and coordination that exist today. The functions of these international institutions have changed dramatically, but their fundamental purposes continue to be directed toward preventing states from turning toward self-interested policies that can undermine the economic welfare of the global community. The institutions remain in place despite a very different distribution of economic resources and power today than existed in 1945 as well as a vastly more integrated global economy. The states and leaders who created these institutions, over the course of an extended conference in Bretton Woods, New Hampshire, beginning in 1944, did so with the aim of offering rewards and punishments so that states would avoid the types of policies that led to the dramatic collapse in world trade in the 1930s, and arguably fueled the unemployment and nationalist tendencies that led to the rise of extreme political movements in Europe and Asia, and eventually to world war.

The Bretton Woods institutions reflected the power of the United States and its weaker ally Great Britain and their mutual interests in reviving the war-ravaged economies in Europe and Asia. Preventing the spread of communist ideology and political movements in these and other regions, part and parcel of U.S. containment policy during the Cold War, was a core American interest underlying the design of the Bretton Woods institutions. By placing emphasis on the principles of a liberal, or open, economic system in which states agreed collectively to reduce barriers to trade, the assumption was that national economies would flourish and thereby weaken the appeal of ideologies and parties that offered alternatives to liberalism and democracy.

The World Trade Organization

After the U.S. Congress in the late 1940s rejected the original Bretton Woods proposal for an "International Trade Organization" as too intrusive in regulating national trade policy and laws, a far more benign-sounding organization, known as the General Agreement on Tariffs and Trade (GATT), came into being as a weaker substitute. The GATT operated on flexible and even idealistic notions—for example, decisions to lower trade barriers were to be made collectively, based on the unanimous consent of all members. In addition, developing countries enjoyed an ample loophole that let them bail out of provisions to lower trade barriers if they could come up with a good reason to exempt themselves. A state found to be in violation of GATT articles could simply bring to a halt any proceedings to punish it by vetoing the report of the GATT panel that leveled the charges against it. Yet remarkably, through a series of long, drawn-out trade talks, or "rounds," (often named after the city in which the talks were begun), trade barriers came down dramatically in the decades after 1945. The value of world trade rose from only $57 billion in 1947 to $6.6 trillion by the late 1990s, and the average **tariff** rates among industrialized countries dropped from 40 percent to 6 percent.

In the early 1990s, the GATT talks known as the **Uruguay Round** came to a conclusion, and GATT members (and their legislatures) agreed that a new body, the World Trade Organization (WTO), would replace GATT with stricter provisions for handling disputes among members and with a far broader mandate to reduce barriers to trade in complex goods such as intellectual property (e.g., software, music, film) and services (e.g., banking, insurance, legal advice). From that point on, the dramatic success of GATT in creating a multilateral forum for trade negotiations gave way to a very mixed record under the WTO. The WTO's greatest achievement has come as a dispute settlement forum: member states, including the most powerful states, have generally taken each other to arbitration (i.e., the WTO's Dispute Settlement Body) over trade policies they find objectionable in their partners rather than engaging in bilateral battles with threats of sanctions and other forms of trade conflict. In fact, a state that receives a favorable ruling from the WTO can legitimately levy trade sanctions on the losing party. Most often, however, the two parties work out a timetable in which the offending state agrees to dismantle the trade barrier in question.[5]

Yet the WTO has failed to live up to its promise as a venue for member states to jointly agree upon lowering trade barriers that would in principle benefit the consumers in all states. Part of the problem arises from the fact that the GATT's trade rounds handled the relatively easy or politically more palatable issues of simple tariff reductions on manufactured goods. The WTO has been able to make very little headway on remaining trade barriers, whose existence is supported by well-organized interest groups in the most powerful states. Farm lobbies in the United States, Japan, and the EU have successfully thwarted attempts in WTO trade rounds in the 1990s and 2000s to dismantle agricultural **subsidies**, tariffs, or outright bans on the import of certain agricultural commodities. Developing countries, such as India and Brazil, have been unwilling in the current **Doha Round** (begun in 2002) to agree on the reduction of barriers to trade in services, or on the protection of intellectual property such as patents that rich country corporations deem critical for their ability to sell pharmaceuticals and other research-intensive products in developing countries.

But the most important reason why the Doha Round, and the future of multilateral trade negotiations generally, remains in peril is that the United States no longer makes global trade talks a serious commitment. This failure of leadership in trade policy has many causes, but they can be boiled down to a new American preference for regional and bilateral trade agreements and a general disdain among American politicians and the public for trade liberalization. The successes of GATT/WTO arose in part because of considerable U.S. leadership and a bipartisan consensus on trade policy. The subsequent demise of multilateral trade negotiations can be attributed in part to the failure of both Republican and Democratic administrations since the mid-1990s to exert the same level of leadership that brought success in earlier trade rounds.[6]

The International Monetary Fund

The International Monetary Fund (IMF) has enjoyed much more limited successes than the GATT/WTO in achieving the aims its founders established for it in the years immediately following World War II. At Bretton Woods, American and British leaders debated extensively over the ideal system for circulating money in the global community. British representatives, led by the distinguished economist **John Maynard Keynes**, pushed for a new global currency that would replace the national currencies of states. This proposal proved entirely too optimistic, as the American representatives, and those of other states at the conference, insisted on maintaining their own national currencies. In part, national currencies bestowed a sense of national unity and pride—having one's own currency was, after all, a core feature of sovereignty and nationhood. But an even more important reason that the conference participants rejected the British proposal lay with the implications that a global currency had for monetary and fiscal policy.

The British proposal did not get very far because generally speaking, states and the politicians who run them are extremely reluctant to abandon their ability to exert control over the money supply in their domestic economy. Leaders want to be able to expand the money supply (through various means ranging from lowering interest rates to printing money) if the economy looks to be entering a recession. Conversely, if inflation looms as a threat, they would like to contract the money supply (through higher interest rates and other means of reducing the money supply). When a state decides to unify its currency with that of another state, or to jointly create a new currency with a group of other states, it does so with the acute realization that this means highly restrictive curbs on its ability to regulate the money supply. After unification, a central bank appointed by members of the **monetary union** makes such decisions for all states in the currency union. A recession in one state does not necessarily mean that the central bank will expand the money supply for the currency union, because doing so might create inflation threats in other members. For these and many other complex reasons, the dream of Keynes and others since him for a global currency has fallen well short of realization.

The IMF became an international institution that, short of global currency unification, tried to ensure that member states would cooperate on keeping their currencies aligned in such a way that trade and other forms of economic integration could continue. Originally, the United States agreed to link the U.S. dollar to gold. In theory, the amount of dollars in circulation would be equivalent to a certain amount of gold, such that anyone holding dollars could trade $35 for one ounce of gold. In turn, the other major economies in the global economy agreed to set their national currencies to a certain amount of U.S. dollars. As economic cycles came and went, this practice would be challenging for all parties to uphold—the temptation would be to weaken the value of one's currency in order to induce exports and stimulate one's national economy. This is where the IMF's core purpose was established: a state facing a downturn in its national economy could come to the IMF for a loan, in exchange for which the country agreed to keep its currency aligned to the U.S. dollar (Eichengreen 2009).

This IMF-backed arrangement facilitated the rapid growth of trade and the recovery of the European and Japanese economies in the 1950s. The Soviet bloc retained its own system of trade and exchange, largely without contact between these states and the U.S.-led Bretton Woods system. A simple glance at today's price of gold reveals that something went wrong with the U.S. dollar-gold standard. By August 2010, gold was being traded at about $1,200 per ounce on commodity markets. To oversimplify, the U.S. government during the 1960s simply printed so much money, to support its foreign policy goals of containment of communism and to allow U.S. consumers to import goods from its allies, that by the early 1970s the credibility of the dollar had fallen considerably. President Nixon's administration made it official by announcing to a distressed group of Europeans and Japanese holding U.S. dollars that the American government would abandon its assurance of keeping the dollar linked to gold at the past price of $35 per ounce. European and Japanese financial officials followed suit, removing their assurance to maintain the value of their currencies to the dollar. Since that time, the world's currency system has been one of **floating currencies,** or currency values determined by the decisions of thousands of traders and their firms each hour of the day. States lost the benefits of stable currencies, but they retained their vital ability to control their monetary policy.

Once the major economies of the world had moved to a system of floating currencies, many claimed that the IMF lost its core purpose. In large part this claim is true, though the IMF somewhat reinvented itself during the 1970s by dispensing loans and policy advice to countries that came to it asking for assistance with currency instability and other economic challenges. Although the IMF conducts annual reports on each of its members—reports that often serve as a kind of credit rating for developing countries wishing to borrow on international capital markets—its most important function remains to offer emergency loans to countries facing economic crises. Conventional wisdom claims that the IMF forces states to take its loans in exchange for austere policies that hurt consumers and especially poor households in the national economy. But strictly speaking, a state's leaders have to make the political decision first to invite the IMF to initiate consultations over a loan package, after which negotiations follow with IMF officials over the terms of the loan. A now infamous photograph shows the then head of the IMF standing with his arms folded and looking down impatiently at a seated President Suharto of Indonesia as the latter signed the terms of a loan package in late 1997. The photography is rich in symbolism, with one of Asia's then most powerful dictators who oversaw three decades of rapid economic growth in Indonesia acquiescing to the apparent power of the IMF.[7]

The fact that riots and political turmoil following the loan package brought down Suharto's regime in spring 1998 offers only richer context for the apparent power of the IMF to hold sway over the sovereignty of states. However, the apparent power of the IMF only reflects the real power of its leading members. The IMF Board of Governors is composed of representatives of the world's largest economies, who enjoy voting rights in rough proportion to their economic size. Thus, any coalition consisting of the United States, Japan, West European economies, and to some extent China can veto any measure or loan that they wish. The putative assertion of power by the IMF when it makes headlines in negotiating loans with states suffering from recessions is in fact an indirect reflection of the world's most powerful states, not the IMF per se.

While the idea of a global currency remains far-fetched, the case for regional currencies can be seen in the euro zone (with sixteen member states in 2010), and in the decision by a number of Central American countries (as well as Ecuador) to abandon their currencies and adopt the U.S. dollar. For one, currency unity means that traders and investors do not have to worry about fluctuations in the value of their assets as national currencies shift, often rapidly, in value. Goods, services, and even wages are also much more simply priced and can be transacted without the endless amount of time and resources spent converting the prices of one good into a local currency. There may be political reasons also for currency unification, such as deepening economic integration that presumably induces cooperation in other areas.

The World Bank

A third Bretton Woods institution, the World Bank, was founded as a multilateral institution to provide development aid. In other words, major development loans could come from the World Bank, rather than powerful states, who might be tempted in making loans to smaller and weaker economies to ask for exclusive trade ties or natural resource contracts, not unlike the colonial relationships that the Bretton Woods founders sought to avoid. The idea of multilateral development aid quickly foundered when in the late 1940s the West European economies faced grave economic challenges and the United States moved ahead in unilateral fashion with development assistance under the Marshall Plan. Moreover, the seeming neutrality of development assistance from the World Bank masked the fact that to qualify for World Bank loans, member states had to first be in good standing as members of the IMF. IMF membership of course entailed annual economic check-ups and policy reviews. The power of the United States and other major economies was reflected in the board of governors of the World Bank, which like the IMF could veto assistance packages put before it by the bank's officers if a small coalition of the United States and a few other large economies decided to act against it. This veto power in practice meant the bank's officers, rather than proposing aid packages that got vetoed, had to design them so that they would meet the expected preferences of the United States. Thus, World Bank loans went to Cold War allies and other states that the United States viewed as politically acceptable. The IMF–World Bank leadership lock by the United States and European economies has resulted in a long-standing agreement by which the Americans and Europeans would vote in such a way that a European would always hold the top position in the IMF, and the presidency of the World Bank would go to an American. These leading posts in the two organizations are powerful only in symbolic terms, but the continued monopoly of the positions by Americans and Europeans does a lot to undermine efforts to make the IMF and World Bank appear more inclusive of smaller non-Western economies.

Throughout the existence of the World Bank, the world's most powerful states have continued to make unilateral loans that, while in no way violating World Bank or any other provisions in international institutions, come with many strings attached for recipient states and overlook some of the provisions that the World Bank has tried to foster in terms of improving governance and transparency in the dispersal of aid. The United States maintained a robust aid program, especially during the Cold War, to channel money for governments of its allies and client states to build roads and transportation infrastructure, schools, and so forth. The Japanese and European governments followed in the footsteps of the United States to build up regional economies, including those of their former colonies, with official development projects. As positive as this support seems at first glance, it is quite common for loans to include provisions that benefit firms or interest groups in the lending state. For example, loans or other development assistance can stipulate that construction contracts, or the machinery imported by local construction firms, must be provided by corporations based in the donor state. This support for corporations in the donor state means that competitive bidding for the aid projects can be sharply restricted.[8]

A more recent controversy in World Bank lending projects has been its efforts to improve governance in the state of recipient countries. During the late 1990s and first decade of the 2000s, World Bank officials drew up much stricter monitoring regulations for how and to whom the bank's aid was disbursed. World Bank loans still must go to government agencies in recipient states (as opposed NGOs and others), but the bank attempted to pay much closer attention to the use of its funds. This commendable goal of lessening the corruption that arose in the distribution of aid from the bank was met with fierce opposition by recipient countries. Bank president Paul Wolfowitz's campaign against corruption ended with his resignation in 2007 over a personal scandal with a World Bank employee. Some have argued that those who opposed his campaign against corruption engineered his downfall (Weisman 2007). A second effect of the bank's anti-corruption crusade has been that would-be borrowers have turned to states such as China for development assistance and loans that require less monitoring of potential corruption in aid distribution.

THE FUTURE OF THE GLOBAL ECONOMIC COMMUNITY

The preceding discussion of the Bretton Woods institutions showed that despite the design of such institutions as multilateral forums for resolving problems of trade barriers, currency coordination, and development assistance, the most powerful states have held sway either explicitly or behind the scenes. This point does not mean that the GATT/WTO, IMF, and World Bank have failed in their stated missions and purposes. In historical context going back more than sixty years, these institutions have by a significant measure met the aspirations of their founders to create a more open global economy in which flows of goods, capital, and loans were subject to a kind of shared governance under multilateral principles. My point is that without the power and leadership of the major economies, first and foremost the United States, these international economic institutions would have been vastly weaker and their progress toward even limited goals would have been hindered. Turning to the economic future of the global community, troubling signs have emerged that suggest the post-war multilateralism has given way to a far more unilateral, uncoordinated, and at times nationalist response to the challenges of the global economy.

The United States

Future historians of the global economy will no doubt debate what event best serves as a landmark for when the United States began to abandon its leadership role in the global economy. My own selection for this turning point would be when the U.S. Congress took up and eventually passed legislation to approve the formation of **the North American Free Trade Agreement (NAFTA)** and to ratify the GATT round that concluded with the formation of the WTO, in 1993 and 1994, respectively. While these two monumental trade agreements were ultimately successful as legislative measures, in that Congress approved them, they also catalyzed currents of protectionism and nationalism that have made it nearly impossible for future trade liberalization agreements to be brought before Congress for debate, let alone approval. What caused the United States to abandon its leadership of the global economy?

The reasons are complicated but can be boiled down to three. First, the end of the Cold War brought a realigned view of global economics in which American administrations, beginning with the Clinton administration, placed much greater emphasis on economic competition over cooperation among its trading partners. Second, an important shift in American public opinion took place. Once mildly supportive of global economic ties and the net benefits of **globalization**, the American public turned resoundingly skeptical of global economic linkages and their effects on American employment patterns and the American economy as well as national security. Third, the emergence of China as a new perceived rival in global affairs created much angst about the U.S. role in the global economy among politicians and the public.

The end of the Cold War brought an entirely new group of states into the global economy, but it also led to new considerations among the American foreign policy community. While the former states of the Soviet Union and the economies of Eastern Europe more or less joined the global economic community with drastic reforms of their economies, this was of lesser importance than the sea change in how American leaders viewed the whole concept of multilateralism in resolving global economic problems. As the sole superpower, the temptation to engage in the unilateral and bilateral pursuit of economic advantages was too much to overcome for successive American administrations. Clinton administration financial and trade officials applied strong political pressure on states of high-growth economies, such as those in East Asia and elsewhere, to open their economies not only to goods and services, but also to financial flows, including foreign (read American) bank loans and foreign (read American) stock market investors. While the same officials shepherded the legislation on the WTO and NAFTA through a highly reluctant but obliging Democratic majority in Congress, American economic strategy by the mid-1990s was clearly one of exerting influence on emerging economies and even its allies in Japan to open markets and accept new forms of financial inflows. Even the onset of the **Mexican peso crisis** in 1995 and the **Asian Financial Crisis** in 1997, which President Clinton first assessed as a "few bumps in the road," did little to stem the enthusiasm for vigorous U.S. promotion of open product and financial markets. One could argue that the United States had designed the Bretton Woods institutions to achieve the same outcome, but what mattered more after 1990 was the means by which American policymakers chose to pursue these ends. While the United States certainly continued to pursue these ends through the WTO, the IMF, and the World Bank, it worked even more enthusiastically through bilateral and regional channels that often undermined the very intent of the Bretton Woods institutions. A succession of regional (e.g., Central American Free Trade Agreement[9]) and bilateral (e.g., United States–Chile Free Trade Agreement) trade deals taken up under the Bush administration in the 2000s gave pause to negotiators at the WTO talks and in other fora about U.S. commitments to multilateral agreements (Erikson 2004–2005). Regional and bilateral agreements are by definition exclusionary, and they undermine the very principles of multilateralism, in which trade openings granted to one state are supposed to apply to all states.

The extremely narrow margins by which even these exclusive trade agreements passed the U.S. Congress underscored the lack of political support for trade and for globalization generally among the American public. In the Pew Global attitudes survey, the percentage of Americans who assessed trade with other countries as good for their country fell from 78 percent in 2002 to 59 percent in 2007 (Pew Research Center 2007, 14). A Fortune poll in early 2008 found that Americans were split on whether international trade benefitted consumers, and 78 percent concluded that it harmed American workers (Easton 2008). The American people's suspicion about the country's role in the global economy comes from perception as much as reality. An essential feature of the rhetoric of each American administration dating back to the Reagan administration (and even before) has been the promise to bring a tough approach to countries with whom the United States runs a trade **deficit**. Starting with Japan and Western Europe under the Nixon administration, and continuing during the Reagan years, such rhetoric was always offset by the fact that the states with whom the president was promising to "get tough" on trade issues were the closest of American security allies. Such rhetoric coincided with a long-term structural decline in the size of the American manufacturing workforce, which dwindled down to 11.6 million or under 10 percent of the total workforce, from 25 percent of the U.S. workforce in 1970. While this decline in the size of the manufacturing workforce can be offset with numbers showing increases in higher productivity service sector jobs, plenty of American politicians sought to pin the blame on America's trade partners. During the 1970s and 1980s, the main target for such criticisms was the trade policies of Japan. Later, with the end of the Cold War and the emergence of China as America's main perceived economic competitor, it was easy to associate employment troubles in the American economy with the deliberate policies of the Chinese government. Rather than use this challenge to call for the resolution of multilateral trade negotiations within the WTO framework,

American politicians demanded restrictions on the import of Chinese goods and on Chinese investments (*Economist* 2007).

This brings us to the third and final factor in America's abandonment of multilateral principles and institutions in the global economy: the rise of China. It is with rich irony that China's rapid economic growth has occurred in the context of the decline of the Bretton Woods system, since China, more than any other country, has been treated among policymakers as a master of gaming the Bretton Woods system to its advantage. As a country that was not even a member of the Bretton Woods institutions in 1980, it has now become the leading recipient of World Bank development loans, a very influential member of the WTO, and living proof to many of the wrong-headed policies of the IMF. China maintains strict capital controls on the inflow and outflow of foreign currencies and investments, advice that the IMF in the 1990s argued would damage long-run prospects for growth in China or any other economy. But in the perception of Americans and in terms of America's leadership role in the global economy, China's economic rise presents a challenge that makes the WTO, IMF, and World Bank, as multilateral institutions under U.S. leadership, seem irrelevant. After all, if the United States and China are or will soon be the top-two economies in the world, then bilateral negotiations and coordination on their respective global economic concerns is a natural strategy to undertake. The twice-yearly **United States–China Strategic and Economic Dialogue**, initiated by the two countries in 2006, has quickly taken up as much if not greater financial press coverage and attention than the annual meetings of the IMF and World Bank, not to mention ministerial meetings of the WTO (Atlantic Council 2009).

All three of these sources in America's gradual withdrawal from multilateral approaches to the global economy and from leadership in the Bretton Woods institutions were well under way, it should be stressed, before the September 11, 2001, terrorist attacks on the United States. The subsequent wars in Afghanistan and Iraq, and the rise of a new American national security doctrine with them, were dramatic displays of American unilateralism. This new doctrine, to the extent it had implications for America's foreign economic policy, only reinforced unilateral tendencies in its economic relations. In addition, the war on terrorism created a political climate to impose a vast new infrastructure of government monitoring over the flows of goods, services, money, and people in the global economy. While the September 11 attacks and subsequent attempts to carry out various bombings and other attacks on civilian infrastructures were certainly aimed at disrupting the global economy, the security countermeasures taken in the United States and virtually every other country have at the very least impeded transnational economic exchanges.

When the most powerful state and guarantor of an open global economic community adopts unilateral or even protectionist tendencies in its economic relations, it is easy for other states to weaken their commitment to multilateralism, to pursue bilateral and regional agreements to the exclusion of other states, and even to view global economic relations in terms of a scramble for limited benefits. Such has been the case with the two other central actors in the global economy, the EU and China.

The European Union

The EU experiment is a model in cooperation leading to economic integration, but it also shows clearly how regional agreements undermine multilateral principles. To their great credit, the powers of Europe that waged bitter and calamitous wars against one another in the nineteenth and twentieth centuries had by the start of the twenty-first century agreed not only to liberalize the flow of goods and services across national boundaries—the creation of a common market—but also to abandon their national currencies in favor of a unified currency, the euro.[10]

Alongside this impressive degree of liberalization in the flow of goods, services, and money across national boundaries within the EU, a negative consequence arose when certain countries, in harmonizing their trade policies with other EU members, had to impose tighter restrictions on some imports, especially agricultural commodities, from economies outside the region. Any regional trade agreement carries the threat to exclude from the benefits of trade liberalization the trading partners outside the region. NAFTA, for example, imposed onerous restrictions such that Japanese auto firms could not assemble cars in Mexico or Canada and sell them into the American market under lower tariff provisions of NAFTA. NAFTA members are free to impose whatever trade restrictions they wish on states outside the trading zone. The EU took integration a step further by requiring unified provisions for tariffs, duties, and so forth on products from outside the EU market. This requirement left a relatively more liberal state such as Germany having to raise trade restrictions on agricultural products, the most infamous case of which was bananas imported from Central and South American producers. The United States and other WTO members filed one of the most protracted and contentious cases against EU agricultural policies in what became known as the **banana wars** in the 1990s and early 2000s. Before it was over, the United States and the EU had retaliated back and forth with threats of sanctions on an array of consumer products having nothing to do with bananas (Shah 2010).

In terms of the monetary union, troubling signs were on the horizon soon after the adoption of the euro. In abandoning their own currencies, states also gave up the ability to control the money supply—they could no longer respond to recessions and inflation threats by printing money or taking it out of circulation. That was now the job of the **European Central Bank**, which had to carefully monitor economic activity in euro zone members and make monetary policy accordingly. On the other hand, euro zone states retained a lever of economic policy that would prove crucial, and deeply problematic, by 2010: member states relinquished control over monetary policy, but they insisted on retaining their ability to tax and spend, also known as fiscal policy.

It is not surprising that euro zone members wanted to preserve their ability to allocate tax revenues as they wished, toward education, social services, security, and so forth. But as members of a monetary union, member states had to promise to keep their budgets close to balanced, and membership in the euro zone required that governments keep budget deficits under 3 percent of GDP. When France broke this pledge for a few years in the mid-2000s, the credibility of the threshold may have weakened, especially for smaller economies in the euro zone. By the end of the decade, countries such as Greece, Spain, Portugal, and Ireland had racked up spending well above the 3 percent threshold, such as the 13 percent levels reached by Greece. Just as Thailand or Korea in the late 1990s had to go hat in hand to the IMF—and by implication to U.S. Treasury officials—to negotiate short-term government loans in exchange for long-term permanent cuts in government spending, Greece was in a similar position when international capital markets refused to extend loans to the Greek government by purchasing its sovereign debt (or government bonds). When faced with a situation where it would soon run short of funds to operate its basic government functions, the Greek government had to go to the EU and its most powerful state, Germany, to negotiate credit in exchange for deep cuts in government spending. As was the case in the Asian economies afflicted in what amounted to a debt crisis in the late 1990s, ordinary Greeks who had little exposure to global finance suddenly found their jobs and livelihood at risk by seemingly uncontrollable actions of the global economy and those who managed it.

European responses in the aftermath of the GFC were to impose restrictions on each other and to take steps to curb imports from America. In France, the government's stimulus package steered funds toward its own (French) companies, a move that the U.S. Congress also considered but eventually rejected when it approved the American stimulus package. German Chancellor Angela Merkel criticized U.S. efforts to prop up its automobile industry as protectionist. Workers in many European countries went on strike to protest management's hiring of foreign labor or to object to plans to sell firms to foreign companies (King, MacDonald, and Walker 2009).

While trade remains robust within EU member states, it is clear that the GFC and the debt crisis that followed have sapped the political will among the Europeans to pursue further trade liberalization in multilateral institutions such as the WTO. European leaders have followed in the footsteps of American trade strategy. They have bypassed the current round of trade negotiations in pursuit of preferential trade and aid arrangements with African economies, among others.

China

No country has benefited more in terms of GDP growth from the open global economic system than has China. The evidence is plain: China was largely in self-imposed isolation from the global economic community before the late 1970s, and since that time has become the largest trading state and leading recipient of foreign direct investment. It has done so in many respects by relying on markets in the United States, Canada, EU, and Japan for exports, and on investors from those countries to build factories in China that served as export platforms.[11] It took China fourteen years from the first application to join the then GATT before it made sufficient promises to the United States and all other members of the WTO to gain membership, as it did formally in 2001. The terms that China agreed to were the most intrusive yet for a WTO member in terms of demands made for dismantling various trade and investment barriers, but the latter were admittedly very high in China to begin with. Moreover, China has been a model citizen of organizations such as the World Bank, as its leading recipient of development loans and as apparent proof that liberalization can bring about substantial reductions in poverty.

Despite these comprehensive reforms, China retains a number of crucial institutions from the old days of the planned economy. The most obvious example is of course the authoritarian political system under the Chinese Communist Party, but in economic terms China's small number of powerful state-owned enterprises have become highly influential actors in the global economy, as they have sought investment and resource deals in Africa, Latin America, and the Middle East. Whether encouraging state-owned enterprises to pursue energy and natural resource contracts abroad, protecting the same firms from foreign competition at home in the Chinese market, or most controversially, pegging its currency to the U.S. dollar in ways that artificially lower the prices of Chinese exports, the Chinese government engages in far greater macro- and micro-economic management than is the case in America or Europe.

China has always had a **mercantilist**,[12] or state-managed, approach to its role in the global economy. The political justification was that integrating with the global economy could make China into the wealthy and powerful state that it had been in global affairs before the disastrous nineteenth century. China's participation in the global economy is thus best thought of as a means to the long-term end of achieving national power, and much less about a commitment to some abstract goal of an open and more prosperous global economic community. It was only a matter of time, therefore, before this means-end reasoning would turn back on itself. Now that China has attained a substantial degree of global power and influence, it is changing its view about the purpose and governance of the Bretton Woods institutions.

The year 2010 is very likely to go down as a game-changer in U.S. and EU economic relations with China. The most telling turnaround came from the chief executive officer (CEO) of General Motors (GM), who said to an audience of Italian executives in July, "I really worry about China. I am not sure that in the end they want any of us to win, or any of us to be successful." Immelt said nothing different from what China critics suspicious of the benefits of American engagement with China had long noted. But for the CEO of GM to say this, and for his remarks to be echoed by leading industrial associations in the United States and in Europe, was a truly stunning turnaround for groups that had often been derided in their own country as "Chinapologists" or defenders of China who urged patience and understanding of China's domestic and foreign policies (Drezner 2010). A year earlier, as chronicled by Richard McGregor, Chinese economic officials began to openly chide Western leaders and representatives from global financial institutions at various international fora. Chinese officials smugly told American and European leaders how the global financial crisis had turned the tables, and now it was time for their American teachers to learn some lessons from the student about how to approach economic policy (McGregor 2010, x–xi).

There is much irony in the current tensions between the United States and the EU versus China: The country that has benefited most from the liberal global economy, China, carries legacies of state socialism and retains a repressive political system. The creator and defender of that same global economic order, the United States, classifies China under U.S. trade law as a "non-market economy" so that the American government can more easily impose duties on certain Chinese imports. EU member states, which for decades struggled to coordinate their currencies among themselves to achieve some stability in their exchange rates (and in their economies) before finally taking the drastic step of currency unification, insist along with America that China should remove its peg to the U.S. dollar and "float" its currency.

Finally, and most oddly, a country whose per capita income is about 20 percent of American and EU levels—and whose overall economy is about the size of California's—is essentially exporting over $1 billion per day to the United States in the form of purchasing U.S. government debt. Money is flowing "uphill," from a relatively poorer economy to the world's richest economy, so that households in America can consume more than they produce (they borrow to make up the difference). Meanwhile Chinese workers and firms produce far more than Chinese households consume, and thus China exports these surpluses to the rest to the world, especially to America. This complex imbalance in the global economy that foreshadowed the American credit crisis and global recession should recede as American households reduce their debt, but it would be rash to expect that Chinese consumers will pick up the slack and replace America's lowered consumption patterns. In addition, the real tensions in the U.S.-China relationship, which stem from lingering suspicions over military and security goals, will keep economic relations from being easily resolved.

China is unquestionably now a major player in the global economy. Much of China's rise had to do with its domestic policies, but in some respects its newfound status is part of a general emergence of large economies to prominent positions in the global economy. Brazil and India now account for considerable shares of the global economy (see table 4.1), with India ranked between industrial powers Germany and Japan with a 5.4 percent share of global output. In part, the rapid growth of Brazil and India, as well as China, illustrates a long-standing source of wealth and power in the global economy. States that are endowed with large populations (China, India) or natural resources (Brazil) have a distinct advantage if they can devise policies that turn those endowments into productive assets. That has been the case in recent decades for China, India, and Brazil, but their continued growth will depend on their ability to move beyond the original foundations of exporting labor-intensive goods and services or natural resources to developed economies. Assuming that China, India, and Brazil (as well as the less-mentioned Indonesia) can continue their growth trajectories, the share of the global GDP would be more evenly distributed than was the case for the past half century. One of the most intriguing questions for the future of the global economy will be whether leaders of states such as China, India, and Brazil will seek to maintain the remnants of the Bretton Woods system or choose to adopt new developmental models and global institutions to address poverty and underdevelopment in regions such as Africa, South Asia, and Latin America.

CONCLUSION

In his classic treatise on the global economy published in the year 2000, Robert Gilpin noted that for an open and stable global economy to survive, three political requirements had to be fulfilled. First, one or more powerful states had to exert political and economic leadership by engaging in the heavy lifting of managing and enforcing trade and currency rules for global exchanges. Second, the small group of the most powerful economies in the world had to cooperate, since no single state regardless of its power could manage the global economy for very long. Finally, an open and stable global economy required the political support of the people in the major economic powers. By this Gilpin meant that the leaders of these states would quickly abandon the hard work necessary to maintain the liberal economic order if the people in their respective states concluded that openness was costlier than the alternatives of a more closed, and presumably more stable, global economy (Gilpin 2000, xv).

All three of these political prerequisites for an open and stable global economic community have suffered substantial erosion since the 1990s. As the preceding discussion has shown, the Bretton Woods institutions enjoyed the limited successes that they did in large part because of U.S. leadership, U.S.-induced cooperation among the major economic powers, and the broad popular support for the liberal economic order that was established after World War II. The decline of these institutions has proceeded in lockstep with the gradual abandonment of American commitment to multilateralism in trade and other economic exchanges.

Many other crucial actors besides the states discussed above are important in the global economic community, but the most powerful states remain firmly in charge and will determine the future direction of the global economic community. The dominance of these powerful states in the global economic community means that it is entirely inaccurate to assume that the trend of "globalization," so much discussed in governments, universities, and elsewhere during the 1990s, is somehow a permanent and ever-expanding state of affairs. Globalization proponents and critics both more or less argued that the rapid integration of the global community, through the rapid movements of huge amounts of capital and through the seamless integration of supply chains across dozens of countries to create a single and miraculous product like the personal computer—which allowed users to make global connections through the Internet—was forever dismantling the barriers that states had once controlled with relative ease. But states have figured out ways to cope with and even control such flows—witness the Chinese government's ability to filter content from easy access by Internet users in China and the U.S. government's massive deployment of resources to create an intelligence industry that monitors closely the comings and goings of foreigners, foreign corporations, and its own citizens. Globalization has been a powerful force for the integration of the global economic as well as cultural communities. But the global economic community has seen considerable fluctuation in terms of openness and closure over the past century and a half.

The sources of these fluctuations, as the preceding discussion points out, has much to do with the willingness of states to assume the costs of leadership in creating a relatively open global economy. But as Gilpin hinted at when he discussed public support for openness, the sources of movement toward relative closure in the global community may have as much to do with human nature as with the power of states. As the economic historian Harold James concluded in his magisterial work on the collapse of the global economy in the 1930s, "globalism [i.e., globalization] fails because humans and the institutions they create cannot adequately handle the psychological and institutional consequences of the interconnected world" (James 2002, 4).

It is important to underscore that history will not repeat itself, at least in the same bleak scenarios as the 1930s. But the historical trends outlined above will repeat themselves. Financial crises caused by the rapid and unrestricted flows of capital to trendy investment venues globally will recur during periods of relative global economic openness. Movements against globalization—including those that offer nationalist or cultural alternatives to dominant ideologies—will form to highlight and criticize the costs of globalization. Governments, especially those of the most powerful states, will eventually abandon their commitment to the further opening of the global economy and pursue policies of self-interest and national power at the expense of the institutions meant to prevent states from engaging in such behavior.

NOTES

1. Estimates of gross world product vary considerably. The World Bank estimates for 2008 were $60.5 trillion at official exchange rates; the Central Intelligence Agency lists in its World Factbook a gross world product of $58.1 trillion for 2009 ($70.3 trillion in purchasing power parity terms).

2. For more precise measurements of the global economy and what each state contributes to it, now and in the past, please see the comprehensive dataset assembled by the late Angus Maddison at www.ggdc.net/maddison.

3. In fact, for much of its rise as a global power between 1850 and 1950, America was an export-driven, surplus economy dependent on other states running deficits to import American goods.

4. Different approaches to the study of power and politics in global economic relations can be found in Frieden, Lake, and Broz 2009.

5. For a useful summary of dispute settlement procedures and American trade policy, see Lawrence 2007.

6. For a highly accessible analysis of the failures of the Doha Round, see Blustein 2009.

7. This photograph can be found, along with very useful current information and analysis of global economic relations, at the International Political Economy Zone blog at http://ipezone.blogspot.com. The specific location of the photograph of Suharto and Camdessus is at http://ipezone.blogspot.com/2007/09/flashback-camdessus-suharto-pic.html.

8. A detailed critique of the World Bank, seen through a profile of its president, James Wolfensohn (World Bank president, 1995–2005), can be found in Mallaby 2006.

9. Even the CAFTA agreement was essentially written by powerful economic interests such as textile manufactures, who made sure that any imports from Central American signatories to CAFTA had to be sourced with American-made inputs such as yarn.

10. The EU consists of twenty-seven states, seventeen of which have joined the euro zone, with Great Britain remaining the most notable exception.

11. China has drawn an even larger share of foreign direct investment from overseas Chinese living in Taiwan, Hong Kong, and elsewhere.

12. Mercantilist policies generally emphasize the benefits of trade surpluses (exports exceeding imports) and avoid trade deficits by protecting domestic

producers from imports and encouraging local firms to sell abroad. China has pursued **mercantilism** with its mixed economy of state-owned and private firms; Japan after World War II did so through bureaucratic management of large private sector corporations.

REFERENCES

Atlantic Council. 2009. "The U.S.–China Strategic and Economic Dialogue." August 7. www.acus.org/new_atlanticist/us-china-strategic-economic-dialogue.

Blustein, Paul. 2009. *Misadventures of the Most Favored Nations: Clashing Egos, Inflated Ambitions, and the Great Shambles of the World Trade System.* New York: Public Affairs.

CIA World Factbook. www.cia.gov/library/publications/the-world-factbook/geos/xx.html.

Drezner, Daniel W. 2010. "The Death of the China Lobby?" July 20. http://drezner.foreignpolicy.com/?page=1.

Easton, Nina. 2008. "America Sours on Free Trade." Fortune.com, January 25. www.cfr.org/us-election-2008/fortune-america-sours-free-trade/p15430.

Economist. 2007. "China and U.S. Trade: Lost in Translation." May 17. www.economist.com/node/9184053?story_id=9184053.

Economist. 2009. "The Long Climb." Special Report on the World Economy. October 3.

Eichengreen, Barry J. 2009. *Globalizing Capital: A History of the International Monetary System.* 2nd ed. Princeton, N.J.: Princeton University Press.

Erikson, Daniel P. 2004–2005. "Central America's Free Trade Gamble." *World Policy Journal* (Winter): 19–28.

Frieden, Jeffry A., David A. Lake, and J. Lawrence Broz, ed. 2009. *International Political Economy: Perspectives on Global Power and Wealth.* 5th ed. New York: W.W. Norton.

Gilpin, Robert. 2000. *The Challenge of Global Capitalism: The World Economy in the 21st Century.* Princeton, N.J.: Princeton University Press.

James, Harold. 2002. *The End of Globalization: Lessons from the Great Depression.* Cambridge, Mass.: Harvard University Press.

King, Neil, Jr., Alistair MacDonald, and Marcus Walker. 2009. "Crisis Fuels Backlash On Trade." *Wall Street Journal,* January 31. http://online.wsj.com/article/SB123331716317333093.html.

Lawrence, Robert Z. 2007. "The United States and the WTO Dispute Settlement System." Council Special Report no. 5 by Council on Foreign Relations. www.cfr.org/trade/united-states-wto-dispute-settlement-system/p12871.

Maddison, Angus. Global Economy Data. www.ggdc.net/maddison.

Mallaby, Sebastian. 2006. *The World's Banker: A Story of Failed States, Financial Crises, and the Wealth and Poverty of Nations.* New York: Penguin, 2006.

McGregor, Richard. 2010. *The Party: The Secret World of China's Communist Rulers.* New York: HarperCollins.

Pew Research Center. 2007. "Global Attitudes Project: World Publics Welcome Global Trade—But Not Immigration." October 4. http://pewresearch.org/pubs/607/global-trade-immigration.

Shah, Anup. 2010. "The Banana Trade War." *Global Issues* (January 3). www.globalissues.org/article/63/the-banana-trade-war.

Weisman, Steven R. 2007. "Wolfowitz Resigns, Ending Long Fight at World Bank." *New York Times*, May 18. www.nytimes.com/2007/05/18/washing ton/18 wolfowitz.html.

Part II

Regional Perspectives

5
China

PETER HAYS GRIES

This chapter begins by exploring three "pasts" central to constructions of Chinese nationalism today: the "five thousand years," the "hundred years," and the "ten years." These pasts together help constitute what it means to be Chinese at the dawn of the twenty-first century. The chapter then turns to an examination of how nationalism can help us understand the dramatic domestic political transformation from Maoist to Reform China as well as China's twenty-first-century foreign relations.

"HARMONIOUS" CHINA

At the third plenary session of the tenth **National People's Congress** in 2005, the **Chinese Communist Party** (CCP) officially declared "**harmonious society**" (和谐社会) to be its new paramount goal. Over a quarter century of capitalist development had created sharp divisions in China's economy and society, with the rich getting richer and the poor getting poorer. The losers from economic development were becoming restless, protesting in unprecedented numbers. The focus on a harmonious society was meant to quell this dangerous instability. The mottos of the 2008 Beijing Olympics, "One World, One Dream" (同一个世界, 同一个梦想), and the 2010 Shanghai Expo, "Better City, Better Life" (城市, 让生活更美好), sought to sell a new middle-class dream, obscure class divisions, and promote social harmony. The CCP goal of harmony has been pursued with progressive economic policies, such as the abolition of agricultural taxes and a new emphasis on developing China's poor western provinces. But it has also been pursued with repressive political policies, such as greater Internet censorship and less tolerance for any form of dissent. Indeed, Chinese **netizens** now sarcastically refer to state censorship of online Internet postings as "being harmonized away" (被和谐了).

A similarly "peaceful" framework for describing Chinese foreign policy has accompanied the "harmonious" mantra for domestic policy. To reassure the world about China's benign intentions, "**China's rise**" (中国崛起) was first reformulated as "**peaceful rise**" (和平崛起). When that did not appear to reassure China's neighbors, the potentially threatening "rise" was also replaced, culminating in the innocuous phrase "**peaceful development**" (和平发展). Convincing the world of China's benign intentions is vital if China is to avoid confronting neighbors and superpowers arming themselves and creating alliances to counterbalance against China's rise.

Yet Chinese foreign policy behaviors have recently appeared increasingly belligerent. In 2008, China first exchanged barbs with German chancellor Angela Merkel and then snubbed French president Nicolas Sarkozy over their meetings with the **Dalai Lama**, the exiled Tibetan spiritual leader. Then, at the 2009 climate change conference in Copenhagen, China thwarted the Obama administration's desire for a substantial global commitment to reduce **greenhouse gas emissions**. Chinese premier Wen Jiabao, furthermore, appeared to snub Obama personally by declining to attend scheduled meetings with him. And angry about arms sales to **Taiwan**, China did not invite U.S. defense secretary Robert Gates to visit China during his summer 2010 tour of Asia. Meanwhile, provocative Chinese military maneuvers in the East and South China Seas are fostering naval arms races in Northeast and Southeast Asia.

THE ENIGMA OF CHINA'S RISE

What should we make of these developments? Is China "harmonious" and "peaceful" as its leaders claim, or not? With the world's largest population (over 1.3 billion), the world's largest standing army (over two million active military personnel), and a nominal 2011 **gross domestic product** (GDP) of close to $7 trillion that continues to grow at around 10 percent a year, China is simply too big to be ignored. Students of the global community must come to grips with the implications of China's rise.

This chapter will contend that if one were to pick just one framework for understanding China in the twenty-first century, it should be nationalism. Nationalism is central to an understanding of domestic Chinese politics: it can help us make sense of the dramatic transformation from Mao's China of the 1950s, 1960s, and 1970s to the "**Reform and Opening**" China of the 1980s, 1990s, and today. Nationalism can also help us better understand Chinese foreign policy. Chinese today share a strong desire to see China returned to what they see as its rightful place at the top of the international hierarchy (Gries 2004).

Understanding China may be particularly challenging for Americans. The study of foreign affairs always involves a certain amount of navel gazing: how we understand others inevitably reflects a great deal about how we understand ourselves. Just as being a student is constituted in part through interactions with teachers, what it means to be an American is constituted in part through our interactions with foreign countries like China. Perhaps because China is such a big, different, and remote country, it has long loomed larger than most other countries in the American imagination. Our founding fathers and other Enlightenment thinkers tended to depict China's emperors as

"**Oriental despots**" tyrannizing over the "**yellow horde**," the exact opposite of the land of reason and individualism that they sought to create in the New World. The Cold War and the confrontation between the **Free World** and the **Communist bloc**, seen as the land of the "un-free," only reinforced this habit of viewing China as our very opposite. And although the Cold War is now long gone, **Chinese communism** persists as a symbol of the very negation of everything that a patriotic American should cherish: freedom and individualism. This dualistic mode of thinking makes it very difficult for Americans to grasp the profound changes occurring in China today (see Wasserstrom 2000). There are many differences between Chinese and Americans, to be sure, but we are all humans and as such share a great deal as well. If we are to understand China, therefore, we must try to move beyond our preconceptions and stereotypes to understand China in its own terms. That does not imply **moral relativism**, however: we can seek to understand another's views or actions without necessarily agreeing with or condoning them.

NATION AND NATIONALISM IN CHINA

How should Chinese nationalism be understood? Is Chinese nationalism a threat to the West and to China's neighbors? Or is it a natural product of China's developmental experience? The dominant Western view of Chinese nationalism today is that it is party **propaganda** constructed by the CCP to legitimize its rule. With the crisis of communism, the party elite is seen as fomenting nationalism to maintain its grip on power. Thomas Christensen (1996, 37) expressed this dominant view succinctly in an influential *Foreign Affairs* article: "Since the Chinese Communist Party is no longer communist, it must be even more Chinese."

This party propaganda view of Chinese nationalism is not wrong—the CCP clearly seeks to use nationalism—but it is far from complete (Gries 2004). By focusing exclusively on the CCP and its "state" or "official" nationalism, the orthodox view fails to capture the independent role that the Chinese people are increasingly playing in nationalist politics. A genuinely bottom-up and popular nationalism has emerged in China that the CCP has its hands full just containing. The view of Chinese nationalism as propaganda is also rationalist and thus fails to explain the passions so clearly evident in Chinese nationalist politics today. Chinese nationalism is not just about the instrumental pursuit of China's national interest; it is also about what it means to *be* Chinese today. Indeed, sense and sensibility often conflict, as when popular anti-Japanese protests contribute to the deterioration of Sino-Japanese relations, jeopardizing the Chinese government's interest in maintaining stable relations with a vital trade partner.

Where do popular Chinese nationalist passions come from? To understand Chinese nationalism today, we must engage Chinese understandings of their **identity**, which are constituted in large part through stories told about the national past. Historian F. W. Mote (1999, p. xv) has rightly argued that "ignorance of China's cultural tradition and historical experience is an absolute barrier to comprehending China today." To comprehend Chinese nationalism today, however, even more important than understanding the Chinese past itself is apprehending how Chinese themselves understand their national past. Narratives are the stories that we tell about our pasts. These stories, personality psychologists have argued, infuse our identities with unity, meaning, and purpose (McAdams 1996; Singer and Salovey 1993). We cannot, therefore, radically change them at will. Sociologists Anthony Giddens and Margaret Somers maintained that narratives infuse identities with meaning. Giddens (1991, 5) argued that narratives provide the individual with "ontological security": "The reflexive project of the self . . . consists in the sustaining of coherent, yet continually revised, biographical narratives." Somers (1994, 618) contrasted **"representational narratives"** (selective descriptions of events) with more foundational **"ontological narratives"**: "the stories that social actors use to make sense of—indeed, to act in—their lives. [They] define who we are." The storied nature of social life, in short, infuses our identities with meaning. "Identities," Stuart Hall noted, "are the names we give to the different ways we are positioned by, and position ourselves in, the narratives of the past" (see Olick and Robbins 1998, 122).

Following Elie Kedourie (1960/1993, 141)—who noted that nationalism "is very much a matter of one's self-view, of one's estimation of oneself and one's place in the world"—this chapter takes a social psychological approach to nationalism. Specifically, it follows social identity theorists (SIT) in defining **national identity** as the aspect of an individual's **self-concept** that derives from his or her perceived membership in a national group (Tajfel 1981, 255). Nationalism is here understood as the commitment to protect and enhance national identity.

Like our personal identities, our national identities are constituted in part through the stories we tell about our (personal and national) pasts. In the case of Chinese nationalism today, three "pasts" are central: the "five thousand years," the "hundred years," and the "ten years." Together, these pasts help constitute what it means to be Chinese at the dawn of the twenty-first century.

FIVE THOUSAND YEARS: THE BURDENS OF "CIVILIZATION"

Pride in the superiority of China's five thousand years of "Civilization" (文明) is central to nationalism in China today. Xiao Gongqing (1994), an outspoken neoconservative intellectual, advocated the use of a nationalism derived from **Confucianism** to fill the ideological void opened by the collapse of communism. The mid-1990s, indeed, witnessed a revival of interest in Confucianism. The CCP, which only twenty years earlier in 1974 had launched a campaign to "Criticize Lin Biao, Criticize Confucius," ironically became an active sponsor of Confucian studies. President Jiang Zemin himself attended the 1994 celebration of Confucius' 2,545th birthday (Guo Yingjie 2004, 35). As of late 2010, the Chinese government had established over three hundred Confucius institutes around the world, with a goal of a thousand by 2020. Popular nationalist writings also frequently evince pride in China's "Civilization." The cover of a 1997 *Beijing Youth Weekly*, for instance, had "Chinese Defeat Kasparov!" splashed across a picture of the downcast Russian grandmaster chess player. Two of the six members of the IBM research group that programmed the chess-playing Deep Blue computer, it turns out, were Chinese Americans. "It was the genius of these two Chinese," one article asserted, "that allowed 'Deep Blue' to defeat Mr. Kasparov." Entitled "We Have the Best Brains," the article concluded that "we should be proud of the legacy of '5,000 years of civilization' that our ancestors have left for us" (*Beijing qingnian zhoukan* 1997, 30). Blood and culture are frequently fused in Chinese discourses of "Civilization."

The five thousand years are more frequently deployed, however, to construct Chinese superiority over a threatening United States—not lowly Russia. For instance, in the 1996 diatribe *Surpassing the USA*, authors Xi Yongjun and Ma Zaizhun amuse themselves with "a few theatrical and rather comical juxtapositions." They begin with clichés. China is the world's richest spiritual civilization, America the most advanced material civilization; China is the collectivist capital, America an individualist's heaven. Xi and Ma then become playful and self-indulgent: America has but two hundred years of history, while China's Tongrentang Pharmacy alone is 388 years old; the American Declaration of Independence was a handwritten document of but four thousand words, while China's **"Four Books"** were printed on the world's first press and contain over three billion characters (Xi and Ma 1996, 3–4). The authors clearly intend to establish Chinese superiority at America's expense.

Just as many in the West use the **Orient** to define themselves, many in the East clearly deploy the **Occident** to the same ends. The text on the back cover of the "Sino-American Contest," a special 1996 issue of the provincial Chinese magazine *Love Our China*, for instance, begins with some contrasts: "China has 5,000 years of civilized history . . . while America has only 200 years of history." It then turns to insults: "Facing an ancient Eastern colossus, America is at most a child." "Emotion-cues," sociologist Candace Clark (1990, 314) reminds us, "can be used to manipulate, reminding and counter-reminding each other of judgments of the proper place." By **altercasting** America as a child, China can play the superior elder (see Weinstein and Deutschberger, 1963). Following Edward Said's discussion of "Orientalism," such Chinese uses of the West have been labeled "Occidentalism," a "deeply rooted practice [in China] of alluding to the Occident as a contrasting Other in order to define whatever one believes to be distinctively 'Chinese'" (Chen Xiaomei 1995, 39).

The five thousand years are also central to the dream of a "prosperous country and a strong army," which still inspires Chinese nationalists over a century after it was first promoted by late Qing dynasty reformers. People's Liberation Army writer Jin Hui (1995, 186–87) wrote that "For over one hundred years, generation after generation of Chinese have been dreaming that since we were once strong, although we are now backwards we will certainly become strong again." The "unlimited cherishing of past greatness," he lamented, is tied to overconfidence that "in the future, we will certainly be 'first under heaven.'" Such "illusions," Jin warned his compatriots, are "even worse than spiritual opiates."

The burdens of Civilization can certainly lead to self-delusions, as Jin argued; they can also lead to racism. In 1995, vice chair of the National People's Congress Tian Jiyun declared that "The IQs of the Chinese ethnicity, the descendants of the Yellow Emperor, are very high" (Sautman 1997, 79). "Confucian nationalism" is not an oxymoron: Confucianism allows for the reinforcement of cultural boundaries when barbarians do not accept Chinese values. The "universal," "all under heaven" can and often has become a closed political community (Duara 1995). Historian Lei Yi (1997, 49–50) of the Chinese Academy of Social Sciences in Beijing has used the phrase "'Sinocentric' cultural nationalism" to describe such views. The Confucian world was not "one big happy family," but extremely **Sinocentric**, involving a "fierce racism, rejection of other cultures . . . and cultural superiority." In China, cultural and ethnic nationalism are frequently intertwined.

ONE HUNDRED YEARS: A "CENTURY OF HUMILIATION"

Narratives about the "**Century of Humiliation**" frame the ways that Chinese interact with the West today. This period began with China's defeat in the First Opium War and the British acquisition of Hong Kong in 1842. The period was marked by major wars between China and Western powers or Japan: the two **Opium Wars of 1840–1842 and 1856–1860**, the **Sino-Japanese "Jiawu" War of 1894–1895**, the Boxer Rebellion of 1900, and the "**War of Resistance against Japan**" of 1931/1937–1945.[1] Many educated Chinese today are painfully aware of the "unequal treaties" signed with the British at Nanjing in 1842 and the Japanese at Shimoneseki in 1895. Unilateral concessions forced on the Chinese in these treaties, such as **indemnities, extraterritoriality**, and foreign settlements in the treaty ports, are still perceived as humiliating losses of sovereignty. Other symbols of the period still resonate with today's nationalists. The stone ruins of the Old Summer Palace outside Beijing, looted and burned by Europeans in 1860, are a reminder of the "rape" of China. Lin Zexu, a famous Chinese crusader against opium and British aggression, still stands for Chinese courage and virtue.

The "Century of Humiliation" is neither an objective past that works insidiously in the present nor a mere invention of present-day nationalist entrepreneurs. Instead, it is a continuously reworked narrative about the national past central to the contested and evolving meaning of being Chinese today.

Furthermore, the century is a traumatic and foundational moment because it fundamentally challenged Chinese views of the world. In Chinese eyes, earlier invaders became Chinese, while barbarians beyond the border paid humble tribute to "Civilization." Both practices reinforced a view of Chinese civilization as universal and superior. Early encounters with "big noses," from **Marco Polo** to pre-nineteenth-century European and American traders and missionaries, did not challenge this view. "Our ancient neighbors," wrote one young Chinese nationalist, "found glory in drawing close to Chinese civilization" (Li Fang 1996, 23). The violent nineteenth-century encounter with the West was different. The **Central Kingdom** was not only defeated militarily, but was also confronted by a civilization with universalist pretensions of its own. "The Western impact," wrote Tu Weiming (1991, 2), "fundamentally dislodged Chinese intellectuals from their Confucian haven . . . [creating a] sense of impotence, frustration, and humiliation." The "Western devils" had a civilization of their own that challenged the universality and superiority of Confucian civilization. The traumatic confrontation between East and West fundamentally destabilized Chinese views of the world and their place within it. "Trauma brings about a lapse or rupture in memory that breaks continuity with the past," wrote historian Dominick LaCapra (1998, 9) in a discussion of the Holocaust. "It unsettles narcissistic investments and desired self-images." Just as the trauma of the Holocaust led many in the postwar West to reexamine their tradition (see Horkheimer and Adorno, 1947/2002), the "Century of Humiliation" threatened a Chinese identity that was based upon the idea of a universal and superior civilization. "The Israelis' vision of the Holocaust has shaped their idea of themselves," Tom Segev (1993, 11) wrote, "just as their changing sense of self has altered their view of the Holocaust and their understanding of its meaning." Stories about the past both limit and define our national identities in the present, which is also true in the case of the Chinese and the "Century of Humiliation": Chinese visions of this century have shaped their sense of self, and these changes to Chinese identity have altered their views of the century.

Today, Chinese struggles to come to terms with this period of trauma are reflected in the emergence of new narratives about the century. Under Mao, China's pre-"Liberation" (解放, 1949) sufferings were blamed on the feudalism of the **Qing Dynasty** and Western imperialism, and the anti-feudal, anti-imperialist masses were valorized for throwing off their chains and repelling foreign invaders. This "heroic," or "victor," national narrative first served the requirements of communist revolutionaries seeking to mobilize popular support in the 1930s and 1940s and later served the nation-building goals of the

People's Republic in the 1950s, 1960s, and 1970s. One 1950s movie about the First Opium War, for instance, changed its title from *The Opium War* to *Lin Zexu* (林则徐) to glorify Chinese heroism. New China needed heroes.

During the 1990s, however, the official Maoist victor narrative was joined by a new and popular victimization narrative that blames the West, including Japan, for China's suffering. This new storyline actually renews the focus on victimization in pre-Mao Republican-era writings on the "Century of Humiliation" (Cohen 2002, 17). Indeed, the metaphor of China as a raped woman, common in **Republican China** but unpopular during the Maoist period, has reemerged. In Republican China, playwrights like Xiao Jun used rape in nationalist plays such as *Village in August*, in which Japanese soldiers rape a patriotic peasant woman (see Liu 1994). The return of the "rape of China" theme may be seen in such bestsellers as Chinese American Iris Chang's 1997 *The Rape of Nanking*. This book helped transform the 1937 Nanjing massacre into a "rape."

The contrast between victor and victim national narratives is nicely captured in two Chinese movies about the First **Opium War of 1840–1842**. The first, 1959's *Lin Zexu*, mentioned above, is a story of the Chinese people's heroic anti-imperialist struggle. Named *Lin Zexu* to highlight resistance, it does not focus solely on Commissioner Lin but emphasizes his close relations with a peasant couple who seek vengeance against Eliot, the evil British trader who had killed the peasant woman's father. Lin and the Chinese people are one in an upbeat tale of popular defiance. The second movie, 1997's *Opium War*, by contrast, is a dark and depressing tragedy of the past (Karl 2001). It is only at the very end of the movie, with the image of a stone lion and the message that "On July 1, 1997 the Chinese government recovered sovereignty over Hong Kong," that China is redeemed. Director Xie Jin's vision of the past is one of opium addicts and humiliation; his vision of the present and future is one of mighty lions awakening to exact their revenge. A victim in the past, China will be a victim no longer.

The year 1997 seems to have been a pivotal moment in the re-emergence of the victimization narrative in China. The countdown to Hong Kong's "Return to the Motherland" in the spring and summer of 1997 created a strong desire to wipe away the "National Humiliation." And in the fall of 1997, sixtieth-anniversary commemorations of the Nanjing massacre, as well as Iris Chang's book about it, directed Chinese attention to their past suffering as never before. Anticipating closure on the "Humiliation," many Chinese paradoxically reopened a long-festering wound. For many Chinese nationalists, this painful encounter with past trauma was expressed in the language of victimization. Thus, 1997 China may prove to be comparable to 1961 Israel, when Eichmann's trial precipitated a dramatic shift in Israeli attitudes toward the Holocaust. The repression of Holocaust memories in the name of the nation building (creating a "New Israel") that prevailed in the late 1940s and 1950s gave way to a new identification with victimization in the 1960s. The early postwar Israeli rejection of victimhood is reflected in the evolution of **Holocaust Day**, which was established only in 1953 and did not become a mandatory national holiday until 1959 (Zerubavel 1995). Early Holocaust Day commemorations emphasized the "martyrs and heroes" of the ghetto resistance, not the victims of the concentration camps who were memorialized in later tributes. China is now undergoing a similar process, as long-suppressed memories of past suffering resurface. Chinese nationalism since the 1990s cannot be understood without taking note of this new encounter with the traumas of the past.

Despite the new focus on victimization, heroic narratives about the "Century of Humiliation" have not disappeared. Narratives of "China as victor" and "China as victim" coexist in Chinese nationalism today. The century is arguably both what psychologist Vamik Volkan calls a "chosen glory" and what he calls a "chosen trauma" (Volkan and Itzkowitz 1994). The publisher's preface to a series of books entitled Never Forget the History of National Humiliation is typical, describing the century as both a "history of the struggle of the indomitable Chinese people against imperialism" and a "tragic history of suffering, beatings, and extraordinary humiliations" (Zhou 1991). Many Chinese nationalists, it seems, are eager to capitalize on the moral authority of their past suffering. But there is a downside to the new victimization narrative. It entails confronting vulnerability and weakness. The enduring need for heroism and a victor narrative serves, it seems, to allay the fears of those who are not yet ready to directly confront the trauma of the hundred years.

"THE LOST DECADE": MAOIST MELANCHOLY, RED GUARD ENVY

The **Great Proletarian Cultural Revolution**, later known as the Ten Years of Chaos, engulfed China from 1966 to 1976, when Mao Zedong died. Mobilized by Mao to attack his enemies in the party bureaucracy, young Red Guards both denounced and violently attacked their teachers, local party officials, their parents, and each other.

The young (thirty-something) so-called **fourth generation nationalists** of today grew up after the Cultural Revolution in the relative prosperity of China under reform. The Ten Years of Chaos has nonetheless left an indelible imprint upon them. Ironically, the fourth generation appears to find the new victimization narrative of Chinese suffering at the hands of Western imperialists appealing precisely because they, unlike their elders, have never suffered. The first generation of revolutionaries endured the hardships of World War II and the civil wars of the 1930s and 1940s. The second generation suffered during the **Anti-Rightist Campaign** and the Great Leap Forward of the late 1950s. And the third generation of Red Guards was sent down to the countryside during the Cultural Revolution of the late 1960s and 1970s. The fourth generation of PRC youth, by contrast, grew up with relative material prosperity under reform in the 1980s and 1990s.[2] In their 1997 psycho-autobiography *The Spirit of the Fourth Generation,* Song Qiang and several of his coauthors of the 1996 nationalist diatribes *China Can Say No* and *China Can Still Say No* are envious of the third generation, who, "proud of their hardships," can celebrate them at Cultural Revolution restaurants like Heitudi ("The Black Earth") in Beijing, nostalgically eating fried corn bread, recalling the good old, bad old days. They then ask, "Are we an unimportant generation?" In a section entitled "How Much Longer Must We Be Silent?" they lament that "We in our thirties are without a shadow or sound . . . it seems that we will perish in silence" (Song, Qiao, Caiwang, Xia, and Liu 1997, 206, 202). Many of this generation, it seems, have a strong desire to make their mark. And they seek to do so through nationalism.

In the early 1990s, young Chinese conservatives compared **Beijing Spring** 1989 to the Cultural Revolution to justify the government clampdown on June 4th. The specter of chaos was brandished to assert the need for national unity and authoritarian CCP rule. More broadly, many fourth generation nationalists today have self-consciously defined themselves against the "Liberal '80s." Sociologist Karl Mannheim (1952) long ago argued that the formative events of youth mark each generation (Halbwachs 1980). Late-1980s experiences like the pro-Western *River Elegy* television sensation and Beijing Spring 1989 came at a pivotal time in the lives of Chinese nationalists now in their thirties. Today's nationalists frequently dismiss the 1980s as a period of dangerous "romanticism" and "radicalism"; they then depict themselves as "realistic" and "pragmatic" defenders of stability and order (Xu Ben 2001).

Even as they condemn the Ten Years of Chaos, however, many Chinese nationalists are both nostalgic for Mao and have embraced the Red Guard style.[3] The Mao craze of the mid-1990s was motivated in part by a pronounced nostalgia for Mao's tough, stand-tall image (Barmé 1996). Many young Chinese nationalists did not have the patience for Deng Xiaoping's economics-first strategy of biding one's time. Instead, they were wistful for the days of Mao's tough talk and violent confrontation with the United States in Korea and Vietnam.

The Red Guard style of take-no-prisoners nationalism in China today is well exemplified by the popular reactions to the "Zhao Wei wears the Imperial Japanese flag" and "Jiang Wen goes to Yasukuni" affairs that occurred in late 2001 and the summer of 2002 (Gries 2005). The September 2001 issue of the state-run *Fashion* magazine featured a picture of Chinese model/actress Zhao Wei wearing a short dress with an Imperial Japanese flag imprinted upon it. On December 3, 2001, a Hunan newspaper ran an exposé on the photo, igniting widespread Internet condemnation and national coverage (Zhang Datian 2001). During the week of December 3–10, over 6,000 mostly angry messages about the Zhao Wei affair were posted on the popular website Sina.com

(*Japan Economic Newswire* 2001). And words were linked with action: protestors used bricks and bottles to smash Zhao's house back in China (*Straits Times* 2001).

On December 10 Zhao Wei made a public apology, which was first circulated on the Internet and later broadcast on national television. Zhao declared that she had learned "an excellent lesson" about this period of history. "In the future, I will be more careful about what I say and do . . . and work hard to improve myself" (*Beijing qingnianbao* 2001). Some Chinese nationalists, however, refused to accept Zhao Wei's apology. At a New Year's Eve event held at Changsha on December 28, an enraged man rushed up on stage, pushed Zhao over, and smeared excrement on her dress.

During most of the controversy, Zhao Wei herself was in Xinjiang filming *Warriors of Heaven and Earth*. Coincidentally, the film's male protagonist, played by actor/director Jiang Wen, became the subject of another Japan controversy the following summer. On June 27, 2002, a Tianjin newspaper ran an exposé that Jiang had been to Yasukuni Shrine several times (*Beijing chenbao* 2002). Yasukuni is a shrine in Tokyo where Japanese go to honor their war dead, including executed war criminals from World War II. When Japanese politicians go there to worship, Chinese nationalists view it as a sign of Japanese militarism and Japan's continuing lack of repentance for wartime aggressions against China. Some Chinese thus took offense at Jiang's Yasukuni trip. In the view of many Chinese nationalists, Jiang's "nationalist integrity" was now in doubt (Shen Xiaoma 2002).

Many in China's cultural elite, however, boldly and publicly defended Jiang. They argued that Jiang had gone to Yasukuni to do research for his film *Devils on the Doorstep*, and that "visiting" Yasukuni was a far cry from "worshipping" there. Author Shi Tiesheng declared, "a director trying to understand the crimes of militarism is not the same as standing on the side of militarism" (Yu Shaowen 2002). Director Tian Zhuangzhuang similarly insisted, "Jiang Wen is an artist with a clear sense of right and wrong, and an extremely strong sense of racial responsibility" (Chen Yifei 2002). Director Feng Xiaogang, "indignant" at the anti-Jiang media coverage, claimed that it was using "Gang of Four" (read: Cultural Revolution) style methods: "The shadow of the extreme 'left' persists in the thinking and behavior of many people today" (Yu Shaowen 2002).

Feng is right that a winner-takes-all, show-no-mercy style reminiscent of the Cultural Revolution is prevalent in much Chinese nationalist discourse today. Many **cybernationalists** exhibit a ferocious, Red Guard-style: words and deeds that seek to literally silence one's opponents, from physically assaulting both Zhao Wei's house and her body to accusations of treason against Jiang Wen to widespread death threats against Chinese liberals.

Thus far I have argued that the nature of Chinese nationalism can be understood as constituted in part by evolving stories about China's Five Thousand

Years of Civilization, the One Hundred Years of Humiliation, and the Ten Years of Chaos. I will now contend that nationalism can help us better understand the dramatic transformation in domestic Chinese politics from Mao's China to Deng's China. I will then conclude by arguing that nationalism is also vital to an understanding of China's external relations with its Asian neighbors and the United States.

MAO'S CHINA

Over sixty years ago, on October 1, 1949, **Mao Zedong** (毛泽东) stood on the rostrum in Tiananmen Square in Beijing to declare the founding of the People's Republic of China (PRC). It was a proud moment for most Chinese. Ever since losing the First Opium War (1839–42) and being forced to cede Hong Kong to the British in the humiliating **Treaty of Nanking** (1842), Chinese had suffered at the hands of Western and Japanese imperialism. Still fresh in the minds of most Chinese present was the Japanese invasion and colonization of **Manchuria** in 1931, which was followed in 1937 by the Japanese invasion of China proper; most of the country was colonized by 1945. It was a brutal war and occupation, symbolized for many by the December 1937 **Nanjing Massacre**, which involved the slaughter of two to three hundred thousand Chinese soldiers and civilians. Given this century of suffering, it is perhaps not surprising that what Mao is best remembered for declaring on that day in 1949 is "China has stood up!" It was a profoundly *nationalist* (and *not* communist) declaration, and nationalism has remained central to CCP claims to legitimate rule ever since.

Mao was thus a nationalist leader; he was also of course a communist leader. **Maoism**, his unique adaptation of Marxism, dominated not just elite Chinese politics but indeed the very lives of all Mainland Chinese over the next three decades. Maoism discounted workers in favor of peasants and economics in favor of politics. Given that Marxism is a fundamentally economic theory, and that Marx believed that the working classes (*not* the "reactionary" peasantry) must lead the revolution to overthrow capitalism and create communism, Maoism is arguably not fundamentally **Marxist** at all. It did, however, provide Mao with an integrated ideology that he utilized to both govern and mobilize the Chinese nation until his death in 1976 (Meisner 1999).

Two major political movements dominated Mao's China. Economic development in the first years of the PRC was quite successful, as the PRC state, led by **Liu Shaoqi** (刘少奇) and **Deng Xiaoping** (邓小平), directed its limited resources at industrialization after the **Soviet model**. By the mid 1950s, however, Mao grew tired of the methodical pace of planned economic development. He believed that the Revolution was being stifled by bureaucratization and feared that the CCP was becoming a new "capitalist class" living off of the common man. He therefore launched the **Great Leap Forward** (大跃

进) in the late 1950s, seeking to rapidly drive China from capitalism to communism. Private plots were socialized and large communes were created in which people worked and lived together—the goal was to rapidly propel Chinese industrialization past the American and British economies. The Great Leap ended in disaster, with a massive famine that killed some thirty million Chinese, mostly peasants.

In the early 1960s, the communes were disbanded. Under the leadership of Liu and Deng again, China's economy rebounded dramatically. But disaster struck again. In the mid-1960s, Mao launched the Great Proletarian Cultural Revolution (文化大革命). Mao again claimed that there were "bourgeois elements" within the CCP who sought to restore capitalism and thwart the Revolution. He may, however, have been motivated by a simple jealousy for his power. He mobilized China's youth, who joined groups of **Red Guards** (红卫兵) to struggle against CCP leaders. Liu, Deng, and their families were some of the first victims of the Red Guards. But the Cultural Revolution was not limited to Beijing. It spread across the nation, leading to political, economic, and military disarray. Chinese today call the period from the start of the Cultural Revolution in 1966 to Mao's death in 1976 the "ten lost years."

The failures of the Great Leap Forward and the Cultural Revolution fundamentally delegitimized communism. These circumstances helped clear the ground for the fundamental change in China's political and economic systems that began after Mao's death and has continued to this day.

CHINA UNDER REFORM

Liu Shaoqi died at the hands of the Red Guards. Deng Xiaoping survived the Cultural Revolution and emerged after Mao's death to quickly push aside Mao's chosen successor, Hua Guofeng (华国锋), and launch "Reform and Opening" (改革开放) in 1978. These economic reforms essentially acknowledged that the Chinese economy had yet to achieve communism and still needed to go through the capitalist stage of development. Soviet-style central planning and price controls were reduced, as markets emerged and economic decision making was slowly devolved from Beijing to the localities. Mao's worst fears eventually came true: the CCP became a massive bureaucracy presiding over the largest capitalist economic transformation in history.

Politics began to change as well. For the most part, Mao-style social movements became a thing of the past. Elite politics became less **Darwinian**, with losers in political struggles now allowed to live. While there were swings between periods of political freeze and political thaw in the 1980s, the overall political direction was initially one of slow liberalization. "Opening" referred to a stance of openness toward the world, not just in terms of economics but also in terms of politics, culture, and ideas. Indeed, the mid to late 1980s have been dubbed China's second **New Enlightenment** following the first New

Enlightenment of the 1910s and 1920s. Western ideas and fashions were all the rage. For instance, some students at Beijing University in 1988 would give something a "thumbs up" and call it *"international!"* (国际!) if they thought it was cool.

That all ended in 1989, the seventieth anniversary of the **May Fourth Movement** of 1919, which had been at the heart of the first New Enlightenment. On April 15, university students began gathering in **Tiananmen Square** to mourn the passing of Hu Yaobang (胡耀邦), a former secretary general of the CCP who was seen as a political progressive unfairly sacked by Deng just a few years earlier during a political freeze. Students, upset about the rising corruption that had accompanied reforms, stayed in the square, growing in numbers as the weeks passed. Indeed, it became a national movement as students came to Beijing from across the country and started their own protests and demonstrations in other cities.

The confrontation between civilian protestors and the Chinese leadership escalated on the night of June 3–4, when Deng ordered **People's Liberation Army** (PLA) troops brought in from distant provinces to clear Tiananmen Square. The PLA killed hundreds, if not thousands, of innocent Chinese civilians. And because the international media were in Beijing to report on general secretary of the Communist Party of the Soviet Union Mikhail Gorbachev's visit and the historic PRC-USSR summit, they covered the massacre in real time on new 24-7 cable news channels like CNN. The effect on western audiences was profound. Deng went from being celebrated in the western press as a heroic capitalist reformer to being scorned as a brutal communist dictator. Sanctions were imposed, and China became an international outcast.

The CCP again survived the turmoil. **Zhao Ziyang** (赵紫阳) was sacked, and **Jiang Zemin** (江泽民) was installed as the new secretary general of the CCP, although Deng continued to wield real power behind the scenes. In the spring of 1992, Deng reasserted his economic policy of reform with his famous "southern tour" (南巡), visiting Guangzhou, Shenzhen, and Zhuhai. He is credited with saying "To get rich is glorious" (发财是光荣的) and with unleashing Chinese entrepreneurship. By the time of Deng's death in 1997, China's economy was again growing rapidly. The 1997 leadership transition was smooth, as was the subsequent one, when **Hu Jintao** (胡锦涛) replaced Jiang in 2002. These leaders continued Deng's economic policy of reform, and Chinese capitalism continued its rapid development. The political liberalization of the late 1980s was not repeated, however. Instead, the last few years under Hu have arguably witnessed political retrenchment, as the CCP has reigned in political liberties through tightening controls over the Internet and imposing tougher prison sentences on protestors, dissidents, or anyone deemed in any way threatening to the state.

The sixty-year history of the PRC thus appears to be divided into two periods that are roughly equal in length but are very different: a communist China under Mao from the 1950s through the 1970s, and a capitalist China under

Deng and his successors from the 1980s to the present. How can we understand the smooth transition between very different communist and capitalist ideologies? I contend that nationalism is a key to this puzzle. If communist and capitalist ideologies were not ends in themselves, but rather means to the more fundamental nationalist ends of recovering the national greatness seen as lost during the "Century of Humiliation," it becomes clearer how this major shift could occur. If communism was largely a tool to be used to achieve nationalist ends, it is easy to see how once it became fully discredited after the Cultural Revolution it could be easily discarded in favor of the new tool of capitalist markets as another means to the same old goal of nationalist renewal.

CHINA'S RELATIONS WITH EAST ASIA

In addition to helping us make sense of China's dramatic domestic political transformation over the past sixty years, nationalism is also central to an understanding of Chinese foreign policy in general and of its relations with its East Asian neighbors in particular. The Koreas, Japan, Vietnam, and the more distant Southeast Asian nations are seen by most Chinese as part of **Sinic Civilization** and the China-centered **tributary system**. This view creates a set of expectations about their deference toward China in the present as well. Japan is a special case, because it is seen as not just part of this ancient Sinocentric East Asian system, but also as one of the worst of the imperialist aggressors that victimized China during the "Century of Humiliation."

For many Chinese, China has for millennia been the center of "Civilization" (文明), with barbarians at the periphery. Neighboring states could gain a degree of Civilization through the adoption of Chinese practices and through a tributary system in which diplomats from Korea, Japan, Vietnam, and elsewhere came to the Chinese imperial court to pay tribute, literally kowtowing before the Chinese emperor and acknowledging their vassal status. Thus, the East Asian order was seen as fundamentally hierarchical, with China at the top.

This assumption of hierarchy appears to persist in Chinese views of their bilateral relations in East Asia. Chinese largely expect that China's neighbors be appropriately deferential and acknowledge Chinese superiority. In such circumstances, China, like a Confucian father, should in return be beneficent toward its children. Scholars like David Kang (e.g., 2003) believe that most Asians accept Chinese superiority, and that this will allow the future of East Asia to be hierarchical but peaceful.

It appears, however, that not all East Asians are comfortable with the idea of a hierarchical East Asian community with China at the top (e.g., Acharya, 2003–2004). For instance, Southeast Asian nations have banded together to form the Association for Southeast Asian Nations (ASEAN). While ASEAN has worked hard to develop robust trade and economic relations with China, it has nonetheless maintained solid diplomatic and military relations with the United States to hedge against the potential security threat that many Southeast Asians perceive in China's rise. They have also, as noted above, begun building up their navies in response to what they view as provocative Chinese activities in the South China Sea. Similarly, while diplomatic and economic relations took off between South Korea and China in the 1990s, starting in the mid-2000s a series of historical disputes have rekindled South Korean concerns about Chinese regional dominance. As a result, South Korea has strengthened its security alliance with the United States.

Japan is a special case. Anti-Japanese sentiment in China has a depth not present in other Chinese anti-foreignisms. This depth is because Chinese view Japan through the prisms of both "Civilization" and the "Century of Humiliation." Japan is seen as having borrowed from Chinese civilization a millennium ago during the **Tang Dynasty**, creating a very long history of indebtedness to China. But beginning with the Sino-Japanese War of 1894–1895 through the Nanjing Massacre of 1937 and until the end of World War II in 1945, little brother Japan did not just victimize China physically, but humiliated China as well. This state of affairs is seen as the height of ingratitude, and it lends anti-Japanese sentiment in China a righteous sense of injustice that helps sustain it as an issue of national pride (Gries 2005).

GLOBAL CHINA

The Chinese government spent over $30 billion (U.S.) on hosting the 2008 Beijing Olympics. Impressive new sports stadiums and an airport terminal were built. Factories were closed or moved well out of the city to reduce pollution. The Chinese government clearly wanted to put on a good show and spared no expense to do so. Why? The answer lies in the nationalist politics of state legitimation. Although Beijing during the Olympics may have appeared to be a **Potemkin village**, a fake display for the benefit of foreign viewers, the show was ultimately put on for the Chinese people. The CCP was claiming nationalist legitimacy before the Chinese people by seeking to make China look good before foreign, and particularly Western, opinion. Chinese today are understandably proud of China's accomplishments after thirty years of "Reform and Opening," and they expect that their government will "earn face/glory for China" (光宗耀祖). In many ways the Beijing Olympics was like a debutante's ball: China, coming out into international society, wanted to show off and be admired. China has come out in another way as well: like a teenager no longer largely confined to home, China has grown into an international player. While China has long played a major role in Asia, it is now a global actor. China is a major contributor to international problems like energy scarcity and global warming. And global issues like genocide and nuclear proliferation cannot be resolved without China's involvement.

Chinese growth can be expected to continue to contribute to global problems of energy and natural resource scarcity. Thirty years of Chinese growth has unquestionably driven up the prices of oil, natural gas, and a wide variety of natural resources. While this has been a boon to exporters of these products in places like the Middle East, Brazil, and Australia, it has also come at a significant cost.

First and foremost, China's inefficient use of coal and other natural resources is a major contributor to global warming. Air and water pollution are already huge problems within China (Economy 2004). Blue skies are rarely seen in China's major cities, and airborne pollution contributes to a variety of health problems in China. Airborne pollutants from China increasingly follow the jet stream east to foul the air in Korea, Japan, and even the west coast of the United States. And while China and the United States are the two largest sources of greenhouse gas emissions, China successfully opposed efforts at Copenhagen to develop an international strategy to address global warming (Watts 2010).

Chinese growth and its attendant energy and resource demands have also led the Chinese government to greater support for authoritarian regimes around the world. China's "go out" energy strategy (走出去战略) presents a mixed picture for the rest of the world. On the one hand, the development of new oil fields and energy sources in Africa and elsewhere increases global supply, which in turn results in decreasing global prices. On the other hand, support for dictators and the proliferation of Chinese small-arms destabilize weak states and contribute to the violation of human rights. For instance, China's support for the authoritarian rule of Omar al-Bashir in the Sudan has arguably contributed to the genocide in Darfur (Leverett and Bader 2005–2006).

China's close relationships with North Korea and Iran also make China a vital player in addressing the growing global problem of nuclear proliferation. The Chinese largely view North Korea as a little brother that they do not much like but must tolerate and protect (Gries 2012). As a result of Chinese protection, global pressures on North Korea to give up its nuclear program have been ineffective. Similarly, China's perceived need for Iranian oil has led it to shelter Iran from international pressures on their nuclear program. In both the North Korean and Iranian cases, China uses its veto power as a permanent member of the United Nations Security Council to water down international sanctions seeking to curtail the development and spread of nuclear weapons.

U.S.-CHINA RELATIONS IN THE TWENTY-FIRST CENTURY

On October 25, 1950, the PLA crossed the Yalu River and entered the Korean War. Over sixty years later, another conflict between the United States and China remains a real possibility. Although the chances of another U.S.-China conflict are low in probability, the consequences would be devastating. U.S. military dominance and China's rise have led to an extensive debate over the inevitability of a U.S.-China conflict. Realists argue over the **balance of power**: Is it stabilizing or destabilizing? Can a stronger China and a weaker United States replicate the relative stability of Cold War bipolarity, or are a rising China and a declining **hegemon** fated to fight? Will twenty-first century China become a "dissatisfied challenger" out to upset the status quo, or will the United States follow the more prevalent historical pattern and initiate a preventative war against a rising China? Understanding the likely determinants of conflict in U.S.-China relations is, therefore, an urgent task.

What can we safely assume about the future of U.S.-China relations? Demography, geography, and natural resources/energy are all material factors that will play near-certain constraining roles in the evolution of U.S.-China relations. And relatively enduring Chinese and American national identities are ideational elements likely to place definite limits on U.S.-China relations over the next ten years (Gries 2006).

Size matters. China's tremendous population is a source of pride and psychological strength that Chinese nationalists can be expected to continue to draw on in the future. Of course, China's 1.3 billion people also represent a tremendous challenge to China's continuing economic development and political stability. Even if a strong overall Chinese growth continues, we can expect an increasing number of the hundreds of millions of China's poor—the losers of three decades of "Reform and Opening"—to make demands of the CCP leadership that are likely to force them to increase the provision of social welfare services. This fundamental demographic challenge suggests that China's leaders will have their hands full with domestic discontent and will not willingly instigate trouble in China's foreign relations.

A nation's geographic boundaries are a relatively stable factor predetermining its security environment. As Tang Shiping (2004, 5) has noted, "separated from other great powers by vast oceans (and neighbored by two much less powerful countries), the security environment of the United States has been (and will likely remain) the best among the major powers." China, by contrast, shares land borders with over a dozen countries (including great powers Russia and India) and confronts over a dozen more countries to its east and southeast in the Pacific Ocean (including great power Japan and superpower United States). China has a long history of being invaded by its neighbors, and we can expect that Chinese will remain anxious about their security environment in the future as well.

What role will geography play in the future of U.S.-China relations? Robert Ross (1999) has argued that because China is a continental power and the United States is a maritime power, geography mitigates the security dilemma. A division of spheres of influence in East Asia, therefore, is likely to be stable and peaceful. This argument depends upon both Beijing and Washington respecting the legitimacy of each other's spheres of influence. That the United States intervened in World Wars I and II once it had become clear that Germany had become a regional hegemon in continental Europe suggests that Washington may not be willing to accommodate a future Chinese sphere of influence in continental East Asia. And China's rapid acquisition of blue water naval capabilities suggests that China is not likely to cede maritime East Asia to the United States.

Surging demand for energy and natural resources to feed China's massive economy has already begun a major debate in China: can China rely on free markets to meet its energy and resource demands? Will the United States continue to guard Middle Eastern oil as a public good, or will it begin to monopolize the Middle Eastern oil market? China has already begun adopting a mercantilist strategy of owning and/or politically controlling needed resources in South America, in the Middle East and Africa, and in Central Asia and the Russian Far East (Zweig and Bi 2005). But this approach is more costly than relying on free market supplies. Should China continue in this mercantilist direction?

Energy anxiety is increasing in the United States as well. Many Americans already view China as a zero-sum energy and natural resource competitor with the United States, and those fears have translated into action: Congressional opposition killed the **China National Offshore Oil Corporation**'s (CNOOC) bid to buy the American energy company Unocal in 2005. With the failure of CNOOC's Unocal bid, many Chinese now view the United States as blocking China's access to the resources it needs to continue its rise. Indeed, Men Honghua (2005, 147–48) of the CCP Central Party School has argued, "Energy security is not just an economic issue, but a geopolitical strategic issue as well" because it implicates China's "political stability and national security." A U.S.-China energy insecurity spiral has thus begun and can be expected to continue.

Differences between Chinese and American national identities virtually predetermines that China and America will not become genuine allies over the short term. Aaron Friedberg (2005, 33) noted that "Ideological differences, and ideologically rooted animosities, may . . . reinforce the dynamics of mutual insecurity at work in the U.S.-China relationship." As noted above, Chinese identity today involves an ethno-cultural nationalism that highlights a pure **Han ethnicity** and pride in China's Five Thousand Years of Civilization. But it is also a wounded nationalism that is currently confronting the long-suppressed trauma that China experienced at the hands of Western and especially Japanese imperialism during the "Century of Humiliation" from the mid-nineteenth to the mid-twentieth century. National narratives about defeat in the Sino-Japanese War of 1894–1895, the humiliating Treaty of Shimonoseki of 1895, the "21 Demands" of 1915, and the "Rape of Nanking" of 1937 conspire to make the Japanese the most reviled target of Chinese nationalism today. But Taiwan's continued separation from China, symbolizing China's humiliating past of being carved up by imperialism, lingers on as the greatest threat to Chinese national identity today. "Reunification" is thus not simply a matter of consolidating territory, but of shoring up national self-esteem. In China's eyes, U.S. support of Taiwan, starting with U.S. naval intervention in the Taiwan Strait in 1950 with the outbreak of the Korean War and continuing on to U.S. political and military support of Taiwan today, is the cause of Taiwan's continued separation from China. As former PRC vice president Zeng Qinghong said in 2002 (cited in Bush 2005, 206): "The United States bears a big responsibility for the fact that the Taiwan issue remains unresolved. The United States sheltered the Taiwan authorities continuously for over twenty years after ordering the seventh fleet into the Taiwan Strait . . . [and] it has never stopped selling advanced arms to Taiwan . . . help[ing] 'Taiwan independence' forces." Therefore, so long as Taiwan remains de facto independent of China—a safe assumption over the short term—Chinese nationalism will set a clear limit on Chinese friendship toward the United States.

By contrast, American identity is largely ideological and not ethno-cultural. It is a **civic nationalism** centered on a particularly American liberalism that has at its heart a fierce insistence on individual freedom set against an authoritarian state. In American national narratives, the United States won its independence and freedom by fighting against the tyranny of King George and the British. But American fears of the individual's enslavement at the hands of a strong state lives on today in a fear of communism. This concern helps explain why so much U.S. discourse on China today says so little about China and so much about American values. Decrying a "China threat" and the evils of communism becomes a way of defining what it means to be a freedom-loving twenty-first-century American. Because it is fairly safe to say that China will remain in name (though not in practice) a communist country for the near future, it is also safe to say that at a very deep-rooted level, most Americans will not trust China as a genuine friend.

What policy implications flow from this analysis? If U.S.-China conflict is a low-probability outcome, we should not let it dominate our thinking and thus become a self-fulfilling prophesy. Of course, the United States should prepare for conflict by maintaining its general deterrence posture through both internal and external balancing—both maintaining its military capabilities and its Asian alliances, particularly with Japan and South Korea. But worst-case thinking should not be allowed to govern our security analysis.

And if we believe that the worst-case scenario of U.S.-China conflict is most likely to be the product of the United States getting drawn into a China-Japan or China-Taiwan dispute, then we should focus on crisis avoidance and management strategies. If the accidents of history are to continue to play a central role in the U.S.-China relations, then China and the United States' need to prepare for such crises. More clearly established crisis management mechanisms may help China and the United States avoid a future conflict. The inability of U.S. leadership to get their Chinese counterparts on the phone in the initial days after the 1999 **Belgrade bombing** and 2001 **spy plane incident** exacerbated each crisis and should be lessons to learn from. Improved channels of communication should be more clearly established so that Chinese and American diplomats are better able to manage crises before nationalists in China and the United States exacerbate them.

Finally, if we believe that the most likely scenario over the intermediate term is either a continuation of the current state of rivalry or marginal moves toward partnership, then we should hedge between these two scenarios. And this is indeed what we are already doing. Both Washington and Beijing are currently confronting uncertainty in their bilateral relationship by hedging their policies toward each other. Hedging is a wise "geopolitical insurance strategy" (Medeiros 2006) for the United States in its China policy because it does not make rivalry or enmity a self-fulfilling prophecy and allows for the possibility of movement toward partnership.

NOTES

1. The Japanese invaded and colonized Manchuria following the Mukden Incident of 1931. However, the invasion of the rest of China did not begin until after the Marco Polo Bridge Incident of 1937. Chinese from the northeast invariably cite 1931 as the onset of the war; others frequently cite 1937.

2. Note that this categorization of Chinese youth generations conflicts with the delineation of generations of political leadership. To distance himself from Mao, leader of the "First Generation," Deng declared himself leader of the "Second Generation," despite the fact that they both participated in the Long March and the War of Resistance. Hence, Jiang is of the "Third Generation," and Hu Jintao now leads the new "Fourth Generation" of technocratic leadership (Li Cheng 2001).

3. A few members of the "New Left" of nationalist intellectuals in China were an exception, having actually sought to affirm the Cultural Revolution (Guo Yingjie 2004, 32).

REFERENCES

Acharya, Amitav. 2003–2004. "Will Asia's Past Be Its Future?" *International Security* 28, no. 3: 149–64.

Barmé, Geremie R. 1996. *Shades of Mao: The Posthumous Cult of the Great Leader.* Armonk, N.Y.: ME Sharpe.

Beijing chenbao [*Beijing Morning Post*]. 2002. "'Jiang Wen qianwang jingguo shenshe' shijian youlai" [The origins of the "Jiang Wen Went to Yasukuni" affair]. July 1.

Beijing qingnian zhoukan [*Beijing Youth Weekly*]. 1997. "Women you zui youxiu de rennao" [We have the best brains]. May 20, no. 98.

Beijing qingnianbao [*Beijing Youth Daily*]. 2001. "Zhao Wei: Wode xingwei shang-haile henduoren de ganqing" [Zhao Wei: My behavior has hurt the feelings of many people]. December 20.

Bush, Richard C. 2005. *Untying the Knot: Making Peace in the Taiwan Strait*. Washington, D.C.: Brookings Institution Press.

Chen Xiaomei. 1995. *Occidentalism: A Theory of Counter-Discourse in Post-Mao China*. New York: Oxford University Press.

Chen Yifei. 2002. "Qinqxuhua de aiguozhuyi bushi zhenzheng de aiguozhuyi: gejie renshi tan 'Jiang Wen qianwang Jingguo shenshe'" [Emotional patriotism is not true patriotism: Everyone's talking about "Jiang Wen Goes to Ya-sukuni Shrine"]. *Beijing qingnianbao* [*Beijing Youth Daily*], July 1. Accessed July 2, 2004. http://bjyouth.ynet.com/article.jsp?oid=743841&pageno=1.

Christensen, Thomas. 1996. "Chinese Realpolitik." *Foreign Affairs* 75, no. 5: 37–52.

Clark, Candace. 1990. "Emotions and Micropolitics in Everyday Life." In *Research Agendas in the Sociology of Emotions*, edited by Theodore D. Kemper, 305–33. Albany: State University of New York Press.

Cohen, Paul A. 2002. "Remembering and Forgetting: National Humiliation in Twentieth-Century China." *Twentieth-Century China* 27, no 2: 1–39.

Duara, Prasenjit. 1995. *Rescuing History from the Nation: Questioning Narratives of Modern China*. Chicago: University of Chicago Press.

Economy, Elizabeth. 2004. *The River Runs Black: The Environmental Challenge to China's Future*. Ithaca, N.Y.: Cornell University Press.

Friedberg, Aaron L. 2005. "The Future of U.S.-China Relations: Is Conflict Inevitable?" *International Security* 30, no. 2: 33.

Giddens, Anthony. 1991. *Modernity and Self-Identity: Self and Society in the Late Modern Age*. Stanford, Calif.: Stanford University Press.

Gries, Peter Hays. 2004. *China's New Nationalism: Pride, Politics, and Diplomacy*. Berkeley, Calif.: University of California Press.

———. 2005. "China's 'New Thinking on Japan.'" *The China Quarterly* 184 (December): 831–50.

———. 2006. "Forecasting US-China relations, 2015." *Asian Security* 2, no. 2: 1–23.

———. 2012. "Disillusionment and Dismay: How Chinese Netizens Think and Feel About the Two Koreas." *Journal of East Asian Studies* 12:31–56.

Guo Yingjie. 2004. "Barking up the Wrong Tree: The Liberal-Nationalist Debate on Democracy and Identity." In *Nationalism, Democracy and National Integration in China*, edited by Leong H. Liew and Shaoguang Wang, 23–43 London & New York: RoutledgeCurzon.

Halbwachs, Maurice. 1980. *The Collective Memory*. New York: Harper & Row.

Horkheimer, Max, and Theodor W. Adorno. 1947/2002. *Dialectic of Enlightenment: Philosophical Fragments*. Edited by Gunzelin Schmid Noerr and translated by Edmund Jephcott. Repr. Stanford, Calif.: Stanford University Press.

Japan Economic Newswire. 2001. "China Pop Star Apologizes for Japan Flag Look-Alike Outfit." December 11.

Jin Hui. 1995. *Tongwen cangzang: Rijun qinHua baoxing beiwanglu* [*Wailing at the heavens: The violence of the Japanese invasion of China*]. Beijing: Jiefangjun wenyi chubanshe.

Kang, David. 2003. "Getting Asia Wrong: The Need for New Analytic Frameworks." *International Security* 27, no. 4: 57–85.

Karl, R. E. 2001. "The Burdens of History: Lin Zexu (1959) and the Opium War (1997)." In *Whither China? Intellectual Politics in Contemporary China*, edited by Zhang Xudong, 229–62 Durham, N.C.: Duke University Press.

Kedourie, Elie. 1960/1993. *Nationalism*. Repr., 4th exp. ed. Cambridge, Mass: Blackwell.

LaCapra, Dominique. 1998. *History and Memory after Auschwitz*. Ithaca, N.Y.: Cornell University Press.

Lei Yi. 1997. "Xiandai de 'Huaxia zhongxinguan' yu 'minzu zhuyi' [Modern "sino-centrism" and "nationalism"]. In *Zhonguo ruhe miandui Xifang* [*How China faces the West*], edited by Xiao Pang. Hong Kong: Mirror Books.

Leverett, Flynt, and Jeffrey Bader. 2005–2006. "Managing China-US Energy Competition in the Middle East." *Washington Quarterly* 29, no. 1: 187–201.

Li Cheng. 2001. *China's Leaders: The New Generation*. Lanham, Md.: Rowman & Littlefield.

Li Fang. 1996. "Chongjian Zhongguo youxi guize" [Rewriting China's rules of the game]. In *Zhongguo ruhe shuobu* [*How China should say no*]. Special issue, *Zuojia tiandi* [*Writer's world*] no. 6, 21–30.

Liu, Lydia. 1994. "The Female Body and Nationalist Discourse: Manchuria in Xiao Hong's Field of Life and Death." In *Body, Subject & Power in China*, edited by Angela Zito and Tani E. Barlow, 157–77 Chicago: University of Chicago Press.

Mannheim, Karl. 1952. *Essays on the Sociology of Knowledge*. London: Routledge & Paul.

McAdams, Dan P. 1996. *The Stories We Live By: Personal Myths and the Making of the Self*. New York: Guilford Press.

Medeiros, Evan S. 2006. "Strategic Hedging and the Future of Asia-Pacific Stability." *Washington Quarterly* 29, no. 1: 147.

Meisner, Maurice. 1999. *Mao's China and After: A History of the People's Republic*. 3rd ed. New York: Simon & Schuster, Free Press.

Men Honghua. 2005. *Goujian Zhongguo dazhanlue de kuangjia: Guojia shili, zhanlue guannian yu guoji shidu* [*Constructing a framework for China's grand strategy: National power, strategic concept, and the international system*]. Beijing: Beijing daxue chubanshe.

Mote, Frederic W. 1999. *Imperial China, 900–1800*. Cambridge, Mass.: Harvard University Press.

Olick, J., and J. Robbins. 1998. "Social Memory Studies: From 'Collective Memory' to the Historical Sociology of Mnemonic Practices." *Annual Review of Sociology* 24:105–40.

Ross, Robert. 1999. "The Geography of the Peace: Great Power Stability in Twenty-First Century East Asia." *International Security* 23, no. 4, 81–118.

Sautman, Barry. 1997. "Racial Nationalism and China's External Behavior." *World Affairs 160*, no. 2: 78–96.

Segev, Tom. 1993. *The Seventh Million: The Israelis and the Holocaust.* New York: Hill and Wang.

Shen Xiaoma. 2002. "The Popular Judgment" [Liuxing pipan]. *Southern Daily* [*Nanfang dushibao*], July 10. Accessed December 16, 2003. Reprinted on Sina.com, http://cul.sina.com.cn/l/d/2002-07-10/14918.html.

Singer, Jefferson A., and Peter Salovey. 1993. *The Remembered Self: Emotion and Memory in Personality.* New York: Free Press.

Somers, Margaret R. 1994. "The Narrative Constitution of Identity: A Relational and Network Approach." *Theory and Society* 23: 605–49.

Song Qiang, Qiao Bian, Caiwang Naoru, Xia Jilin, and Liu Hui. 1997. *Disidairen de jingshen: xiandai Zhongguoren de jiushi qinghuai* [*The spirit of the fourth generation: The savior feeling of the modern Chinese*]. Lanzhou: Gansu wenhua chubanshe.

Straits Times (Singapore). 2001. "Actress Sorry for Wearing 'Wartime Japan Flag' Dress." December 11.

Tajfel, Henri. 1981. *Human Groups and Social Categories: Studies in Social Psychology.* New York: Cambridge University Press.

Tang Shiping. 2004. "A Systemic Theory of the Security Environment." *Journal of Strategic Studies* 27, no. 1: 1–34.

Tu Weiming. 1991. "Cultural China: The Periphery as Center." In "The Living Tree: The Changing Meaning of Being Chinese Today," special issue, *Daedalus* 120, no. 2: 1–32.

Volkan, Vamik, and Norman Itzkowitz. 1994. *Turks and Greeks: Neighbors in Conflict.* Cambridgeshire, England: Ethoden.

Wasserstrom, Jeffrey. 2000. "Big Bad China and the Good Chinese: An American Fairy Tale." In *China Beyond the Headlines,* edited by Timothy Weston and Lionel Jensen. Boulder, Colo.: Rowman and Littlefield.

Watts, Jonathan. 2010. *When a Billion Chinese Jump: How China Will Save Mankind—Or Destroy It.* New York, N.Y.: Scribner.

Weinstein, Eugene A., and Paul Deutschberger. 1963. "Some Dimensions of Altercasting." *Sociometry* 26, no. 4: 454–66.

Xi Yongjun, and Ma Zaizhun. 1996. *Chaoyue Meiguo: Meiguo Shenhua De Zhongjie* [*Surpassing the USA: The end of the American myth*]. Harbin, China: Neimenggu daxue chubanshe.

Xiao Gongqing. 1994. "Cong minzuzhuyi zhong jiequ guojia ningjuli de xinziyuan" [Deriving from nationalism a new resource that congeals the state]. *Zhanlue yu guanli* [*Strategy and management*] 4:21–25.

Xu Ben. 2001. "Chinese Populist Nationalism: Its Intellectual Politics and Moral Dilemma." *Representations* 76, no. 1: 120–40.

Yu Shaowen. 2002. "Zhendui 'Jingguo shenshe' shijian Feng Xiaogang ti Jiang Wen ma bu ping" [On the "Yasukuni" incident, Feng Xiaogang comes to Jiang Wen's defense]. *Beijing qingnianbao* [*Beijing youth daily*], July 2. Accessed December 24, 2003.http://bjyouth.ynet.com/article.jsp?oid=749158.

Zerubavel, Yael. 1995. *Recovered Roots: Collective Memory and the Making of Israeli National Tradition*. Chicago: University of Chicago Press.

Zhang Datian. 2001. "Zhao Wei zhao 'Riben junqizhuang' yinlai juda fengbo" [Zhao Wei wears a "Japanese military flag outfit" and creates a furor]. *Beijing chenbao* [*Beijing morning post*], December 4. Reprinted on the People's Forum, www.people.com.cn/GB/wenyu/64/129/20011204/618330.html.

Zhou Gucheng. 1991. "Preface" [*Xu*]. In Never Forget the History of National Humiliation book series [wuwang guochi lishi congshu], 1–2. Beijing: Zhongguo huaqiao chubanshe.

Zweig, David, and Bi Jianhai. 2005. "China's Global Hunt for Energy." *Foreign Affairs* 84, no. 5: 25–38.

6

The European Union

MITCHELL P. SMITH AND ROBERT HENRY COX

More than sixty years after the official founding of the **European integration** project with the 1951 **European Coal and Steel Community**, the European Union (EU) confronts an existential crisis. The financial turmoil of the late 2000s led to massive bank losses and government budget deficits in several EU countries—especially Greece, Ireland, Portugal, and Spain—that required joint action and common sacrifice by member states.[1] Some governments, especially the EU's leading economic power, Germany, which sustained stable finances throughout the downturn, proved reluctant to come to the economic rescue of their troubled fellow members. In response, many observers began to question whether citizens and governments of EU countries are losing the commitment required to sustain monetary union, the euro, and the European integration project itself. Will Europeans tolerate the transfers of their tax revenues to fund a union-wide economic stability? Are governments willing to facilitate a swift and certain response to episodes of financial instability in other EU member countries? If not, has European integration reached political limits that may culminate in an unraveling of the entire project? Should an unraveling come to pass, it would be a stunning irony that the creation of a single European currency—the ultimate act of economic union—had within a little more than a decade sown the seeds of discord and disintegration in Europe.

In addition to the fundamental challenge of financial cohesion, EU countries also bear the vulnerability of extensive dependence on Russia for energy supplies, including 33 percent of oil imports and 21 percent of natural gas imports.[2] More generally, the EU is struggling to define a meaningful global role commensurate with its standing as the world's single largest economy. Many observers see deterioration in political relations between the EU and the United States that continue to have deep economic links. According to one perspective, as the United States experiences a relative decline in its global standing, it is shifting its attention to an ascendant Asia. Under this scenario, Europeans are uncertain about whether to redefine or reinforce partnership with the United States. Some advocate a more independent European approach to relations with China, Russia, Turkey, and the Middle East.

Given these areas of major uncertainty, how are we to evaluate the historic project of European integration? Is there an alternative to the potential disintegration outlined above and anticipated by numerous observers? For example, might efforts to overcome the Eurozone's financial turmoil produce deeper fiscal and, ultimately, political union? Four points are essential to any assessment of the meaning and trajectory of the EU: (1) an appreciation of the origins and initial objective of integration; (2) recognition that the EU has faced periods of uncertainty and loss of direction at several junctures in its history; (3) acknowledgement that the achievements of European integration have emerged from acts of political will rather than either necessity or coincidence, and that, in the process, the EU has developed powerful mechanisms of improvisation and conflict resolution; and (4) an understanding that steps toward European integration stem not from the decisions of member state governments to *set aside* national interests, but from their mutual conviction that *they may more effectively pursue those interests at a European level.*

EU CRISIS IN PERSPECTIVE

Origins and Initial Objectives of European Integration

Conceived in the wake of World War II's devastation, the project of integration emerged from the ideas of French planning commissioner Jean Monnet. Monnet shared the ultimate goal of European federalists who believed the only way to escape the "Europe of wars" was to transcend the nation state. However, while the federalists wished to create a United States of Europe, Monnet had the political vision to recognize that such an outcome was unattainable without concrete mechanisms to move incrementally in this direction. As a result, Monnet proposed an approach of **economic gradualism**, beginning with an integrated mechanism for overseeing the production and distribution of European coal and steel resources. Monnet chose these sectors strategically: aside from their significance for industrial production, coal and steel were the principal mid-century components of war-making capacity. Supporting this approach with a set of institutions for common decision making, Monnet argued, would generate a dynamic that "replaces the efforts at domination of nation states by a constant process of collective adaptation to new conditions, a chain reaction, a ferment where one change induces another" (Monnet 1962, 208). Viewed from this perspective on the roots of European integration, the turmoil of recent years seems less threatening to the very existence of the EU.

Monnet's strategy took shape in the plan for a European Coal and Steel Community (ECSC) officially proposed by French prime minister Robert Schuman in 1950. Reflecting Monnet's concept of gradualism, Schuman announced, "Europe will not be made all at once, or according to a single plan. It will be built through concrete achievements which first create a de facto solidarity."[3] The proposal supplemented the vision expressed by Winston Churchill, who asserted in a dramatic 1946 speech given in Zurich that "The first step in the re-creation of the European family must be a partnership between France and Germany" (Churchill 1946). With Britain as an outside supporter rather than a participant, it fell to the French government to take the lead in launching the process. The ECSC that emerged from the **Schuman declaration** was designed to make war between France and Germany "not merely unthinkable, but materially impossible."[4] Judged by this standard—the quest to firmly institutionalize peace among member states—the European integration project achieved stunning success.

The visions of Monnet, Schuman, and other postwar leaders committed to European peace took hold. The ECSC was expanded in the 1957 **Treaty of Rome** to include plans for a broader European Economic Community (EEC). The EEC was to be a **customs union**, meaning that the member states would eliminate tariff barriers between themselves and also establish common tariffs on goods from outside the Community. Membership initially included the original six states of the ECSC: France, West Germany, Italy, Belgium, the Netherlands, and Luxembourg. The EEC established a schedule for realizing the economic community by January 1, 1970.[5] The result of the EEC was a sharp growth in trade between member states, especially France and Germany. The latter quickly began to emerge as a global export leader, boosted by post–World War II recovery. Franco-German cooperation intensified along with trade, and the threat of armed conflict between the two European powers gradually faded into oblivion.

Losing a Sense of Direction

With the EEC in place between the original six member states, European integration appeared to have built a firm foundation for the deeper integration envisaged by Monnet and others. However, the project faced fundamental challenges, including absence of a shared sense of purpose and clear source of leadership. How could the member states of the EEC forge a common response in the face of the global economic turmoil of the 1970s, which came in two forms: the collapse of the U.S. dollar-led **Bretton Woods monetary system**, and the energy price shocks associated with the formation of the **Organization of Petroleum Exporting Countries (OPEC)** oil cartel?

Bretton Woods referred to a U.S.-forged system for global monetary stability designed to support economic growth and recovery after WWII. The system revolved around the U.S. dollar as an anchor that was exchangeable for gold at a fixed rate, with other global currencies tied to the dollar also at fixed rates. However, recovery of European countries and the onset of U.S. trade deficits, along with the huge increase in U.S. military spending associated with the war in Vietnam, contributed to a global oversupply of dollars that meant the dollar's fixed rate was unsustainable. As the United States abandoned **convertibility** to gold in 1971, the EEC countries faced the question of how to establish an area of monetary stability in Western Europe. Stability was important to sustaining gains in trade and investment throughout the region. In an environment in which an economically struggling United States sought to pass along some of the costs of its adjustment to its now recovered allies, European efforts to develop a stable monetary order floundered, although the experience would generate lessons later applicable to the successful launch of European monetary union in 1999.

In addition, the decision of OPEC to use their control over markets to cut supply produced a quadrupling of oil prices in 1973 and a tripling later in the decade in the wake of the 1979 **Iranian Revolution** and the outbreak of war between Iran and Iraq the following year.[6] With different levels of dependency on oil and diversely structured economies, the EEC countries struggled to find any common ground on which to forge a cooperative response. Governments sought their own paths of adjustment, and the European integration project seemed to have lost its sense of direction. With most of the benefits of the customs union already attained, governments inwardly focused on economic adjustment and elusive monetary cooperation. Numerous observers bemoaned a condition of "eurosclerosis." As the 1970s ended, the U.S. economy reestablished its footing, and economic dynamism began to surge in East Asia. It was unclear whether European integration would retain its relevance into the 1980s.

The Community Expands

Meanwhile, the membership of the EEC had expanded from its original six with the addition of Britain, Ireland, and Denmark in 1973. French president Charles de Gaulle had twice vetoed British membership in the 1960s, concerned that Britain would both challenge French leadership of EEC institutions and bring in unwelcome U.S. influence.[7] But by the early 1970s, de Gaulle had passed from the scene, and both the United Kingdom and existing members saw economic and political advantages in British accession.

The next enlargement of the European Community (EC) took place with Greece becoming a member in 1981, followed by Spain and Portugal in 1986. There was a dual significance to these three countries joining. First, all three had only recently made internal transitions from authoritarian to democratic government. EC membership, therefore, not only had economic significance, but was also meaningful as a mechanism for institutionalizing stable commitments to democracy, a requirement of membership. Second, these countries also were economically poorer than the average member state, with far larger agricultural sectors. The accession of these three Mediterranean countries produced new mechanisms for the provision of EC financial support to less developed and more heavily agricultural regions.

The fourth enlargement, which took place in 1995, contrasted sharply with the expansions that brought Greece, Spain, and Portugal into the (now re-named) EU. Austria, Sweden, and Finland were all considerably wealthier than the EU average. Far more complex was the so-called big bang of May 1, 2004, that added ten members to the EU, eight of which were former social-ist countries under Soviet tutelage.[8] In 2007, Bulgaria and Romania became the twenty-sixth and twenty-seventh members of the EU, with their accession considered the delayed tail end of the fifth enlargement.

The process by which new members accede to the EU is rigorous and pro-tracted, involving scrutiny and reform of all elements of the candidate coun-try's economy and political system. According to criteria agreed by member state governments in 1993,[9] candidates must demonstrate stability of **demo-cratic institutions** and commitment to the rule of law, the existence of a func-tioning **market economy**, and the ability to take on all of the obligations of membership in order to join the EU.[10] The essence of the enlargement criteria is that countries must achieve these qualities *prior to* membership, not after they accede, so that the EU does not import political or economic instability.

The next country aligned for EU membership is Croatia. The European Parliament gave its consent to Croatia's Treaty of Accession on December 1, 2011, and on December 9 the governments of Croatia and all EU member states signed the treaty. Assuming successful ratification in Croatia and all EU member states, Croatia will become the EU's twenty-eighth member on July 1, 2013. Upon the signing of the accession treaty, EU leaders expressed hope that Croatia's successful transformation would produce a demonstration ef-fect in the western Balkans, so that enlargement could "continue to serve as an anchor of stability, a driver of democracy and the rule of law, and as a catalyst for economic prosperity."[11]

Other countries in line for membership include Iceland, Macedonia, and Montenegro. Turkey remains the most contentious potential member. Un-like other candidates, Turkey is a large country by European standards, with a population expected to surpass the eighty-two million of Germany, cur-rently the EU's largest member, within a decade or so.[12] In addition, Turkey is a predominantly Islamic country. Although there is a deeply institutionalized tradition of **secularism** in Turkish government, some European leaders and substantial shares of the citizenry of EU member states insist that Turkey is not "European" and, while a valued ally of the EU, should be granted special partnership status rather than full membership.[13] This perception explains why the EU controversially reinforced in 2006 the additional criterion of "absorption capacity"—that granting membership to the candidate country not diminish the EU's capacity "to maintain the momentum of European integration."[14]

Additional potential members include the remaining Balkan countries: Al-bania, Bosnia and Herzegovina, Kosovo, and Serbia. Of course, the precise boundaries of "Europe," and of potential EU membership, remain indeterminate, as do the prospects for distant future membership of east European countries such as Ukraine, Belarus, and Moldova and countries of the Southern Caucasus (Armenia, Azerbaijan, Georgia). Russia even enters the discussion, although Russia's size, level of economic development, and democratic deficits leave it very far short of suitability for EU candidacy in the foreseeable future.

For the time being, the EU has developed an Eastern Partnership program designed to develop stable relations and closer economic ties with the former Soviet Republics of Ukraine, Belarus, Georgia, Moldova, Armenia, and Azerbaijan. The objective of the Eastern Partnership, launched in May 2009, is to stimulate economic, political, and environmental reforms in these countries and to enhance the EU's **energy security**. In a sense, we may view the Eastern Partnership as a test of the transformative capacity of the EU as a community of values (rule of law, protection of human rights and the rights of minorities) outside the sphere in which it can offer the incentive of the promise of membership. Instead, the payoff for Eastern Partnership countries of advancing liberty, democracy, and rule of law will be deeper political and economic integration with the EU through movement toward visa-free travel of their citizens and "Deep and Comprehensive Free Trade Areas." While it is early to judge the impact of the Eastern Partnership, the results of the first two to three years suggest political dynamics in each of these countries proceed more or less independently of EU influence.

Explaining Integration

If the advance of European integration depends upon agreement between national governments, how has integration of states with diverse political economies, cultures, and interests been possible at all? Does progress hinge on a coincidence of national needs and perspectives? Some scholars, such as the renowned late historian of Europe, Tony Judt, claim this is indeed the case. Judt argued that the conditions producing postwar integration were historically unique and unlikely to be reproduced (Judt 1996). Yet, rather than an integration process that stagnates much of the time, punctuated by brief eras of agreement and progress, we in fact find the inverse: significant periods of progress interrupted by periods in which the process seems stuck. How might we explain this phenomenon?

In his widely cited work on the early post-WWII origins of the European integration project, the historian Alan Milward writes that national governments in the aftermath of World War II came to value integration as a means to boost their abilities to address the most pressing national economic and political concerns. In other words, "without the process of integration the west European nation-state might well not have retained the allegiance and support of its citizens in the way that it has. The European Community has been its buttress, an indispensable part of the nation-state's post-war construction" (Milward 1992, 3).

Milward's perspective is extremely helpful for understanding the drive behind European integration: the tendency of national governments to view the EU as an opportunity to more readily address *national* economic and political challenges. Viewed from this vantage point, the advance of integration becomes less mysterious. As government officials interacted within EU institutions more intensively over time, they came to see the EU as useful for addressing a growing array of policy problems.

For example, EU institutions could be useful for solving problems of coordination across member states. Consider the issue of declining mining, shipbuilding, and steel industries across Western Europe in the 1970s and early 1980s. These industries experienced excessive domestic production, a problem exacerbated by increased production (at lower cost) in emerging economies (shipbuilding in South Korea, for example). Each government faced an incentive to spend money to keep loss-making industries operating in order to protect jobs. If several governments did this simultaneously, each would then be squandering funds, collectively perpetuating the problem of overproduction. By relying on the **European Commission**—the administrative body of the EU—to develop a plan for reducing production and subsidies across member states, governments could bring an end to this wasteful process in a gradual and orderly fashion. In another example, the finance ministers of member state governments reached agreement in the December 1991 **Maastricht Treaty** to create the conditions for a single currency by reducing government deficits to a common level (below 3 percent of gross domestic product [GDP]); each national finance minister did so as a means of locking their government into a path of fiscal austerity. As we know from the **eurozone** crisis of 2010–2013, this commitment to fiscal responsibility did not work out precisely as planned, but the intention was to make an irreversible commitment to sound budget practices. Europe, in this instance, provided an opportunity to buttress the objectives of national governments, precisely as Milward described.

EUROPE'S SOCIAL DIMENSION

In terms of areas of policy competence, the expansion of the EU has been successful mainly in areas related to economic policy. However, since the beginning, European leaders and the treaties they have signed have explicitly affirmed their desire to make the process of integration bring together the people who inhabit the European continent. This goal is broadly referred to as the social dimension of European integration, and it has been pursued in a number of important ways that reflect a desire to widen and deepen European integration. Deepening the EU involves a number of initiatives to create a common identity and sense of belonging among European citizens, or to enhance the degree to which Europeans see the EU as important to their lives. Widening reflects an effort to expand the areas where the EU operates into policy areas beyond economic cooperation, especially by promoting harmonization of social policies. Both of these areas of integration have been difficult to achieve, and they provide poignant illustrations of the broader challenges that face the process of European integration. Citizenship, and the common identity that ought to accompany it, is not fully developed in the EU and is based on principles that show a preference for national over European citizenship. Efforts to coordinate social policies among member states are limited by the constitutional boundaries of the EU. These limits have led to some creative mechanisms for policy coordination, but this, too, is an area where member states still have a dominant role.

The issue of European citizenship is almost as old as the EU itself and is an outgrowth of the idea that economic integration requires the free movement of labor. The ECSC initially promoted the free movement of labor as a right, prompting discussion about what other rights citizens of the EU should enjoy. In the first three decades after World War II, migrant workers, who came primarily from Italy to work in north European factories, discovered that as they moved, they gave up some of their rights. Residing in Belgium, Germany, and the Netherlands, these migrants held roughly the same status as foreign workers who came from other parts of the world. The problem became more severe as years passed, and it became clear that these workers were going to stay. As these workers raised families and became members of their communities, their status as migrants seemed out of place (Maas 2007).

In 1972, Belgium and Italy proposed allowing citizens in member states to vote in local elections where they reside, which would have allowed these "migrant" workers to enjoy important political rights in their new residences. A high-level commission, established to revive the process of European integration that had been threatened by the global economic crises of the early 1970s, pushed the issue of political rights even further. The **Tindemans Commission**, named for the Belgian prime minister Leo Tindemans, who served as its chair, issued a number of recommendations, including a suggestion that common citizenship be established.

In the wake of the economic crises of the 1970s, citizenship took a back seat but was revived in the 1980s with the Treaty on European Union that helped to define European citizenship. It stated that citizens of the member states are also citizens of the EU, but that citizenship only comes from being a citizen of a member state. In other words, citizenship in one of the member states was to be *primary*, and EU citizenship would be *derivative* and *secondary*. The determination of citizenship, therefore, is controlled by each member state; however, once such citizenship is recognized by a member state, EU citizenship became automatic. In practical terms, one cannot apply to be a citizen of the EU, but one can apply to become a citizen of a member state. Though there is a great deal of coordination on immigration and naturalization issues, as well as some convergence in regulations, member states are the primary controlling authority. For example, passports for EU citizens are issued by each member state. The member states have agreed that these passports would have similar designs, and that they would bear the words "European Union" along with the name of the member state, but the EU does not itself issue passports.

When it was passed in 1992, the Treaty on European Union also enumerated many rights of EU citizens. First, the right to freedom of movement was expanded to allow for all forms of movement, not only for employment. Second, some important political rights were granted to EU citizens that allow them to vote in elections where they reside and to stand for office to the **European Parliament** in their place of residence. Third, the treaty assured all EU citizens of common diplomatic protection abroad, which has led to a great deal of coordination and cooperation of diplomatic staff from member states.

The granting of common rights and citizenship was an important step in creating a common status, but the greater challenge has been to instill a common sense of identity. Getting citizens of the EU to think of themselves as Europeans, and not as Germans, Italians, Estonians, and so forth, has taken longer. In recent years, public opinion suggests that a sense of European identity is beginning to emerge (Risse 2010). It is most evident among the younger generation. This finding is not surprising. Young Europeans are exposed to the EU more frequently than their parents' generation. The EU is taught more in schools, and travel among European countries is easier and more common. Moreover, the EU itself sponsors many programs that bring students together across national boundaries. The Erasmus Programme, for example, encourages universities from different member states to build common degree programs and exchange agreements that allow students from each university to study at one or more of the other partner universities. The Leonardo da Vinci Programme does the same for technical colleges. By the time students in these programs finish their degrees, they have already met fellow students from different parts of the EU and have learned to work together in the classroom. As the graduates of these programs enter the workforce, they already have a more European outlook.

In addition to the deepening of the EU, a widening of efforts has fostered policies to encourage "social cohesion." This term is based on the idea that the integration of markets affects European citizens unevenly. For those who are adversely affected by market integration, social cohesion policies provide resources to help them adjust to market integration. The oldest, and indeed the most important, example of social cohesion is the Common Agricultural Policy (CAP). Adopted in 1962, the CAP was intended to achieve a number of objectives. First was the goal of achieving a stable food supply. The experience of widespread hunger before and during World War II made Europeans sensitive to the need to ensure an adequate supply of food. Second, the CAP was intended to stabilize the economies of rural regions. The major mechanism for achieving these objectives has been price supports given to farmers.

The effect of the CAP has been profound. Since its inception, the CAP has consistently been the single largest line item in the EU budget. At its peak, 60 percent of the EU budget went to the CAP, and even today it consumes one third of the EU budget. In terms of providing an adequate supply of food, the CAP has been a success. Today the EU is self-sufficient in every agricultural product it can produce within its own climate. Indeed, the EU is also a major exporter of many agricultural products, which often leads to charges that it dumps surpluses on global markets.

The success of the CAP has not come without complaint. Not only is it expensive, but the system of agricultural price supports is more valuable to some countries, especially those that still have a large sector of the workforce in agriculture. In recent years, numerous efforts have been forwarded to reduce and reform the levels of subsidies, but the different perspectives of member states often stymie reform. Some of the EU's largest countries, such as France, benefit greatly from the CAP and consequently are among its strongest supporters.

Nonetheless there have been important reforms to the CAP. In recent years it has expanded beyond providing support for farm income. Now, in addition to this objective, CAP projects also strive to maintain the integrity of landscapes by, for example, encouraging farmers to preserve wetland habitats or by establishing landscapes for recreational use. Over the years, the focus on rural areas has broadened from one of intensifying agricultural output to one of creating sustainable rural environments.

Aside from the CAP, the goal of social cohesion is also pursued by efforts to foster coordination in the social policies of member states. Here the process is slowed by something Fritz Scharpf calls the "constitutional asymmetry" between the **single market** and social policy (Scharpf 2002, 647). Because the EU was designed to promote economic integration, its instruments of policy control are strongest where they help to create and expand the single market. When social policy interferes with the operation of the single market, the EU has strong instruments to compel states to adjust social policy in favor of the single market. To date, EU treaties have not articulated a commitment to social policy on par with the status of the single market. In the constitutional language of EU treaties, the single market represents an area where the EU exercises "exclusive" competence, meaning that member states cannot make their own laws on such subjects as tariffs, monetary policy, and competition policy. Consequently, efforts to build and enhance the social dimension of Europe can only operate via so-called soft mechanisms of coordination, or policy instruments that encourage voluntary compliance.

Under the EU system of multilevel governance (Hooghe and Marks 2003), strong distinctions exist between policy areas where the EU is solely in charge (exclusive competences), areas where the member states have sole control (no competence), and areas where competence is shared between the EU and member states. Most areas of social policy are the domain of each member state, where the EU has no competence to govern. In a few policy areas, such as employment policy, the EU and member states share competences. In the absence of a constitutional power to control policy development, the EU has invented some creative policy instruments to induce coordination among member states.

One example of a new policy instrument is the **Open Method of Coordination**. Invoking its shared competence, the EU announced in 2000 a broad strategy to help foster the skills European workers will need to succeed in a more global and technological economic environment. Dubbed the **Lisbon Strategy**, the plan was to encourage member states to invest more in education, especially technological programs, to facilitate a transition from an industrial to a high-tech service economy. In an area where the EU lacked the competence to carry out the policy on its own, the Open Method of Coordination became a process by which member states would agree to certain targets for reducing unemployment, instituting retraining programs for jobless workers, and reforming welfare assistance. Each state would then report on its own progress toward achieving the goals, after which the European Commission would evaluate the reports and offer suggestions for improvement. Along the way, the member states were to meet periodically to share their best practices with each other.

Under the Open Method of Coordination, however, social policy coordination proved rather elusive.[15] The problem is that without a means to compel member states to cooperate, many of them abided by the objectives of the Lisbon strategy only when it was convenient to do so. In the areas where the EU has exclusive competence, such as the single market, it has strong policy instruments at its disposal to make member states comply with its decisions. In the area of social policy, by contrast, so-called soft policy instruments use incentives and moral persuasion to induce member states to take the appropriate measures. The low level of compliance led many observers, including the European Commission, to conclude that the Lisbon Strategy had fallen far short of its goals (European Commission 2010).

Today, a revised version of this program, called Europe 2020, still encourages member states to take steps to prepare their workers for a more technological workplace, and it encourages growth in the development of green jobs, in such areas as renewable energy and recycling. Without strong policy instruments, however, the success of Europe 2020 is uncertain.

Indeed, part of the resistance to EU influence in the area of social policy is due to the perception that the EU is committed to rolling back welfare support in the member states. The constitutional bias in favor of the single market often leads critics to accuse the EU of representing an ideological preference for **neoliberal** policies that encourage market forces. Many national welfare states were based on alternative, namely social democratic and Christian democratic ideological, perspectives and were explicitly designed to offer security against the vagaries of market forces (van Kersbergen and Manow, 2009; Berman 2006). Within the member states, many of the institutions and programs that define the welfare state are deeply entrenched and popular, making it difficult to introduce change. EU efforts to introduce reform, even by such innocuous means as the Open Method of Coordination, are seen as threats to national control. The perception that these efforts have a neoliberal bias stems from the fact that where the EU has a strong capacity to act, it promotes expansion of the single market at the expense of welfare support. For example, to promote the free competition among market forces, the EU challenges the relationships between hospitals, insurance companies, and patients in the health care regimes of many member states.

In short, the social dimension of European integration is a bold effort to push the European project beyond the boundaries of economic integration. This goal strives to deepen integration by strengthening the common bonds among European citizens and to broaden integration by encouraging convergence in social policy. In this area, however, progress is slower. Identities are resistant to change, and the popular policies of the welfare state have strong support, leading many member states to assert their control.

ECONOMIC INTEGRATION

Transcending Eurosclerosis

From the perspective of the stagnation of the 1970s, few could have imagined that the integration project's most dramatic forward movement was still ahead. What made it possible for Europe to escape the stagnation that characterized the latter 1970s?

The institutions of the EC were central to this process. The European Commission, the EC's bureaucracy that is situated in Brussels, is charged both with overseeing implementation of the treaties undergirding European integration (such as the 1957 Treaty of Rome that created the EEC) and driving the European entity in the direction of its deliberately vague and timeless objective of "ever closer union."[16] With the appointment by the member state governments of Jacques Delors, a former French finance minister, to the post of president of the European Commission in 1985, the Commission took bold steps to advance the cause of integration. Delors was determined to move the Community from its status of increasing irrelevance as a "taker of history," to being a "maker of history."[17] Supported by leaders of Europe's leading multinational businesses, Delors led an effort to set the groundwork for creation of a single European market. To be achieved by January 1, 1993, this monumental step in the construction of European integration called for the free movements of goods, capital, services, and labor across the borders of member states. A huge leap from the customs union, the European single market would eliminate the countless non-tariff barriers that slowed the flow of goods and services across borders and would thereby produce a surge in investment, trade, growth, and job creation in the EC.

Delors applied a brilliant tactic to the task of winning support for the single market. As with any step toward deeper integration, the endorsement of national governments was absolutely necessary. To garner this support, Delors sanctioned a series of sector-by-sector studies of the costs of *not* integrating markets—termed "the costs of non-Europe." These studies showed that the member states of the EC were missing opportunities to capture vast economic gains.[18]

Achieving the single market was not a simple matter. The ultimate approach derived from the principle of "mutual recognition"—a good produced in, and meeting the standards of, one member state could circulate throughout all member states. Professionals with training and qualifications in one member state (e.g., architects) could gain recognition of that professional qualification in another member state. Though the single European market largely was in place by January 1, 1993, the institutions of the EU continue to this day to remove remaining barriers (e.g., integration of financial services markets, which was advanced only in the mid-2000s) in an effort to perfect the single market and maximize its benefits.

From Single Market to Single Currency

Drawing on the lessons of the 1970s, when the benefits of the EEC had peaked and there was an absence of strategic follow up, Delors and others sought to build on the foundation of the single market—the next major step in the economic integration of Europe. This progression took the form of plans for economic and monetary union (EMU) codified in the December 1991 Maastricht Treaty (named for the Dutch town in which the treaty was signed by the leaders of national governments). Maastricht established the conditions for the creation of a single currency, the euro. Integrating the currencies of some of the world's major economies was a complex operation. The treaty identified a set of conditions that countries would have to meet to participate in EMU, involving reducing government deficits and debts and bringing inflation and interest rates in line with the best performing countries in the group. These conditions reflected another lesson learned from the experience of the 1970s—in particular, the failed attempt to achieve monetary coordination among EC member states. The lesson learned from that short-lived experiment was that it was a mistake to create a mechanism for monetary cooperation and then expect economic coordination to follow; rather, economic convergence would have to *precede* monetary cooperation if the process was to be stable. The Maastricht Treaty involved application of this lesson.

As it turned out, the Maastricht convergence process was an initial success, as governments worked to make the policy adjustments needed to qualify for Eurozone membership. Several member states, such as Portugal, Spain, and Italy, made important strides in improving their fiscal conditions. On January 1, 1999, the euro came into existence for eleven countries;[19] Greece qualified after a two-year delay in which it was supposed to undertake sharp cuts in public spending. Since that time, Slovenia (2007), **Cyprus** and Malta (2008), Slovakia (2009), and Estonia (2011) have qualified for membership, bringing the number of countries in the Eurozone to seventeen. At the same time, two sets of countries remain outside: first, older EU member states that have abstained by choice (the UK, Denmark, Sweden); and, second, newer members that also belong to the single market but have not yet met the conditions for Eurozone membership (as of 2011, Bulgaria, Czech Republic, Hungary, Latvia, Lithuania, Poland, Romania). The newer members do not have the option of choosing (the UK and Denmark negotiated a right to "opt out" in the Maastricht Treaty) and must work toward meeting conditions for eurozone entry.

Plans for economic and monetary union reflected the successes of Jean Monnet's design for ever-closer union through economic gradualism. Some scholars highlight as a primary motive for monetary union the shared desire of national finance ministers to lock in a commitment to control deficits, a means of keeping down inflation and stimulating investments.[20] Others place emphasis on the Franco-German deal forged in the wake of German unification in 1990, in which the French government agreed to support unification in exchange for a German pledge to deepen their commitment to European integration.

Introducing the new currency into circulation on January 1, 2002, presented serious technical challenges. Vending machines throughout Eurozone member countries would have to be retrofitted to accept euro coins, as would toll booths and parking meters, requiring modifications by actors across the private and public sectors. ATM machines also would have to be stocked with euro notes for dispensing at the stroke of midnight on January 1. New euro coins would similarly have to be front-loaded in the hands of banks and merchants, who would receive payment in national currency and return change in euros in order to withdraw national notes from circulation and introduce euro notes in their place.[21]

What was to be gained from this massive undertaking? First, businesses conducting transactions across several single-market countries would now be insulated against currency movements. An Italian furniture maker with accounts payable to input suppliers from France and accounts receivable from customers in Austria would not have to worry that adverse currency movements would eat into profits. A sharp rise or fall in the value of the euro relative to major currencies such as the dollar or the yen would have no effect on trade taking place within the Eurozone. The anticipated result would be an increase in trade among countries using the euro. Second, the reduced budget deficits and lower inflation created by the convergence process would create a stable investment climate in which investors would gain confidence, enhancing creation of growth and jobs. Anchoring this dynamic was the **European Central Bank** (ECB). Established in Frankfurt, signifying both that Germany had become the EU's principal economic power and that the ECB would model its approach to monetary policy on the behavior of the German Bundesbank that had managed (West) German economic stability throughout the postwar era, the ECB was committed by its charter to a sole objective: price stability. With a target of an inflation rate at or below 2 percent, the theory behind the ECB's charge was that price stability was the cornerstone of a virtuous economic cycle, from which higher rates of investment, growth, and job creation would follow.

The Eurozone Crisis of 2009–?

The first ten years of the single currency appeared in many respects to be a qualified success. Mid-decade, critics did complain that the single monetary policy of the ECB was not appropriate for countries facing different economic conditions. While some countries (e.g., Ireland and Spain) were growing rapidly, others (Italy and Germany, ironically) experienced stagnation. With less-than-spectacular growth throughout the Eurozone, the benefits brought by the common currency were not visible to citizens, and many judged the euro a disappointment. Still, the euro came to represent an increasing share of global transactions and reserves, and while the euro did not threaten to supplant the dollar, it did establish itself as the major alternative global **reserve currency**.[22] So what went wrong?

From the inception of EMU, proponents of currency union were well aware of the need for rules to keep governments committed to sound finances. This necessity was reflected in both the Maastricht convergence criteria and the Stability and Growth Pact, designed to keep deficit limits in place even after completion of EMU. However, oversight of deficit limits proved elusive. The authority of EU institutions is constrained in the face of willful resistance from a national government. Furthermore, monetary union gave all member states ready access to global capital markets, meaning they could individually borrow virtually unlimited amounts of money at low interest rates—a recipe for excess debt on the part of countries with poor fiscal discipline. One of the virtues of EMU was also a vice; in late 2009 it became clear that Greece had engaged in excessive borrowing.

Most critically, the crisis revealed the most fundamental tension of the entire European integration project: political union has not accompanied attainment of economic union. Put differently, the citizens of EU member states do not, by and large, consider themselves part of a single political community.

Accordingly, when asked to contribute to rescuing Greece from its debt crisis, German citizens did not feel compelled to do so.

Nonetheless, the political will behind the creation of the euro was incredibly strong, and EMU will not easily unravel. Indeed, many observers forecasted the imminent breakup of the Eurozone as the crisis dragged on from 2010 into 2012. Leaders of member state governments, responding in the cumbersome fashion characteristic of decision making in a community of numerous sovereign nations with a complex institutional architecture, sifted through a menu of options in successive attempts to contain the crisis. The immediate term challenge consisted of providing governments such as Greece, Italy, and Spain with enough capital to continue to repay existing debt and issue new debt, and shoring up banks in the EU holding substantial amounts of sovereign debt of these governments.[23] The most contentious issue concerned whether or not the ECB would become a "lender of last resort" akin to the Federal Reserve Bank of the United States, which has the power to create virtually unlimited amounts of money and which was instrumental to lifting the United States from the depths of financial crisis in 2009. While the ECB did engage in significant purchases of the bonds of highly indebted governments, it refrained from fully embracing this role. Still, over time, citizens in Germany and other member states progressively acknowledged that the costs of a Eurozone breakup would exceed those of saving monetary union. Today, the member states and institutions of the EU are engaged in a familiar process: collectively developing new mechanisms to negotiate their way through turbulent times.

THE EU AS A GLOBAL ACTOR

The EU's Quest for Relevance

While the architects of European integration seek to compete on an equal footing with the United States economically—and do so in setting rules and regulations governing global exchange—they do not aspire to match U.S. military capability. They do, however, wish to play a larger global role in exercising political and diplomatic influence.

In addition to the significant advance of economic union in the postwar era, the EU has developed as a community of values. The EU is defined by its commitment to tolerance, human rights, and especially the rule of law. Consistent with this identity, the EU has emerged as a global leader in the provision of humanitarian and development aid. The European Commission's humanitarian aid division, for example, provides nearly $1 billion a year in relief aid in response to natural disasters and to zones of conflict in a wide range of countries. The **Community's Development Fund** also provides for nonemergency assistance to promote development in African, Caribbean, and Pacific states; the budget for this aid totals nearly $30 billion for the 2008–2013 period.[24]

Speaking most directly to the global aspirations of the EU is the creation in 2009 of a European External Action Service (EEAS)—in essence, the EU's own diplomatic corps. The **Treaty of Lisbon**, which entered into force on December 1, 2009, provided for the creation of the EEAS and a **High Representative of the Union for Foreign Affairs and Security Policy**—similar to the EU's own Secretary of State—to oversee the EEAS and provide direction and coherence to an emerging common EU foreign and security policy. However, the division of labor between the High Representative and the EEAS, on the one hand, and the foreign ministries of national governments, on the other, remains a work in progress.

Unquestionably, the EU is actively engaged in the advancement of development, markets, and the rule of law through diplomatic means across the globe.[25] Through its Common Security and Defense Policy (CSDP), the EU is involved in numerous civilian and military missions of capacity building (preparing the national police force in the Democratic Republic of Congo to help preserve order during a transition to democracy, for example, or training a **Palestinian Authority** police force) and peacekeeping (monitoring the return of displaced persons following the 2008 conflict in Georgia, for example).[26] But how far does the influence of the EU truly extend, and how effectively can the EU foster internalization of its values beyond the sphere of countries to which it can promise membership?

The transformative impact of the EU was highly visible in the central and eastern European countries that went through the process of accession between the early 1990s and 2007. There is some evidence, on the other hand, that EU influence may be waning as a thriving and strategically located Turkey uses its resources to cultivate its relations to the east. Will the EU's eastern partnership program have a formative impact on economic and political conditions in Ukraine, Belarus, Moldova, and countries of the Southern Caucasus that have proven long resistant to reform? More broadly, will the EU complement the United States in efforts to provide leadership to meet the challenges of global financial instability and climate change? Will the EU be a competitor of the United States for close economic ties and partnership with China?

In the end, the crucial question to ask about the EU in the second decade of the twenty-first century is not whether it will survive, but whether it will continue to be a maker of history, as Jacques Delors wished, or will once again fade into the background amidst a shifting global configuration of power.

NOTES

1. In May 2010, the Greek government was able to draw on rescue funds from the EU and the International Monetary Fund (IMF) in the amount of $150 billion (110 billion euros) over a three-year period, and it subsequently enacted severe budget cuts, including reductions in public-sector wages and pensions and in spending on everything from health care to defense. In late November 2010,

Ireland, whose banks had accumulated massive losses that the Irish government decided to fully guarantee in order to prevent a run on the banking system, was rescued by $114 billion (about 85 billion euros) of EU and IMF funds. In turn, the Irish government embarked on a four-year plan of $20 billion in budget cuts to slash its budget deficit from an astonishing 32 percent of gross domestic product (GDP). Inflicting pain on a wide swath of Ireland's middle and lower-middle class, the cuts would involve significant shrinkage in the number of public-sector workers, stiff reductions in social welfare spending, and a sharp cut in the minimum wage as well as an increase in the value added tax paid by consumers. Both Greece and Ireland experienced substantial public protest in response to the cuts. While Greek and Irish citizens bemoaned their loss of domestic sovereignty regarding government spending choices, citizens in Germany, Austria, and other EU member countries expressed their distaste for rescuing governments whose practices were not as fiscally responsible as their own. A particular source of tension was the Irish government's fixed 12.5 percent business tax rate, which was designed to lure businesses to Ireland and was a significant contributor to the rise of the "Celtic tiger" in the 1990s and 2000s, but which policy makers in other member states viewed as a massive loss of potential tax revenue.

2. See the European Council's background report on EU Energy Policy, February 4, 2011, accessible on the website of the European Council at www.european council.europa.eu/media/171257/ec04.02.2011-factsheet-energy-pol_finaldg .en.pdf.

3. The full text of the Schuman Declaration, issued on May 9, 1950, may be found on the Europa website at http://europa.eu/abc/symbols/9-may/decl_en.htm. To this day, May 9 is celebrated as "Europe Day" throughout the EU and is considered one of the core symbols of the identity of the EU, along with its flag (which consists of a circle of twelve gold stars, representing solidarity and harmony between the citizens of Europe, on a blue background), anthem (Beethoven's "Ode to Joy"), and motto ("Unity in Diversity").

4. The Schuman Declaration.

5. In fact, the member states took the steps necessary to complete establishment of the EEC by July 1, 1968.

6. Crude oil was priced at about $3.00 per barrel in 1972; two years later the price was about $12.00 following the embargo on oil supplies. The price rose to $35 in 1981. See WRTG Economics at www.wtrg.com/prices.htm.

7. The accession of any country to the EU requires negotiation of a treaty, which must be ratified by all existing member states. Accordingly, any single member state government can veto a new application for admission.

8. These countries were the Czech Republic, Hungary, Poland, Slovakia, Slovenia, and the Baltic countries of Estonia, Latvia, and Lithuania. The Greek portion of Cyprus and the tiny Mediterranean archipelago of Malta also joined the EU in 2004.

9. This took place at the Copenhagen meeting of the council of heads of state and government of the member states (the "European Council," not to be confused

with the "Council of Europe," a deliberative body located in Strasbourg, France, founded in 1949 to advance democracy and human rights in Europe).

10. The full "Copenhagen criteria" may be found on the EU's Enlargement website at http://ec.europa.eu/enlargement/enlargement_process/accession_process/criteria/index_en.htm.

11. Statement by European Commission president José Manuel Durão Barroso at the signature ceremony of the Accession Treaty of Croatia, December 9, 2011. Accessed on December 30, 2011, at http://europa.eu/rapid/pressReleasesAction.do?reference=SPEECH/11/869&format=HTML&aged=0&language=EN&guiLanguage=en.

12. Turkey's population in 2011 is approximately seventy-five million. The Population Division of the UN Department of Economic and Social Affairs projects a Turkish population of nearly ninety-eight million in 2050, compared with a decline to seventy-nine million for Germany. See table A11 in the Population Division's document "World Population to 2300" at www.un.org/esa/population/publications/longrange2/WorldPop2300final.pdf.

13. French President Nicolas Sarkozy was the principal European proponent of this view, having repeatedly stated that Turkey is not geographically part of Europe. Sarkozy took this position during his campaign for the French presidency in 2007, and he reaffirmed his preference for a "privileged partnership" as recently as February 2011 while on a state visit to Turkey. See "Sarkozy Reaffirms Opposition" (2011).

14. The June 2006 European Council meeting concluded that the next council meeting would continue the debate on enlargement, "including the Union's capacity to absorb new members and further ways of improving the quality of the enlargement process on the basis of the positive experiences accumulated so far. It recalls in this connection that the pace of enlargement must take the Union's absorption capacity into account." See the Presidency Conclusions of the June 15/16 Brussels European Council at www.consilium.europa.eu/uedocs/cms_Data/docs/pressdata/en/ec/90111.pdf.

15. For an assessment of the impact of the Lisbon Strategy on national economies, including macroeconomic performance, social policy, employment policy, and other areas, see Smith (2012).

16. The phrase is from the first line of the preamble to the 1957 Treaty of Rome, which reads, "Determined to lay the foundations of an ever-closer union among the peoples of Europe . . ." and continues to list other motives and objectives for the creation of the EEC. For the text, see http://ec.europa.eu/economy_finance/emu_history/documents/treaties/rometreaty2.pdf.

17. Speaking before the College of Europe (established to train civil servants for the institutions of the EC) in Bruges, Belgium, in October 1989, Delors said, "The founding fathers wanted to see an end to internecine strife in Europe. But they also sensed that Europe was losing its place as the economic and political centre of the world. Their intuition was confirmed before our very eyes, to the point in the 1970s when we had to choose between survival and decline." Speaking

in the context of the incipient crumbling of socialist regimes in central and eastern Europe, Delors proclaimed, "There is a need for urgency, for history does not wait. As upheavals shake the world, and the other 'Europe' in particular, our re-invigorated Community must work for increased cohesion and set objectives commensurate with the challenges thrown down by history." The full text of the address is available on the European Navigator website at www.ena.lu/address_given_jacques_delors_bruges_17_october_1989-02-10171.

18. The "Cecchini Report," named in recognition of the senior European Commission official, Paolo Cecchini, who led the committee responsible for overseeing the study, found that the single market would produce two million new jobs in the medium-term (five to six years), would add approximately 5 percent to the EU's GDP, and would reduce consumer prices through greater competition. For the text of the summary report, see "Europe 1992" (1988).

19. The initial members were Austria, Belgium, Finland, France, Germany, Ireland, Italy, Luxembourg, the Netherlands, Portugal, and Spain.

20. The seminal article here is Sandholtz's "Choosing Union" (1993). Sandholtz addresses the intriguing question of why governments were willing to make this dramatic commitment to abandon national control over monetary policy.

21. According to the ECB, approximately 70 percent of euro notes would be put into circulation through ATM machines. Overall, introduction of the euro required the distribution of 14.25 billion banknotes and more than 50 billion coins. See Duisenberg's (2001) speech.

22. At the end of 2009, the dollar's share of global foreign exchange reserves was about 62 percent; that of the euro was approximately 27 percent. The euro circulates in an integrated market of more than 325 million consumers (a subset of the larger single market, with approximately 500 million people). See statistical table no. 8 in ECB (2010).

23. The medium-term challenge is to restore growth in those states (especially Greece) engaged in severe fiscal austerity, since the critical ratio of debt (the numerator) to GDP (the denominator) will not decline in the absence of economic growth, which both increases government revenues and enlarges the denominator of the debt to GDP calculation.

24. See the website of the European Commission's Humanitarian Aid & Civil Protection department at http://ec.europa.eu/echo/index_en.htm.

25. This is the central message of Mark Leonard's interesting, well-argued, but exceptionally optimistic *Why Europe Will Run the 21st Century* (2005).

26. For details of completed and ongoing CSDP missions, see the EU External Action CSDP web page at www.consilium.europa.eu/showpage.aspx?id=268&lang=EN.

REFERENCES

Berman, Sheri. 2006. *The Primacy of Politics, Social Democracy and the Making of Europe's Twentieth Century*. Cambridge: Cambridge University Press.

Churchill, Winston. 1946. "The Tragedy of Europe." Speech given on September 19. Available at numerous websites, including the Churchill Society of London, www.churchill-society-london.org.uk/astonish.html.

Duisenberg, Wim. 2001. "The Euro, Our Money." Speech by president of the European Central Bank at the first conference of National Central Banks, Brussels, March 6. www.ecb.int/press/key/date/2001/html/sp010306.en.html.

"Europe 1992: The Overall Challenge [Summary of the Cecchini Report]. SEC (88) 524 final, 13 April 1988." 1988. Archive of European Integration, University of Pittsburgh. http://aei.pitt.edu/3813/.

European Central Bank. 2010. "The International Role of the Euro." July, statistical table no. 8. www.ecb.int/pub/pdf/other/euro-international-role201007en.pdf?3ed08f8c845f3b7bbcdd9b592fec8826.

European Commission. 2010. *Commission Staff Working Document: Lisbon Strategy Evaluation Document.* Brussels, February 2. Accessed March 24, 2011. http://ec.europa.eu/archives/growthandjobs_2009/pdf/lisbon_strategy _evaluation_en.pdf.

Hooghe, Liesbet, and Gary Marks. 2003. "Unraveling the Central State, But How? Types of Multilevel Governance." *American Political Science Review* 97, no. 2 (May): 233–43.

Judt, Tony. 1996. *A Grand Illusion: An Essay on Europe.* New York: Hill & Wang.

Leonard, Mark. 2005. *Why Europe Will Run the 21st Century.* London: Fourth Estate.

Maas, Willem. 2007. *Creating European Citizens.* Lanham, Md.: Rowman and Littlefield.

Milward, Alan. 1992. *The European Rescue of the Nation State.* London and New York: Routledge.

Monnet, Jean. 1962. "A Ferment of Change." *Journal of Common Market Studies* 1, no. 1: 203–11.

Risse, Thomas. 2010. *A Community of Europeans? Transnational Identities and Public Spheres.* Ithaca, N.Y.: Cornell University Press.

Sandholtz, Wayne. 1993. "Choosing Union: Monetary Politics and Maastricht." *International Organization* 47: 1–39.

"Sarkozy Reaffirms Opposition to Turkey's EU Membership." 2011. *Euronews,* February 25. Accessed February 26, 2011. www.euronews.net/2011/02/25/ sarkozy-reaffirms-opposition-to-eu-membership/.

Scharpf, Fritz W. 2002. "The European Social Model." *Journal of Common Market Studies* 40, no. 4: 645–70.

Smith, Mitchell P., ed. 2012. *Europe and National Economic Transformation: The EU After the Lisbon Decade.* London and New York: Palgrave Macmillan.

van Kersbergen, Kees, and Philip Manow. 2009. *Religion, Class Coalitions and Welfare States.* Cambridge: Cambridge University Press.

7

Latin America

ALAN MCPHERSON

No kidding: Brazil's nude carnival queen may best express Latin America's foreign policy. Viviane Castro, who held the title in 2009, painted the smiling image of President Barack Obama on one of her thighs as she paraded down the streets of Rio. The gesture was no doubt taken lightly by most. But what appeared as a mere sign of adulation for the popular new president was not so. Those looking closer at the thigh in question—and there were no doubt many—noted that Castro painted Brazilian president Luiz Inácio Lula da Silva on her other thigh. Completing the fresco *al fresco* was the word *vendese* (for sale) on her stomach. It was not adulation but an expression of the Brazilian fear that U.S. corporations are destroying the Amazon.

Those who know Latin America should not have been surprised. To begin with, they know that carnivals have long been opportunities for the "street" to thumb its collective nose at the powers that be. In this case, the message was that behind the admiration and hope generated by the election of Obama lay a slew of serious, long-term disagreements over policy that betray a tectonic shift in the region's outlook on the world.

Of course, there is no such thing as a "Latin American" foreign policy. The chapter in this volume by Mark Frazier makes the point that international relations are conducted primarily by nation-states, not by regions or "international systems," and experts of Latin America have long observed that things are no different in their region. In fact, Latin Americans are perhaps some of the peoples of the earth most proud of their national identity and jealous of their national sovereignty. Latin America remains, as it has been since gaining independence in the early nineteenth century, a diverse set of republics that have kept their distance from each other as well as from any imperial power. Latin American leaders are still not nearly as united or coordinated as the European Union.

Yet there *are* discernible trends in the region's international relations, and this chapter identifies them. The chapter begins by showing how, since the end of the Cold War, trends have mostly percolated from the bottom of the socioeconomic ladder, where ordinary Latin Americans have increasingly been dissatisfied, to affect the foreign policy attitudes of those at the top.

Those attitudes have included a split between those who still favor the **neoliberal economics** championed by the United States and those who openly challenge them. Next, the chapter shows that, regardless of the split, both sides have been in favor of **globalization** and, particularly, of efforts to integrate the region itself so that it may begin to act as one before the other consolidating regions of the world—North America, Europe, East Asia. So the story comes full circle: the unhappiness with the status quo of many at the bottom (and middle and top) has prompted international changes that in turn caused greater discontent at the bottom. All is not dark, to be sure, and the last section identifies more positive trends. Overall, what is certain is that, for the first time in the history of Latin American international relations, the bottom is having its say.

INEQUALITY AND POVERTY

The poor are speaking partly because they are more numerous and more desperate than ever. Latin American citizens are largely skeptical about their own governments. With the spread of free media and democracy—constitutional government has been the norm for a generation now—has come more criticism of incompetence, corruption, and human rights abuses. The institutions of good government—legislative houses, courts, the police—are still largely undeveloped and weak, leaving most Latin Americans to fend for themselves. The result? The people are not amused; in fact, they are downright cynical. In 2008 only 44 percent of them said they had "a lot" or "some" faith in government. (Yet confidence is rising: in 2010, 17 percent of Latin Americans thought that government could solve "all" their problems, up from 8 percent in 2003; Latinobarómetro polls, 2008 and 2010).

In an indication that people do not trust their representatives to conduct foreign policy, just about every meeting of world leaders, it seems, prompts a parallel meeting of civil society groups with their own agenda for democracy and development. Brazil has hosted five out of nine World Social Forums, and the Fifth Summit of the Americas in Trinidad in 2009 ran alongside a smaller "Peoples' Summit," the fourth of its kind. The World Social Forum is not an anti-globalization protest. It is, itself, a global event that gathers thousands of groups and hundreds of thousands of activists from around the world to discuss, advertise, and exchange information about favorite causes, most of which revolve around local environmental or human rights issues. The forum has no fixed agenda, produces no common resolution, and passes no laws. Critics may see this lack of focus as a weakness, but to the organizers it is an alternative form of meeting, highly symbolic because no single voice dominates. Its motto is "Another World is Possible."

Much of the talk at these events revolves around the continuing—indeed, growing—poverty and inequality in the region. The rapid globalization of the continent since the 1980s has not resolved these problems and may have, in fact, worsened them. And this is strange because Latin America is relatively rich. Its **gross domestic product (GDP)** per person is three times that of East Asia and seven times that of South Asia and sub-Saharan Africa. Yet about one Latin American out of every ten lives on less than $2 per day, and another one out of twenty lives on a measly dollar a day. This statistic suggests the obvious: income distribution in the region, measured in the "Gini coefficient," is the worst in the world (Kacowicz 2009).

The devastation began as soon as globalization sped up—in the 1980s. Known as the "lost decade," the eighties in Latin America were marked by governments' inability to repay the massive foreign debts taken out in the 1970s. This debt drove governments to slash social spending. Per capita income actually fell by 1.1 percent on average that decade, and the poor rose from 41 percent of the population to 44 percent (Kacowicz 2009). In the 1990s GDPs rose but could not keep up with population growth. In the best years, around the middle of the nineties, Latin America's poor numbered 210 million, 50 million more than in the lost decade (Kacowicz 2009). By the end of the 1990s, the top tenth owned 2.5 percent more than at the beginning of the decade. So the region was not well prepared for the economic shocks of the late 1990s and the 2000s that occurred in Mexico, Brazil, and Argentina, especially. These economic shocks were largely caused by globalization in that unregulated foreign investors pulled their money out of these countries when signs of instability appeared.

The result today is that the income of the top 5 percent of Latin Americans is one quarter of the income pie, whereas the poorest 30 percent take a slim 7.5-percent slice even though the global recession of 2008 threw 9 million more into poverty. The middle class has been seriously eroded, too (Kacowicz 2009). Is globalization the only culprit? Probably not, considering much of the recent growth in inequality has little to do with it. Unequal land ownership going back centuries and skewed education levels—only 62 percent even enroll in high school—have played their part (Singh and Collyns 2005). Yet trade liberalization, the lowering of trade tariffs and barriers, has undone many of the **protectionist policies** that provided jobs at decent wages to workers. The many losers of a globalized trade—mostly peasants—have become the urban poor, those who swell the ranks of the disadvantaged.

There are exceptions. Chile, the most globalized country in Latin America with twenty-eight trade agreements signed, averaged a growth rate of 6.5 percent and doubled its per capita income from 1982 to 1997. And, unlike in other countries, growth overall *did* mean growth for the poor. Poverty in the geographically slim country declined from 39 percent in 1990 to 11.5 percent in 2009. Chile's success was mostly due to its fiscal prudence, control of inflation, free floating exchange rate, and average **tariffs** of only 2 percent. Chile notably socked away a rainy day fund when it had a surplus (Singh and Collyns 2005).

And when that rainy day came in 2008–2009, the government kept up its social payments, to the delight of Chileans.

Perhaps Latin Americans should never have expected so much positive change so quickly from **neoliberalism**; much anger stems from unmet expectations. Whatever its source, it is real anger, and since the middle class is traditionally the guarantor of robust democratic institutions, its disappearance threatens the political stability of the region as a whole. Country by country we have seen societies deeply marked by inequality—Venezuela, Bolivia, Honduras—fall into political crises that pitted small groups of wealthy citizens versus large groups of desperate ones who cling to grandiose promises of populists.

IMMIGRATION AND REMITTANCES

The bottom of Latin American society has its own foreign policy: it leaves and sends back money. Immigration and **remittances** have become the two most important international issues to the poor of Latin America. In 2007, the foreign-born—both legal and illegal—comprised one of every eight people in the United States, compared with one of twenty-one in 1970 (Camarota 2007). Well over half of these foreign-born people were from Latin America and the Caribbean, and about half of those were from Mexico. The money that these mostly young, working-class males send back to their families is tremendously important. In 2007 again, remittances back to the region rose to $66.5 billion. The biggest recipients were Mexico and Brazil, but the dollars meant more in Guyana (where they made up 43 percent of the GNP), Haiti (35 percent), and Honduras (25 percent; **Inter-American Development Bank** [IADB] 2009). In almost all countries remittances far outweigh any international aid payments. And remittances help the poor far more: no administrative costs for armies of aid workers, no "overhead" to corrupt local governments, just a commission to wire the funds and the rest can be applied to food, shelter, clothing, and school.

Of course, immigration is not the salvation that it may appear. Life in *el norte* is difficult, especially for **undocumented immigrants**. Immigrants work hard at jobs for which they are often overqualified, and they are frequently underpaid and discriminated against by those who know they can exploit them. They live away from their families, sometimes not seeing them for years. Some suffering is not worth it. Hundreds die every year trying to cross over from Mexico to the United States through barren, arid deserts and mountains. Thousands more are caught and deported. And most nefarious are the immigrant smugglers, or coyotes, many of whom help immigrants cross only in exchange for a massive debt to the sending family. Rodrigo, a father from El Salvador who migrated in 2001, had his family put up their house as collateral for a $6,000 coyote fee. The smuggler kept none of his promises of an easy voyage, and the Border Patrol caught Rodrigo. He spent two months in a foul jail in Arizona, then was transported to California, and finally was sent back to El Salvador. Undeterred, he tried again. As a reminder to Salvadorans that such stories are not unique, a monument to the "faraway brother" stands at the entrance of San Salvador (Agrego 2009).

The faraway brother also has to navigate significant hostility from U.S. groups opposed to undocumented immigrants. These groups highlight the illegal nature of their immigration and encourage draconian laws such as Arizona's SB 1070, passed in 2010, which required that police detain any person who prompted a "reasonable suspicion"—apparently race or ethnicity did not qualify—of being undocumented. The federal government immediately challenged the law on the basis that states cannot legislate immigration (Bacon 2008; Castañeda 2007; Chomsky 2007; Guskin and Wilson, 2007).

BOTTOM-UP, TOP-DOWN ANTI-NEOLIBERALISM

In many ways, civil society—defined as organized groups beyond the traditional spheres of government, corporations, military, and church—is organizing in response to the economic misery suffered by so many people and to the new possibilities afforded by expanded democracy and political rights. Many of the grievances of civil society are internal; for example, the continuing power of *machismo*, racism, and unfair land ownership are all well documented. Other grievances are international. The largely **indigenous** Bolivians who protested the selling of water rights in Cochabamba in 1999–2000 to the Bechtel corporation—and won—were, in very direct ways, waging a crusade against the **privatization** enshrined in **free trade** ideology. Shortly after a similar struggle over natural gas, indigenous leader Evo Morales explained that "from the point of view of the indigenous people here, [free trade is a way] to legalize the colonization of the Americas" (Dangl 2005). The indigenous rebellion in Chiapas, Mexico, began the day in 1994 when the **North American Free Trade Agreement** (NAFTA) went into effect as a way to protest the loss of autonomy and livelihood that poor southern Mexicans feared from corporate-led globalization. Indigenous groups have begun organizing everywhere, especially where they realize they have a majority or **plurality**, such as Bolivia, Guatemala, and Ecuador. Women, too, have achieved greater representation. In 1980 they accounted for 8 percent of national legislatures in Latin America. By 2012 Latin America joined Europe as the only two regions to have more women in these bodies than the world average.

The most important example of a bottom-up leader is Morales, now the president of Bolivia. An Aymara Indian, he is the first fully indigenous head of state in the hemisphere since the Spanish Conquest. He rose from the struggle begun in the 1980s by *cocaleros*, or coca farmers, to protect their livelihood—mostly against U.S.-aided repression from La Paz. Morales, himself, claims to have been tortured while U.S. Drug Enforcement Agency employees looked on. By 2005, the year of his election, Morales was the head of an alliance between (1) the largely indigenous coca farmers, the miners, and other workers and (2) urban middle-class students and intellectuals. His rhetoric was sometimes frightful—"Death to the Yankees!" chanted his supporters—but it was also based on Morales's own indigenist, **nationalist** issues: promoting the culture of the coca leaf, renegotiating natural gas contracts with foreign corporations, and ending the so-called war on drugs. White, wealthy Bolivians by and large hated him, and the four provinces dominated by them waged an autonomist struggle after Morales came to power.

But Morales has not been the only example of civil society elevating one of theirs to the presidency. Brazil's Lula, a former shoeshine boy, worked his way up the ranks of the ironworkers' union before he won the presidency in 2002. In El Salvador after the 1992 Chapultepec Accords that ended the civil war there, the Farabundo Martí Liberation Front (FMLN), an armed group, laid down its weapons. During the next decade and a half, the FMLN rebuilt itself as a major electoral party. It opposed the U.S.-inspired privatization of medicine, for example, winning to its cause the country's health care workers. Its presidential candidate, Mauricio Funes, triumphed in 2009. Though Funes himself was a former journalist and an outsider to the party, he was nevertheless the representative of a long-simmering organizing effort.

In 2006, Venezuela's Hugo Chávez walked up to the podium at the United Nations (UN) General Assembly and proceeded to rhetorically blast the president of the United States, George W. Bush. He said it smelled of sulfur around the podium because "the devil" (Bush) had been there the previous day. For most of the world's media, that quote provided the headline and, in fact, the entire story. Yet those who listened to Chávez's entire speech noticed that it was a comprehensive attack not just on Bush or even the United States, but also on neoliberalism's "current pattern of domination, exploitation and pillage of the peoples of the world," as he put it. "The American empire is doing all it can to consolidate its system of domination" (Wikipedia 2011). Neoliberalism, goes the argument of Chávez and others, equals selling national economies to a small number of capitalist investors. These investors buy up more and more capital until they monopolize markets to drive down salaries, bribe politicians to promote their interests, and rewrite the rules of the global game to benefit only themselves.

Chávez, however, did not emerge from civil society. He came up through the military, and he gained power and maintained his hold on the presidency through populist policies that redistributed petroleum profits to the poor and the sick, thus cementing their allegiance. He has also acted against foreign investors in his country; for instance, he passed the Hydrocarbons Law of 2001 that raised royalty taxes on oil companies, and then in 2006 he forced those companies into joint ventures with Venezuela's government-owned petroleum giant. Many have predicted that sustained dips in petroleum prices would mean the end of Chávez. His lack of roots in civil society is also reflected in the fact that many of his critics are to be found among union members and students. And while many no doubt are grateful for his food and medical subsidies, they fear his motto: "Socialism for the 21st Century." Seventy-two percent of Venezuelans, in fact, want to keep the free-market model.

To encourage his brand of international defiance, Chávez has created the Bolivarian Alliance for the Peoples of Our America (ALBA), an integration scheme that includes eight full member states and promotes bartering among the members instead of liberalization. From 1999 to 2006 Venezuela benefited from high oil prices and spent $16 to $25 billion on foreign aid, including paying off $7 billion of Argentina's and Ecuador's debt. Cuba, long a self-declared enemy of neoliberalism, has probably benefited the most from high oil prices, sending its surplus of doctors abroad in exchange for much-needed petroleum at prices so low it has enabled doubling the minimum wage and increasing pensions to the elderly. Through ALBA, Cuba and Venezuela now offer free eye surgery to anyone in the hemisphere.

Also top-down but somewhat less populist are the governments that arose in Chile and Argentina since the turn of the century. They have been far more open to business interests but still drive hard bargains with international organizations. Argentina under President Néstor Kirchner, for instance, refused to pay the **International Monetary Fund (IMF)** its debt incurred under previous governments until the IMF agreed to renegotiate. The IMF caved. Néstor's wife, Cristina Fernández de Kirchner, herself won the presidency in 2007, demonstrating the popularity of Kirchner policies (Edwards 2010; Hershberg and Rosen 2006; Kozloff 2008; Silva 2009; Weyland, Madrid, and Hunter 2010).

JAMES MONROE, R.I.P.

Anti-neoliberalism has put the final nail in the coffin of the Monroe Doctrine. The doctrine first announced by U.S. president James Monroe in 1823, which claimed that Europe should stay out of Latin American affairs, has finally breathed its last. Some might think the demise of this doctrine is attributable to the end the Cold War—Washington can no longer use the bugbear of Soviet influence to help overthrow regimes like it did in Guatemala in 1954, Chile in 1970, Grenada in 1983, and Panama in 1989. This explanation is, of course, partly true (Brands 2010; Grandin 2004; McPherson 2006).

But the Monroe Doctrine was always about more than U.S. military intervention. In the 1990s, the **Washington Consensus** on neoliberalism, promoted actively by George H. W. Bush and Bill Clinton, was also Monroe's legacy since it assumed U.S. leadership and the hemispheric pursuit of U.S. priorities—in this case, a reduction of barriers for capital, a privatization of the public domain, and reduced spending on social services like health and education. Latin America followed the advice. Argentina sold off fifty-one firms and made $18 billion. Mexico sold a whopping thousand firms for $12 billion. From 1986 to 1995, tariffs on imports dropped from 42 percent to 14! In Colombia alone they dropped from 83 to 7 percent. In the 1990s the region seemed to be doing well, with growth rates of 3.2 to 4 percent (Kacowicz 2009).

Now, however, Latin American political leaders all along the political spectrum are predisposed to reject U.S. leadership on hemispheric issues. To be sure, we have the neglect, incompetence, and fear mongering of the George W. Bush administration to thank for this situation. Reacting to the brusqueness of U.S. diplomacy and to its faulty intelligence, for instance, both Mexico and Chile, members of the UN Security Council during the run-up to the Iraq War, refused to support a U.S. resolution. Otherwise Bush showed his ignorance of Latin America when in 2002 he asked his Brazilian counterpart, "Do you have blacks, too?"

But the defiance that we witness today would have emerged with or without Bush. The United States is no longer *numero uno* in Latin America. During the Cold War, it consistently led the Soviets, Europe, and Cuba in favorability ratings as polled by the U.S. Information Agency and others. In an October 2008 poll, Spain, Japan, the European Union, and China rated higher than the United States in the eyes of Latin Americans. In fact, the favorability of the United States was at its lowest ever, 58 percent, down from 73 percent in 2001 (Latinobarómetro poll 2008). An even more recent multi-country poll from April 2009 showed that only 43 percent of Latin Americans had a positive image of the United States. The Chinese fared better by 4 points and Europe, by 14 (Oppenheimer 2009). Numbers went up with the arrival of Obama but did not close the gap.

Reflecting this new low, the United States is losing its hold on institutions that provided it with leverage in Latin America. The IMF, facing a full-bore challenge to its austerity programs from free-spending social democracies, has lost much of its ability to lend in the hemisphere. One scholar calls the loss of the IMF's power in Latin America the greatest change in the financial world since the collapse of **Bretton Woods Monetary System** (North American Congress on Latin America [NACLA] 2009). Another institution losing its clout is the military. Militaries in the Americas are increasingly subordinate to civilians and less willing to follow the guidelines of their traditional taskmasters at the Pentagon and the Central Intelligence Agency (CIA). When the United States signed a pact with Colombia in 2009 to keep its base rights for its 1,400 personnel there—a commonplace deal during the Cold War—Chávez warned Venezuelans that imperialism was creeping ever closer and predicted "one hundred years of war" (Basas 2009).

As a result of all this, Latin American leaders are now openly celebrating the inability of the United States to direct Latin America's affairs. In 2008 in

Bolivia, for instance, Morales expelled U.S. ambassador Philip Goldberg for meddling in Bolivian politics, and Washington retaliated by banishing Bolivia's man, Gustavo Guzmán. Guzmán noted a shift in the bilateral dynamic. "The U.S. embassy is historically used to calling the shots in Bolivia, violating our sovereignty, treating us like a banana republic." "Morales's victory," as he called it, "represented both a defeat of past U.S. policies and a challenge to see if the United States could bend itself to the new realities of Bolivia" (Burbach 2009).

To make things worse for Washington, the Union of South American Nations (UNASUR), a new forum for diplomacy that excludes the United States, *did* meddle in the Bolivian crisis, and *it* did so successfully. It declared its "'full and decided support" for Morales, a statement that helped diffuse a provincial challenge to Morales. The Bolivian president was ecstatic: "For the first time in South America's history," he crowed, "the countries of our region are deciding how to resolve our problems without the presence of the United States" (Burbach 2009).

For its part, Venezuela is aggressively trying to exclude and replace the United States as an arm-twister of small countries. ALBA and the Bank of the South, both of them **multilateral** economic schemes led by Venezuela, are explicitly designed to keep Washington out. Venezuela also has a controlling interest in Telesur, a television network beamed to twenty nations that presents itself as an alternative to CNN and other "northern" cable news channels. And Chávez has the *bolívars* (the Venezuelan currency) to do it: In one year he provided $9 billion in aid and loans to finance the purchase of his petroleum by the Caribbean, more than four times what the United States spent in the region. Venezuela is also providing an alternative source of financing to a myriad of countries. Because of its help, Bolivia ran a **current account** surplus equal to 14 percent of its GDP (NACLA 2009).

Even Mexico, the Latin American country most linked to the United States, has an increasingly liberated foreign policy. Mexico City was traditionally leftist in its internal politics but guarded in its encouragement of Latin American revolution. But now the fear of upsetting the gringo is gone. In 2008 Mexico slapped tariffs on ninety U.S. goods in retaliation for restrictions on cross-border trucking. And where Mexico *does* agree with the United States it now often takes the lead, for instance in crafting the anti-drug, $1.4 billion Mérida Initiative.

Perhaps the most potent sign of U.S. impotence was the death of the Free Trade Area of the Americas (FTAA), which failed to materialize by its deadline of 2005. South America's opposition to U.S. agricultural **subsidies** mercilessly killed this attempt, launched in 1994, to extend NAFTA to the rest of the hemisphere. To take just one statistic, Washington gives its farmers a $20 billion shot in the arm every year, whereas Mexico City can only afford $3.5 billion. The result has been that U.S. corn, dumped on Mexican markets, has lowered the price so much that thousands of producers abandoned the crop, either switching to other crops, moving to cities, or migrating . . . to the *Estados Unidos*. The motor of the FTAA was to be the Summit of the Americas. But by the time it gathered for a fifth meeting in April 2009, its agenda had strayed from mostly promoting corporate trade toward more diverse and less controversial goals: "Human Prosperity, Energy Security, and Environmental Sustainability."

Candidate Obama's sole campaign speech focusing on Latin America in May 2008 was titled "Renewing U.S. Leadership in the Americas." It was full of progressive ideas for the continent. But few assumed that Latin America wanted to be led by an outside power—because that is what the United States has become.

BRAZIL: THE NEW LEADER OF LATIN AMERICA?

The largest and most populous nation in Latin America—fifth in the world on both counts—Brazil may be the true spearhead of Latin America's foreign policies, not Venezuela. Latin Americans polled in 2010 certainly thought so (Latinobarómetro poll 2010). After all, half of the people and GDP of South America are Brazilian. Brazil has going for it not only size but also economic success and ideological flexibility. It has also proven itself as a great democracy. Since his first election in 2002, Lula has consistently been the most popular leader in Latin America, far above Chávez. And Lula's predecessor, Fernando Henrique Cardoso, also proved himself an able and honest two-termer who passed on the presidency without violence—in itself a feat for Brazil. Brazil used to be the perpetual "country of the future," but its time may have arrived (Shifter and Joyce 2009).

Much of the reason for Brazil's ascendancy is attributable to intelligent economic choices. Under Cardoso's watch, the government addressed a major inflation crisis—it ran near 2,500 percent—by giving the Central Bank the autonomy to keep prices low and by allowing their new currency, the *real*, to float. It also encouraged the formation of home-grown **multinational corporations**—Petrobras for petroleum, Vale for mining, and Embraer for aircraft—out of what were, in some cases, slow-moving state companies. The government has also continued to invest hundreds of billions in **infrastructure**. Lula, who left the presidency on January 1, 2011, did most to pair this financial wizardry with generous social policies, namely the doubling of the minimum wage and the introduction of the Bolsa Familia, which paid poor families to send their children to school, thus reducing poverty, child labor, and crime and investing in the country's future ("Brazil Takes Off" 2009). Lula left office with approval ratings of 87 percent, and his handpicked successor, Dilma Roussef, a former **Marxist guerrilla**, promised more of the same.

Because of its solid bases, Brazil has recovered well from the recession that hit the globe in 2008. Its economy is growing annually at a rate of 5 percent and the *real* is gaining on the dollar. By mid-century Brazil will be the fifth largest economy in the world—behind China, the United States, India, and Japan. Offshore oil discoveries in 2007 are helping fuel the optimism, as is petroleum self-sufficiency. And Brazil has not gone the way of Venezuela in pegging its success only to petroleum; it has diversified its economy. Rio de Janeiro's success in winning the right to host the 2016 Olympics has been a kind of recognition of its achievements from the global community ("Brazil Takes Off" 2009).

Reflecting its new status, Brazil has taken a role in the mediation of Latin American conflicts, for instance in a cross-border conflict between Ecuador and Colombia in March 2008. It is also a leader of the **Group of 20,** a gathering of finance ministers and central bank governors. President-elect Obama wisely engaged Lula early on, phoning him the day after Obama's victory and stating that Brazil should be included in the G-8 group of industrialized nations.

Brazil is also becoming a global example. In 2003 the investment house Goldman Sachs designated it one of the **BRICS countries**—along with Russia, India, China, and South Africa, all new leaders of the developing world. Many at the time were skeptical, but no more. Brazil has treated its foreign investors with respect and is exporting ever more petroleum, minerals, and agricultural goods. As a result, investment is flowing into Brazil as it leaves other countries. Early in 2009 China announced that it would lend Petrobras $10 billion in exchange for as much as 200,000 barrels a day of crude for the following ten years ("Brazil Takes Off" 2009).

Brazil has also emerged as a world diplomat. The much-admired **Sérgio Vieira de Mello** was UN ambassador to Iraq until on August 19, 2003, terrorists bombed the building he was in, taking de Mello's life. And in 2010, Lula, named by *Time* magazine the globe's most influential leader, negotiated a **uranium** swap between Iran and Turkey meant to avert UN sanctions on Iran. (It failed.)

INTEGRATING FOR STRENGTH

In December 2008, thirty-three Latin American and Caribbean nations convened in Brazil for a mega-summit that, among other things, formally included Cuba. They did not, however, invite the United States. In February 2010 thirty-two of these (Honduras was not invited) banded into the Community of Latin American and Caribbean States, an embryonic **Organization of American States** (OAS) without the United States and Canada. Washington was also not sent invitations to join UNASUR, a Latin American NAFTA; the South American Defense Council, a Latin American **NATO**; or the Rio

Group, a multilateral diplomatic forum of twenty-three Latin American countries that may also one day become an OAS without the United States. And let us not forget the sub-regional trade compacts—Mercosur, the Andean Group, and the Central American Group—that also exclude the United States. This regional integration coupled with an exclusion of Washington signals that Latin America wants to approach the United States the way Europe does—as a separate and equal competitor on the global stage.

Latin Americans are integrating the continent not just to exclude the United States. They also do it to prosper and to avoid conflicts, and at a more inchoate level they do it to affirm their common identity. A $600 million highway across the imposing Andes, for instance, will soon link Brazil to Chilean ports. Chávez has been especially clever to sell his multilateral schemes as efforts to unite Latin Americans. The idea is so attractive that even U.S. allies such as Colombia, Peru, and Mexico are discussing joining the Bank of the South (NACLA 2009). Chávez's financial diplomacy is also working for Argentina and Ecuador—as mentioned previously, he's paid off $7 billion worth of their debt. And Chile's trade agreements should certainly not be deemed anti-U.S. but, rather, pro-Latin America (Suggett 2008). Brazil and Venezuela have also argued for years that there should be a South American defense organization, with Chávez justifying it on the grounds that, "from Mexico to Argentina, we are one whole nation" (Shifter and Joyce 2009). Under UNASUR, that vision came together on March 10, 2009, when, in Santiago, Chile, the defense ministers of every country in South America formed a formal "defense council" that would fall short of NATO's international army but still provide a forum where Latin America's militaries can discuss common issues and collaborate on solutions.

LATIN AMERICA'S NEW WORLD

Because of the diminished role of Washington, Latin America's foreign policy is becoming what it probably should always have been—global. Normalcy is finally here. For almost two centuries, Latin America operated under the shadow of the Monroe Doctrine, unable to define itself in the world as anything other than a "little brother," a **dependency**, or a weaker "neighbor." Now Latin American nations are deepening their formal and informal ties both with each other and beyond the Americas.

It should be no surprise that Latin American societies are rapidly globalizing. To be sure, Latin America has been part of the global economy for four centuries, since Europeans subjected its civilizations—and the millions of slaves they added to the mix—as a lesser labor force making exports for the rest of the world. Yet the newer definition of globalization, the interconnectedness to the world, has accelerated since the 1980s, when many governments abandoned the Import-Substitution-Industrialization (ISI) schemes inspired by leftist economists that were supposed to encourage domestic industry. ISI languished and created massive debts. So a new batch of leaders began to aggressively open their economies to privatization, **deregulation**, and foreign investment. The world poured into Latin America. To take just one index of that change, from 2002 to 2010 Internet use in Latin America increased from 19 to 39 percent (Latinobarómetro poll 2010). More meaningfully, trade with Europe in 2006 was worth $177 billion, about a third of trade with the United States. Spain especially has a strong presence there in banks, hotels, airlines, and phone companies such as Telefónica. There have been some clear winners of globalization. Chile, Costa Rica, Panama, and northern Mexico have all found something of value to export to the global marketplace. There is no reason, then, that Latin Americans should not globalize their foreign policies to match their new self-image.

Also key for much of the continent is the outreach beyond the seas. Apart from the traditional investment and involvement of East Asia and Europe, new powers now seek a foothold in Latin America, punctuating the displacement of the United States. Chávez, as usual, has been overt in courting U.S. adversaries like Iran and competitors like Russia, buying over $4 billion in military equipment from Moscow. Since 2001 Iran and Venezuela have signed a whopping 180 agreements, especially on oil and gas, and announced a $2 billion development fund for "anti-imperialist" countries. Chávez has vowed to "unite the Persian Gulf and the Caribbean" (Erikson 2007).

China has been the more delicate elephant in the room—but still an elephant. Compared with Russia and Iran, its interests have been more economic but far larger. It is a top-five trading partner to most Latin American countries, totaling $80 billion in trade in 2007. In Venezuela alone, Chinese trade totals $10 billion, up from $200 million when Chávez came to power. Chinese-Venezuelan partnerships notably have built cheap computers and cell phones for low-income Latin Americans (Al Jazeera English 2009). China especially competes with the United States for the region's energy resources. In 2004 Venezuela sold only 12,000 barrels per day of petroleum to China; in 2011 it sold 460,000 per day, about half what it exported to the United States (Romero and Barrionuevo 2009). And China doubled its development fund with Venezuela to $12 billion and lent similar sums to Ecuador and Argentina in a bid to meet future energy needs. Washington certainly is noticing that Beijing's $10 billion payment to Brazil's Petrobras is almost as much as the IADB gave to all Latin America that same year (Romero and Barrionuevo 2009).

MITIGATING FACTORS:
INTERDEPENDENCE AND DIVISION

Chávez has long talked about realizing the Bolivarian dream of uniting South America—not surprisingly under a Venezuelan icon, Simón Bolívar—and the recent changes mentioned above might lead us to think that the dream has been realized. But there are several mitigating factors holding back integration.

First among these is the continuing interdependence between the United States and Latin America. Despite the Bush-era anti-Americanism from the south and neglect from the north, both will long be involved in each other's affairs and should not pretend otherwise. About half of U.S. trade is with Latin America, and about half of Latin America's exports end up in the United States. The global economic crisis further showed how the U.S. economy's troubles are also Latin America's troubles: the recession hit all the hemisphere's countries, many would-be immigrants to the United States stayed home, and some families even sent money *to* relatives north of the border. Lula notably stated that the best thing Washington could do for Latin America was to get its own economic house in order.

The most obvious involvement of the United States will be in Mexico, where the killing of 50,000 in drug-related violence along the border from 2006 to 2012 and the continuing movement of drugs northward and weapons southward are stinging reminders of the importance of good U.S.-Mexican relations. U.S. investment in Mexico has not slowed its flow since the signing of NAFTA in 1992, growing from $1.3 billion that year to $97.9 billion by 2011. As a result of NAFTA, Mexico's trade deficit with the United States has turned into a surplus and its northern region is prospering: there, only 12 percent live below the poverty line compared with to 47 percent in the south. Eighty-five percent of the country's exports end up in the United States.

Central America is also ever closer to the United States. Along with the Dominican Republic, it has emulated Mexico in signing a sweeping trade agreement, called DR-CAFTA, that will transform these small economies as not only more integrated into that of the United States but also more bound to free market principles. The Washington Consensus lives on in Central America and the Caribbean. Because of the trade ties, of remittances, and of the vast swath of humanity that lives in the United States, polls of Latin American public opinion consistently show that Central Americans are the most pro-U.S. Latin Americans.

As if Mexico and Central America and the Dominican Republic were not enough, Peru, Chile, Panama, and Colombia have also ratified free trade pacts with the United States. What these agreements do is not only reduce tariffs on goods but also provide easier access for capital. For example, they provide training and standards for customs procedures and food sanitation. They also shift intellectual property rights away from government and individuals and onto corporations.

Even the most critical Latin American leaders will continue to depend on the United States, and it on them. The United States continues to buy 10 percent of its imported oil from Venezuela, and Caracas needs those oil dollars—which account for 40 percent of its income—more than ever. Quito, the seat of the Ecuadorian government, is in the same boat. And despite their harsh rhetoric, Bolivia and Ecuador do not wish to lose U.S. trade preferences. If all the free trade deals now being negotiated go through, the United States will trade freely with a majority of the twenty Latin American republics. Even Nicaragua's president, Daniel Ortega, has championed DR-CAFTA despite his closeness to Chávez. Perhaps Nicaragua's eightfold increase in U.S. trade since 1993 has something to do with it (Roberts 2008).

Recognizing the trend of interdependence, President Obama has promised to expand, not retract, U.S. involvement in the region. The week before the 2009 Summit of the Americas, he penned an editorial for Latin American newspapers that promised movement on common initiatives such as drug trafficking, crime, and an "Energy and Climate Partnership for the Americas" (Tedford 2009). Obama also wants to triple the lending of the IADB, and the Summit of the Americas moved toward that goal (Romero and Barrionuevo 2009). The figure of Obama himself signals hope for U.S.–Latin American relations since he is among the most popular leaders in Latin America (Oppenheimer 2009). And, unlike during the Cold War, younger Latin Americans tend to be friendlier to Washington than their elders (Latinobarómetro poll 2008). But the second and more important factor mitigating Latin America's total independence from the United States is Latin America's own disunion. Perhaps one should never expect a united foreign policy to emerge from a few dozen republics, especially ones so divided by geography, history, language, religion, and race. Remember that South American Defense Council? Rumor is that it's really a Brazilian proposal to pre-empt Chávez's more aggressive alternative. And nasty rhetoric has marred many multilateral meetings between Latin Americans divided by arms races (Chile and Peru) and border troubles (Ecuador and Colombia). Make no mistake: domestic politics, nationalism, and plain old pettiness are alive and well and still shaping policies in Latin America.

The most serious dispute pits the two most ideological regimes in South America, Chávez's Venezuela against Colombia, where in 2010 right-wing Álvaro Uribe passed on the presidential sash to another conservative, Juan Manuel Santos. The conflict stems largely from the ongoing civil war between the Colombian government and the guerrillas of the Revolutionary Armed Forces of Colombia (FARC), who claim to be Marxists but find their true power from protection rackets, kidnapping, and controlling an area larger than Maryland. In 2008 Colombians captured a FARC laptop apparently showing that Chávez made payments of more than $300 million to the guerrillas. Chávez, who had already called Uribe a "shameless liar," denied it all but also defused the situation by helping liberate some FARC hostages. In 2009 Colombia found among FARC's cache some anti-tank rockets that used to belong to the Venezuelan government. The conflict eased with the arrival of Santos, but it did not dissipate completely.

SIGNS OF PROGRESS

The gloomy picture of international relations in Latin America can make us forget one bright side: the persistence of democracy. Even before the end of the Cold War, Latin Americans were choosing rule by the people rather than dictatorship. Between 1978 and 1991, fifteen Latin American nations turned to or returned to electoral democracy. Since then, there have been only three successful coups or forcible removals of elected leaders: Haiti in 1991 and 2004 and Honduras in 2009.

As important as the very existence of democracy has been its institutionalization by the inter-American system. At a meeting of the OAS in 1991 in Chile, delegates accepted the Santiago Declaration, in which members agreed to meet whenever any democracy was threatened. The process notably succeeded during the self-coup of Peru's Alberto Fujimori in 1992, pressuring him into early elections and restoring democracy within a year. In 2001's Summit of the Americas in Quebec City, a so-called democracy clause linked free trade agreements with democracy. Then on the fateful day of September 11, 2001, the OAS codified the clause into its Inter-American Democracy Charter, thereby enabling the suspension of an OAS member who did not adhere to "no democracy, no trade."

The transnational network of activists and diplomats who pushed through democracy institutions also celebrated important wins on the human rights front. For far too long, Latin American dictators and military regimes committed atrocious human rights abuses on their own civilians and even hunted down the exiles of other autocratic regimes in a multinational conspiracy called Operation Condor. While these regimes imprisoned, tortured, killed, or **"disappeared"** tens of thousands, the inter-American system worked to pursue human rights cases. Backed by the American Convention on Human Rights, the OAS created a commission to investigate violations and then a court to prosecute. But their efforts were largely in vain during the Cold War because abusers, often backed by U.S. support, could simply refuse to be investigated or brought to court.

Again it was the end of the Cold War that opened the floodgates for finding out the truth about the disappeared and bringing rights violators to justice. The dam broke in October 1998 when a Spanish judge named Balthasar Garzón issued an international warrant for the arrest of former Chilean dictator Augusto Pinochet, who was at the time in London. The charges were murder, conspiracy to murder, hostage taking, torture, and kidnapping. Pinochet resisted, with an army of lawyers this time. After Pinochet spent fifteen months under house arrest, the British government ruled that he had dementia and should be sent back to Chile. The next several years were a cat-and-mouse game between Pinochet and his Chilean supporters and a Chilean judge who was inspired by the Spanish example and prodded by the families of the victims. Pinochet died in 2006 before he was ever punished. But he *was* formally indicted, a great symbolic victory for human rights activists.

The ripples of the Pinochet wave are now rolling over the continent. Chile has convicted 150 former Pinochet cronies for human rights violations, and over 400 more are now under investigation or indictment. Former autocrats Gregorio Álvarez of Uruguay and Alberto Fujimori of Peru are both now spending twenty-five years in prison for their crimes. Argentina has also handed down hundreds of indictments. Even Cuba has released half its political prisoners under Raúl Castro. Perhaps most symbolic is that Michelle Bachelet, a former student activist tortured by Pinochet's secret police, won the presidency of her now-liberated country in 2006. In late 2009 another former prisoner who was tortured, José Mújica, took the presidency in Uruguay (Feitlowitz 1998; Payne 2008; Roht-Arriaza 2005).

CRIME ACROSS BORDERS

Right after Brazilians celebrated their successful bid for the Olympics, a drug **cartel** shot down a São Paulo police helicopter less than a mile from where the sports complexes will host the games. The crash was a devastating reminder of the growing ability of criminal organizations to threaten the security of international relations. Transnational crime can be summarized as two overlapping, intertwined problems: drug trafficking and gangs. Both are nefarious, society-destroying phenomena. That has long been known. But what is relatively new is that drugs and gangs are increasingly destabilizing whole governments and forcing security agencies to refocus themselves outward.

The basic problem is that drugs are such a lucrative business that there is little incentive for traffickers to stop moving them to other countries. Today half a gram of marijuana costs $1.70 to produce but sells on the street at $8.60. The coca leaf, once processed into cocaine, earns even more and gives farmers three to four harvests a year. Profits *just at the Mexican border* are about $80 billion per year. In the United States, the federal government spends about $12 billion yearly trying to staunch the flow of drugs northward, but the crops keeps growing and the twenty million U.S. users show little sign of cleaning up their act (Arias 2006; Carpenter 2003; Marcy 2010; Youngers and Rosin 2005).

Since the 1980s, the U.S. government has defined the drug problem in two fateful ways: first, as a "war" that must be fought with military hardware rather than development aid or diplomacy, and second, as a problem of "supply" that blames Latin Americans for the drug habits of the United States (and increasingly of Europe and Latin America itself). As a result, the U.S. government has sunk $7 billion into Colombia alone, only one fifth of which is non-military aid. The insistence of pursuing producers rather than consumers has notably heightened tensions with Bolivia, where Morales, a champion of *cocaleros*, has looked the other way as they exceed the limits of licit coca leaf farming.

Drug cartels are especially devastating the U.S.-Mexican border. They long ago corrupted the police. They then controlled municipal governments, newspapers, even civil society groups, instilling in the region an aura of lawlessness. After his election, President Felipe Calderón distrusted even the national police so much that he sent the Mexican military along the border. But soldiers could not resist the lure of the drug world: over 1,300 of them defected to work for cartels. Even dozens of U.S. border agents were discovered to have taken bribes. By 2010 the violence approached the level of an international war, as drug cartels threw a bomb at a U.S. consulate and even set off a car bomb in Ciudad Juárez—the first ever against authorities. At the border itself, the task of preventing trafficking while promoting trade has seemed like an impossible dilemma. Every year over 4 million trucks, 8 million trains, 88 million cars, and 50 million pedestrians cross. They simply cannot all be searched.

The street gangs are the ones who deal a lot of these drugs and protect those dealers. The gangs profit not only from drugs, but also from the absence of many parents from Latin American families and from the other crimes in which one is tempted to engage when armed. They run drugs and guns across borders and, like cartels, often control entire neighborhoods. Brazilian gangs have been made notorious by films such as *City of God* and *Elite Squad*. In Guatemala, transnational organized crime has infiltrated political parties, the National Police, and even the office of the attorney general, whose job it is to prosecute criminals. Gangs such as the **Mara Salvatrucha,** or **MS-13,** plague Central America more than any other area. The Northern Triangle of El Salvador, Guatemala, and Honduras is now one of the most violent areas in the world, and Guatemala has the highest rate of lynching of any country in the hemisphere. Overall, Latin America suffers from the highest homicide rate in the world (Ayers 2008; Bergman and Whitehead 2009; Di Tella, Edwards, and Schargrodsky 2009; Frühling, Tulchin, and Golding 2003).

OUTLIERS: CUBA AND HAITI

Cuba and Haiti stand largely outside the trends that have dominated Latin America and the Caribbean since the end of the Cold War: Cuba because of its ongoing communist regime, and Haiti because of its social blight.

Cuba is an enigma to much of the outside world, even to many Cubans. Its abandonment by the Soviet Union at the end of the Cold War and its economic weakness ever since has made it seem like its communist government, under **Fidel Castro** since 1959, would collapse. But it has withstood poverty, social discontent, and political dissent, most recently by young bloggers in Cuba who bemoan the slow pace of change. Another enigma to many is why U.S. policy toward Cuba has refused to budge much. Some liberalization under Clinton occurred, but then the Bush government tightened travel restrictions to an unprecedented degree, and the fifty-year trade **embargo** against the island continues. The overwhelming factor has been the Cuban American community in Florida, which historically has voted for any U.S. president who proved he was "tough" on Castro—a swing vote in a **swing state**, especially in 2000 and 2004. Many hoped that change would come when Obama won Florida without needing Cuban votes and won the nation without needing Florida. Obama did announce a loosening of travel rules, especially for Cuban families, but he did not venture to end the embargo, a move that needs to go through Congress. And more important, he placed the ball in Cuba's court, and Cuba, under Fidel's brother Raúl's rule since 2008, has been limited in its embrace of reform.

Two developments will likely break the logjam. One is the aging of the Miami Cubans. As they pass away so will their bitter memories of the Castros. The next generation of Cuban Americans is less ideological than their parents. Like the Cubans who left the island in the 1980s and 1990s, young Cuban Americans are generally more ambivalent (or less interested) in the Castros and Cuba's communist past. The second will be the growth of trade. In 2000 Congress approved cash sales of agricultural goods to Cuba. By 2008 the United States had become the island's main supplier of food and farm products, with sales totaling $711 million.

Cuba has already begun to normalize relations with the rest of the hemisphere. Cuba is important to Latin America not because of its economic or strategic value, but because Latin America sees in Cuba's integration into the continent a proof that Latin America can emerge as a collective of sovereign republics with common interests and identities. Venezuela is not the only country that has supported the normalization of relations with Cuba. At the last Summit of the Americas in April 2009, every Latin American leader called for an end to the embargo. Brazil has also given the island $1 billion in credit. Moreover, the presidents of Chile and Guatemala have visited Cuba, the latter apologizing for his country's role in the 1961 **Bay of Pigs attack** (Shifter and Joyce 2009; Chomsky, Carr, and Smorkaloff 2004; Erikson 2008; Suchlicki 2002; Sweig 2009).

Haiti presents a far bleaker picture than does Cuba and did so before the devastating earthquake of January 12, 2010, that killed a reported 300,000 and destroyed Port-au-Prince and the cholera outbreak that occurred later that year. It continually ranks lowest in the hemisphere in all UN human development indices—life expectancy, illiteracy, access to water, and general poverty. The causes are many: centuries of dictatorship, worsened by international ostracism; environmental devastation, exacerbated by frequent hurricanes; and a racial divide between a white and mixed-race French-speaking elite and a black Kreyol-speaking destitute mass. As a result, Haiti has experienced the most traumatic political upheavals since the end of the Cold War. Jean-Bertrand Aristide, its first democratically elected president, was ousted in a coup in 1991 and then restored by the Clinton administration. He proved an ineffective and corrupt leader who was paranoid about foreign intervention and who resorted to armed gangs to protect himself. And he was right to be afraid. In 2004 an alliance of drug-dealing gang members and internationally backed political opponents rose up and forced Aristide to flee. The international community—headed by the United States, Canada, France, and Brazil—has since had various peacekeepers in Haiti, which has prevented the military from taking over again. But elections have been marred by irregularities, and successive leaders have been unable to overcome the culture of corruption and much less to improve the lot of the ordinary Haitian. The earthquake of 2010 only made things worse (Farmer 2005; Girard 2010; Robinson 2008).

PRAGMATISM

All in all, in the nearly two decades since the end of the Cold War, the continent has fared rather well in its foreign policies, with no major wars or fundamental conflicts of interest. But re-invigorating a normal system of nation-states dealing with each other and with the outside world as sovereigns will not be as easy as it may appear.

The good news is that perhaps the most important concept in present Latin American international relations is pragmatism. It seems more than ever that sovereign states, and civil society groups within them, are making policy choices based on hard self-interest rather than ideology. As Secretary of State Hillary Clinton said in 2009, "Let's put ideology aside; that is so yesterday" (Landler 2009). And that is a good thing. What's more, President Obama seems the perfect U.S. president to share that vision. He has neither been seduced by the alluring thigh of the carnival queen nor deterred by her defiant stomach, and neither has Latin America.

REFERENCES

Agrego, Leisy J. 2009. "Rethinking Salvador's Transnational Families." *NACLA Report on the Americas*, November/December 2009, 28–33.

Al Jazeera English. 2009. "Oil Deals Smooth China-Venezuela Trade Ties." August 11. www.youtube.com/watch?v=6GzJvYYsv7c.

Arias, Enrique Desmond. 2006. *Drugs and Democracy in Rio de Janeiro: Trafficking, Social Networks, & Public Security.* Chapel Hill: University of North Carolina Press.

Ayers, Robert L. 2008. *Crime and Violence as Development Issues in Latin America and the Caribbean.* Washington, D.C.: World Bank.

Bacon, David. 2008. *Illegal People: How Globalization Creates Migration and Criminalizes Immigrants.* Boston: Beacon Press.

Basas, Richard. 2009. "Chavez's One Hundred Years War: A Lesson in Diplomacy." November 21. latinamerica.foreignpolicyblogs.com/2009/11/21/chavezs-one -hundred-years-war-a-lesson-in-diplomacy/.

Bergman, Marcelo, and Lawrence Whitehead, eds. 2009. *Criminality, Public Security, and the Challenges to Democracy in Latin America.* Notre Dame, Ind.: University of Notre Dame Press.

Brands, Hal. 2010. *Latin America's Cold War.* Cambridge, Mass.: Harvard University Press.

"Brazil Takes Off." 2009. *The Economist.* November 14. www.economist.com/node/14845197.

Burbach, Roger. 2009. "Treating Bolivia as a Sovereign Partner." *NACLA Report on the Americas*, January/February 2009, 33–35.

Camarota, Steven A. 2007. "Immigrants in the United States, 2007: A Profile of America's Foreign-Born Population." November. www.cis.org/immigrants_profile_2007.

Carpenter, Ted Galen. 2003. *Bad Neighbor Policy: Washington's Futile War on Drugs in Latin America.* New York: Palgrave Macmillan.

Castañeda, Jorge. 2007. *Ex Mex: From Migrants to Immigrants.* New York: The New Press.

Chomsky, Aviva. 2007. *"They Take Our Jobs!" And 20 Other Myths about Immigration.* Boston: Beacon Press.

Chomsky, Aviva, Barry Carr, and Pamela Maria Smorkaloff, eds. 2004. *The Cuba Reader: History, Culture, Politics.* Durham, N.C.: Duke University Press.

Dangl, Benjamin. 2005. "An Interview with Evo Morales (12/08/03)." *Upside Down World*, October 16. http://upsidedownworld.org/main/content/view/38/31/.

Di Tella, Rafael, Sebastian Edwards, and Ernesto Schargrodsky, eds. 2009. *Economics of Crime: Lessons for and from Latin America.* Chicago: University of Chicago Press.

Edwards, Sebastian. 2010. *Left Behind: Latin America and the False Promise of Populism.* Chicago: University of Chicago Press.

Erikson, Daniel P. 2007. "Ahmadinejad Finds it Warmer in Latin America." *Los Angeles Times*, October 3.

———. 2008. *The Cuba Wars: Fidel Castro, the United States, and the Next Revolution.* New York: Bloomsbury Press.

Farmer, Paul. 2005. *The Uses of Haiti.* Monroe, Maine: Common Courage Press.

Feitlowitz, Marguerite. 1998. *A Lexicon of Terror: Argentina and the Legacies of Torture.* New York: Oxford University Press.

Frühling, Hugo, and Joseph S. Tulchin, with Heather A. Golding, eds. 2003. *Crime and Violence in Latin America: Citizen Security, Democracy, and the State.* Washington, D.C.: Woodrow Wilson Center Press.

Girard, Philippe R. 2010. *Haiti: The Tumultuous History—From Pearl of the Caribbean to Broken Nation.* New York: Palgrave Macmillan.

Grandin, Greg. 2004. *The Last Colonial Massacre: Latin America in the Cold War.* Chicago: University of Chicago Press.

Guskin, Jane, and David Wilson. 2007. *The Politics of Immigration: Questions and Answers.* New York: Monthly Review Press.

Hershberg, Eric, and Fred Rosen, eds. 2006. *Latin America after Neoliberalism: Turning the Tide in the 21st Century?* New York: New Press.

Inter-American Development Bank. 2008. "Remittances to Latin America and the Caribbean Slower, IDB Fund Says." March 11. www.iadb.org/news/detail .cfm?language=EN&artid=4459&id=4459.

Kacowicz, Arie. 2009. "Globalization, Poverty, and Inequality: The Latin American Experience, 1982–2007." Paper presented at the International Studies Association, February 14–18.

Kozloff, Nikolas. 2008. *Revolution! South America and the Rise of the New Left.* New York: Palgrave Macmillan.

Landler, Mark. 2009. "Clinton Scores Points by Admitting Past U.S. Errors." *New York Times*, April 17.

Latinobarómetro polls. 2008 and 2010. www.latinobarometro.org.

Marcy, William L. 2010. *Politics of Cocaine: How U.S. Foreign Policy Has Created a Thriving Drug Industry in Central America.* Chicago: Lawrence Hill Books.

McPherson, Alan. 2006. *Intimate Ties, Bitter Struggles: The United States and Latin America Since 1945.* Washington, D.C.: Potomac Books.

North American Congress on Latin America. 2009. "Progressive Policy for the Americas? A NACLA Roundtable." *NACLA Report on the Americas,* January/February, 15–23.

Oppenheimer, Andrés. 2009. "Obama Most Popular Leader of the Americas." *Miami Herald,* April 18.

Payne, Leigh A. 2008. *Unsettling Accounts: Neither Truth Nor Reconciliation in Confessions of State Violence.* Durham, N.C.: Duke University Press.

Roberts, James M. 2008. "Rethinking the Summit of the Americas and Advancing Free Trade in Latin America." *Heritage Foundation Backgrounder,* August 8.

Robinson, Randall. 2008. *An Unbroken Agony: Haiti, from Revolution to the Kidnapping of a President.* New York: Basic Civitas.

Roht-Arriaza, Naomi. 2005. *The Pinochet Effect: Transnational Justice in the Age of Human Rights.* Philadelphia: University of Pennsylvania Press.

Romero, Simon, and Alexei Barrionuevo. 2009. "Deals Help China Expand Its Sway in Latin America." *New York Times,* April 16.

Shifter, Michael, and Daniel Joyce. 2009. "No Longer Washington's Backyard." *Current History,* February, 51–57.

Silva, Eduardo. 2009. *Challenging Neoliberalism in Latin America.* Cambridge: Cambridge University Press.

Singh, Anoop, and Charles Collyns. 2005. "Latin America's Resurgence." *Finance and Development,* December. www.imf.org/external/pubs/ft/fandd/ 2005/12/singh.htm.

Suchlicki, Jaime. 2002. *Cuba: From Colombus to Castro and Beyond.* Washington, D.C.: Potomac Books.

Suggett, James. 2008. "Venezuela and Brazil Advance on South American Defense Council." http://venezuelanalysis.com/news/3361.

Sweig, Julia. 2009. *Cuba: What Everyone Needs to Know*. New York: Oxford University Press.

Tedford, Deborah. 2009. "Obama Reaches Out to Latin America in Editorial." *National Public Radio*, April 16. www.npr.org/templates/story/story.php?storyId=103178217&ft=1&f=1001.

Weyland, Kurt, Raúl Madrid, and Wendy Hunter, eds. 2010. *Leftist Governments in Latin America: Successes and Shortcomings*. Cambridge: Cambridge University Press.

Wikipedia. 2011. "2006 Chávez Speech at the United Nations." Last modified November 11, 2011. http://en.wikipedia.org/wiki/2006_Chávez_speech_at_the_United_Nations.

Youngers, Coletta A., and Eileen Rosin, eds. 2005. *Drugs and Democracy in Latin America: The Impact of U.S. Policy*. Boulder, Colo.: L. Rienner.

8

The Middle East

YARON AYALON

The Middle East is a geographical region that extends from Afghanistan in the east to Morocco in the west and from Turkey in the north to Yemen and the Sudan in the south. Its heartland, known in western literature as the **Levant**, is the area bound by southeastern Anatolia, Iraq, the Arabian Desert, and the Mediterranean. The Middle East is also the birthplace of the three principal Western religions: **Judaism**, **Christianity**, and **Islam**. While the first two originated in Palestine, Islam emerged from the Arabian Peninsula. The majority of Middle Easterners are **Sunni Muslims**, and a minority follow a number of other sects, the largest of which is **Shiism**. Shiites form the majority in Iran—where Shiism is the official religion of the state—and also have significant concentrations in Bahrain, Saudi Arabia, and Lebanon. Besides Muslims, the Middle East has Christian and Jewish populations, the latter living primarily in Israel. Most of the inhabitants of the Middle East are ethnically Arab, with **Persians** (who are mostly Shii Muslim, but not Arab) found mostly in Iran, Turks in Turkey, and Jews (Judaism being a religion and an ethnic identity) in Israel. **Kurds**, the largest ethnic minority in the world without a state, occupy parts of eastern Turkey, northeastern Syria, northern Iraq, and northwestern Iran. The majority of Kurds are Muslims who speak one of many dialects of Kurdish.

This chapter explores the history of the Middle East to the present day. It is divided into five sections. The first, titled "The Arab-Israeli Conflict," explores the dispute that perhaps more than anything has defined the political and social reality of the region in the last century and a half. The second, "Iran and Iraq," deals with the two rivals that have been the focus of Western influences and interests since the nineteenth century, and that are still the source of many upheavals in the region. The third, "Turkey," focuses on the old-new rising power, a successor to the **Ottoman Empire** that is a member of the **North Atlantic Treaty Organization** (NATO), strives to join the **European Union** (EU), yet enjoys strengthening strategic ties with Syria and Iran. The fourth section, "**Radical Islam**," discusses the emergence of movements that project a radical vision, such as the **Muslim Brotherhood** in Egypt, Hamas in **Gaza**, **Hizballah** in Lebanon, and the global network of **al-Qaeda**—all groups that are generally perceived to sponsor acts of terror yet enjoy widespread popularity in some circles. A fifth section looks briefly at the Arab Spring (or Arab Awakening) that started in early 2011 and resulted in widespread protests and demonstrations across the region.

THE ARAB-ISRAELI CONFLICT

No dispute has affected the history of the modern Middle East more than the conflict between Arabs and Jews in Palestine. The origins of the conflict lie in the last quarter of the nineteenth century, when multiple anti-Semitic incidents in eastern Europe prompted Jews to emigrate to Palestine in great numbers. **Zionism**, or the expression of Jewish national consciousness, was an idea first propagated by intellectuals such as Leo Pinsker (d. 1891) and Theodore Herzl (d. 1904). As the plight of Jews in Europe worsened, support for the Zionist cause among European Jews increased. The first International Zionist Congress was held in Basel, Switzerland, in 1897. During the 1890s, and until his death, Herzl was involved in a series of negotiations with world leaders and wealthy Jews to gain support for the idea of an independent Jewish state in Palestine. The Ottoman Empire that ruled Palestine at the time tried to thwart Jewish immigration into the country, but the number of Jews in Palestine rose steadily from 1881 until the outbreak of World War I in 1914. Although the newcomers were mostly of modest means and worked in agriculture in undesirable conditions, they were financially backed by wealthy European Jews, such as Edmund de Rothschild, who supported the Zionist enterprise in Palestine through the purchase of lands from Arabs. The settlement of Jews drove many Arab farmers who had lived there for centuries off their lands. It was a source of great contention and the reason for violent clashes between Arabs and Jews even before the British mandate over Palestine began in 1920 (Laqueur 2003).

During the British mandate (1920–1948), Jews in Palestine fared better than their Arab counterparts. The British assured the Jews of their support for the Zionist project in the **Balfour Declaration** of 1917, which spoke of a future Jewish national home in Palestine. Despite a few setbacks—and contradictory promises the British had made to other parties, such as the Husayn-McMahon Correspondence of 1915 that spoke of Arab independence and the Sykes-Picot Agreement of 1916 that divided the Middle East between England and France—British policies throughout the mandate years reflected the spirit of Balfour's promise. This British commitment to a Jewish homeland was partly a result of intensive Jewish efforts to influence decision making in London, a lobbying power the Palestinians lacked. Unlike the Jews in Palestine, who received European financial aid, the Palestinians received little help from the Arab world. From 1920, Jews in Palestine had their own political leadership and gradually developed some state-like institutions. These included an elected government, education and health systems, labor unions, and even a militia, the **Haganah**, which operated at first clandestinely and from the late 1930s out in the open. Because of both British favoritism of the Jews and internal disputes, the Palestinians were not as successful in creating similar structures. In 1936, the Palestinian leadership announced a general strike in an attempt to weaken the Jewish economy. In what turned out to be a three-year-long violent confrontation with the Jews and the British, the Palestinians worsened their political position, and most of their leaders were arrested or forced into exile (Khalidi 2006). In 1937 the British asked the League of Nations to seek a solution for Palestine. The League responded by sending the **Peel Commission**, which toured the land and submitted its proposal for the partition of Palestine into Jewish and Arab states. The Jews accepted these recommendations with reservations; the Palestinian leadership rejected them. World War II put the discussions about the future of Palestine on hold. During the war, the Jewish leadership in Palestine decided to support the British struggle against Nazi Germany while opposing the British decision to limit immigration of Jewish refugees from the **Holocaust**. When the war ended, Britain found itself under pressure to allow Jewish refugees into Palestine, and it had to face financial constraints that prompted a reevaluation of the colonial enterprise. The British thus turned to the **United Nations** (UN) to seek a solution for the problem of Palestine. The UN responded by sending the **United Nations Special Committee on Palestine** (UNSCOP) to Palestine in the summer of 1947. UNSCOP met with Jewish representatives, but the Arab leadership boycotted it. UNSCOP's recommendations again included the partition of the land. The UN General Assembly voted to adopt UNSCOP's proposal on November 29, 1947; the United States and Soviet Union supported the proposal, while the Arab states voted against it. Consequently, the British announced that the mandate over Palestine would terminate by May of 1948 (Krämer 2008).

An open military confrontation between Jews and Arabs in Palestine began immediately after the UN vote in November. In its first stage, lasting until May 1948, the Palestinians fought the forces of the Haganah on a number of fronts. By the time the leader of the Jews in Palestine, David Ben Gurion, declared independence on May 14, 1948, the Haganah had already captured areas not included in the original partition resolution. Once the British left Palestine and the state of Israel was declared, the second phase of the war ensued, with the newly formed **Israeli Defense Forces** (IDF) confronting the invading regular armies of Egypt, Jordan, Syria, Lebanon, and Iraq. The war continued until January 1949 and ended with a victory for the fledgling Jewish state. There were two main outcomes. First was the success of Israel to withstand an attack from all its borders despite all odds. This success was the result of careful planning and nearly three decades of state building and military training—an invaluable experience the Palestinians and Arab armies did not have. Second was the displacement of hundreds of thousands of Palestinians, who were either forced to leave or fled their homes and who ended up in refugee camps in Syria, Lebanon, Jordan, the West Bank, and Gaza (Morris 2001).

Between 1948—when Israeli independence was declared—and 1973, Israel fought four wars with its Arab neighbors. The first was the **Sinai War** of 1956, where Israel joined a French-British alliance that sought to drive the forces of **Gamal 'Abd al-Nasser**, Egypt's president, away from the **Suez Canal**. Militarily, the operation was a great success: Egypt was forced to withdraw, and Israel captured the entire **Sinai Peninsula** in eight days of fighting. Politically, the **Suez crisis** was a victory for Nasser, who played the delicate balance between the United States and the USSR to his advantage. The Soviets threatened to attack Israel, and the United States exerted pressure that led the British and the French to withdraw and Israel to give up the Sinai in March 1957 (Rabinovich 1990).

The next confrontation occurred in 1967 when Nasser closed the straits of Tiran in the Red Sea, blocking Israeli ships from reaching the south port of Eilat, and ordered UN troops to evacuate Sinai. Israel opted for a preemptive attack on Egypt, Syria, and Jordan. Within six days, the IDF had recaptured the Sinai and Gaza Strip from Egypt, had conquered the **West Bank** and east Jerusalem from Jordan, and had taken control of the **Golan Heights** from Syria. In the **Six Day War**, as it would come to be known, Israel more than doubled its area and dealt a final blow to Arab attempts to annihilate it. The war exacerbated the Palestinian refugee problem as many Palestinians fled or were forced to abandon their villages in the West Bank, and especially in areas surrounding Jerusalem. The war also marked the clear division of the Middle East into regions of influence—Russian and American—as part of the Cold War; the USSR cut its diplomatic relations with Israel, which began to enjoy extensive U.S. support (Oren, 2003).

The impression of Israeli invincibility began to erode in 1969, when the IDF fought a **War of Attrition** with Egypt on the Suez Canal. It was completely shattered when in 1973 Egyptian and Syrian forces managed to surprise Israel on **Yom Kippur**, the holiest day on the Jewish calendar, and launch a joint attack. The unpreparedness of the IDF cost thousands of lives, and many more were imprisoned. Israel managed to regain lands lost in the first week of fighting, and the war did not change the borders between Israel and its neighbors. The **Yom Kippur War**, as that conflict came to be known, paved the way for peace talks between Egypt and Israel. From the perspective of Egypt's president, **Anwar al-Sadat**, the war had changed Israel's arrogant approach to the Arab world, proved it was not invincible, and allowed negotiations on better terms. Sadat arrived on a first visit to Jerusalem in November 1977. Direct negotiations between the Israeli prime minister Menahem Begin and Sadat began shortly after, with U.S. president Jimmy Carter serving as a mediator. The two countries signed a peace treaty in 1979, in which Israel agreed to withdraw from the Sinai, and a general formula was set to resolve the Palestinian issue in the future (Stein 1999).

After the war of 1948, the Palestinian leadership scattered all over the Arab world. Most of the Palestinian elite left for Gaza, Cairo, or other countries, and in the international scene, the Palestinians practically ceased to exist. In 1959, a Palestinian engineer living in Kuwait, **Yasser Arafat**, formed a group later to be known as **Fatah**, whose main goal was the liberation of Palestine from foreign occupation and the establishment of an independent Palestinian state. Arafat was instrumental in rallying support for the Palestinian cause through diplomatic efforts and later through a series of violent attacks on Israeli and Jewish targets. In 1964, Fatah joined a number of smaller Palestinian groups to form the **Palestine Liberation Organization** (PLO). In 1974, the PLO obtained an observer status in the UN General Assembly, and Arafat received international recognition as the representative of the Palestinian people. From its inception, the PLO was only a political framework for promoting the Palestinian cause. In practice, the PLO supported the paramilitary activities of its member organizations. Attacks against Israel were at first carried out from the West Bank, and, after 1967, from Jordan. The Palestinians' setting up of a state within a state in Jordan, and the inability of Jordanian security forces to control Palestinian refugee camps, prompted Jordan's King Hussein to launch a wide-scale attack on the Palestinians in September of 1971. In what came to be known as **Black September**, the Jordanian military forced the entire Palestinian leadership to leave; they ultimately settled in Lebanon (Rubin 1994). Throughout most of the 1970s, Arafat and his men coordinated attacks on Israeli and Jewish targets from Beirut, and from 1975 they were involved in a bitter civil war within Lebanon. Because of the attacks Fatah carried out against Israel from south Lebanon during the 1970s, the Israeli government launched what is now known as the **First Lebanon War**. Originally intended to drive Palestinian fighters away from the border a distance of 40 kilometers—the range of Palestinian rockets—the IDF continued to advance and reached the capital Beirut within a week. After a siege on the area of Beirut where the Palestinian leadership was hiding, Arafat and thousands of PLO fighters agreed to leave Beirut for good, headed for Tunis. Shortly after Arafat's departure, on September 16 and 17, the IDF allowed the forces of the **Christian Falanges**, Israel's ally in the war, to enter the Palestinian refugee camps of **Sabra and Shatila** in south Beirut. In what seemed to have been revenge for the assassination of the Christian president of Lebanon, Bashir al-Jumayyil, on September 14, the Falanges murdered thousands of Palestinians, including many women and children. The international community saw the Israeli government, whose army de facto controlled the area, as responsible for the massacre, and so did most Israelis (Schiff and Ya'ari 1984). Despite the criticism of Israel's presence in Lebanon, it took until 1985 for Israel to withdraw its forces from most of Lebanon. Israel kept a security zone in the south of Lebanon, where it set up military outposts, until its complete withdrawal in May 2000.

Israel's presence in Lebanon was one of the factors promoting the rise of Shiite militias **Amal** and Hizballah (Party of God, also spelled Hezbollah). Amal was a Shiite political party, initially formed with the goal of promoting Shiite welfare within Lebanon. When Israel invaded in 1982, Amal supported Israel's quest to rid Lebanon of Palestinians. When Israel stayed, Amal's views changed. A group of young Shiites, among them Abbas al-Mussawi, Hasan Nasrallah, and Imad Mughniyyah, were not content with what they saw as Amal's soft approach to Israel's occupation and formed Hizballah. From its early days, the new group carried out attacks against Israeli and American targets in Lebanon, including the bombings of the U.S. embassy and the Marines barracks in Beirut in 1983. Hizballah pledged to fight not just until Israel's complete withdrawal from Lebanon, but until Israel's destruction. After Israel consolidated its forces to the security zone, Hizballah continued to attack IDF bases daily. It also carefully planned attacks on Jewish targets worldwide, including the bombings of the Israeli embassy in Buenos Aires, Argentina, in 1992 and later the Jewish cultural center in the same city in 1994. As a result, Hizballah was declared by the U.S. State Department and most European countries as a terrorist organization, and Mughniyyah, the mastermind behind Hizballah's international operations, was placed on the Federal Bureau of Investigation's (FBI's) most wanted terrorists list, where he remained until his mysterious assassination in Damascus in February 2008 (Norton 2009).

With the Palestinian leadership far away in Tunis, it was left to local leaders in the Israeli-occupied West Bank and Gaza strip to carry on the Palestinian struggle. Without any coordination, a Palestinian popular uprising broke out in various locations in the West Bank in December 1987. The outbreak of the first **intifada** caught Arafat and the PLO by surprise, and it was only after a month of protests that the Palestinian leadership in Tunis managed to assert its control over the uprising. In the intifada, Palestinians demonstrated against the IDF's presence in the West Bank by throwing stones and **Molotov cocktails** at Israeli soldiers and vehicles and by burning tires (Morris 2001). Attempts to negotiate peace between Israel, the Palestinians, and other Arab countries failed at first, primarily because of Israel's right-wing **Likud** government's uncompromising approach. Change came only after the Gulf War, when the United States pressured the different parties to begin peace talks. In October 1991, Israeli and Arab leaders met for the first time in Madrid, a conference that marked the beginning of multilateral negotiations between Israel and Jordan, Syria, and the Palestinians. These talks led to the **Oslo Accords** with the Palestinians, a general name for the interim agreements that provided for the establishment of Palestinian self-rule in parts of the West Bank and the Gaza strip, in preparation for a future state. Israel also signed a peace treaty with Jordan in October 1994. The talks with Syria, however, deadlocked, with the Syrians demanding complete Israeli withdrawal from the Golan Heights to the 1967 border, a request the Israeli government was not willing to meet. The assassination of the Israeli prime minister **Yitzhak Rabin** of the left-wing Labor Party on November 4, 1995, and the subsequent election of **Benjamin Netanyahu** of the Likud in June 1996 led to an almost complete standstill in the peace talks with Syria and the Palestinians (Enderlin 2003).

Despite a number of summits held between Netanyahu and Arafat in the years 1996 to 1999, no significant advances were achieved. The election of **Ehud Barak** of the Labor Party in 1999 marked a new yet brief era in Israeli-Palestinian and Israeli-Syrian relations. Barak's government embarked on intensive negotiations with the Palestinian Authority (PA) and called for a meeting between Israeli and Syrian leaders. The latter took place in Shepherdstown, West Virginia, in January 2000, when Barak met Syrian foreign minister Farouk a-Shara. The talks, however, led to no agreement, as Syria refused to accept any solution that would not grant it sovereignty over all lands Israel took in 1967 and Israel refused to completely withdrawal to the 1967 border, which would have brought Syrian forces to the banks of the **Sea of Galilee**, Israel's main source of drinking water. Barak then turned to negotiate with Arafat. The two leaders met in **Camp David** in July 2000. According to various reports, Barak offered Arafat a Palestinian state on most of the West Bank and Gaza Strip but refused to recognize the right of return of Palestinian refugees from 1948. Although Arafat reportedly agreed to compromise on the latter point, he refused to comply with Barak's demand to declare that the Israeli-Palestinian conflict had been resolved. In October 2000, the second intifada broke out. This time, it was carefully planned and directed by Arafat and the leaders of the PA, and it involved the use of guns that had been acquired during the 1990s from Israel for the Palestinian police (Jamal 2005).

The collapse of the peace process, the second intifada, the violent suppression of Arab Israeli protesters in October that resulted in thirteen deaths and many injured, and internal political problems led to the collapse of Barak's coalition and to the election of **Ariel Sharon** as prime minister in February 2001. Sharon took a tough stance toward suicide bombings in Israeli cities. After over eighty Israelis died in such attacks on buses and shopping malls in March 2002, Israel launched **Operation Defensive Shield**. By the end of April, the IDF recaptured West Bank cities, besieged Arafat in his compound in Ramallah, and the PA effectively collapsed. From then until days before his death in November 2004, Arafat was not allowed to leave his headquarters. In the meanwhile, Sharon's government decided to increase security in Israel by building a barrier between the areas that roughly constitute the West Bank and Israel. Construction began in 2003. The barrier mostly comprises a twenty-six-foot-high concrete wall that has trenches on both sides, with passage from and to the West Bank possible at designated checkpoints only. Because of various topographical, demographic, and security concerns, certain areas of the West Bank are now on the Israeli side of the barrier. The construction of the wall thus involved the isolation of some Palestinian villages, limitations on movement for many, and the confiscation of private lands of Palestinians. Because of budgetary issues and an ongoing Palestinian struggle against the wall that has involved Israel's supreme court time and again, the wall is yet to be completed (Jacoby 2007).

In January 2005, **Mahmud Abbas** (Abu Mazen) became the new president of the PA and chair of the PLO. Cooperation between Abu Mazen and Sharon facilitated the execution of the plan to dismantle remaining Israeli **settlements** in the Gaza strip in August 2005—a plan Israel had announced unilaterally more than a year before. In 2006, elections in the PA resulted in the victory of **Hamas**, an Islamist-militant group that has refused to recognize Israel or the agreements the PLO has signed with it. The new Palestinian government formed shortly after the elections, with Isma'il Haniyya from Hamas as prime minister. Israel, the United States, and EU supported free elections in the PA, yet when Hamas turned out the winner, they severed ties with the PA. The government of **Ehud Olmert**, Sharon's successor, announced it would not have any contact with the PA until Hamas recognized Israel. On June 25, 2006, Hamas operatives kidnapped an IDF corporal, Gilad Shalit, and demanded the release of over a thousand of its members imprisoned in Israel. Israel responded by sending its troops into the Gaza Strip (Schanzer 2008). The military operation had limited success and was called off when on July 12 Hizballah attacked an IDF patrol on the Israeli side of the border, kidnapping two of its soldiers and killing three. Israel responded with bombardments of infrastructure and various targets across Lebanon. Hizballah responded by launching rockets toward Israel. The confrontation, known in Lebanon as the **July War** and in Israel as the **Second Lebanon War**, lasted till a UN-brokered ceasefire went into effect on August 14, 2006 (Harel and Issacharoff 2008).

In the autumn of 2006 tensions between Fatah and Hamas continued to escalate. Attempts to form a Palestinian national unity government in March 2007 proved unsuccessful. An open military confrontation began on June 10, and five days later, Hamas gained control of the entire Gaza strip. Abu Mazen then dissolved the government and moved to take measures against Hamas in the West Bank. By early July, two Palestinian political entities had emerged: the PA in the West Bank and a Hamas-controlled government in Gaza (Schanzer 2008). The split in the Palestinian leadership paved the way for direct talks between Israel and the PA in 2007–2008. These took place from late 2007 till December of 2008. In the meanwhile, the southern Israeli town of Sderot and neighboring areas continued to be targeted by Hamas' rockets daily. On December 27, 2008, Olmert's government set out to end Hamas' attacks in operation **Cast Lead**. After three weeks of air strikes and a massive ground assault, Israel and Hamas independently announced a ceasefire, which has since been preserved with few interruptions. Cast Lead brought much destruction to the Gaza strip and subjected Israel to international criticism for deliberately targeting civilians and for the high death toll: between 1,100 and 1,450 casualties on the Palestinian side (Harel and Issacharoff 2010).

Operation Cast Lead and the subsequent election of the Likud Party, headed again by Benjamin Netanyahu, put the Israeli-Palestinian negotiations on hold. Although Netanyahu, a staunch opponent to a two-state solution, announced in June that he supported a compromise in Palestine, Abu Mazen refused to enter direct talks with Israel until further assurances were made. The Palestinians' main demand was that Israelis freeze construction in all its West Bank settlements. Pressure from the United States eventually led to Netanyahu's announcement, in November 2009, of a ten-month freeze on all Jewish building in the West Bank. When the moratorium expired in September 2010, the Palestinians announced that they would not return to the negotiations as long as Israel continued building settlements in the West Bank.

After two decades of intermittent negotiations between Israel, the Palestinians, and the Arab world, the demands of each side are apparent. In 2002, the **Arab League** reached a decision to offer Israel normalization of relations with all league member states in return for Israel's withdrawal to the 1967 borders, the foundation of a Palestinian state whose capital is Jerusalem, and an agreed solution to the refugee problem. Known as the Arab or **Saudi peace initiative**, it outlines elements of a future peace between Israel and its neighbors. The Arab peace initiative does not ask Israel to accept responsibility for the refugee problem, as the Palestinians have done in the past, but merely calls for a suitable solution both sides would agree to abide by. Furthermore, the initiative could offer Israel and the United States an opportunity to thwart Iran's ambition to govern the Middle East. Although Israel has officially rejected the Saudi peace plan, successive Israeli prime ministers—Sharon, Olmert, and Netanyahu—have acknowledged that it could form a basis for negotiations, provided Israel's security concerns were addressed (Eisenberg and Caplan 2010).

Resolving the conflict with the Palestinians will end Israel's occupation of another people and will pave the way for diplomatic and economic relations with other Arab countries, which in turn will earn Israel more recognition and support in the international community. A lasting peace will help defuse Israel's fierce enemies, Hizballah in Lebanon and Hamas in Gaza. In the long run, peace between Israel and the Arab world might also improve the image of Israel and the United States in the Arab media. At the time these words are written, however, peace seems unlikely, and for two main reasons. First, even though the Netanyahu government—in office since March 2009—has accepted the two-state solution in principle, it has continued to expand settlements in the West Bank to reduce the possibility of withdrawal from Palestinian-claimed territory in the future. And second, the recent reconciliation between Fatah and Hamas, signed in April 2011 but yet to be implemented, threatens the possibility of Israeli-Palestinian negotiations, so long as Hamas openly calls for the destruction of Israel.

IRAN AND IRAQ

The modern period in Iranian history began with the establishment of the **Safavid dynasty** and of Shiism as the official religion of the state in 1502. The Safavids, who built an empire that competed with the Ottomans for hegemony in the eastern parts of the Middle East, ruled Iran from their capital of Isfahan till 1722. A period of instability and turmoil followed for most of the eighteenth century, until the rise of the **Qajar dynasty** in 1794. The Qajars ruled Iran at a time of progress, innovation, and foreign intervention and influences in the Middle East. Like the Ottomans, they invested in education and infrastructure and at the same time allowed Western powers to strengthen their influence over the economy by granting them concessions. In 1890, the Iranian ruler Nasir al-Din Shah granted the British a monopoly over the production, sale, and export of tobacco for fifty years in return for revenues that would enrich the shah's treasury. The Shiite clerics, unhappy with foreign takeover of their economy, issued a religious ruling (fatwa) calling for the boycotting of tobacco products. The clergy were successful—Iranians nearly stopped smoking—and the **shah** eventually had to rescind the agreement with the British. The episode emphasized the extent of popular support the clergy in Iran enjoyed and outlined the limits of the shah's power (Keddie 2006).

Despite the experience of the tobacco boycott, Iran's shah from 1896, Mozaffar al-Din, signed more economic deals with European companies. Members of noble families and the clergy called for limiting the shah's authority and for allowing popular representation in government. A joint uprising of the merchants and religious establishment began in 1905 in the capital Tehran and soon spread to other cities. In August 1906, the shah agreed to form a parliament and hold elections, and the new parliament drafted a constitution that placed the shah under the rule of law (Abrahamian 1982).

In 1921, Reza Khan staged a coup in Iran, which led to the overthrowing of the Qajar dynasty and Reza's appointment as shah in 1925. The **Pahlavi dynasty**, which consisted of Reza and his son, Muhammad Reza Shah, ruled Iran, with a few interruptions, until 1979. The Pahlavis modernized their country and maintained good relations with the West (and relied on U.S. and later Israeli support), but they left limited room for dissenting political expressions (Keddie 2006).

During his reign, Muhammad Reza Shah made efforts to curtail forces that posed a potential risk to his rule. In the early 1950s, popular support for the prime minister, **Muhammad Mossadegh**, nearly removed the shah from power. Mossadegh nationalized Iran's oil, violating agreements the shah had with the British, and he introduced land laws that limited private ownership. With the support of the communist Tudeh Party, the Soviets increased their influence in Iran. The shah then turned to the United States and the Central Intelligence Agency (CIA). Already wary of Mossadegh's pro-Soviet inclinations, the Americans helped stage a coup against him while the shah waited in the wings in exile in Italy. The shah then returned to Iran and had Mossadegh arrested and tried for treason. The years following the overthrow of Mossadegh were marked by a crackdown on communists and individuals and groups that posed a threat to the shah's rule. The United Kingdom, the United States, and Israel backed the shah and helped create his secret police, **Savak**, in 1957. Until its dissolution in 1979, Savak arrested, tortured, and executed tens of thousands of Iranians for various allegations and was hated by ordinary Iranians (Abrahamian 1982).

In January 1963, the shah announced the **White Revolution** that offered many reforms in the spirit of Westernization, including land ownership and some rights for women and non-Muslims. Such measures were not popular in Iran, whose population was largely religious and conservative. One of the most outspoken opponents to the shah's reforms was **Rohallah Khomeini**, who issued statements and delivered speeches strongly criticizing, and eventually denouncing, the shah. When the shah realized that support for Khomeini was growing, he placed Khomeini under house arrest. Khomeini's imprisonment resulted in major riots all over Iran, and hundreds of people lost their lives. The government released Khomeini in August, but he was later exiled from Iran. He spent more than fourteen years in Turkey, Iraq, and France. He gained many followers among the Shiite diaspora, and his recordings and writings were smuggled into Iran (Keddie 2006).

Popular discontent of the shah's rule became widespread during the 1970s. Khomeini, still in exile in 1977, became the leader of the opposition to the shah, openly criticizing his corrupt and pro-Western regime. Widespread demonstrations began in Iran in October 1977 after the death of Khomeini's son of a heart attack; many believed Savak's dark hand was behind his death. Other clashes between the shah's forces and supporters of the **ulama** produced hundreds of casualties in each city. By late 1978, the streets of Tehran were the site of massive public protests. Facing a revolution, the shah appealed to the United States for help. The Carter administration rebuffed his request for U.S. intervention. On January 16, 1979, the shah left Iran and never returned. Shapour Bakhtiar, the oppositionist prime minister the shah had appointed a few weeks earlier to appease the public, dissolved Savak, freed political prisoners, ordered the army to allow people to demonstrate, and invited Khomeini to return from exile in France. By February, the forces loyal to Khomeini controlled all government buildings and police stations and had the army on their side. Khomeini dissolved Bakhtiar's government and appointed Mehdi Bazargan the interim prime minister. Bazargan, an advocate for democracy, civil rights, and the preservation of U.S.-Iran relations, soon found himself under the authority of the **Revolutionary Council** led by Khomeini. In the three years that followed, Bazargan and other moderates who supported the revolution at first ended up politically marginalized, under house arrest, in exile, or dead. In November 1979, a referendum approved the constitution Khomeini and his supporters had drafted, which made Khomeini the **Supreme Leader of the Islamic Republic**—the head of state who appoints the commander of the armed forces, the chief justice, and many other key positions. In February 1980, Abulhassan Banisadr was elected to be the first president (Keddie 2006).

One incident that shaped the direction the revolution would take in the coming years was the Iran hostage crisis. It started with the takeover of the U.S. embassy in Tehran by a group of pro-Khomeini students on November 4, 1979. Khomeini did not sanction the takeover, but he later gave it his support. The United States attempted to send a rescue mission, but it failed. Fifty-two of the hostages were kept in captivity for 444 days, first at the embassy, then in other locations in Iran. The hostage episode marked the beginning of a sharp decline in U.S.-Iran relations. During the crisis, Iranian assets in the United States were frozen, and diplomatic relations between the two countries were cut off—they remain closed to this day (Bowden 2006).

Even before the hostage crisis was resolved, Iran had to face an Iraqi invasion, which led to the eight-year-long **Iran-Iraq war**. Unlike Iran, Iraq did not have centuries of imperial history. In fact, Iraq had not existed as one political entity before the British and French redrew the map of the Middle East during World War I. When the British were fighting the Ottomans, they enlisted the help of local Arabs who wanted to see the Ottomans go. One such ally was Husayn of **Mecca**, who offered to revolt against the Ottomans in return for a British pledge to the formation of a future independent Arab state under his family's rule. After the war, the British appointed Husayn's younger son, Abdallah, king over Transjordan (now Jordan; Abdallah was the great grandfather of the current king, Abdallah II). The British tried to do the same with Husayn's older son, Faysal, by offering him the kingdom of Syria. Entangled in contradictory promises, the British eventually permitted the French to drive Faysal out of Syria. As compensation they offered Faysal the kingdom of Iraq—a new state emerged from the combination of three Ottoman provinces. Faysal, his son Ghazi, and his grandson Faysal II, ruled Iraq until 1958. They were then removed in a military coup staged by ʿAbd al-Karim Qasim, whose rule ended similarly in 1963. Another coup, in 1968, brought the secularist-socialist Baʿath party to power. From then until July of 1979, Iraq experienced a period of political instability, which ended when one of the propagators of the 1968 coup, Saddam Hussein, managed to push his opponents aside and become the president of Iraq. Fearing insurgency among Iraq's Shiite population because of Iranian attempts to export its revolutionary message, and continuing border disputes, Saddam invaded Iran on September 22, 1980. Although Saddam hoped for quick territorial gains amidst Iran's revolutionary chaos, Iraq's forces achieved only modest gains that were quickly reversed. When the war ended in August 1988, neither side had gained any territory, and both had suffered tremendous losses in lives— over half a million deaths are estimated on both sides—and to the economies. Since the end of the war, Iran-Iraq relations have been on a slow curve of improvement (Tripp 2000).

Khomeini died on June 3, 1989. Initially, Khomeini intended for Hussein Montazeri to succeed him as Supreme Leader. According to the constitution, only a person of the highest level of learning, one who is a **marja'-i taqlid** (source of imitation) or **grand ayatollah**, may serve as the Supreme Leader. When Montazeri began to support a more liberal approach in the late 1980s and openly criticized Khomeini's policies, the latter switched his support to Ali Khamena'i. Since Khamena'i lacked the religious qualifications for the position, the constitution had to be revised. On June 4, 1989, Khamena'i succeeded Khomeini as the Supreme Leader. **Hashemi Rafsanjani**, who served two four-year terms, followed Khamena'i, who was until then the president of Iran. Rafsanjani was then succeeded by the reformist Muhammad Khatami. Khatami's presidency, from 1997 to 2005, was characterized by internal dissents between the government and the more traditionalist clergy and by relative reconciliation with the West. Khatami's presidency also saw a number of student and popular riots (Keddie 2006).

In 2005, **Mahmud Ahmadinejad**, the mayor of Tehran, defeated Rafsanjani in the second round of the presidential elections. Ahmadinejad, a conservative hard-liner, approached economic problems by increasing spending and providing subsidies to the poor, pushed family planning legislation that was unfavorable to women, and introduced an uncompromising attitude to Iran's development of a nuclear plan. The plan, which Iran claims was intended for peaceful uses, became the main source of contention between Iran and the West. Despite several rounds of negotiations with the International Atomic Energy Agency (IAEA), the EU, the United States, Russia, and China, Iran has refused to heed international demands to put its nuclear plan on hold and has denied any intentions to develop nuclear weapons. Iran's failure to meet the West's demands led to economic sanctions against it in the UN, promoted by the United States and its western European allies (Ebel 2010). Iran's nuclear question was a key issue in the 2008 presidential elections in the United States, serving as the epitome for U.S. foreign policy and influence in the Middle East. The Obama administration, opting for diplomacy before considering other options, has emphasized that all options, including a military strike, are on the table if Iran continues to develop its nuclear capabilities (Tezcür 2010). The Americans have taken that stance primarily to appease Israel, whose government continues to stress the possibility of a military strike against Iran's nuclear plants if diplomatic measures do not bear fruit.

Before the Islamic Revolution, Israel was a close ally of Iran. When Khomeini came to power the new regime cut off ties with Israel, calling it the "small Satan" (the "large" being the United States). The revolutionary leaders of Iran have issued numerous anti-Israeli statements in the past three decades. During the presidency of Khatami, fewer such statements were made, and at one press conference Khatami even responded to a question by an Israeli reporter—something no Iranian leader has done before or after him. But since Ahmadinejad became president in the summer of 2005, anti-Israeli, anti-Semitic, and anti-American statements—including denial of the Holocaust and calls for the destruction of Israel—have increased dramatically. During a speech at the UN General Assembly in September 2010, Ahmadinejad suggested an American conspiracy was behind the attacks of September 11, 2001. Such statements have had a negative effect on Iran's relations with the West and even with its relative allies, Russia and China (Lynch 2010).

Iran is widely considered to have a poor human rights record, including under the shah, when Savak was arresting and torturing thousands of Iranians for holding views or taking actions considered dangerous to the regime. The trend of silencing the opposition continued under the Islamic Revolution. The political system in Iran allows for a relative plurality of views, and elections for parliament and the presidency are open and—at least until 2009— have been fair by all standards. All candidates, however, have to be approved by the **Guardian Council**, a body of twelve jurists that elects and dismisses the Supreme Leader, yet in fact is subject to his authority. As a result, only candidates whose message and lifestyle fit that of the revolution may be allowed to run for office. Furthermore, Iran's penal code has provisions for the use of corporal punishment for offenses such as theft, fornication, or homosexuality, and its methods include public execution by hanging, cutting off limbs, and stoning. The silencing of opponents of the regime, which has taken place from the very first days of the revolution, was demonstrated clearly in the aftermath of the presidential elections of 2009. When Mahmud Ahmadinejad defeated Mir Hussein Musavi by a considerable margin, protests broke out all over Iran. Supporters of Musavi challenged the authenticity of the results and did not cease demonstrating even when security forces clashed with them, arrested many, and prevented communication with the outside world by banning foreign media from the streets and blocking Facebook and other websites. The protests subsided when the Supreme Leader, Khamena'i, announced his support for Ahmadinejad, ordered a partial recount that determined Ahmadinejad was indeed the winner, and called for the complete cessation of the disturbances (Ebel 2010).

Neighboring Iraq has faced even more turmoil in the last decade. The events of September 11, 2001, prompted the United States to launch an attack against Afghanistan, where the forces responsible for the attacks (al-Qaeda and Taliban) were believed to have been hiding. Two years later, benefitting from the momentum of the war in Afghanistan and believing Saddam Hussein was hiding weapons of mass destruction, a multinational force of U.S., British, and other countries' militaries invaded Iraq on March 20, 2003. By May the regular armies of Saddam surrendered, yet pockets of resistance remained and continued to attack allied forces. After months in hiding, Saddam was captured in December 2003. He was handed to Iraqi authorities in 2004, and his trial began in October 2005. Saddam was found guilty of crimes against humanity, sentenced to death, and hanged on December 30, 2006 (Carlisle 2007).

The passing of Saddam, who had ruled Iraq for over twenty years, brought instability to the country. Under Saddam, the Sunni minority formed the political and economic elite, while the Shiite majority was generally poor and disenfranchised. Kurds, the third major segment of Iraqi population, occupying most of the northern provinces, were targeted in the 1980s, from waves of mass arrests to chemical weapons attacks, most famously in the city of Halabja (Kelly 2008). In a country torn by competing ethnic and religious identities, Saddam's harsh treatment of anyone suspected of criticizing his regime created a relatively stable political setting, albeit at a great cost. When Saddam was removed, old rivalries resurfaced and threw Iraq into a bloodbath—a crisis that has only recently abated. From the summer of 2003, Sunni and Shiite insurgents have carried out attacks against **mosques** and neighborhoods and confronted the multinational force frequently. In the process of trying to bring order and stability to Iraq, the participating allies sent over 300,000 troops there, who remained in the country in the first two years following the invasion, and of whom more than 4,700 were killed and over 32,000 wounded. The majority of soldiers and most casualties were American (CNN 2010).

After occupying Iraq, the U.S.-led coalition established the **Coalition Provisional Authority** (CPA) to serve as a governing body until Iraqis formed new institutions. On June 28, 2004, the CPA handed authority over to the Iraqi interim government, which was in charge of preparing Iraq for democratic elections and rebuilding state institutions in the post-Saddam era. The first prime minister was Ayad Allawi, a Shiite. Iraq's first legislative elections were held on January 30, 2005. Most Sunni politicians, angry with the U.S. intervention (and some still supporters of the old regime and members of Saddam's Ba'ath party), boycotted the elections. The Shiites, a majority in Iraq, achieved the highest number of seats in parliament; a Kurdish coalition of parties came in second. By April, a new government was appointed, with the Shiite Ibrahim al-Ja'afari as prime minister. Jalal Talabani, a Kurd, was elected to serve as president of Iraq, a post he still holds (Allawi 2007).

Despite handing over authority to the Iraqis, the United States continued to intervene in local politics. An October 2005 referendum was held to approve a constitution proposal reached after months of U.S.-brokered negotiations between Sunnis, Shiites, and Kurds. The approval of the constitution meant that new elections for the **Council of Representatives** (parliament) were to be held in December. Although the 275 seats in the council were allocated regionally to guarantee a Sunni majority—the only way to bring Sunnis back to the political game—the elections produced a complicated political constellation and a period of violence that subsided only in 2007, in part thanks to the American substantial increase of soldiers that year known as the Surge. Eventually the Shiite Nuri al-Maliki formed a government and was sworn in on May 20, 2006. In March 2010, elections for the council were held again, with the number of representatives now increased to 325. The official results, contested by some parties, reflected a slight advantage for the **Iraqi National Movement** of former prime minister Ayad Allawi. The **State of Law Coalition** of the incumbent Nuri al-Maliki came in second. The new parliament opened on June 14, but the new government's stability is not assured. Overall, the United States alone has spent more than $700 billion in Iraq since the invasion in 2003. In the summer of 2010, the United States declared an end to all combat missions in Iraq, leaving 50,000 troops there to advise and assist the Iraqi government (Kahl 2010).

Iraq's experience with democracy is very recent. Traditionally, Iraqi political power was obtained by force or through the backing of a foreign power. With decreasing U.S. presence and intervention in Iraq in the coming years, the question of whether Iraqi democracy remains stable is a pertinent one.

TURKEY

In recent years, Turkey has attracted much attention as an old-new rising power in the Middle East, the bridge between East and West, and the example of a successful Muslim democracy. The Republic of Turkey was founded in 1923 on the ashes of the Ottoman Empire, a state that had ruled over vast lands from Hungary through Greece to present-day Turkey, and from Syria and Palestine through Egypt to the western parts of North Africa. The Ottomans, named after the founder of their dynasty, Sultan **Osman I**, conquered most of the Arabic-speaking lands nowadays considered the heartland of the Middle East in 1516–1517. A series of smaller wars from the early nineteenth century to the eve of World War I deprived the Ottomans of most of their possessions in Europe. In World War I, the Ottomans joined a German-Austrian alliance but were defeated by the British and French. Following World War I, the allies sought to impose a division of former Ottoman lands into various areas of influence. A very small portion, not including the capital city of Istanbul, was left for a future Turkish state. The weak Ottoman sultan agreed to the terms dictated by the allies in the Treaty of Sèvres, signed on August 10, 1920. The treaty, however, was never implemented (Lewis 2002).

After the war, Mustafa Kemal, an Ottoman officer, was sent to the eastern provinces of **Anatolia** to regroup military forces remaining there. Kemal refused to carry out his orders and instead started a movement that would change the course of Turkish history. Kemal and his supporters, known as the nationalists, elected an assembly, declared the rule of the Sultan void, gathered an army, and set out to defend Turkey from the Greek invasion that had started in 1919. Soon Kemal's forces, stationed in Ankara in central Anatolia, drove the Greeks out, entered Istanbul, and forced the allies to recognize the sovereignty of the Turkish people and the nationalists as their sole representatives, which they did in the **Treaty of Lausanne** of 1923 (Zürcher 2004).

Throughout the 1920s, the nationalists sought to disassociate Turkey from its Ottoman past and to create a modern, secular republic. Until his death in 1938, Kemal as the president of the Turkish republic introduced a series of reforms, including outlawing traditional dress, closing down religious schools, abolishing the sultanate, changing Turkey's capital city to Ankara, and reforming the Turkish language to purge from it Arabic and Persian words and to introduce the Latin script to replace the Arabic one in which Turkish had been written until then. Kemal also required Turks to adopt last names—a European practice uncommon in the Ottoman Empire—and set an example by taking the somewhat presumptuous surname **Atatürk** (father of the Turks) for himself (Lewis 2002). Today, Atatürk's legacy is well apparent in Turkey, embodied in the still relatively secular character of the state, modern infrastructure, capitalist economy, grand shopping malls, and his own image or statue overlooking every square, public building, and school yard.

Atatürk's Turkey was a one-party state. The ruling party, the **Republican People's Party** (RPP), allowed the formation of competing parties for the first time in 1946. In 1950, it lost elections to the **Democratic Party** (DP). The DP and its prime minister, Adnan Menderes, reversed some of the policies of the RPP, allowed a resurgence of Islam at the popular level, joined NATO, and became a close ally of the United States, which provided Turkey with significant financial assistance. Despite imposing limitations on certain civic liberties, the DP won two more elections in 1954 and 1958. Its mismanagement of the economy yielded a steep rise in national debt and inflation. The military, the guardian of Atatürk's legacy according to the constitution, rebuffed the policies of Menderes and, after issuing a number of warnings, staged a **coup** in 1960 that removed Menderes from power. The military also banned the DP and suspended the constitution. Menderes and other leaders of the DP were tried and executed in 1961. In 1962 the military allowed civilian politicians to return but only after a referendum approved a new constitution that was supposed to prevent future political upheavals. The new constitution could not make politicians of different factions get along, however, and Turkey was soon thrown into political instability and another economic crisis. In 1971 and 1980, the military again intervened—the first time behind the scenes, the second by taking charge—to restore order. The generals staging the coups of 1960 and 1980 did not, however, seek to remain in power. In both cases, after purging the system of "corrupt" elements, the military allowed political parties to form and eventually also accepted the return of old politicians it previously condemned (Zürcher 2004).

The 1990s saw the emergence of an Islamist party in Turkey, the **Welfare Party** (WP). Led by Necmettin Erbakan, the WP won a modest number of seats in the General Assembly (parliament) elections of 1991. It more than doubled its size in 1995, making it impossible for the secularist parties to form a coalition without it. Erbakan became the prime minister in 1996 (Pope and Pope 1997). Pro-Islamic statements by Erbakan and other members of his party drove the military to issue a list of secularist demands to the government in February 1997. To demonstrate its seriousness, the military sent its tanks to patrol neighborhoods in Ankara. Erbakan announced that he would comply with the military's wishes, but he took no practical measures to meet their demands. Between February and June the military embarked on a quest to purge its ranks of officers suspected of Islamist inclinations. The military soon followed up with an ultimatum demanding Erbakan's resignation. To avoid another military takeover, Erbakan stepped down. A case against the WP was opened in the constitutional court in Ankara, which banned the WP and Erbakan from political activity in January 1998 (Zürcher 2004).

Although a new government set out to implement the military's recommendations to rid the political system of any religious elements, the Islamists did not disappear from the political arena. In the 1999 elections, the successor to the WP, the **Virtue Party** (VP), finished third and was left out of the government. This third-place finish did not stop the secularists from leveling accusations against the VP and eventually, in 2001, winning a case against it in the constitutional court that brought about its disintegration. The leaders of the VP then split into two camps, radicals and moderates. The latter, under the leadership of the former popular mayor of Istanbul, Recep Tayyip Erdoğan (pronounced Erdo-aan), and Abdullah Gül, formed the Justice and Development Party (better known by its Turkish acronym, AKP) in August 2001. In the November 2002 elections, AKP came out first with 34 percent of the votes, leaving the RPP far behind with only 19 percent. The high electoral threshold of 10 percent in Turkey allowed only these two parties entry into the National Assembly and granted the AKP a majority of seats. It thus ruled as a single-party government, with the RPP serving as the opposition. In the 2007 elections, the AKP received 46 percent of the votes but lost seats in the assembly (Yavuz 2006).

The AKP has been successful with voters in eastern and central Turkey, in villages and small towns, and where the population is more traditional than in the western part of the country or in large cities such as Istanbul, Ankara, and Izmir. Yet one should not attribute AKP's success only to its religious message. Its initial appeal to voters had more to do with people's desire to rid Turkey of its old politicians, combat the financial crisis, and seek a party that offers hope for a better future. Erdoğan's message was one of conservative democracy, which would successfully combine moderate Islam with democratic and Western principles. Officially, the AKP rejected religion as its main line, claiming to be a conservative party instead. Its leaders talked about the importance of globalization and being part of the Western world, as opposed to the separatist Turkish nationalist agenda that had governed Turkey since the foundation of the republic. This emphasis meant a willingness to allow public display of ethnic identity that was not Turkish, an ideology especially appealing to the Kurdish minority. Indeed the AKP promoted a message of human rights and promised to allow further room for Kurdish culture and language in the political and educational spheres as well as the media (Yavuz 2006).

In its first term, Erdoğan's government's most noteworthy achievement was resolving the financial crisis. Inflation was brought down to normal levels, a new currency (New Turkish Lira, now again Turkish Lira) was introduced, foreign investments grew many fold, and the annual growth of the Turkish economy rebounded from a negative 9 percent to 7.5 percent in four years. The AKP government also presented a compelling case that Turkey was a fitting candidate for joining the EU. Turkey had been trying to join the EU and its predecessor, the European Economic Community (EEC), since 1959. It officially submitted its candidacy for full membership in the EEC in 1987, but it was denied. After repeating attempts throughout the 1990s, Turkey's candidacy for membership was finally approved in 1999, but the long list of demands Turkey had to comply with was de facto an insurmountable obstacle. Reforms in the judiciary system, changes in government policies, and an improvement in Turkey's human rights and civic liberties records prompted the EU to start accession negotiations with Turkey in 2005. However, these negotiations have been put on hold almost entirely, officially because of Turkey's refusal to recognize the Greek-controlled **Republic of Cyprus** (an EU member state) and its ill treatment of the Kurdish minority living within its borders (Yavuz 2009).

In its first term the Erdoğan government had a majority in parliament and thus tried to promote legislation that the RPP deemed too religious in nature, including an attempt to ease the ban on wearing headscarves in government buildings and educational institutions. The president at the time, Ahmet Necdet Sezer, a secularist who was the chief justice of Turkey's constitutional court, mostly vetoed the legislation. Lacking the two-thirds majority necessary to override a veto, the AKP could not fully pursue its agenda. It did, however, have enough votes to ensure the next president would be more sympathetic to its agenda.

The AKP started its second term with the political conundrum of electing a successor to Sezer, whose term expired up in 2007. The AKP chose Abdullah Gül. When the secularists managed to block his election through the constitutional court and the military posted a warning on its website that it would not view changes to the secularist nature of the state favorably, Erdoğan called for new elections. The AKP's victory secured the election of Gül to the presidency through a plebiscite. Gül's election allowed the party to continue its slow takeover of civic society, by appointing school principals and university rectors sympathetic to the AKP and by using legislation to limit the military's checks against the government. Members of the party also supported the international network of private schools of Fethullah Gülen that aims to combine science and religion, as well as other Muslim charitable organizations, some of which have suspected ties to terrorist cells (Yavuz 2009).

Erdoğan's government has changed its foreign policy dramatically in a short period. Traditionally, Turkey and Israel have been strong allies that maintained close economic and military cooperation. Turkey's relations with its neighbors Syria and Iran were not nearly as warm. Turkey also assisted the United States in the war in Iraq by sending troops and by securing its border to prevent insurgents fleeing into Turkey. After 2007, the relations between Turkey and Syria improved and Erdoğan offered to broker a peace treaty between Israel and Syria. A series of indirect negotiations took place in the summer and fall of 2008 in Istanbul and Ankara. Syria walked away from the talks when Israel launched operation Cast Lead in Gaza and Erdoğan endorsed Hamas, criticizing Israel for committing a massacre. Relations between Turkey and Israel have declined rapidly, and on May 31, 2010, a Turkish-led flotilla trying to break the Israeli siege on Gaza was stopped by the Israeli navy in international waters. Five of the six ships were taken over without resistance, but a violent confrontation developed on one vessel resulting in the deaths of nine passengers, all Turkish citizens, and injuries to many others, including a number of Israeli soldiers. Turkey blamed Israel for the incident, demanding an apology and compensation to the victims' families. The Turks withdrew their ambassador from Tel Aviv. At the same time, Turkish officials increased their support for the Palestinians, including Hamas. Turkey has also tightened its relations and cooperation with Iran, to the dismay of the United States and the EU and despite UN sanctions prohibiting international business in Iran. Some explain Turkey's recent change of orientation from West to East by its disappointment in the EU accession process that has demanded time and again that Turkey change while not showing any signs of willingness to seriously consider their candidacy. Others point to a hidden Islamist agenda that drives Erdoğan to distance Turkey from its former ally, Israel, and thus from the United States, and to seek the friendship of Iran and Syria. The overwhelming support the AKP enjoys in Turkey, driven mostly by its internal policies, will likely give the party some more time to clarify its foreign policy intentions (Danforth 2009; Davutoğlu 2010).

RADICAL ISLAM

Radical Islamist ideas developed differently among Sunnis and Shiites, although today there is some cooperation between fundamentalist groups of both traditions. In the modern Sunni world the Muslim Brotherhood (MB) of Egypt was among the earliest and most influential radical Islamist movements. Founded in 1928 by Hasan al-Banna (d. 1949), its ideology called for a return to the early days of Islam and opposed Western influences in the Middle East. Another leading ideologue of the MB, **Sayyid Qutb** (d. 1966), is considered the most influential intellectual among radical groups. Qutb was an author of many books, an educator, and a commentator on the **Qur'an**. In his works, he criticized modern Islamic society and the United States, where he had spent time in the late 1940s, and whose society he perceived to have been corrupt and materialistic. The MB and Qutb supported the 1952 Free Officers coup that ended the British-backed monarchy in Egypt and brought Gamal 'Abd al-Nasser to power. When it became clear that Nasser's socialist agenda did not fit in with that of the MB, the latter began to criticize his rule. In 1954 the Egyptian government used an unsuccessful attempt to assassinate Nasser to crack down on the MB, and Qutb and other leaders of the MB were arrested. Except for an eight-month period in 1964, Qutb spent the rest of his life behind bars. His prison experiences influenced his conflict with the government. The MB resumed activities openly only during the presidency of Anwar al-Sadat, who replaced Nasser in 1970 (Rubin 2010).

The MB's ideology helped attract many to its ranks, especially among the lower classes and those disappointed by the government. The MB also introduced a welfare system that provided the poor with food, clothing, shelter, and education at levels the Egyptian government could not compete with. In addition, the MB had a military arm, which the organization employed until the 1990s to attack government, secular, and foreign targets in Egypt (Rubin 2010). This model of gaining political support by providing services to potential voters has been mimicked across the world from the Irish Republican Army in Ireland to Hizballah in Lebanon. The political reality, however, is that the MB does not allow for a plurality of views.

In 1987 Ahmad Yassin founded Hamas, a social-political movement that aims to replace Israel and the PA's rule with an Islamic-Palestinian state on all the lands of Palestine. Hamas, inspired by the MB, operates an extensive network of social services in Gaza (and formerly in the West Bank). The movement also staffs teachers and workers in the UN's schooling and relief agencies for refugees in the Gaza strip. In addition to its civic operations, Hamas has a military wing called the **'Izz al-Din al-Qassam brigades**. Named after a Palestinian nationalist from the 1930s, the brigades were responsible for attacks in Gaza, the West Bank, Israel, and Egypt starting in the early 1990s. Hamas has sent suicide bombers to Israeli cities (until 2005) and launched rockets from the Gaza strip into southern Israel. The United States, Canada, the EU, and Israel formally define Hamas as a terrorist group (Tamimi 2007).

In the 1980s and early 1990s the ideas of Sayyid Qutb became very popular among traditionalist circles in the Middle East. Al-Qaeda emerged from these groups sometime in the late 1980s. A group of Egyptian Islamists that included Ayman al-Zawahiri, the operating and strategic commander, and Osama bin

Laden, a member of the wealthy Saudi Bin Laden family, formed al-Qaeda in Pakistan. The founders of al-Qaeda were most influenced by Sayyid Qutb's ideology. According to some testimonies, al-Qaeda believes in restoring a true Islamic state based on Islamic law (the Shari'a); purging the Muslim world of foreign ideologies, such as nationalism or socialism; and eliminating the enemies of Islam, such as Jews and Westerners in general, with emphasis on the United States. Radical Islamists have long sanctioned the killing of non-Muslims. Al-Qaeda, however, justifies the targeting of other Muslims, which Islamic law generally prohibits, by pointing to a religious obligation to execute apostates, or those who pretend to be true Muslims (Burke 2004).

Bin Laden's and al-Qaeda's enmity toward the United States began during the first Gulf War, when bin Laden criticized the decision of King Fahd of Saudi Arabia to allow the United States military to operate from Saudi Arabia, the home of Islam's holiest sites of Mecca and **Medina**. In response to his criticism, the Saudis banished bin Laden, and from 1992 to 1996 he lived in Sudan. The Saudis also stripped him of his citizenship, and his family cut off financial ties with him in 1995. In 1996, after the Egyptian **Islamic Jihad**—a movement whose members helped found al-Qaeda—attempted to assassinate Egyptian president **Hosni Mubarak**, Sudan expelled bin Laden and his most loyal followers. Al-Qaeda then moved its headquarters to Afghanistan, where the **Taliban**, a group of hard-liner Islamists, had emerged in the void created after the Soviet withdrawal in 1989. Al-Qaeda operated from Afghanistan in the five years leading up to September 11, 2001. The U.S. war in Afghanistan toppled the Taliban regime, and many members of al-Qaeda fled the country. Since then, the United States has been involved in operations in Afghanistan and neighboring Pakistan to fight Taliban resistance and hunt down al-Qaeda operatives. The most noteworthy success of the years-long war in that region has been the killing of bin Laden, who was found in a compound in Abbottabad, Pakistan, on May 2, 2011. After bin Laden's death, Aiman al-Zawahiri replaced him as leader of al-Qaeda. Beyond Afghanistan and Pakistan, where al-Qaeda clearly operated, it is believed that the group has cells in other Middle Eastern and African countries. Although they claim to represent all Muslims, al-Qaeda has been denounced and condemned by moderate and traditionalist leaders in the Muslim world, most of whom saw bin Laden as a threat to stability and good relations with the West (Jones 2010).

In the Shiite world the main propagators of fundamentalist ideology are the clerics of the Islamic Revolution in Iran. The Ayatollah Khomeini suggested in his book *Vilayet-e Faqih* the idea that an Islamic state, led by a jurist who serves as the source of inspiration, will replace a corrupt regime backed by non-Muslims (Khomeini 1979). When the Islamic Revolution broke out, Khomeini sought to implement his ideas in government. The principles of the revolution, however, were soon deemed universal and exported to other parts of the Islamic world. Throughout the 1980s relentless efforts were made to appeal to Shiite populations in countries governed by Sunnis. In the western parts of Saudi Arabia, a large Shiite minority lived in relatively poor conditions. The message of the revolution was also delivered to the Saudi Shiites through books and recordings of Iranian clerics. The Saudis, however, were clever to confront the threat to their rule by pouring money into the Shiite areas and improving the socioeconomic status of their inhabitants. Similar attempts to export the revolution were made in the Persian Gulf area, mostly through supporting small Shiite organizations or political parties represented in the Kuwaiti parliament under the name the **National Islamic Alliance** (Ramazani 1990).

The one success story of the Islamic Revolution outside Iran has no doubt been Hizballah of Lebanon. In recent years, and especially since Israel's withdrawal from South Lebanon in 2000, Hizballah has positioned itself as a legitimate political party within Lebanon and as the defender of the country from external threats. Through its extensive network of schools, hospitals, community centers, and soup kitchens, Hizballah has gained supporters even among non-Shiites. Its prestige in Lebanon skyrocketed after the war with Israel in 2006, and many now see the organization as the symbol of Lebanese resistance against Israeli (and thus also American) threats. In addition, Hizballah's participation in Lebanese democratic political system and government has positioned it as a mainstream political party in recent years. Gradually, Hizballah is gaining political legitimacy outside of Lebanon as well (Norton 2009).

The change in Hizballah's position within Lebanon is characteristic of a process radical Islamist groups have undergone in recent years. Hamas has attempted to transition from a paramilitary group known mostly for its suicide bombers to a legitimate political party by participating in and winning the elections for the PA in 2006 and by portraying itself as the vanguard of the struggle against Israeli occupation. Hamas exchanged using suicide bombings for launching rockets, a tactic that seemed more conventional and helped portray Hamas as the victim. Since its takeover of Gaza, and even more since its confrontation with Israel in December 2008, Hamas has managed to achieve some recognition in Turkey, Russia, and even the EU. As its leader, Khaled Mash'al has claimed Hamas should be seen not as part of the problem, but rather part of the solution for the question of Palestine. Time will tell whether such groups will integrate fully into the political systems of their societies and gain international recognition. Such integration would require radical groups to adapt and compromise—something they have thus far failed to do.

THE ARAB SPRING

There were no scholars, journalists, or observers of the Middle East who predicted the sweeping events of 2011 in the region. Popular demonstrations and protests emerged, seemingly out of nowhere, and led to the downfall of long-standing autocratic governments in Tunisia, Egypt, Libya, and Yemen as well as to violence and significant unrest in Syria, Bahrain, and elsewhere. The reverberations from the social-media-inspired movement shook the foundations of nearly every country in the region.

In hindsight, however, there had perhaps been some unusual signs of discontent with the old order of dynastic and anti-democratic rule that was waiting for the right spark to start the wildfire that led to the Arab Spring. An early warning sign that the popular **Arab Street** might be turning the corner against traditional despotic rule in the region came in 2005 in Lebanon during the **Cedar Revolution.** Racked by civil war and competing religious factions for the last quarter of the twentieth century, Lebanon remained under the political and military thumb of neighboring Syria and the regime of **Bashar Assad** as late as 2005. In February of that year a massive car bomb killed the popular prime minister of Lebanon **Rafik Hariri**. While it was unclear who murdered Hariri, all signs pointed to the Syrian-backed Hizballah (Hoge 2005). Popular protests in the streets of Beirut soon led to demands that all Syrian forces leave Lebanon and that the Syrians end their heavy-handed influence in the political life of the country. Despite some violence and counter-protests in support of Syria, Assad announced the withdrawal of Syrian troops by April, and the protests lost their steam. A similar outpouring of popular defiance occurred in 2009–2010 in Iran, where thousands took to the street to protest fraudulent national elections that returned Mahmud Ahmadinejad to power. As a sign of how much technology had changed since the protests in Lebanon, the young Iranian demonstrators in the so-called Green Revolution confounded the Islamic regime and their police forces by taking advantage of Twitter, blogging, and using Facebook to quickly organize rallies and deliver their message to the world. The mass demonstrations in Iran ended, but not before there were arrests, scores of wounded or dead protestors, and international condemnation of the Iranian government (Keller 2010).

Despite the events in Lebanon and Iran, there was no indication that a larger regional movement might challenge long-standing rulers such as Ben Ali (Tunisia: twenty-four years), Mubarak (Egypt: twenty-nine years), Saleh (Yemen: thirty-three years), or Gaddafi (Libya: forty-two years). The match that ignited the proverbial fire began in Tunisia, modestly enough, in December 2010 when a fruit and vegetable vendor committed an act of self-immolation to protest the corruption and repression of the Ben Ali government (Blight, Pulham, and Torpey 2012). Local protests in provincial Tunisian towns soon followed and spread to Tunis, the capital. Middle East analysts were perplexed by the rapid nature of the protest. Tunisia had little history of popular demonstration against the government, which was widely viewed as corrupt but which had also expanded economic opportunities (Borger 2010). By mid-January, less than a month after the initial protests, Ben Ali had fled the country for Saudi Arabia. Events in Tunisia, however, were just a warm-up for what was about to unfold in Egypt.

Less than two weeks after Ben Ali had fled Tunis, thousands of Egyptians decamped to Tahrir Square to protest the repressive and corrupt Mubarak regime and call for his removal from office. Like their Iranian counterparts in 2009, the Egyptians were young, Internet savvy, and frustrated by the lack of economic opportunity or a meritocracy. Egypt had long been considered a cultural core of the Middle East, with a significant population (81 million) and a pro-American government. A regime change in Tunisia was one thing, but Egypt was a crucial geopolitical pivot point. The international community was riveted by a standoff that quickly developed between Mubarak and the protestors. World leaders anxiously watched as increasingly violent clashes between loyalists and protestors unfolded online. All eyes were set on the Egyptian military. Would they decide to back their patron Mubarak or side with the growing numbers of citizens in Tahrir Square? The United States, quiet throughout the first weeks of the Egyptian protests, finally called for Mubarak's ouster after an uncomfortable wavering. Just eighteen days after the protests began, Mubarak was placed under house arrest.

Similar protests soon spread to the Gulf States, across North Africa and the wider Middle East. While the revolts carried "a common call for personal dignity and responsive government," they were each unique. Different economic and social variables that included high unemployment and lack of opportunity had an impact, but so too did unique relations with the West and their irregular rule of each modern regime (Anderson 2011).

Libya had, perhaps, the most distinctive of the region's odd and repressive modern regimes. Dominated for more than forty years by the eccentric Muammar Gaddafi, whose megalomania knew no bounds, the oil-rich nation of six million people was rocked by the Arab Spring. Just as the protests in Cairo reached their peak in February 2011, anti-Gaddafi demonstrations started in Libya. These protests soon led to a protracted all-out war, with the better-armed and trained Libyan armed forces loyal to Gaddafi holding the upper hand. The international community, sensing that Gaddafi had the firepower to ride out the challenge, intervened via the UN Security Council's authorization of NATO to assist the rebel forces. NATO's help, which included air strikes and logistical support to the rebels, made all the difference. By late October 2011 Gadaffi was dead, wounded first by a French missile strike and then dragged from his car and shot by rebels who captured the melee on cell phone video and posted it online for the world to see. Libya's brush with the Arab Spring ended with regime change, but much less clear (in early 2012) is what will become of Syria, where a civil war, for all practical purposes, is underway. What is clear, however, is that the regional legacy of the Arab Spring of 2011 will be felt in years ahead in ways that are unpredictable. While there have been regime changes and some modest reforms enacted as a result

(Jordan and Morocco are examples of countries where the royal families have dealt more adroitly with the protests by offering improvements), democracy and economic development have not yet been realized.

CONCLUSION

The Middle East is a region where intricate social and political problems pose numerous challenges for the years to come. The Arab Spring has changed the dynamic in the region. As Arab nations turn inward and try to improve their own societies and to institute self-government, the rule of law, economic opportunity, and the conflict between Israel and its Arab neighbors have received less attention. The Arab-Israeli conflict embodies many of the challenges the region has faced and will confront in the future, but it is not the only issue. One hopes that an eventual resolution between the Israelis and the Palestinians will relieve the plight of the Palestinian people, lead to the Arab world's acceptance of Israel, strengthen relations between moderate Arab states and the West, and weaken reactionary elements in the region, such as Iran, Hizballah, Hamas, and al-Qaeda. The resolution of the conflict could alter alliances in the region, most notably those of the United States with moderate Arab regimes and those of Turkey with Iran and Syria. It is difficult to assess, however, how the Arab world's reconcilement with Israel might change Turkey's foreign policy and its attempts to join the EU on the one hand, and its growing investment in Iran and Syria on the other. A solution to the Arab-Israeli conflict might affect American involvement in the region and perhaps even bring stability to Iraq and Afghanistan. These are wishful thoughts given the events on the streets of Tunis, Cairo, Damascus, and Tripoli during 2011. The internal reconstruction of a region rocked by domestic protest, violence, regime change, and in some cases civil war leaves very little room in the near term for finding a sustainable relationship with Israel. What is clear, however, is that the situation in the Middle East remains a fluid one, and that trying to predict the future is anyone's guess.

REFERENCES

Abrahamian, Ervand. 1982. *Iran between Two Revolutions*. Princeton, N.J.: Princeton University Press.

Allawi, Ayad. 2007. *The Occupation of Iraq: Winning the War, Losing the Peace*. New Haven, Conn.: Yale University Press.

Anderson, Lisa. 2011. "Demystifying the Arab Spring." *Foreign Affairs*, May/June: 2–7.

Blight, Garry, Sheila Pulham, and Paul Torpey. 2012. "The Path of Protest." *The Guardian*, January 5. Accessed January 22, 2012. www.guardian.co.uk/world/interactive/2011/mar/22/middle-east-protest-interactive-timeline.

Borger, Julian. 2010. "Tunisian President Vows to Punish Rioters After Worst Un-
    rest in a Decade." *The Guardian*, December 29. Accessed January 22, 2012.
    www.guardian.co.uk/world/2010/dec/29/tunisian-president-vows-punish
    -rioters.

Bowden, Mark. 2006. *Guests of the Ayatollah: The Iran Hostage Crisis*. New York:
    Grove Press.

Burke, Jason. 2004. *Al-Qaeda: The True Story of Radical Islam*. New York: Palgrave
    Macmillan.

Carlisle, Rodney. 2007. *Iraq War*. New York: Facts on File.

CNN. 2010. "Casualties of the Iraq War." Accessed January 12, 2011. http://edition
    .cnn.com/SPECIALS/war.casualties/.

Danforth, Nick. 2009. "How the West Lost Turkey." *Foreign Policy*, November
    25. Accessed January 12, 2011. www.foreignpolicy.com/articles/2009/11/25/
    how_the_west_lost_turkey.

Davutoğlu, Ahmet. 2010. "Turkey's Zero-Problems Foreign Policy." *Foreign Pol-
    icy*, May 20. Accessed January 12, 2011. www.foreignpolicy.com/articles/
    2010/ 5/20/turkeys_zero_problems_foreign_policy?page=0,0.

Ebel, Robert. 2010. *Geopolitics of the Iranian Nuclear Energy Program: But Oil and
    Gas Still Matter*. Washington, D.C.: Center for Strategic and International
    Studies.

Eisenberg, Laura, and Neil Caplan. 2010. *Negotiating Arab-Israeli Peace: Patterns,
    Problems, Possibilities*. Bloomington: Indiana University Press.

Enderlin, Charles. 2003. *Shattered Dreams: The Failure of the Peace Process in the
    Middle East, 1995–2002*. New York: Other Press.

Harel, Amos, and Avi Issacharoff. 2008. *34 Days: Israel, Hezbollah, and the War in
    Lebanon*. New York: Palgrave Macmillan.

———. 2010. "A New Kind of War." *Foreign Policy*, January 20. Accessed January
    12, 2011. www.foreignpolicy.com/articles/2010/01/20/a_new_kind_of_war.

Hoge, Warren. 2005. "U.N. Cites Syria as Factor in Lebanese Assassination."
    The New York Times, March 25. Accessed January 22, 2012. www.nytimes
    .com/2005/03/25/international/middleeast/25hariri.html.

Jacoby, Tami Amanda. 2007. *Bridging the Barrier: Israeli Unilateral Disengage-
    ment*. Burlington, Vt.: Ashgate.

Jamal, Amal. 2005. *The Palestinian National Movement: Politics of Contention,
    1967–2005*. Bloomington: Indiana University Press.

Jones, Seth. 2010. *In the Graveyard of Empires: America's War in Afghanistan*. New
    York: W. W. Norton & Company.

Kahl, Colin. 2010. "Breaking Dawn: Building a Long Term Strategic Partnership
    with Iraq." *Foreign Policy*, August 31. Accessed January 12, 2011. http://mid
    east.foreignpolicy.com/posts/2010/08/31/breaking_dawn.

Keddie, Nikkie. 2006. *Modern Iran: Roots and Results of Revolution*. New Haven,
    Conn.: Yale University Press.

Keller, Jared. 2010. "Evaluating Iran's Twitter Revolution." *The Atlantic*, June 18.

Accessed January 22, 2012. www.theatlantic.com/technology/archive/ 2010/ 06/evaluating-irans-twitter-revolution/58337/.

Kelly, Michael. 2008. *Ghosts of Halabja: Saddam Hussein and the Kurdish Genocide.* Westport, Conn.: Praeger.

Khalidi, Rashid. 2006. *The Iron Cage: The Story of the Palestinian Struggle for Statehood.* New York: Beacon Press.

Khomeini, Ruhollah. 1979. *Islamic Government.* Arlington, Va.: Joint Publications Research Service.

Krämer, Gudrun. 2008. *A History of Palestine: From the Ottoman Conquest to the Founding of the State of Israel.* Princeton, N.J.: Princeton University Press.

Laqueur, Walter. 2003. *A History of Zionism.* London: I. B. Tauris.

Lewis, Bernard. 2002. *The Emergence of Modern Turkey.* Oxford: Oxford University Press.

Lynch, Colum. 2010. "Ahmadinejad: 9/11 Was a US Conspiracy." *Foreign Policy,* September 23. Accessed January 12, 2011. http://turtlebay.foreignpolicy.com/ posts/2010/09/23/iranian_president_911_was_a_us_conspiracy.

Morris, Benny. 2001. *Righteous Victims: A History of the Zionist-Arab Conflict.* New York: Vintage Books.

Norton, Augustus. 2009. *Hezbollah: A Short History.* Princeton, N.J.: Princeton University Press.

Oren, Michael. 2003. *Six Days of War: June 1967 and the Making of the Modern Middle East.* New York: Presidio Press.

Pope, Hugh, and Nicole Pope. 1997. *Turkey Unveiled: A History of Modern Turkey.* New York: Overlook Press.

Rabinovich, Itamar. 1990. "The Suez-Sinai Campaign: The Regional Dimension." In *The Suez-Sinai Crisis, 1956: Retrospective and Reappraisal,* edited by S. I. Troen and M. Shemesh, 162–71. New York: Columbia University Press.

Ramazani, R. K. 1990. "Iran's Export of the Revolution: Politics, Ends, and Means." In *The Iranian Revolution: Its Global Impact,* edited by John Esposito, 40–62. Gainesville: University Press of Florida.

Rubin, Barry. 1994. *Revolution until Victory?: The Politics and History of the PLO.* Cambridge, Mass.: Harvard University Press.

———. 2010. *The Muslim Brotherhood: The Organization and Policies of a Global Islamist Movement.* New York: Palgrave Macmillan.

Schanzer, Jonathan. 2008. *Hamas vs. Fatah: The Struggle for Palestine.* New York: Palgrave Macmillan.

Schiff, Ze'ev, and Ehud Ya'ari. 1984. *Israel's Lebanon War.* New York: Simon and Schuster.

Stein, Kenneth. 1999. *Heroic Diplomacy: Sadat, Kissinger, Carter, Begin and the Quest for Arab-Israeli Peace.* New York: Routledge.

Tamimi, Azzam. 2007. *Hamas: A History from Within.* Northhampton, Mass.: Olive Branch Press.

Tezcür, Güneş. 2010. *Muslim Reformers in Iran and Turkey: The Paradox of Moderation*. Austin: University of Texas Press.

Tripp, Charles. 2000. *A History of Iraq*. New York: Cambridge University Press.

Yavuz, Hakan, ed. 2006. *The Emergence of a New Turkey: Democracy and the AK Parti*. Salt Lake City: University of Utah Press.

———. 2009. *Secularism and Muslim Democracy in Turkey*. Cambridge: Cambridge University Press.

Zürcher, Erik. 2004. *Turkey: A Modern History*. New York: I. B. Tauris.

Conclusion

ZACH P. MESSITTE

Forgotten during the 2011 National Basketball Association (NBA) Western Conference Finals between the Oklahoma City Thunder and the Dallas Mavericks was the international background of the teams on the floor. In one sequence, during game 3, the Mavericks' Jose "J. J." Berea (Mayagüez, Puerto Rico) dribbled up court and passed the ball to future Hall of Famer Dirk Nowitzki (Würzburg, Germany), who was guarded by the Thunder's Serge Ibaka (Brazzaville, Republic of Congo). Nowitzki then flipped the ball beyond the three-point arc to Peja Stojakovic (Požega, Croatia),[1] who missed a long arching shot. The ball was rebounded by Oklahoma City's Thabo Sefolosha (Vevey, Switzerland), who then passed the ball to all-star Kevin Durant (Maryland, USA). On the Mavericks' bench, reserve players Rodrigue Beaubois (Pointe-à-Pitre, Guadeloupe)[2] and Ian Mahinmi (Rouen, France) watched the game unfold. Professional basketball, much like other team sports such as soccer, baseball, and hockey, no longer knows borders (Wolff 2002). Today we expect advertisements in Spanish about the "éne-bé-a"; take for granted the ability to watch global soccer stars like Argentine Lionel Messi, who plays for Barcelona in the Champions League; or check on the Japanese slugger Ichiro as he goes for his third Major League Baseball batting title.

The rapid globalization of culture, politics, economics, and our daily lives has been, to keep the analogy going, a game changer. This book examines how that growing internationalism impacts critical issues (American foreign policy, international security, humanitarian intervention, and the global economy) and affects key parts of the world (China, the European Union, Latin America, and the Middle East). As an editor of *Understanding the Global Community*, I challenged our colleagues to write chapters that would be straightforward but also intellectually interesting. I asked them for words that would be more accessible than an academic conference paper yet more stimulating than an introductory textbook. Students embarking on an academic path of international and area studies should look closely at the reference list of each chapter. These recommended readings are a road map. Should you choose to major in international and area studies, pursue an advanced degree, enter into a career that takes you overseas, or just want to learn more about a specific topic, these suggested books and articles are a great place to begin the journey.

THE MISSING CHAPTERS

This book is by no means comprehensive. There are critical issues and areas that are absent, and we will be the first to admit that there are gaps. It is simply not possible to cover every important global issue and all the regional perspectives. It is no accident that the chapters in this book focus heavily on economic, historical, and political issues. The editors and authors of this book overwhelmingly hold degrees in, and study, history, economics, and political science. Nevertheless, the field of international and area studies is by its very nature interdisciplinary. Most, but not all, of our colleagues eschew rigid methodological formulas in favor of practical and mixed techniques to solve problems and try to reach solutions. This mélange approach is the reason why many of the chapters mix history, politics, economics, and cultural references in order to illuminate larger points. That said, however, there are still some vital areas and issues that we would wish could be included in a future edition of this book.

For example, an analysis of global music, food, sport, film, literature, and so forth (what we might call global culture) would be welcome. There are many students of international affairs who believe that cultural exchange builds trust so that thornier problems can eventually be addressed with greater ease. It is certainly less complicated for the Iranians and the Americans to play out their tensions at soccer's World Cup than it is for Washington to figure out whether Tehran is developing nuclear energy for peaceful purposes.[3] The theory holds that if we can celebrate our basic humanity by rejoicing at the Olympics or by enjoying the pandas on loan from China at the zoo, then we will eventually be more willing to solve the more serious stuff, like nuclear proliferation or trade disputes.

The importance of religion, communication, natural resources, and transportation are also chapters that we would wish for in a future edition. The issue of religion is certainly touched upon by Yaron Ayalon in his chapter on the Middle East, but a more systematic understanding of religion's role in the global twenty-first century is crucial to any student of the discipline (Kimball 2011). Similarly, one could argue that the role of communication and how we move (and perhaps will eventually move) about the planet are topics for further exploration. Even though environmental concerns are briefly examined in the chapter on international security, the great debate about the world's reliance on fossil fuels and the race to find alternative energy perhaps also merits its own chapter.

Harder to rationalize away are the missing regional perspectives: where are the chapters on Africa, Russia, and the rest of Asia (in addition to China)?

Do Brazil and India not merit their own chapters? There are no defensible answers to this critique. These are critical regions of the world with unique viewpoints. We hope to have contributors from these important regions in future editions of this book. In the end, while this volume cannot claim to be all-inclusive, there are certain collective lessons to be gleaned from its chapters.

THE CONTINUED POWER OF THE STATE SYSTEM

Major strides have been made to harmonize global governance since the end of World War II (the creation of the United Nations, the World Bank, the International Monetary Fund, and a host of international and regional organizations), and the importance of nongovernmental organizations in solving transnational issues cannot be understated. Yet the essays in this book highlight the sustained and primary role of states. As Alan McPherson points out in his chapter on Latin America, the United States may no longer be *numero uno*, but without a strong system of global governance, a comparative superpower rival, and the military force to back it up, America remains the big *enchilada*, so to speak, in every region and on virtually all international issues. As I noted in my chapter on American foreign policy, President Barack Obama (or any sitting American president) is still the single world leader with enough power to truly define a global era. Yet Obama's power to lead and shape the world is vastly diminished from that of his not-so-distant predecessors.

When the Allies (primarily the United States, England, and the Soviet Union) emerged victorious over fascism in 1945, they faced a world devastated by years of conflict. Hunger, disease, poor governance, and ruined infrastructure dominated nearly every corner of globe, save the United States. American resolve in the aftermath of the Second World War, along with key allies, to galvanize the creation of international governmental organizations, foster regional development, and usually (but not always) promote democracy has led to dramatic change for the good. The progress that has been made in the past half century to solve some of the basic needs of human life are significant and should not be blithely dismissed (Kenny 2011). Nevertheless, as Suzette Grillot details in her chapter on international security issues, today's global problems—the spread of weapons of mass destruction, poverty and the growing gap between the rich and poor, global health epidemics, and environmental degradation—will take more than American leadership. It will take an invigorated international community, regional security organizations, and nongovernmental organizations to solve the transnational problems of the coming decades.

The key to whether or not the international community can mobilize collectively in the near term—on everything from climate change to trade—may well hinge on the evolving U.S.-China relationship. As Peter Gries highlights in his chapter on China, understanding the factors that define U.S.-China relations is "an urgent task" because armed conflict is a real, even if distant, possibility. China's economic and political aspirations now reach into what have been traditional spheres of American influence. China is the "elephant in the room" in Latin America, with increasingly large economic and political clout throughout the region. China's ability to gain a toehold in Latin America (as well as Africa) may have much to do with the still embryonic sense from Bogota to Buenos Aires of a common regional identity. Latin America remains a "diverse set of republics" that "has kept their distance from each other as much from any imperial power."

While Venezuela's Hugo Chavez may get the world's media attention for his theatrics and vocal anti-Americanism, Brazil is clearly the one state in Latin America with the potential to break through and become a major player on the world stage. With going on three decades as a successful democracy, a booming economy, and popular political leadership during the past decade, Brazil will play host to soccer's 2014 World Cup and the 2016 Summer Olympics. Nevertheless, Latin America as a united regional entity is still a long way off.

The European Union (EU), however, is far more coordinated than Latin America and already has a seat at the table of world power. The European regional identity has grown quickly—and perhaps even too fast—in the last two decades. By taking in the former satellite states of the Soviet Union, introducing a common currency, and trying to establish a cohesive foreign policy, there is a sense that perhaps the EU has overreached. As Mitchell Smith and Robert Cox explain in chapter 6, the EU's ambitious agenda has ironically led to an existential crisis that calls into question six decades of largely successful cooperation.

COMPETITION, CONFLICT, AND OUTLIERS

The EU's identity crisis and Latin America's dysfunctional relationship with the United States both pale by comparison to the problems in the Middle East, a region that has persisted—more or less—for the past half century in a permanent state of turmoil. The tumultuous political history of the region and the religious importance of the land make it nearly impossible to be a dispassionate observer. Yaron Ayalon is right when he points out in chapter 8 that the "intricate social and political problems pose numerous challenges for the years to come." How has the Arab Spring altered the region's future? Is there a lasting solution to the Israeli-Palestinian conflict? Will Iran remain a rogue state? Can Iraq end the sectarian violence and prosper? Is Turkey a model of Islamic democratic success, or does radical Islam threaten Atatürk's experiment with secularism? These are just a few of issues that must be addressed in the coming decade.

If the Middle East is to pull itself out of the mire of conflict and tension, the pathway to a better future will likely start with economic development. Middle Eastern countries will need to move beyond the export of oil and integrate fully into the global economy. In chapter 4, Mark Frazier offers a skeptical assessment of the future of international economic cooperation. He calls out the United States, China, and the EU for abandoning their responsibilities to adhere to the common principle that a rising economic tide lifts all boats. Instead of promoting the benefits of working together through multilateral institutions that try to promote fair trade, economic growth, and currency stability, the United States, China, and the EU have returned to the unilateral and nationalist policies that prevailed in between the First and Second World Wars. In the wake of the worst economic crisis since the Great Depression, the world financial community seems to have forgotten some of the lessons of the 1930s, mainly that protectionism, barriers to free trade, and self-interested policies do more damage in the long run to the economic well-being of the global community than the short-term domestic political benefits they are designed to satisfy.

It is not only the economic lessons of the World War II era that have been forgotten in the past two decades. It is in many ways remarkable that the international community still has not learned the lessons of inaction in the face of fanaticism and brutality. Millions of Jews and other Europeans perished at the hands of Hitler and the Nazis during the lifetimes of either the parents or grandparents of most of those reading this book. The Japanese Army's disregard for the treatment of civilians in wartime is well documented and remains in the news almost seven decades later.[4] And yet, in the past twenty years, ethnic cleansing in the former Yugoslavia, genocide in Rwanda, and the wanton slaughter of women and children in Darfur, Sudan, have joined the ranks of modern global failures, mocking the "never again" promise made by the Allies in the wake of Nazi and Japanese atrocities. When, and perhaps equally important, how, does the international community intercede when internal conflict spirals out of control and thousands (and even millions) of innocent lives are threatened? Eric Heinze's chapter examines this issue that continues to bedevil the international community despite the opportunity for concerted action by the great powers created by the end of the Cold War. In the end, a definable solution for effective humanitarian intervention remains both elusive and problematic.

Even within the state system there are rogue nations that actively choose not to participate in international cooperation: North Korea and Myanmar are probably the best example of outlier states that actively shun the forces of the outside world. There are still others factors, such as failed states, that are contributing to everything from the spread of infectious disease to the arms trade and piracy. These failed states (such as Somalia or Haiti) also hinder what could be a consistently more positive and cohesive joint response to crises such as famine, AIDS, or disaster relief by the international community.

NATIONAL HISTORY AND IDENTITY STILL MATTER

A large part of the problem behind mobilizing the United Nations (or any international organization or coalition of states) to take bold action in the face of a common problem is that historical patterns, nationalism, and identity still matter as much (if not more) than the emerging global identity. The political push and pull between domestic interests and international concerns is a common theme that runs through every chapter.

In the first part of the book, we see how American political leaders keep a close eye on voters' opinions (lest they be voted out of office) and how this colors foreign policy decision making about nearly everything from the hunt for al-Qaeda's leadership to whether or not to sign on with most of the rest of the world to limit greenhouse gases. In the second chapter, on global security issues, we see how it becomes hard for failed states to divert precious national resources away from education or national defense to combat health epidemics or other issues that might impact the rest of the world. In the third chapter, on humanitarian intervention, the importance of the concept of "selectivity," which is in part defined by the unpredictable domestic political willingness of countries to support risky interference in another nation's conflict, remains crucial. For example, why do some decide to respond to violence in Kosovo but not respond to violence in Rwanda? Similarly, the final chapter of part I, on the global economy, outlines how economic and domestic demands (perhaps of steel workers in Pennsylvania, heavy industry in China, or farmers in France) lead to generally higher prices and ultimately substandard goods for people all over the world.

In the second part of the book, the regional perspectives similarly highlight the importance of identity in hindering the development of a global community. Our identity, or what the scholar Benedict Anderson has called our "imagined community" (which might include nationality, religion, and shared history and morals), determines how we interact with others from different parts of the world (Anderson 1983). Chinese nationalism is at the very root of that country's domestic political transformation of the past forty years. China's foreign relations with the rest of the world are filtered through the lens of what it means to be Chinese.

The EU has also had to wrestle with nationalism in the form of historical enmity between member states that in some cases goes back centuries. Conceptions about the social, economic, and political role of the state have put the EU's own future into question. As the chapter's authors point out, "Identities are resistant to change, and the popular policies of the welfare state have strong support, leading many [European] member states to assert their control." Similarly, Latin America's diversity and different histories make each country unique. While Chile may be the most globalized, Cuba and Haiti remain painfully isolated. The critical importance of history in the shaping of the modern Middle East cannot be underestimated. The interpretation and passion attached to the importance of a specific place extend from the ancient to the more recent. For example, within several hundred yards of each other in Jerusalem's old city, Jews, Christians, and Muslims have enshrined their holiest of holy sites. In an area little more than the size of a few football fields, Christians believe Christ was crucified; Muslims hold ground sacred because they believe it is where Muhammad ascended to heaven accompanied by the angel Gabriel; and Jews doven at the Western (or Wailing) Wall, an ancient remnant of the Second Temple, which is nearly 2,000 years old. It is no wonder that Jerusalem remains a key sticking point in resolving the conflict not only between Israelis and Palestinians, but also between Israel (and its ally the United States) and the rest of the Arab world. History, and in particular the record between the local population and the colonizing West, has been critical to the formation of the modern-day countries of Iran, Iraq, Turkey, Egypt, and Lebanon among others.

COMMON CONCERNS AND HOPES

Despite the divisive nature of the modern state structure, and the limitations that national history and identity place on the global community, there are several common concerns that are also shared by most people, regardless of boundaries or preconceived notions. This book highlights at least three large, shared interests. First, humankind's continued quest to find solutions to limit war, conflict, violence, and destruction remains elusive, but there have been positive strides forward in recent decades. It is now coming in on seventy years since the end of the last truly world war. While the second part of the twentieth century and first decade of the twenty-first has certainly seen its share of violence and destruction, there are a growing number of people throughout the world, linked by technology, that keep a close eye on international events as they unfold in real time. More perfect and diffuse information makes it considerably more difficult for tyrants or organized thugs to commit gross acts of brutality without someone finding out about it and posting the details online for all to read, see, and hear. As the popular demonstrations of the Arab Spring attest, the use of Facebook, Twitter, blogs, and the Internet in general can be used to organize supporters around the world to demand more accountability and openness from dictatorships. Taking coordinated international action against intransigent autocrats remains more problematic, but the improvement over the past century is real and sustained.

Second, economic growth and development in order to reduce poverty and hunger and to increase human security is also a largely shared goal of the global community. Whether states will lead the way by creating a relatively open global economy remains a riskier proposition. The past suggests that there are periods of fluctuation where a more closed and protected global economy occasionally rules. While history may not repeat itself in the second decade of the twenty-first century and follow the counterproductive whirlpool of measures that stemmed the flow of trade and deepened the worldwide economic depression of the 1930s, there is no guarantee that the largely uninterrupted progression toward greater economic internationalization of the past half century will continue forever.

Nontraditional security concerns are a third area where global actors are now at least paying lip service to a desire to find sustainable solutions to common problems. These emerging issues are outlined in the chapter on international security. Many of these new areas spring from the rapid advances in communication, transportation, and technology of the past half century. Terrorism—because of the spread of weapons of mass destruction and our reliance on technology—has taken on a new urgency in recent years. Terrorists have so many entry points into the global system that intelligence about their plans has become crucial. Cyberterrorism and cyberwarfare have entered the world's lexicon as new words in the past twenty years. Efforts to break the linkages between areas of scarce natural resources (such as water or diamonds) and violence are increasingly fertile areas for policy makers looking to solve age-old conflicts. Global health epidemics are a long-standing problem, but they have been exacerbated and sped up because of advances in the movement of people and goods on ever-faster and more affordable planes, ships, cars, and trains. There are similar shared concerns about the impact of modern society on the environment, from the accidental introduction of invasive, non-native species spoiling an ecosystem to global warming and unpredictable weather. The world's ability to begin to understand and chart these nontraditional security concerns is a first small step toward concretely addressing these kinds of issues. While some concerted action has already been taken, there is clearly much more work yet to do done.

FINAL THOUGHTS

If the world is, indeed, on an inevitable and continuing pathway toward greater globalization, what does it mean for the years 2040, 2070, and beyond? Of course, this question is meant to be more rhetorical than real. Fundamentally, however, an increasingly globalized world means we need to have a greater understanding and appreciation of many of the issues and regions detailed in this book. It is ever more likely that many of us will work and live in a different country than the one we reside in now. A college-aged reader of this book has a better chance than his or her parents' or grandparents' generations of doing business, sharing a meal, or singing a popular common song with someone who grew up on a different continent. These kinds of interactions will have unintended and unimagined ripple effects on international political, economic, and social issues that make understanding the global community so critically important.

As we have said several times, this book is a complimentary side order to a more traditional introductory textbook of terms, theories, and ideas. While it is suitably designed for a first course in international studies, it is also a compendium of chapters about critical ideas and concepts for the internationally curious. Being globally adventurous is not only desired, it is essential for the next generation of policy makers, business leaders, academics, journalists, community leaders, and so forth. As a professor (and previously as a student), the best classroom discussions and courses I have been a part of were the ones when the participants augmented what they gleaned from their assigned readings or scholarship with their own real-life experiences.

Getting beyond the syllabus is absolutely required for the student of international studies. There are always more books and articles to read or lectures to attend, but equally important is travelling overseas for pleasure and studying abroad. There is extraordinary value in leaving the comfort zone of your home culture and trying to put yourself in the shoes of people living thousands of miles away. Seeing where different people live, and at least glimpsing the daily rhythms of life in another culture, has immeasurable importance on intellectual development and the richness of the human experience. While some American public universities are contracting their departments of modern languages, it remains essential to learn to speak at least one foreign language with some degree of fluency. Language critically enhances your perspective on the world. This is particularly true for native English-speakers, who often feel they don't need other languages since "everyone speaks English." Not only is this statement untrue, but more important, learning another language is the ultimate sign of respect for another culture. Taking the time to understand language and culture helps to break down communication barriers, providing greater insight about the nuances of why different people, in the end, believe what they believe. Of course, there is no single book or set of courses that can give us a complete picture of how to view the world. It is only by getting out beyond our own borders that we can come to our own understanding of what the global community truly means.

NOTES

1. Stojakovic is a Serbian.

2. Guadeloupe is a small island in the Lesser Antilles and a region of France.

3. The United States and Iran have, in fact, played each other at the World Cup. The Iranians eliminated the Americans from the 1998 World Cup in France with a 2-1 victory.

4. The issue of compensation for "comfort women," who were forced into prostitution across Asia during World War II, remains a topic of relatively current

discussion between the Japanese government and many of their regional partners. See http://news.bbc.co.uk/2/hi/asia-pacific/6530197.stm (accessed May 29, 2011).

REFERENCES

Anderson, Benedict. 1983. *Imagined Communities.* London: Verso Books.

Kenny, Charles. 2011. *Getting Better: Why Global Development Is Succeeding—And How We Can Improve the World Even More.* New York: Basic Books.

Kimball, Charles. 2011. *When Religion Become Lethal: The Explosive Mix of Politics and Religion in Judaism, Christianity and Islam.* San Francisco: Jossey-Bass.

Wolff, Alexander. 2002. *Big Game, Small World: A Basketball Adventure.* New York: Warner Books.

Glossary

Abbas, Mahmud (Abu Mazen; 1935–). Palestinian leader elected as chairman of the Palestinian Liberation Organization in 2004 and president of the Palestinian Authority in 2005.

Abu Ghraib. A Baghdad prison used by the American military to house suspected insurgents during the Iraq War. It received worldwide attention for graphic photos depicting acts of torture and sexual abuse on Iraqi detainees by American soldiers.

Ahmadinejad, Mahmud. First elected president of the Islamic Republic of Iran in 2005, he won a second term in the disputed elections of 2009 that led to the Green Revolution. He has fiercely defended Iran's nuclear development and has described the Holocaust as a myth while calling for the destruction of Israel.

AIDS/HIV. Acquired Immune Deficiency Syndrome (AIDS) is a disease of the immune system caused by the Human Immunodeficiency Virus (HIV) that weakens the human immune system and makes it less resistant to infections. The disease is transmitted by direct contact with infected bodily fluids.

Alliance for Progress. Created by U.S. president John F. Kennedy in 1961 to increase cooperation between North and South America.

altercasting. Invoking a role or relationship to persuade or pressure others to comply with one's wishes, for example, "Friend, could you buy me a beer?"

al-Qaeda. A radical Sunni movement founded in the late 1980s and composed of networks of multinational, stateless armies who call for a global jihad and are generally perceived to sponsor and perpetrate terrorist acts worldwide.

Amal. A Lebanese Shiite political party that supported Israel's campaign to rid Lebanon of Palestinians in the First Lebanon War in 1982.

Anatolia. A geographic region that denotes the westernmost extension of Asia and comprises the majority of modern Turkey.

anti-globalization. The opposition of a single world market that is dominated by multinational corporations that often reside in wealthy countries.

anti-rightist campaign (反右运动). Instigated by Chairman Mao Zedong in the late 1950s, it involved the persecution of "rightists" believed to be capitalists opposing socialism.

Arab League. A regional organization of twenty-two Arab states in the Middle East and North Africa that was founded in Egypt in 1945.

Arab Spring. A wave of protests that began in early 2011 across North Africa and the greater Middle East that led to the toppling of autocratic governments in Tunisia, Libya, and Egypt. Making use of social media, the demonstrations have also led to violence in a host of other countries, most notably Syria, Yemen, and Bahrain.

Arab Street. Popularly used during the Arab Spring to refer to what common people were saying, doing, and thinking around the Middle East.

Arafat, Yasser (1929–2004). President of the Palestinian National Authority (1996–2004), long-serving chairman of the Palestinian Liberation Organization, and Nobel Peace Prize winner (1994).

Armitage, Richard (1945–). The U.S. deputy secretary of state (2001–2005).

Asian financial crisis. A currency crisis that started in Thailand in July 1997 when it appeared that the Thai government could no longer support the Thai currency at fixed rates of exchange. Other states in East Asia, most notably South Korea and Indonesia, suffered currency crises that led to emergency IMF loans and regional recession.

Assad, Bashar. Dynastic leader of Syria since 2000 after succeeding his father, Hafez; he has presided over a civil war since late 2011.

Atatürk (1881–1938). First president of Turkey (1923–1938), he helped shape Turkey into a modern, secular republic.

balance of payments (BOP). A system of accounting for the international transactions of a given state, including trade in goods and services, capital flows, and other exchanges of money.

balance of power. A stable equilibrium between nations within a regional or global system.

Balfour Declaration. A 1917 British expression of support for a Jewish national homeland in Palestine.

Banana Wars. An economic conflict between the United States and the EU over the EU's preferential treatment of former colonies in the import of bananas. This preferential treatment negatively impacted the ability of American-owned, Latin America-based banana companies to export to Europe. The dispute was taken to the WTO, which ruled in 2001 that the import tariffs placed on Latin American bananas by the EU were illegal.

Barak, Ehud (1942–). The prime minister of Israel (1999–2001), Israeli minister of defense (2007–present), and former chair of the Israeli Labor Party.

Bay of Pigs attack. A CIA-funded attempt to invade Cuba in April 1961 with Cubans exiled in the United States. The attack against Castro's Cuba failed and caused a hemisphere-wide decrease in American prestige.

Beijing Spring (北京之春). The spring of 1989 when Chinese activists occupied Tiananmen Square in downtown Beijing.

Belgrade Bombing. The U.S. bombing of the Chinese embassy in Belgrade during the war over Kosovo that killed three Chinese and led to several days of anti-American street protests across China. The building was marked on American maps as a Serbian communications center, and President Clinton and NATO later apologized.

Berlin Wall. A wall constructed by the Soviets in 1961 that divided communist East Berlin and Germany from free West Berlin/Germany. The wall "fell" on November 9, 1989, signaling the beginning of the end of the Cold War.

Biden, Joseph (1942–). The forty-seventh vice president of the United States and U.S. senator from Delaware (1973–2009). He was the longtime chair and member of the U.S. Senate Foreign Relations Committee.

Big Three. The leaders of the three major Allied powers of World War II: Soviet premier Josef Stalin, U.S. president Franklin D. Roosevelt, and British prime minister Winston Churchill.

Bill and Melinda Gates Foundation. A non-profit founded by Bill and Melinda Gates for the purpose of increasing healthcare and reducing poverty globally.

Biological Weapons Convention (BWC). A multilateral disarmament treaty that banned the development, use, stockpiling, and transfer of biological weapons.

bin Laden, Osama. The founding leader of al-Qaeda and one of the masterminds of the September 11, 2001, attacks on the World Trade Center and the Pentagon. A Saudi Arabian by birth, he was killed in Pakistan by U.S. forces on May 1, 2011.

bipolar system. An international system characterized by a roughly equal distribution of military, economic, and cultural power between two states or groups of states.

bipolar world. The division of the world into two main major centers of power. An example would be the Cold War era (1946–1991), dominated by the United States and the Soviet Union.

black market. An underground, illicit, and illegal market for the buying and selling of goods in violation of laws, price controls, rationing, or other legal constraints.

Black September. A series of wide-scale attacks on the Palestinians who were living in Jordan that forced much of the Palestinian leadership to leave the country in September 1970.

Bretton Woods Monetary System. A U.S.-forged system for global monetary stability designed to support economic growth and recovery after World War II. Created at a conference held in Bretton Woods, New Hampshire, in 1944, the monetary system revolved around the U.S. dollar as an anchor that was exchangeable for gold at a fixed rate, with other global currencies tied to the dollar at fixed rates.

BRICS countries. Brazil, Russia, India, China, and South Africa—each considered to be an emerging economic and politically powerful country.

Brzezinski, Zbigniew (1928–). U.S. national security advisor (1977–1981).

Bush, George H. W. (1924–). The forty-first president of the United States (1989–1993), forty-third vice president (1981–1989), director of Central Intelligence (1976–1977), ambassador to China (1974–1975), U.S. ambassador to the UN (1971–1973), and U.S. congressman from Texas (1967–1971).

Bush, George W. (1946–). The forty-third president of the United States (2001–2009), governor of Texas (1995–2000).

Camp David. The Maryland country retreat of the president of the United States, it is famous for being the site of peace talks between Egypt and Israel in the late 1970s that led to the Camp David Accords in 1978, which formed the basis of the peace treaty between the two countries.

capitalism. Economic system based on free markets and profit.

cartel. Grouping of illicit drug producers, distributors, or sellers who cooperate to achieve high prices for its product.

Carter, Jimmy (1924–). The thirty-ninth president of the United States (1977–1981), governor of Georgia (1971–1975), and winner of the Nobel Peace Prize in 2002.

Casablanca Conference. Meeting between Franklin Roosevelt and Winston Churchill in Morocco in January 1943 to plan the European military strategy during World War II.

Cast Lead. A military operation carried out by the Israeli armed forces against Hamas in December 2008 in response to Hamas' rocket attacks on Israel.

Castro, Fidel (1926–). Leader of Cuban Revolution, he became the head of government in Cuba in 1959 and passed on his role to his brother Raul in 2008 because of health concerns.

Cedar Revolution. A term coined to encompass the 2005 protest movement in Lebanon following the assassination of Prime Minister Rafik Hariri. The demonstrations led to a withdrawal of Syrian forces from Lebanon and a curtailing of Syrian involvement in Lebanese politics.

Central Kingdom (中国). Refers to China and the idea of China at the center of "Civilization."

"Century of Humiliation" (百年国耻). The evolving Chinese narrative/story about China's past encounter with Western and Japanese imperialism starting with the First Opium War of 1839–1842 up through the middle of the twentieth century.

Chemical Weapons Convention (CWC). A multilateral disarmament treaty that prohibits the development, production, stockpiling, and use of chemical weapons.

Cheney, Richard (1941–). The forty-sixth vice president of the United States (2001–2009), CEO of Halliburton (1995–2000), U.S. secretary of defense

(1989–1993), U.S. congressman from Wyoming (1979–1989), and White House chief of staff (1975–1977).

China National Offshore Oil Corporation (中国海洋石油总公司; CNOOC). One of the three major national oil companies of China, along with SINOPEC and PetroChina.

China's rise (中国崛起). China's growing influence in the world, particularly economically and militarily.

Chinese Communism. Communist Party of China (CPC) is the ruling party of the People's Republic of China (PRC).

Chinese Communist Party (中国共产党). Founded in the early 1920s, it is the only political party in China.

Christian Falanges. A political party in Lebanon that is mainly supported by Maronite Christians. The Falanges were Israel's ally during the First Lebanon War in the early 1980s and played a major role in the Sabra and Shatila massacres. Also called the Lebanese Social Democratic Party.

Christianity. An Abrahamic religion founded in the first century CE that is based on the life, the death by crucifixion, and the resurrection of Jesus Christ as described in the New Testament of the Bible.

Churchill, Winston (1874–1965). British prime minister during World War II (1940–1945) and also from 1951 to 1955.

civic nationalism. Identification with one's nation based on its political institutions, rather than its ethnicity or culture.

climate change. Significant and lasting changes in the weather patterns of a specific area.

Clinton, Bill. The forty-second president of the United States (1993–2001), governor of Arkansas (1979–1981 and 1983–1992).

cluster bomb. A type of bomb that ejects smaller projectiles called "bomblets" over a large area. Cluster bombs are designed to target enemy personnel and nonarmored vehicles.

Coalition Provisional Authority (CPA). A temporary government set up by the United States in Iraq following the American invasion in March 2003. Designed to be a transitional arrangement until Iraq could elect its own leaders, the CPA turned over authority to Iraqi leaders in June 2004.

Cold War (1946–1991). A period of political, military, and economic tension between the United States (and its allies) and the Soviet Union (and its satellite states).

Communist Bloc. The countries that were aligned with the Soviet Union during the Cold War, particularly members of the Warsaw Pact.

communitarian. A political theory that emphasizes the moral value of political or social communities and the need to balance the rights of individuals with interests of the community as a whole.

Community's Development Fund. Part of the European Commission's humanitarian aid division, it provides for nonemergency assistance to promote development in African, Caribbean, and Pacific states.

Comprehensive Test Ban Treaty (CTBT). A multilateral agreement in 1996 to ban all nuclear explosions, regardless of their military or civilian purposes; the treaty has yet to come into force because it has not been ratified by enough countries.

Confucianism (儒家). A complex Chinese philosophical system that aims for the cultivation of human ethics in social life.

consequentialism. An ethical theory that seeks to appraise the moral desirability of an action based on the goodness of the consequences that the act will, or is likely to, bring about.

containment. American foreign policy strategy authored by George F. Kennan that aimed to limit the worldwide expansion of the Soviet Union and communism.

conventional war. A form of violent conflict conducted with the use of conventional military weapons and battlefield tactics between two or more well-defined states.

Convention on the Rights of the Child. A multilateral human rights agreement outlining the political, economic, social, and cultural rights of children.

convertibility. The ability of a government's currency to be converted into another currency or gold.

Copenhagen Summit. UN meeting of world leaders in Denmark in December 2009 to raise global awareness on climate control and change.

cosmopolitan. A political theory that argues that individuals each belong to a universal community based on a common morality, regardless of nationality, citizenship, ethnicity, and so forth.

Council of Representatives. The Iraqi 275-seat parliament that was set up in 2005 under the Iraqi Constitution.

coup. The sudden overthrow of a regime, usually by a small group within the government, such as the military.

Cuban Missile Crisis. A thirteen-day confrontation between the United States and the Soviet Union in 1962 over Soviet missiles being placed in Cuba.

current account. A measure of the yearly financial health of a government that adds exports minus imports to interest and dividends to transfer payments such as foreign aid.

customary international law. Binding international law that is derived from consistent state practice over a period of time and accompanied by the belief that the practice is permitted or required by law (this latter requirement is called *opinio juris*).

customs union. A trade bloc that exercises free trade within its borders and has a common external tariff.

cybernationalists (网络民族主义). The use of the Internet as a communication tool to promote nationalism.

cyberwarfare (or **cyberterrorism**). The use of computers and other electronic devices to attack an enemy's information systems and cause widespread damage or disruption. Cyberwarfare is often characterized by actions among states while cyberterrorism involves terrorist use of the Internet to damage or disrupt a target's information systems.

Cyprus. An island in the eastern Mediterranean that has been the locus of dispute—military and political—between Turkey and Greece. The southern half of the island is known as the Republic of Cyprus and is predominantly Greek. It is also a full member of the EU. Only Turkey recognizes the northern part of the island, the Turkish Republic of North Cyprus.

Dalai Lama (达赖喇嘛; 1935–). The spiritual leader of Tibetan Buddhism and viewed by some as the reincarnation of the Bodhisattva; he is also winner of the 1989 Nobel Peace Prize.

Darwinian. Those who believe in Charles Darwin's theory of evolution.

debt. The accumulation of a nation's deficits.

decolonization. The process of becoming independent and installing self-rule and governance after a period of rule by a colonial power. This term is most often used in association with the removal or relinquishment of colonial powers in Africa and Asia after World War II.

deficit. The amount by which spending exceeds income, which indicates a negative balance of funds.

de Mello, Sergio Vieira (1948–2003). A UN diplomat from Brazil who was killed in Baghdad in 2003 while serving as the UN envoy to Iraq.

democratic institutions. Significant aspects of democratic governance, such as free and fair elections; separation of powers; checks and balances; transparency in governance; freedoms of speech, religion, and association; equality before the law; and protection of minorities.

Democratic Party (DP). A Turkish center-right, conservative political party.

democratic peace theory. A theory suggesting that democratic governments—especially liberal democratic governments—are very unlikely to go to war with one another.

Deng Xiaoping (邓小平; 1904–1997). Chinese politician who was a leader of the Communist Party of China, he helped open China's economy to the global market.

dependency. A territory that may or may not be a legally sovereign state but one that has surrendered some of its sovereign rights, for instance its ability to sign treaties, to defend its own territory, or to collect its own customs duties.

deregulation. The dismantling of state-imposed regulations on private corporations, such as health and safety rules or limits on pollution.

desertification. The process by which desert boundary areas lose topsoil and plant life, thus causing the desert to spread. The process is most often the result of natural drought and human populations overusing and exploiting grasses and vegetation.

Desert Storm (1990–1991). A military operation led by the United States and the Coalition Forces (thirty-four nations) against Iraq in what is also known as the Persian Gulf War.

deterrence. The ability to deter an attack by another with the deployment of a particular weapon or combination of weapons.

development. The act or process of developing, growing, or making progress. The term is typically used in the context of economic development, although it is also appropriate with political and social development.

disappeared. A noun describing those individuals kidnapped by repressive governments and whose whereabouts are never confirmed. Most are presumed to be killed by their captors.

Doha Round. The name of the current round of WTO multilateral negotiations that began in 2001 and sometimes known as the "development round." The negotiations have been both protracted and contentious in an attempt to reduce agriculture and textile subsidies in North America, Europe, and Japan in exchange for reduced barriers to trade in goods and services among developing countries.

dual-use targets. Military targets that serve both a civilian and military purpose, for example, bridges, airports, roads, and power grids.

economic gradualism. The belief that economic change should be brought about gradually and in small increments.

economic structuralism. A theory of international relations that characterizes relations between the developed and developing world based on inequality, dependency, and exploitation. The approach emphasizes the world capitalist system as the mechanism by which such relations emerge and are perpetuated.

Eisenhower, Dwight (1890–1969). The thirty-fourth president of the United States (1953–1961), supreme allied commander of NATO (1950–1952), president of Columbia University (1948–1950), five-star general in the U.S. Army, and supreme allied commander of U.S. Armed Forces during World War II.

embargo. The banning of trade with a country in order to isolate it and weaken it.

energy security. The ability of a nation to have stable access to the resources and commodities it needs for the productive functioning of the state and society.

entangling alliances. A phrase coined by George Washington in his farewell address in 1796, it refers to his advice to his countrymen to avoid foreign commitments, particularly in Europe.

environmental degradation. A gradual deterioration of the environment as natural resources such as air, water, and soil are depleted through overuse and/or pollution; such deterioration damages and potentially destroys ecosystems and may lead to the extinction of wildlife.

environmental refugees. People forced to migrate from their homeland because of rapid, gradual, or long-term negative changes to their local environment.

ethnic cleansing. A term coined during the Balkan wars of the 1990s wherein an ethnic group seeks to create an ethnically homogenous state by "cleansing" it of people of different ethnicities by either expelling or killing them.

ethnic conflict. A violent conflict between ethnic groups that is often internal rather than international in nature.

euro. The official currency of the Eurozone of the EU.

European Central Bank. The central bank of the EU that administers monetary policy, it was established by the Maastricht Treaty of 1992 and is headquartered in Frankfurt, Germany.

European Coal and Steel Community. A 1951 European integration project that incorporated six European nations, uniting a fractured post-war Europe by creating a common market for coal and steel.

European Commission. The EU's bureaucracy that is located in Brussels, Belgium.

European integration. The process of European states acceding to membership in the EU and integrating certain commonalities.

European Parliament. The parliamentary institution of the EU that is directly elected and serves as the legislative body of the EU.

European Union (EU). An association of European nations formed to achieve economic and political integration.

Eurozone. The area made up of the nations of the EU that use the euro as their currency and is joined in an economic and monetary union.

expansionism. A country's attempt to geographically extend its borders, sometimes by using military force.

expatriate. A citizen of one country who lives in another but still holds rights (such as voting) in his or her home nation.

export. A good or service that a nation produces and transports to another nation.

extraterritoriality. A legal concept under which a foreign national is exempt from being prosecuted under the local law of the foreign territory in which he or she resides.

failed state. A state that has failed to provide many of the basic conditions and responsibilities of a sovereign government.

fascism. First introduced by Benito Mussolini in Italy after World War I and later adopted by the Nazis in Germany, it puts a strong and nationalistic state at the core of its governing philosophy.

Fatah. A major Palestinian political party that is the largest faction of the Palestinian Liberation Organization (PLO) and a left-wing rival of Hamas.

First Lebanon War. An Israeli campaign to subdue Palestinian forces in Lebanon in 1982 by driving them away from the Israeli-Lebanese border. The war ended with a siege of Beirut that forced the Palestinian leadership to leave Lebanon for Tunis.

Fissile Material Cut-off Treaty (FMCT). An international treaty that has been negotiated, but not yet finalized, to prohibit further production of fissile material for nuclear weapons or other explosive devices.

floating currencies. An arrangement in which the values of currencies reflect the supply of, and demand for, currencies in global markets, rather than being fixed or "pegged" by governments to another currency or set of currencies.

Former Yugoslavia. Consists of the new states following the collapse of the Socialist Federal Republic of Yugoslavia—Bosnia-Herzegovina, Croatia, Kosovo, Macedonia, Montenegro, and Macedonia.

Four Books (四书). Chinese texts selected by the prominent Song dynasty scholar Zhu Xi to be the core works of Confucianism.

Fourth Generation Nationalists (第四代民族主义者). The thirty-something and largely middle class, male, and urban professionals who were the driving force behind the emergence of popular Chinese nationalism in the late 1990s and into the new millennium.

Fox, Vicente (1942–). The president of Mexico (2000–2006).

free trade. An economic concept in which countries trade freely with each other with minimal government intervention or additional tariffs placed on imports.

Free World. Cold War term that referred to countries that were not aligned with the Soviet Union, refers today mainly to the Western powers and is a symbol of democracy and economic prosperity.

Gaddafi, Muammar. The leader of Libya from 1969 until his death in 2011 by anti-government rebels. Charismatic, but also harsh, he clashed frequently with the United States and Europe over terrorism, Israel, and human rights.

Gates, Robert (1943–). The twenty-second U.S. secretary of defense (2006–); director of Central Intelligence (1991–1993).

Gaza. An ancient Middle Eastern city and region **(Gaza Strip)** that borders the Mediterranean Sea, Israel, and Egypt. Gaza has been under the control of Hamas since 2006.

GDP. *See* gross domestic product.

General Agreement on Tariffs and Trade (GATT). The predecessor of the WTO, which governed trade among member nations through a series of treaties from 1947 to 1994.

Geneva Convention. The treaties and protocols adopted by most countries during the twentieth century that set standards for international law in the conduct of war.

genocide. The deliberate, systematic, and often violent extermination of a specific group of people based on nationality, race, ethnicity, politics, religion, culture, or some other distinguishing factor.

geopolitics. The interplay of geographical territory and political authority.

global economic inequality. The uneven distribution of economic resources and income across states and regions.

global financial crisis (GFC). The worldwide recession that began with a credit crisis and a series of bank failures in the United States in 2008.

globalization. The political, economic, and cultural connection between the countries of the world due to factors such as free trade and advances in technology, transportation, and communication.

Global North. A social, economic, and political distinction of wealthy developed countries, known collectively as "the Global North."

Global Partnership against the Spread of Weapons and Materials of Mass Destruction. A G8 partnership to prevent terrorists, or those that harbor them, from acquiring or developing weapons of mass destruction.

Global South. A social, economic, and political distinction of poor, lesser-developed countries, known collectively as "the Global South."

Global War on Terror (GWOT). A campaign led by the United States in the wake of September 11, 2001, to counter terrorism.

Golan Heights. A rocky plateau of extreme strategic importance that straddles the borders of Israel and Syria; Israel has occupied the Golan Heights since the Six Day War of 1967.

grand ayatollah. In Shia Islam, an ayatollah who has attained a greater status and position of influence by publishing extensively on issues that relate to ordinary Islamic life.

Great Depression. A severe global economic depression that began in the United States in 1929 following the crash of the stock market and lasted through the Second World War.

Great Leap Forward (大跃进). A political and economic campaign that Chairman Mao Zedong initiated in 1958 to accelerate industrialization, collectivization, and the realization of communism.

Great Proletarian Cultural Revolution (无产阶级文化大革命; 1966–1976). Known also as the "Cultural Revolution" or the "ten years of chaos," this was a political and cultural movement Chairman Mao Zedong launched to rid China of his political enemies and impel China toward communism.

Great White Fleet. Sixteen new U.S. battleships sent around the world at the end of Theodore Roosevelt's administration (1907) as a show of American international military might.

greenhouse gas emissions. Gases generated through human economic activity that are trapped in the earth's atmosphere and contribute to global warming.

Green Revolution (Iran). Widespread protests in Iran in response to the 2009 reelection of Mahmud Ahmadinejad. Demonstrators wore the color green to honor the campaign of the defeated candidate and called the elections fraudulent. Clashes between protestors and the government led to arrests and casualties.

gross domestic product (GDP). The market value of all goods and services produced within a country in a given time period and usually measured annually.

Group of 20 (G-20). A grouping of finance ministers and central bank governors from the twenty of the world's largest or most influential economies that meets regularly to discuss issues critical to the global economy.

Guantanamo Bay (Gitmo). American detainment facility located in Cuba established in 2002 as a prison to hold suspected terrorists captured on the field of battle during the Global War on Terror.

Guardian Council. An Iranian body of twelve jurists that holds the power to elect and dismiss the Supreme Leader of Iran, while simultaneously being subject to his authority.

guerrilla. A person who has been a soldier in a "little war," or insurgency, in which small groups use their disadvantages against their enemy, often hiding in difficult terrain, ambushing more conventional forces, and retreating.

H1N1 (swine) flu. The human version of respiratory illness in pigs that is caused by infection with Swine Influenza A virus.

Haganah. A Jewish paramilitary organization that operated under the British Mandate of Palestine from 1920 to 1948 and later became the core of the Israeli Defense Forces (IDF).

Hamas. A Palestinian Islamist political party founded in 1987 that has actively participated in resistance operations against Israel. Hamas has been classified as a terrorist group by the United States and the EU.

Hamilton, Alexander (1757–1804). The first U.S. secretary of the treasury and one of the principal authors of the Federalist Papers.

Han ethnicity (汉族). The largest Chinese ethnic group, consisting of approximately 92 percent of the Chinese population.

hard power. The use of military or economic power to exert global influence.

Hariri, Rafik. The prime minister of Lebanon from 1992 to 1998 and again from 2000 to 2004, he was assassinated in Beirut in 2005. His death sparked the Cedar Revolution that led to a withdrawal of Syrian troops from Lebanon.

harmonious society (和谐社会). A slogan championed by China's current president Hu Jintao, which aims to promote social and political stability amidst the exploitation accompanying rapid development.

health epidemics. Illness and disease that affect many persons at the same time and spread in areas where the disease is not permanently prevalent or easily controlled.

hegemon. A nation that has military, political, or economic power over other countries.

high representative for the Union in foreign affairs and security policy. A single EU representative designed to give the EU a clearer and more unified voice in global affairs.

Hizballah. A militant Shia group officially founded in 1985 and based in Lebanon that emerged in response to the 1982 Israeli invasion.

Holocaust. The Nazi German massacre of six million European Jews that included large-scale gassings carried out in concentration camps.

Holocaust Day. The Remembrance Day dedicated to the memory of the approximately six million Jews who died during WWII.

Hu Jintao (胡锦涛; 1942–). The current general secretary of the Communist Party of China (2002–) and president of the People's Republic of China (2003–).

humanitarian aid. The provision of goods or services, often by international agencies and organizations, in order to alleviate human suffering, including the provision of food, potable water, and medical supplies and care.

humanitarian intervention. The use of military force by a state or group of states for the purpose of halting or averting large-scale and gross human suffering.

human rights. Rights afforded to the individual by the government and society simply by virtue of being a human being.

human security. A term coined by the UN Development Programme to encompass all possible threats to human well-being that originate from both outside and within the boundaries of states.

human trafficking. The illegal transnational trade in, or movement of, human beings for the purposes of forced labor or commercial sexual exploitation that is often referred to as modern-day slavery.

Hussein, Saddam (1937–2006). The president of Iraq (1979–2003) and leader of the Ba'ath Party vice president of Iraq (1968–1979), he was captured by U.S. troops in Iraq in 2003, tried by an Iraqi court for murder and torture, and executed by hanging in 2006.

idealism. A view of the world that fundamentally believes in the good of humanity and the use of power to protect the rights of the individual.

identity. A person's self-image or mental model of himself or herself.

imperialism. The territorial, political, and economic domination of one country over another.

improvised explosive devices (IEDs). These crude homemade bombs have been used by insurgent forces against more established militaries in recent years. IEDs first came to the attention of many Americans during the Iraq and Afghanistan wars, where they were used against U.S. troops.

indemnities. Compensation paid by party A to party B if A has caused B suffering or loss.

indigenous. Related in Latin America to peoples (and their descendants) who inhabited the Western hemisphere before the arrival of Europeans.

infrastructure. The physical apparatus necessary for development, including roads, bridges, sewers, and communications equipment.

Inter-American Development Bank. A multilateral lending institution founded in 1959 that borrows from a variety of nations and lends to Latin American and Caribbean governments for development projects.

interdependence. A dynamic of being mutually dependent in that the actions of one player impact the circumstances and decisions of another player.

international (governmental) organizations (IOs or IGOs). Groups of states that work collectively and multilaterally to achieve various goals and objectives, with purposes often outlined in an international treaty or charter.

international anarchy. A fundamental concept in international relations theory suggesting that there is no central authority in the international system of states.

International Atomic Energy Agency (IAEA). An international organization that promotes the peaceful use of nuclear energy and seeks to inhibit its military use, including nuclear weapons.

International Campaign to Ban Landmines (ICBL). A global network of more than 1,000 nongovernmental organizations that works for a world free of antipersonnel landmines and cluster munitions.

International Commission on Intervention and State Sovereignty. An international commission of experts convened at the request of the UN, and sponsored by the Canadian government, that drafted a report called *The Responsibility to Protect.*

International Criminal Court. An international organization based in The Hague (Netherlands) that rules on transnational criminal issues, including war crimes and genocide.

international law. Legally binding rules such as treaties that individual states have consented to follow in their relations with one another.

International Monetary Fund (IMF). An intergovernmental organization founded at the Bretton Woods Conference in 1944 that seeks to ensure international exchange rate stability and oversee balance-of-payments between nations.

International Security Assistance Force. A multinational force created by NATO to help provide security for the governance and rebuilding of Afghanistan.

intifada. An Arabic word that means "uprising" and came to signify the insurrections carried out by Palestinians against Israel in the West Bank and Gaza Strip from 1987 to 1993 and from 2000 to 2005.

investment. The commitment of money or capital to purchase financial instruments or assets with the expectation of some amount of financial return.

Iran-Contra affair. A political scandal during the second term of the Reagan administration (1986–1989) when senior U.S. government officials were accused of secretly selling arms to Iran to gain the release of Americans held hostage in Lebanon and diverting the profits to provide funding to the Contras (anti-communist rebels) in Nicaragua.

Iranian Hostage Crisis. Following the takeover of the U.S. embassy in Tehran by a group of pro-Khomeini students in November 1979, fifty-two American employees of the embassy were held in captivity for 444 days before being released in the first hours of the Reagan administration in January 1981.

Iranian Revolution. The 1979 popular uprising in Iran that included the overthrow of Shah Mohammad Reza Pahlavi and the establishment of an Islamic Republic.

Iran-Iraq War. An eight-year-long war (1980–1988) between Iran and Iraq primarily fought over border disputes and the increasing Iranian influence following the 1979 revolution.

Iraqi National Movement. An Iraqi political coalition made up of both Sunnis and Shias that claims to be nonsectarian and secular and was formed to contest the parliamentary elections of 2010.

Islam. An Abrahamic religion founded in the seventh century CE that accepts the doctrine of submission to God and to Mohammad as the last in the chain of prophets.

Islamic jihad. An Egyptian Islamist movement active since the 1970s whose members helped form al-Qaeda.

isolationism. A philosophy that advocates a withdrawal from international affairs and a concentration on domestic concerns.

Israeli Defense Forces (IDF). The military forces of the state of Israel that was founded along with the state in 1948.

Izz al-Din al-Qassam brigades. The military wing of Hamas.

Jiang Zemin (江泽民; 1926–). President of the People's Republic of China (1993–2003), general secretary of the Communist Party of China (1989–2002).

Johnson, Lyndon (1908–1973). The thirty-sixth president of the United States (1963–1969), thirty-seventh vice president of the United States (1961–1963), and U.S. senator from Texas (1949–1961).

Judaism. The oldest surviving monotheistic religion whose spiritual and ethical principles are derived from the Old Testament (Hebrew Bible).

July War. *See* the Second Lebanon War.

Jus ad bellum. A set of ethical criteria to be considered before engaging in war in order to determine whether the conflict is justifiable.

Jus in bello. A set of ethical criteria that serve as guidelines for appropriate means of fighting a war once it has begun.

Just War theory. An ethical discourse of both secular and ecclesiastical origins that theorizes about the moral legitimacy of armed conflict.

Kant, Immanuel. A central figure in modern philosophy, he contributed significantly to contemporary understandings of international relations.

Karzai, Hamid (1957–). President of Afghanistan (2004–).

Kellogg-Briand Pact. Treaty signed in 1928 by the United States, the United Kingdom, France, Germany, Japan, and others that forbade the use of war as a way to solve conflict between countries.

Kennedy, John F. (1917–1963). The thirty-fifth president of the United States (1961–1963), he was a U.S. senator (1953–1960) and U.S. congressman (1947–1953) from Massachusetts.

Keynes, John Maynard (1883–1946). A British economist of the twentieth century who had a major impact on modern macroeconomics, particularly through his advocacy of using fiscal and monetary policy to minimize the negative impacts of the business cycle.

Khomeini, Rohallah. Iranian leader and political figure who led the 1979 Iranian Revolution until his death in 1989.

Kirkpatrick, Jeane. The U.S. ambassador to the UN and close foreign policy adviser of President Reagan, her strong anti-communist views influenced a generation of neo-conservative policymakers.

Korean War (1950–1953). A conflict between South Korea (supported by the United States and the UN) and North Korea (supported by China) and ended by an armistice that separated the two countries at the thirty-eighth parallel.

Kurd. A member of the Kurdish ethnic group that is of Persian descent and primarily located in eastern Turkey, northeastern Syria, northern Iraq, and northwestern Iran—areas that comprise a region known as Kurdistan.

Kyoto Accord. A 1997 UN meeting on climate change in Japan that resulted in Kyoto Protocol that sets national limits on emissions of greenhouse gases.

Lake, Anthony (1939–). Executive director of UNICEF (2009–), national security advisor (1993–1997).

Law of the Sea Treaty. A multilateral treaty that outlines the rights and responsibilities of nations in their use of the world's oceans, it also includes guidelines for the management of marine natural resources.

League of Nations. An intergovernmental organization created following the end of World War I that was a precursor to the UN; among its goals was the prevention of war through collective security, disarmament, and resolution of international disputes through negotiation and arbitration.

lesser-developed countries. Countries of the world that exhibit the lowest Human Development Index ratings as established by the UN.

Levant. The geographic area bounded by southeastern Anatolia, Iraq, the Arabian Desert, and the Mediterranean.

liberal economic order. The economic system characterized by free trade, free market thinking, and minimal government regulation.

liberalism (or **liberal international relations theory**). A theory of international relations that emphasizes the importance of democratic institutions, international trade relations, and societal interactions beyond borders as a way to mitigate war and perpetuate peace.

Likud. A right-wing Israeli political party founded in 1973 by Menachim Begin and Ariel Sharon.

Lisbon Strategy. *See* open method of coordination.

Liu Shaoqi (刘少奇; 1898–1969). The chairman of the People's Republic of China from 1959 to 1968, during which time he tried to implement economic development and was later purged and died during the Cultural Revolution.

loose nukes. Refers to poorly protected nuclear weapons, facilities, materials, technology, and knowledge that are vulnerable to theft or loss, allowing such sensitive nuclear items to be acquired by undesirable actors.

Louisiana Purchase of 1803. The acquisition under the Jefferson administration of nearly a million square miles from France for $15 million.

Luo ethnic group. A Kenyan/Tanzanian ethnic group that consists of nearly five million people; President Barack Obama is a descendent on his father's side.

Maastricht Treaty. A treaty signed on February 7, 1992, in Maastricht, Netherlands, that created the EU and led to the creation of the euro as a common currency.

machismo. Noun derived from *macho*, which encapsulates the male-dominant, patriarchal values that supposedly have long dominated Latin American society.

malaria. An infectious disease in humans that is most often acquired from a mosquito. The disease typically causes fever and a headache but can cause death. There are more than 200 million cases of malaria each year, with approximately 750,000 leading to death.

Manchuria. China's northeast provinces.

Manifest Destiny. A belief that it was the destiny of the United States to stretch its territory from the Atlantic to the Pacific Oceans and across the North American continent.

Maoism. Mao Zedong's unique adaptation of Marxist theory to Chinese realities.

Mao Zedong (毛泽东; 1893–1976). He led the Communist Party of China to victory in their war against the Kuomintang of Chiang Kai-Shek, founded the People's Republic of China in 1949, and was chairman of the Communist Party of China (1943–1976).

Mara Salvatrucha (MS-13). A transnational criminal gang run by Central Americans living throughout the United States, Canada, and Central America. Known for their tattoos and involvement in the drug trade, the group is infamous for their violent tactics.

Marco Polo (1254–1324). A merchant traveler born in Venice, Italy, and one of the first people to travel through Mongolia and China.

Marja'-i taqlid. A word in Persian that means "source of imitation," and a person who has achieved the highest level of Islamic religious learning.

market economy. An economy or economic system in which the value of goods and services are determined by a free price system.

Marxist. One who believes in the ideas of Karl Marx, a nineteenth-century social critic who predicted the end of private property and promoted the common ownership of factories and farms.

May Fourth Movement (五四运动). A brief period of progressive thought in 1920s China prior to the Japanese invasion and the triumph of communism in China that grew out of demonstrations protesting the Treaty of Versailles, which gave German territories in China to Japan, rather than returning them to China.

McCain, John (1936–). U.S. senator from Arizona (1987–), U.S. House of Representatives (1983–1987), 2008 Republican presidential nominee, and a prisoner of war in Vietnam where he was held in captivity for six years.

McCrystal, Stanley (1954–). Retired four-star general in the U.S. Army, commander of Joint Special Operations Command (2003–2006), and commander of U.S. and NATO forces in Afghanistan (2009–2010).

Mecca. The holiest city in Islam; located in present-day Saudi Arabia.

Medina. The second most holy city in the Islamic tradition, located in present-day Saudi Arabia.

mercantilist (mercantilism). A policy and political philosophy that stresses the vital role of states to generate trade surpluses, by protecting domestic producers from imports and incentivizing certain producers or industries to sell to foreign markets.

Mexican Cession of 1848. Mexican land ceded to the United States after the Mexican-American War and comprises 15 percent of the modern United States, including much of the southwest.

Mexican peso crisis. A currency crisis in Mexico in 1994 and 1995 that developed when foreign investors determined that they would reduce or cancel loans to Mexican banks and reduce purchases of Mexican government bonds. The sudden fall in the value of the peso set off a currency crisis and led the U.S. government and the IMF to make emergency loans that were widely criticized as bailouts of the investors who unwisely made the loans in the first place.

Mitchell, George (1933–). Special envoy for Middle East peace (2009–), special envoy for Northern Ireland (1995–2000), and U.S. senator from Maine (1980–1995).

Molotov cocktails. An improvised incendiary weapon that is simple to produce by filling a breakable glass bottle with a highly flammable liquid and cloth wick and throwing it at a target.

monetary union. An arrangement in which two or more states agree to give up their autonomy to set monetary and fiscal policy in order to achieve currency stability and enhanced capital flows by creating a new currency or adopting that of another state.

Monroe Doctrine –U.S. president James Monroe's pronouncement in 1823 that the United States would perceive European attempts to interfere with lands in the Americas as acts of aggression against the United States.

moral relativism. The interpretation of what is morally right or wrong varies can vary between individuals.

mosque. The place of worship of followers of Islam.

Mossadegh, Muhammad (1882–1967). Elected prime minister of Iran in 1951, he nationalized the Iranian oil industry and was removed from office through an American-backed coup in 1953.

Mubarak, Hosni (1928–). The president (1981–2011) and vice president (1975–1981) of Egypt and a former commander of the Egyptian Air Force, Mubarak came to power after the assassination of Anwar Sadat and was removed after widespread popular protests in early 2011.

multilateral. Several countries working collectively on a given topic.

multilateral interaction. Multiple countries collaborating together to address a common issue or problem.

multinational corporations. Private or public-private business organizations that operate in several countries, often with a headquarters in one country but managers and shareholders in many others.

multipolar system. An international system characterized by power being spread across multiple actors.

Muslim. A follower of Islam.

Muslim Brotherhood. An Islamic transnational group founded in 1928 in Egypt that advocates political conformity to Islamic tenets.

Nanjing Massacre (南京大屠杀). The "Rape of Nanking" took place in December after Nanjing fell into the hands of Japanese soldiers during the Second Sino-Japanese War; the number of civilians killed remains a subject of controversy between China and Japan.

Nasser, Gamal 'Abd al- (1918–1970). The President of Egypt (1956–1970).

national identity. The sense of belonging to a nation or country.

National Islamic Alliance. A fundamentalist Shiite political party that is active in Kuwait and aligned with Iranian Islamist groups.

nationalist. Believing in the unity, welfare, and sovereignty of a country and specifically defending against foreigners controlling it from the outside.

National People's Congress (全国人民代表大会). The largely rubber-stamp legislature of the People's Republic of China.

National Security Strategy 2002. A strategy developed in the wake of September 11, 2001, by the administration of George W. Bush that introduced the policy of preemption—to militarily address threats before they reach they reach the United States.

nation-state. A sovereign state that coincides with a national cultural or ethnic identity.

Negroponte, John (1939–). Deputy U.S. secretary of state (2007–2009), the first U.S. director of National Intelligence (2005–2007), and a career foreign service officer who served as the U.S. ambassador to the United Nations, Iraq, Philippines, Mexico, and Honduras.

neoconservative. A school of thought in American foreign policy developed by former liberals that emphasizes the spread of democracy abroad by force if necessary. It is particularly associated with the foreign policy of President George W. Bush.

neoliberalism. A theory of international relations that builds on earlier interpretations of liberalism and emphasizes the role of international organizations as mechanisms by which states can and do achieve international cooperation.

neorealism (or **structural realism**). A theory of international relations that builds on earlier interpretations of realism and emphasizes the structure of the international system, including factors affecting state behavior and the distribution of power capabilities across the international system.

neo-Wilsonian. A school of thought in American foreign policy rooted in the worldview of President Woodrow Wilson. It emphasizes international organizations, free trade, and interdependence as the means to a more peaceful and stable world.

Netanyahu, Benjamin (1949–). A two-time prime minister of Israel (2009–present) and (1996–1999), he is member of the right-wing Likud Party.

netizen (网民). An "Internet citizen," with the implication that Internet activity can contribute to the emergence of civil society.

New Enlightenment (新启蒙). The decades of the 1910s and 1920s was a period of progressive thinking in China.

new world order. A phrase used by President George H. W. Bush to describe the international dynamic following the collapse of the Soviet Union and the end of the Cold War.

NGO. *See* nongovernmental organization.

Nixon, Richard (1913–1994). The thirty-seventh president of the United States (1969–1974), Republican nominee for president in 1960, thirty-sixth vice president (1953–1961), and U.S. congressman from California (1947–1950).

Nobel Prize. An annual international award given to honor outstanding achievement in the sciences, arts, and for peace and named after chemist Alfred Nobel, the inventor of dynamite.

nongovernmental organizations (NGOs). Organizations that operate independently from any government and are generally not-for-profit, often focusing on issues and concerns that governments cannot address alone.

non-state actors (or sub-state groups). Actors, such as insurgent groups or terrorist organizations, operating within a state and/or at the international level.

Noriega, Manuel (1934–). The president of Panama (1983–1989), he was removed from office during the U.S. invasion of Panama in 1989 and later served a fifteen-year sentence in a U.S. federal prison for drug trafficking, racketeering, and money laundering. He was then extradited to France, where he is serving a seven-year sentence for money laundering that is set to expire in 2017.

normative system. A legal system in which participants follow the rules because they believe that the rules prescribe action that is morally desirable.

North American Free Trade Agreement (NAFTA). A trade agreement between the United States, Canada, and Mexico that reduced trade and investment barriers between the three countries but imposed certain restrictions on firms from outside those three countries (especially Japanese auto producers) who might base production in one of the three markets to sell products in the other two markets.

North Atlantic Treaty Organization (NATO). A military alliance created in 1949 among Western democracies whose original purpose was to confront the threat of the Soviet Union during the Cold War and exists today as a collective security organization.

North–South divide. The social, economic, and political divide that exists between the wealthy developed countries of the Global North and the developing countries of the Global South.

nuclear arms race. A competition for nuclear weapons supremacy during the Cold War between the United States, the Soviet Union, and their respective allies.

Nuclear Nonproliferation Treaty (NPT). A treaty signed in 1968 to limit the spread of nuclear weapons to non-nuclear weapon states.

nuclear strike capability. The strategic ability to deploy and use nuclear weapons at a time of war.

Nunn-Lugar legislation. Provides the U.S. government resources by an act of Congress to dismantle weapons of mass destruction found in the former Soviet Union and former satellite states.

Obama, Barack (1961–). The forty-fourth president of the United States (2009–), former U.S. senator from Illinois (2005–2008), and Nobel Peace Prize winner in 2009.

Occident. Refers to the "West." Used in juxtaposition against the "Orient," or the "East."

Olmert, Ehud (1945–). The prime minister of Israel (2006–2009) and former chair of the Kadima Party.

ontological narratives. Stories that give meaning to our lives.

open method of coordination. A process to encourage convergence in the policies of EU member states where leaders from European member states establish common policy goals and implement necessary changes to policies in their own countries.

Operation Defensive Shield. The military operation conducted by the Israeli Defense Forces in 2002 during the Second Intifada to curb attacks by the Palestinians; it included strict civilian curfews and other restrictions.

opinio juris. Latin term that literally means "an opinion of law or necessity" and connotes the belief on the part of states that actions they are employing are required or permitted by law.

Opium Wars of 1840–1842 and 1856–1860 (鸦片战争). Fought between China's last dynasty, the Qing, and Britain in the first case, and both Britain and France in the second case, the Chinese losses mark the onset of the "Century of Humiliation," seen as the beginning of China's traumatic encounter with Western imperialism.

Organization for Cooperation and Security in Europe (OSCE). An international organization of more than fifty countries in Europe and the European region to facilitate security cooperation.

Organization of American States (OAS). A multilateral forum for governments of the Americas—all except Cuba are members—to discuss diplomatic matters; it was founded in 1948 and is located in Washington, D.C.

Organization of Petroleum Exporting Countries (OPEC). An intergovernmental organization of twelve oil-producing states that seeks price stability of oil exports.

organized crime. Criminal activity perpetrated by an organized and extensive group of people that often operates across national boundaries and evades national laws.

Orient. The "East," or Asian countries like China or Japan, used in juxtaposition against the "Occident," or the "West."

Oriental despots. The Asian autocracies that feature a powerful centralized state with total control over its citizenry.

Oslo Accords. Two agreements signed during peace negotiations between Israel and Palestinian representatives concluded in 1993 and 1995 that provide for the creation of the Palestinian National Authority (PNA) and outline parameters for Palestinian self-rule in Gaza and the West Bank.

Osman I. The leader and sultan of the Ottoman Turks from 1299 to 1324 CE and founder of the Ottoman dynasty (later empire).

Ottawa Treaty. An international treaty that is formally titled the Convention on the Prohibition of the Use, Stockpiling, Production and Transfer of Anti-Personnel Mines, which completely bans all anti-personnel landmines.

Ottoman Empire. An empire in the Middle East that lasted from 1299 to 1923 CE and had its capital in Istanbul (in pre-Ottoman times, Constantinople).

Pahlavi dynasty. The dynasty that ruled Iran from the 1920s until the Iranian Revolution of 1979, it had close relations with many Western powers, including the United States and Israel.

Palestinian Authority (PA). The administrative organization created in 1994 as a result of the Oslo Accords to govern parts of the West Bank and Gaza Strip.

Palestine Liberation Organization (PLO). A political and paramilitary organization founded in 1964 to represent the Palestinian people. The PLO holds an observer status at the UN General Assembly and is recognized by most countries as the official representative of Palestinian affairs.

Palin, Sarah (1964–). The 2008 Republican Party vice presidential nominee and former governor of Alaska.

Peace Corps. A U.S. program created under President Kennedy that makes use of American volunteer expertise to promote social and economic assistance in the developing world.

peace dividend. The idea that the end of the Cold War ought to signal a return of overseas defense spending to domestic concerns.

peace-enforcement operation. A military operation undertaken by states with the approval of the UN Security Council where states are permitted to use offensive military force.

peaceful development (和平发展). A turn of phrase deployed by Chinese fearful that "China's rise" and even "peaceful rise" would frighten foreigners, thereby undermining China's security environment.

peaceful rise (和平崛起). A phrase deployed by Chinese fearful that talk of "China's rise" would frighten foreigners, thereby undermining China's security.

peacekeeping. International mediation by personnel (oftentimes armed military), normally sponsored by an international organization such as the UN, which helps countries torn by conflict create the conditions for lasting peace.

Peel Commission. A British Royal Commission of Inquiry that toured Palestine (under the British Mandate) in 1936 and recommended a partition of Palestine into Arab and Jewish states.

Pentagon. The headquarters of the U.S. Department of Defense.

People's Liberation Army. China's military, including its army, air force, and navy.

Persian. A descendent of the peoples of the Persian Empire founded around 500 BCE and the largest ethnic group in modern-day Iran.

Persian Gulf War. A war between Iraqi forces and the United States and its allies that took place after Iraq's invasion of Kuwait in August 1990.

Petraeus, David (1952-). A U.S. Army general who is identified with the counterinsurgency strategy in Iraq, where he served as the commanding general of the multinational force (2007–2008), head of U.S. Central Command (2008–2010), and as the commanding general of U.S. forces in Afghanistan (2010-).

plurality. The largest number among several numbers, but short of a majority.

positivist legal system. A legal system in which the participants follow the rules because they have consented to them, and not necessarily because they consider it morally desirable.

Potemkin Village. Fake villages built to fool outsiders.

Powell, Colin (1937-). The sixty-fifth U.S. secretary of state (2001–2005), chairman of the joint chiefs of staff (1989–1993), national security advisor (1987–1989), and four-star U.S. Army general.

Prague Spring (1968). A period of political liberalization in Czechoslovakia during the height of the Cold War where citizens demanded "socialism with a human face"; the movement was soon crushed by the Soviet Army.

privatization. The selling of state-owned corporations to private investors.

propaganda. The use of rhetoric to guide the opinions and behavior of a targeted audience, it usually carries a negative connotation because it implies the use of manipulation.

proportionality. A principle of Just War theory that says participants in war should weigh the positive effects of an act against the negative and only undertake the act if the positive outweighs the negative.

protectionist policies. Economic policies that include tariffs and import quotas intended to reduce international competition in domestic markets.

Putin, Vladimir (1952–). Prime minister of Russia (2008–), president (1999–2008).

Qajar dynasty. A dynasty that ruled Iran from the late eighteenth century to the early twentieth century and was notable for its education and infrastructure improvements.

Qing dynasty (清代; 1644–1912). The last of China's dynasties, the Qing were Manchu nomads who initially invaded China proper from the north.

Qur'an. Islamic holy scriptures as revealed to the prophet Muhammad in the seventh century CE.

Qutb, Sayyid. Author, educator, and commentator whose ideas were influential among radical Islamist intellectuals.

Rabin, Yitzhak (1922–1995). Israeli prime minister (1974–1977 and 1992–1995), commander of the Israeli Defense Forces during the 1967 Six Day War, and Nobel Peace Prize winner (1994), he was assassinated by an Israeli extremist in 1995.

radical Islam. An extreme, militant form of Islam that emerged in the early twentieth century and is usually associated with modern Islamic terrorist groups such as Hamas, Hizballah, al-Qaeda, and the Taliban.

Rafsanjani, Hashemi (1934–). The president of Iran (1989–1997).

Reagan, Ronald (1911–2004). The fortieth president of the United States (1981–1989) and governor of California (1967–1975).

realism. A theory of international relations that emphasizes power politics on a global scale, including that states are self-interested, power-seeking actors and that the anarchical international environment contributes to state fears and concerns about aggression and attacks.

realist theory. A theory of international relations that emphasizes the centrality of states and the role of state power and self-interest.

recession. An economic contraction generally characterized by a fall in GDP and a rise in unemployment.

Red Guards (红卫宾). Chinese youth organized by Mao Zedong in 1966 and 1967 to help him implement his agenda during the Cultural Revolution.

reform and opening (改革开放). The policy of economic reform and the opening of China to foreign investment and greater entrepreneurship that Deng Xiaoping launched in 1978.

remittances. Money sent by immigrants to their families in their country of origin.

representational narratives. The representation of a series of events.

Republican China (中华民国; 1912–1949). China under the Kuomintang or Nationalist Party following the collapse of the Qing Dynasty and prior to the establishment of the People's Republic of China.

Republican People's Party (RPP). The ruling and only party in Turkey during Atatürk's time, it remains the second largest and opposition party in the Turkish parliament, representing mostly secularist voters.

Republic of Cyprus. *See* Cyprus

reserve currency. A currency held in significant quantities by a government in its foreign exchange reserves; common reserve currencies include the U.S. dollar, the Japanese yen, the Pound sterling, and the euro.

responsibility to protect. A concept developed by the International Commission on Intervention and State Sovereignty as a way to delineate that states have a primary responsibility to look after the welfare of their citizens, and if they fail then this responsibility falls on the international community, which may use force to protect people in extreme cases.

Revolutionary Council. A group formed by Rohallah Khomeini to oversee the Iranian Revolution of 1979.

Rice, Condoleezza (1954–). The sixty-sixth secretary of state (2005–2009), national security advisor (2001–2005).

River Elegy (河殇). A six-part documentary shown on China Central Television (CCTV) in 1988 that promoted modern and Western culture over traditional Chinese culture.

Romney, Mitt. Twice a Republican candidate for president of the United States (2008 and 2012), he served as the governor of Massachusetts (2003–2007), head of the Salt Lake Olympic Games (2002), and was an unsuccessful candidate for the U.S. Senate (1994).

Roosevelt, Franklin (1882–1945). The thirty-second president of the United States (1933–1945) and governor of New York (1929–1932).

Roosevelt, Theodore (1958–1919). The twenty-sixth president of the United States (1901–1909), vice president (1901), and governor of New York (1898–1900).

Roosevelt Corollary. Articulated by President Theodore Roosevelt in 1904 as an addendum to the Monroe Doctrine, it called for the United States to intervene directly in Latin America to help settle the debts and claims of European nations.

rule of law. A general institution of democracy that respects the individual rights and freedoms and emphasizes the importance of legal procedures and precedent in governing members of democratic society.

Rumsfeld, Donald (1932–). The secretary of defense (2001–2006 and 1975–1977), White House chief of staff (1974–1975), U.S. permanent representative to NATO (1973–1974), and U.S. congressman from Illinois (1963–1969).

Russo-Japanese War (1904–1905). Conflict between the Russian Empire and the Japanese Empire over Manchuria and Korea.

Sabra and Shatila. Palestinian refugee camps in south Beirut where the Christian Falanges massacred thousands of Palestinians during the 1982 First Lebanon War.

al-Sadat, Anwar (1918–1981). The president of Egypt (1970–1981) and signer of the Camp David Accords.

Safavid dynasty. A dynasty founded in 1502 that transformed Iran into a Shiite state and is considered the beginning of the modern period in Iran.

Sandinistas. A socialist political party and movement in Nicaragua that overthrew the rule of Anastasio Somoza in 1979. Sandinistas were ideologically aligned with the Soviet Union, and the United States fought a proxy war throughout much of the 1980s against them.

Saudi Peace Initiative. A 2002 plan by the Arab League to offer Israel normalization of relations with all Arab League member states in return for Israel's withdrawal to the 1967 borders, the foundation of a Palestinian state whose capital is Jerusalem, and an agreed solution to the refugee problem.

Savak. Iran's secret police force that operated from 1957 to 1979.

Schuman Declaration. A proposal made in 1950 by French foreign minister Robert Schuman to create the European Coal and Steel Community.

Scowcroft, Brent (1925–). National security adviser (1989–1993 and 1975–1977), lieutenant general in the U.S. Air Force.

Sea of Galilee (also known as Lake Tiberias or Kineret). The largest freshwater lake in Israel and Israel's main source of water.

Second Lebanon War. A thirty-four-day military conflict in Lebanon and northern Israel in the summer of 2006 between Israeli military forces and Hizballah that ended with a UN-brokered ceasefire.

second-strike capability. The strategic ability to deploy and use nuclear weapons in response to and retaliation against a nuclear attacker.

secularism. A belief with origins in Greek and Roman philosophies that a government should be free of religious control or influence.

self-concept. Refers to one's understanding of the "self" based on criteria such as race, gender, or self-esteem.

self-help. A concept derived from realist theory that says that states cannot rely on other states to assist them if they are threatened, so they must provide the means for their own self-defense.

September 11, 2001. A series of coordinated suicide attacks by al-Qaeda against the United States that targeted the World Trade Center Twin Towers in New York City and the Pentagon in Washington, D.C.

settlements. Israeli civilian settlements on land that was captured during the 1967 Six Day War that is a point of fierce contention between Israelis and Palestinians.

Severe Acute Respiratory Syndrome (SARS). An infectious human respiratory disease that is caused by the SARS corona virus and is easily communicable.

shah. Meaning "king" in Farsi, it was the official title of Persian rulers until the 1979 Islamic Revolution.

Sharon, Ariel (1928–). Prime minister of Israel (2001–2006) and major general in the Israeli Army.

Shiism. The second largest branch of Islam, it acknowledges Ali, the fourth caliph, and his descendants as Mohammad's rightful successors rather than the first three caliphs and the Umayyad dynasty founded after them.

Shock and Awe. A doctrine that uses extraordinary military and technological power to dominate the adversary and completely destroy its will to fight, it was used during the initial phases of the 2003 U.S. invasion of Iraq

Sinai Peninsula. A peninsula in Egypt that lies between the Mediterranean Sea to the north and the Red Sea to the south, it was under the control of Israel from 1967 to 1982.

Sinai War. A war fought by Britain, France, and Israel against Egypt following the Egyptian nationalization of the Suez Canal in 1956.

single market. Represents the area where the EU exercises "exclusive" competence, as opposed to national European governments.

Sinic Civilization (中华文明). The Chinese or China-centered civilization of East Asia.

sinocentrism. The ethnocentric belief that China is the center of the world and is superior to other nations.

Sino-Japanese "Jiawu" War of 1894–1895 (甲午战争). The first Sino-Japanese war, which is remembered as a humiliating Chinese defeat codified in the 1895 Treaty of Shimonoseki.

Six Day War. Fought between June 6 and 12, 1967, Israel achieved a swift military victory in which it captured the Sinai Peninsula from Egypt, the West Bank and East Jerusalem from Jordan, and the Golan Heights from Syria.

Smoot-Hawley tariff. Protectionist legislation passed by the U.S. Congress in 1930 that raised U.S. tariffs on imports at the beginning of the Great Depression and led to retaliatory tariffs by U.S. trading partners.

social constructivism. A theory of international relations that emphasizes the role of state interaction in the development of state identities and interests.

soft power. The use of economic, cultural, and diplomatic influence to obtain change or desired outcomes in other countries.

Somoza, Anastasio. The pro-American ruler of Nicaragua from 1967 to 1979. He was overthrown by the pro-Soviet Sandinistas and later assassinated in Paraguay.

sovereignty. A country's or a nation's right to have sole or supreme authority over its territory, such as having the power to make law and administer it.

sovereignty as responsibility. A concept first developed by African scholar Francis Deng that reformulates state sovereignty as a *responsibility* that states have to their people, as opposed to a *right* that allows them to treat their people however they please.

Soviet model. The economic ideas of the Soviet Union, which consisted of a state-run planned economy, centralized administration, and collective farming—ideas that were very influential in China in the 1950s and 1960s.

Spanish-American War of 1898. A brief conflict that developed over the independence of Cuba and resulted in the Spanish relinquishing the Philippines, Cuba, Puerto Rico, and Guam to U.S. control.

spy plane incident. A mid-air collision between an American surveillance aircraft and a Chinese fighter jet on April 1, 2001.

Stalin, Joseph (1878–1953). The general secretary of the Communist Party of the Soviet Union (1922–1953).

Star Wars. *See* Strategic Defense Initiative.

State of Law Coalition. An Iraqi coalition formed in 2009 by Nouri al-Maliki for the Iraqi parliamentary elections.

Stevenson, Adlai (1900–1965). Governor of Illinois (1949–1953), two-time Democratic Party nominee for president (1952 and 1956), and U.S. ambassador to the UN (1961–1965).

stimulus package. The use of government spending to promote economic growth when private investment is absent or inadequate.

Strategic Defense Initiative. A space-based missile defense system promoted by President Reagan in the 1980s as a way to protect the U.S. from a strategic nuclear ballistic strike.

subsidies. Money given by governments to private corporations to help lower the cost of production and thus help industries compete, usually with foreign exporters.

Suez Canal. An artificial waterway in Egypt opened in 1869 that connects the Red Sea and the Mediterranean Sea.

Suez Crisis. *See* Sinai War.

Sunni Muslims. The largest branch of Islam, which accepts the first four caliphs as rightful successors to Mohammad.

superpower. A single country with the ability to simultaneously dominate the international arena politically, economically, and culturally and to singularly influence the behavior and/or decision making of other countries.

Supreme Leader of the Islamic Republic. The Iranian political and religious head of state who appoints the commander of the armed forces, the chief justice, and other key positions.

swing state. Any large U.S. state whose voters are such that majorities can be at times Democratic or Republican and so can "swing" an election one way or the other.

Taiwan (台湾). An island, also known as Formosa, that is located off the southeastern coast of mainland China. The Republic of China took control over the island in 1945, but the People's Republic of China continues to contest its sovereignty.

Taliban. An Islamist militia group that has ruled parts of Afghanistan since 1996.

Tang dynasty (唐代; 618–907). The dynasty that ushered in a period of Chinese cosmopolitanism and openness to the outside world after the Sui dynasty collapsed.

tariff. A tax that a government places on imports or exports.

Tenet, George (1953–). The U.S. director of central intelligence (1997–2004).

terrorism. The use of violence and threats against civilian populations in an effort to intimidate or coerce behavior for political purposes.

Tiananmen Square (天安門). Located in the center of Beijing, it is the biggest square in the world and is known as the place where hundreds of Chinese citizens were massacred by Chinese soldiers while protesting in June 1989.

Tibet. A mountainous region in western China that has had a difficult history regarding human rights and autonomy with the Chinese government in Beijing.

Tindemans Commission. A group of European politicians, civil servants, and experts who met in 1994–1995 to discuss policies of European integration.

trade. The transfer of goods and/or services from one party to another.

trade deficit. Reflects a negative balance in a country's relationship between imports and exports that takes place when the value of a nation's imports is more than the value of their exports.

trade surplus. A condition in which the value of a country's exports exceeds the value of its imports.

transnational actors. Organizations or groups that operate beyond state boundaries and are independent of traditional state authorities.

transparency. Information and decision-making processes that are open and accessible as opposed to being private and secret.

Treaty of Lausanne. Peace treaty signed in Lausanne, Switzerland, in 1923 that led to the international recognition of the Republic of Turkey as the successor to the Ottoman Empire.

Treaty of Lisbon. This treaty was intended to improve democratic legitimacy within the EU when it came into force in 2009.

Treaty of Nanking (南京条约). Signed on August 29, 1842, this treaty ended the First Opium War between England and China. According to its terms, he Qing were forced to pay reparations to the British government and to cede sovereignty over Hong Kong for 150 years.

Treaty of Rome. The 1957 treaty that created the European Economic Community.

Treaty of Versailles. The peace treaty that officially ended World War I on July 28, 1919.

tributary system (朝贡体制). The political and trade relations that existed between the Chinese Empire and their neighboring tribute states.

Truman, Harry S. (1884–1972). The thirty-third president of the United States (1945–1953), vice president (1945), and U.S. senator from Missouri (1935–1945).

tuberculosis. An infectious disease that primarily affects the lungs.

ulama. Muslim religious scholars, often engaged in jurisprudence and interpretation of Islamic law.

UN blue helmets. The UN peacekeepers who are under the command and control of the UN and are distinguished by their blue helmets or berets.

UN Charter. The founding treaty of the United Nations, which was created in 1945.

UN Development Programme (UNDP). A subsidiary body within the UN system that acts as the organization's global development network.

undocumented immigrants. Immigrants who do not have the legal documents that permit them to live in the host country.

UN General Assembly. The organization's plenary body where each member-state has a vote.

unipolar moment. A phrase coined by columnist Charles Krauthammer that referred to the brief geopolitical status of the United States following the Cold War as the only superpower with the political, economic, and cultural power capable of influencing the rest of the world.

unipolar system. An international system characterized by the concentration of power in one country.

United Nations (UN). An international organization with near-universal membership created after the Second World War to promote international peace, cooperation, and security.

United Nations Special Committee on Palestine (UNSCOP). A UN commission sent to Palestine in 1947 that recommended the partition of Palestine into Jewish and Arab states—a recommendation that was supported by the United States and the Soviet Union but was opposed by the Arab states.

United States–China Strategic and Economic Dialogue. A series of regular meetings that began in 2006 between cabinet officials from China and the United States to discuss areas of concern in their economic and later security relationship.

Universal Declaration of Human Rights. A non-binding declaration adopted by the UN in 1948 that outlines and defines thirty human rights to which all individuals are entitled.

UN Security Council. Charged with the maintenance of international peace and security and composed of fifteen members: five permanent members (United States, United Kingdom, France, China, Russia), which each have veto power, and ten rotating members, which serve two-year terms.

uranium. A metallic fissionable element that can be enriched either to produce energy or to manufacture nuclear bombs.

Uruguay Round. The final series of multilateral negotiations (1986–1994) held under the auspices of the GATT that created the WTO.

Vietnam War. The military conflict (1955–1975) between Vietnamese communists and their allies and the government of South Vietnam backed by the United States that resulted in 57,000 American causalities and hundreds of thousands of Vietnamese casualties.

Virtue Party (VP). The forerunner of the current Turkish Justice and Development Party founded in 1998 and later banned from political activity.

War of Attrition. A war fought between Israel and Egypt from 1967 to 1970, with no territorial gains to either side.

War of Resistance against Japan (抗日战争; 1931/1937–1945). Part of the Pacific theater of World War II, it is also known as the Second Sino-Japanese War.

War on Terror. *See* Global War on Terror.

Washington Conference on Disarmament. The first major international conference (1921–1922) held on U.S. soil, it led to an arms control agreement among the great powers.

Washington Consensus. A set of principles that recommends free-market policies in Latin America, it has become synonymous with U.S.-led neoliberalism.

weapons of mass destruction (WMD). Nuclear, chemical, or biological weapons that cause systemic and indiscriminate death and injury on a large scale.

Welfare Party (WP). A Turkish Islamist party founded by Necmettin Erbakan in the 1990s.

West Bank. The territories west of the Jordan River captured by Israel from Jordan in the 1967 Six Day War and populated mostly by Palestinians, governed in part by the Fatah-led Palestinian Authority.

White Revolution. A reform process in Iran that began in 1963 by the shah and offered many Western-style changes, such as land ownership and some rights for women and non-Muslims.

Wilson, Woodrow (1856–1924). The twenty-eighth president of the United States (1913–1921), governor of New Jersey (1911–1913), and president of Princeton University (1902–1910).

Woodstock. A music festival in 1969 in upstate New York that was the culmination of American cultural protests against the Vietnam War.

World Bank. An international financial institution created at the end of World War II that provides economic and technical assistance to developing countries.

World Health Organization (WHO). Established in 1948 as an agency of the UN to focus on improving global health and preventing or controlling infectious diseases.

World Trade Center. The twin towers in lower Manhattan were built in the early 1970s and recognized as symbols of American capitalism. They were the target of terrorist attacks in both 1993 and on September 11, 2001, when more than 2,700 people were killed as the towers collapsed.

World Trade Organization (WTO). An intergovernmental organization created in 1995 to pursue the multilateral liberalization of trade and to adjudicate trade disputes that arise between states that are members.

Yalta Conference. A meeting between U.S. president Franklin Roosevelt, British prime minister Winston Churchill, and Soviet premier Josef Stalin in the Crimea (Soviet Union) in February 1945 to discuss Europe's post–World War II reorganization.

Yellow Horde. A derogatory term used in the West to refer to East Asian peoples, who are perceived as threatening because of their vast numbers and alien culture.

Yom Kippur. The holiest day on the Jewish calendar that commemorates the practice of atoning for sins.

Yom Kippur War. Fought in October of 1973, this war between Israel on one side and Syria and Egypt on the other began when Arab forces surprised Israel by attacking on Yom Kippur, the holiest day on the Jewish calendar.

Zakaria, Fareed (1964–). Foreign policy expert, editor-at-large of *Time Magazine,* and host of CNN show *Fareed Zakaria GPS.*

Zhao Ziyang (赵紫阳; 1919–2005). The premier of the People's Republic of China (1980–1987) and the general secretary of the Chinese Communist Party (1987–1989), he was an advocate of free-market enterprise and was purged from his post in 1989 during the Tiananmen Massacre.

Zionism. A Jewish political-nationalist movement that has historically supported self-determination of the Jewish people in a Jewish national homeland.

Contributors

Yaron Ayalon was the Schusterman/Josey visiting assistant professor in Judaic and Middle Eastern studies in the Department of International and Area Studies and the Program in Judaic and Israel Studies at the University of Oklahoma from 2009 to 2011. His research focuses on the history of the Middle East in the early modern period, social history of the Ottoman Empire, and non-Muslims under Islamic rule. He is currently at Emory University and in the process of writing a book on natural disasters in the Ottoman Empire, which will be partly based on his doctoral dissertation.

Robert Henry Cox is director of the Walker Institute for International and Area Studies and professor of political science at the University of South Carolina. He was previously on the faculty at the University of Oklahoma. He is the author or co-editor of three books, and his articles have appeared in *World Politics, Politics and Society, Journal of Social Policy, Comparative Political Studies, West European Politics, Governance, Publius,* and many other academic journals. His current research interests focus on the politics of sustainability in Europe.

Mark W. Frazier is a professor in the Department of Politics at the New School in New York City, where he also serves as an academic director of the India China Institute. From 2007 to 2012, he was the ConocoPhillips professor of Chinese politics and associate professor of international and area studies at the University of Oklahoma. Frazier teaches and writes about the political economy of China. His recent research examines the politics of labor and social policies in China. He is the author of *Socialist Insecurity: Pensions and the Politics of Uneven Development in China* (Cornell University Press 2010) and *The Making of the Chinese Industrial Workplace* (Cambridge University Press 2002). He has published articles in *Asia Policy, Studies in Comparative International Development,* and *The China Journal.*

Peter Hays Gries is the Harold J. & Ruth Newman chair and director of the Institute for U.S.–China Issues at the University of Oklahoma. He is author of *China's New Nationalism: Pride, Politics, and Diplomacy* (University of California Press 2004) and co-editor (with Stanley Rosen) of *State and Society in 21st Century China: Crisis, Contention, and Legitimation* (Routledge 2004) and *Chinese Politics: State, Society, and the Market* (Routledge 2010). He is also author of dozens of academic journal articles and book chapters.

Suzette R. Grillot is the interim dean of the College of International Studies, the Max and Heidi Berry chair and professor in the Department of International and Area Studies at the University of Oklahoma. She teaches courses on international relations theory, global security, international activism, illicit trafficking, international organization and regimes, American foreign policy, European security, and international politics, literature, and film. She co-edited and contributed to the books *Arms on the Market: Reducing the Risk of Proliferation in the Former Soviet Union* (1998) and *Arms and the Environment: Preventing the Perils of Disarmament* (2001). She also co-authored the books *The International Arms Trade* (2009) and *Protecting Our Ports: National and International Security of Containerized Freight* (2010).

Eric A. Heinze is associate professor of political science and international and area studies at the University of Oklahoma. He teaches courses in the field of international relations, including classes on international relations theory, international law and institutions, and international human rights. Heinze's research deals with normative and ethical issues in international relations, with a focus on global governance, armed conflict, and human rights. His current and recent work is on humanitarian military intervention, the politics of genocide, the ethical and legal implications of the "war on terror," and the role of non-state actors in armed conflict. He is the author of *Waging Humanitarian War: The Ethics, Law and Politics of Humanitarian Intervention* (State University of New York Press 2009), co-editor (with Brent Steele) of *Ethics, Authority and War: Non-State Actors and the Just War Tradition* (Palgrave Macmillan 2010), and editor of *Justice, Sustainability, and Security: Global Ethics for the 21st Century* (Georgetown University Press, under contract). He is currently writing a book on ethics and global violence.

Alan McPherson is the ConocoPhillips Petroleum chair of Latin American studies and associate professor of international and area studies at the University of Oklahoma. He teaches courses in Latin American studies and U.S. international relations and specializes in U.S.–Latin American relations. A historian by training, McPherson is the author of *Yankee No! Anti-Americanism in U.S.–Latin American Relations* (Harvard University Press 2003), which won the A. B. Thomas Award for Best Book of the Year from the Southeastern Council on Latin American Studies and was named Outstanding Academic Title for 2004 by *Choice* magazine. He has since published three more books. The first, *Intimate Ties, Bitter Struggles: The United States and Latin America Since 1945* (Potomac Books 2006) is a concise, up-to-date narrative with primary documents. The second is an edited volume titled *Anti-Americanism* *in Latin America and the Caribbean* (Berghahn Books 2006). The third, co-edited with Ivan Krastev, is titled *The Anti-American* (Central European University Press 2007).

Zach P. Messitte is the president of Ripon College in Wisconsin. He was the first dean of the College of International Studies and vice provost for international programs at the University of Oklahoma from 2007 to 2012. He also served as the William J. Crowe chair in geopolitics. At the University of Oklahoma he taught American foreign policy, American foreign policy and film, an interactive course on the Iraq War, and a capstone class on how Washington works internationally. His work has appeared in the *International Herald Tribune*, the *Baltimore Sun, Slate, Italy Daily*, the *Maryland Daily Record*, the *Johns Hopkins SAIS Review*, the *Johns Hopkins Bologna Center's Journal of International Affairs, Maryland Historical Magazine*, the *Oklahoman, World Literature Today*, the *Tulsa World*, and the *Washington Times*. He also hosted National Public Radio's World Views, an international affairs interview program on KGOU.

Mitchell P. Smith is a professor of international and area studies and the chair of the Department of International and Area Studies at the University of Oklahoma. His work focuses on comparative and international political economy, with a particular emphasis on European integration. Smith is also director of the university's European Union Center. His work has appeared in *West European Politics, Journal of Legislative Studies, Politics & Society, Journal of Common Market Studies, Journal of European Public Policy, German Politics*, and other journals. He is the co-editor of *Legitimacy and the European Union: The Contested Polity* (Routledge 1999), author of *States of Liberalization* (SUNY Press 2005) and *Environmental and Health Regulation in the United States and the European Union: Protecting Public and Planet* (Palgrave Macmillan 2012), and editor of *Europe and National Economic Transformation: The EU After the Lisbon Decade* (Palgrave Series in European Union Politics 2012).

Index

Al-Qaeda: and Afghanistan, 20, 21, 91, 217; America's post-9/11 obsession with, 32; attacks after 9/11 in Madrid and London, 30; defined, 235; founding of by bin Laden, 216–17; links claimed to Saddam Hussein, 21, 86, 91; training camps of, 4. *See also* September 11, 2001

Abbas, Mahmud (Abu Mazen), 203–204, 235

Adams, John Quincy, 12

Afghanistan: and 2001 invasion by coalition, 91; and bin Laden, 19–20; initial support for action in, 20; and al-Qaeda, 20, 21, 91, 217. *See also* Bin Laden, Osama

Ahmadinejad, Mahmud: and anti-American statements, 235; denial of Holocaust, 209, 235; and fixing elections in Iran, 30; identification of, 235; as president of Iran, 208–209; protests of fraudulent elections, 219

AIDS/HIV, 3, 55, 65, 229, 235

AKP (Justice and Development Party), 213–15

ALBA (Bolivian Alliance for the Peoples of America), 179, 181

Allawi, Ayad, 210–11

Álvarez, Gregorio, 189

Álvaro Uribe, 187

American Convention on Human Rights, 188

American foreign policy, 11–38; challenges for, 32–33; idealism and realism in, 11–16; and Obama administration's challenges, 26–32; Obama's worldview, 23–26; and

presidential leadership, 16–19; September 11th attacks, 19–23

Anarchy, international. *See* International anarchy

Annan, Kofi, 3, 7, 58

Anti-globalization, 49, 235. *See also* Globalization

Anti-neoliberalism, 177–79, 254

Arab-Israeli conflict: and Arafat's Fatah, 200; Camp David Accords of 1979, 199–200, 238; and Camp David in July 2000, 202; and dismantling of settlements in Gaza strip (2005), 203; and First Lebanon War, 200–201; and Israeli Defense Forces (IDF), 198; Israeli independence declared in 1948, 198; Netanyahu and the Likud Party, 204; and open military confrontation, 198–99; and operation Cast Lead, 204; and Operation Defensive Shield, 202, 256; origins of, 197–98; peace still unattained in, 204–205; and Saudi peace initiative, 204, 261; and Second Lebanon War, 203, 261; and Sharon's election in 2001, 202; and Six Day War, 199, 262; and Suez crisis, 199; summits held between Netanyahu and Arafat (1996-99), 202; and War of Attrition, 199

Arab League, 93, 204, 236

Arab Spring: defined, 236; and future of region, 228; and Middle East, 218–221; and NATO intervention in Libya, 15, 30–31; and social media, 5

Arafat, Yasser, 200, 201

Armitage, Richard, 21, 236
Assad, Bashar, 219, 236
Atatürk (father of the Turks), 212, 236
Ayatollah Khomeini, 206–207, 208, 217, 250

Ba'ath party, 207, 210
Bachelet, Michelle, 189
Bakhtiar, Shapour, 206
Balance of payments (BOP), 104–105, 236
Balfour Declaration of 1917, 197, 236
Banana Wars, 116, 236
Al-Banna, Hasan, 216
Barak, Ehud, 202, 223, 236, 251
Al-Bashir, Omar, 31, 143
Begin, Menahem, 199, 223, 251
Beijing Olympics (2008), 127, 142
Beijing Spring, 136, 236. See also
    Tiananmen Square in Beijing
Ben Ali, Zine El Abidine, 219–220
Ben Gurion, David, 198
Biden, Joseph, 26, 29, 237
Bill and Melinda Gates Foundation, 103, 237
Bin Laden, Osama: Bush
    administration's unsuccessful hunt
    for, 23, 30; and enmity toward
    U.S., 217; founder of al-Qaeda in
    Pakistan, 216–17; identification
    of, 237; killing of, 5, 15, 29–30, 32;
    pursuit of into Afghanistan, 19–20.
    See also Afghanistan; September
    11, 2001
Black market, global, 54, 237
Black September, 200, 237
Bolívar, Simón, 185–86
Bolivarian Alliance for the Peoples of
    Our America (ALBA), 179, 181
Bolivia, 177, 181, 187, 189, 193
Bolton, John, 20, 34
Brazil: as BRICS country, 238; and
    China, 185; GDP of, 182; and link
    to Chilean ports, 184; potential
    as major player on world stage,
    182–83, 228; and transnational
    crime, 189. See also Latin America

Bretton Woods system: overview,
    106; decline of, 115, 121, 154–55,
    180; International Monetary Fund,
    108–10; leadership role abandoned
    by U.S., 112–13; World Bank, 110–12
BRICS countries, 5, 11, 183, 238
Bush, George H. W., 18, 179, 238, 255
Bush, George W.: and Chávez of
    Venezuela, 178; disputed election
    of, 18–19; identification of, 238;
    and "Mission Accomplished"
    declaration, 22–23; and preemption
    policy after 9/11, 20; and rejection
    of U.S. leadership in Latin America,
    180; and worldview expressed in
    debate, 19

Calderón, Felipe, 190
CAP (Common Agricultural Policy),
    160–61
Carter, Jimmy, 14, 17, 199, 206, 238
Castro, Fidel, 190, 238
Castro, Raúl, 189, 191
Castro, Viviane, 173
CCP (Chinese Communist Party), 118,
    127, 129, 239
Cedar Revolution, 219
Central America, 3, 186, 190, 194
"Century of Humiliation" in China:
    and being Chinese today, 133; and
    major wars between China and
    Western powers, 132; and new
    narratives emerging, 133–34; and
    victimization narratives, 134–35;
    Western impact on Confucianism,
    133
Chávez, Hugo: background of,
    178–79; and criticism of George
    W. Bush, 178; efforts to unite Latin
    Americans, 184, 185–86; and FARC,
    187; media attention of, 182, 228;
    in support of exclusion of U.S.,
    181; Venezuelans warned against
    imperialism by, 180
Cheney, Richard (Dick), 21, 239
Chile: and globalization, 175–76,
    185, 230; government of, 179;

and Pinochet, 188–89; and trade agreements, 184

China, 127–51; overview, 127; and belligerent foreign policy, 128; and East Asia, 141–42; as "elephant in the room" in Latin America, 185, 228; global, 142–43; 'harmonious,' 127–28; and Mao, 135–38; pasts: five thousand years of "Civilization," 130–32; pasts: one hundred years: "Century of Humiliation," 132–35; pasts: Ten years of Chaos, 135–38; under reform, 139–41; rise of, 128–29; and U.S. in 21st century, 143–47; and World Bank development loans, 115. *See also* Global economics and China; Nationalism of China

Chinese Communist Party (CCP), 118, 127, 129, 239

Churchill, Winston, 16, 154

City of God (film), 190

Climate change. *See* Global warming; Kyoto Accord

Clinton, Bill: and Cuba, 190–91; and emphasis on economic competition, 113; identification of, 239; and lack of foreign policy experience, 18; and neoliberalism, 179; as post-Cold War president, 13; as "ruler of the planet," 16

Clinton, Hillary: as presidential candidate (2008), 24, 26, 34n6; as secretary of state, 29, 31, 192; as senator and First Lady, 34

Coalition Provisional Authority (CPA), 23, 210, 239

Cold War period: allies received World Bank loans, 111; and American foreign policy, 13, 15; and armed conflicts, 41; China reinforced as our opposite, 129; and doctrines of deterrence and containment, 20, 106; end of, 3, 18; foreign policy during, 13; interconnectedness following, 3; and nuclear arms race, 50;

protracted nature of, 17; terrorist organizations during, 48–49; U.S. had high favorability ratings in Latin America, 180; USSR relations with Israel severed, 199. *See also* Post–Cold War period

Common Agricultural Policy (CAP), 160

Common Security and Defense Policy (CSDP), 168

Conclusion, 225–234; concerns and hopes for future, 231–32; continued power of state system, 227–28; critical issues absent from this book, 226–27; final thoughts, 232–33; issues to be addressed in coming decade, 228–29; national history and identity matter, 230–31

Confucianism, 130–31, 132, 133, 240

Consequentialism, 76, 240

Containment policy of U.S., 12, 20–21, 106. *See also* Cold War period

Contemporary international security issues: overview, 47; environmental degradation, 57–58; health epidemics, 55–57, 227; international terrorism, 47–50; weapons of mass destruction, 227. *See also* WMD

CPA (Coalition Provisional Authority). *See* Coalition Provisional Authority

Criteria for severity and scale of abuse, humanitarian intervention issue, 75–77

Croatia, future EU member, 156

CSDP (Common Security and Defense Policy), 168

Cuba-U.S. relations, 190–91, 230

Cyberwarfare (cyberterrorism), 49, 241

Dalai Lama, 128, 241

Darfur, 80, 92, 143, 229

Delors, Jacques, 163–64, 168

Democracy in Latin America, 188

Deng Xiaoping, 136, 138, 139, 140

Devils on the Doorstep (film), 137

"Dictatorships and Double Standards"
(Kirkpatrick), 14
Doha Round, 107–108, 242
DR-CAFTA, 186, 187
Dreams from My Father (Obama),
24–25
Drug trafficking in Latin America, 3,
186, 189–190, 192

East Asia, China and, 141–42
EC. *See* European Commission
ECB. *See* European Central Bank
Economic and monetary union
(EMU), 164
Economics and poverty, 52–55
Economic structuralism, 44–45
Economy, global. *See* Global economy
ECSC (European Coal and Steel
Community), 153–54, 159, 243
EEC. *See* European Economic
Community
Eisenhower, Dwight, 17, 242
Elite Squad (film), 190
EMU. *See* economic and monetary
union
Environmental degradation, 57–58
Erbakan, Necmettin, 213, 266
EU: community expansion: countries
in line for admittance, 156–57;
criteria for admittance, 156,
169n7, 169n9, 170n14; and Eastern
Partnership program, 157; and
enlargement, 155–56, 169n8
EU: crisis in perspective: and
community expansion, 155–57; and
European integration, 153–54; and
integration explained, 157–58; and
losing sense of direction, 154–55;
origins and objectives of European
integration, 153
EU: economic integration: and
Eurosclerosis, 163–64; and
Eurozone crisis of 2009–?, 166–68;
and global economy, 116–17; single
market to single currency, 164–66
EU: global actor, 167–68
Euro (EU currency), 116–17, 164–67,
171n21–22

European Central Bank (ECB), 166–67
European Coal and Steel Community
(ECSC), 153–54, 159, 243
European Commission (EC), 158, 162,
163–64, 171n18, 243
European Economic Community
(EEC), 154, 155, 169n5, 169n7
European External Action Service
(EEAS), 168
European Parliament, 150, 156, 243
European Union (EU), 152–72; crisis
confronting, 152–53, 168n1, 228;
crisis in perspective, 153–58;
economic integration, 163–67;
Europe's social dimension, 158–163;
as global actor, 167–68, 228. See
also *entries beginning with* EU
European Union, Treaty on, 159–60
Europe's social dimension: and
Common Agricultural Policy,
160–61; and "constitutional
asymmetry," 161; and European
citizenship, 159–60, 230; need for
in EU, 158–59; and open method
of coordination, 162–63, 230, 256;
and Treaty on European Union,
15–160; and welfare state policies
prevail, 163
Eurozone membership, 165, 171n19
Expansionism, 12, 243

Facebook, 5, 209, 219, 231
Farabundo Martí Liberation Front
(FMLN), 178
FARC (Forces of Colombia), 187
Feng Xiaogang, 137, 151
FMLN (Farabundo Martí Liberation
Front), 178
Forces of Colombia (FARC), 187
Foreign policy of U.S. *See* American
foreign policy
FTAA (Free Trade Area of the
Americas), 181, 182
Fujimori, Alberto, 188, 189
Funes, Mauricio, 178

Gadaffi, Muammar, 15, 30–31, 66, 70,
92–93, 219

Gates, Robert, 29, 128, 274
GATT (General Agreement on Tariffs and Trade), 106–107, 113
GDP (gross domestic product): of Brazil, 182; of Latin America, 175; tables 4.1 and 4.2, 102–103; of world, 101, 102
General Agreement on Tariffs and Trade (GATT), 106–107, 113
GFC (global financial crisis). *See* Global financial crisis
Global economics and China: currency pegged to U.S. dollar, 118; and irony in tensions with U.S., 119–20; open economic system as benefit to, 118, 122n11; and response to global financial crisis (GFC), 117; rise partly due to general emergence of large economies, 120; and state-managed approach, 118, 122n12; and turnaround in 2010, 119; and World Bank development loans, 115
Global economics and the EU, 116–17, 122n10, 236
Global economics and the U.S.: and American unilateralism doctrine, 115–16; Bretton Woods institutions undermined, 113–14, 115; and economic rise of China, 113, 115; and lack of support for global trade, 114–15, 121
Global economy, 100–123; overview, 100–104; basic problem, 104–106; Bretton Woods solution to, 106–12; and GDP in Latin America, 175; largest GDP nominally (table 4.2), 103; largest GDP in terms of purchasing power parity (table 4.1), 102; and protectionist tendencies of sates, 100–101, 229, 258; uneven distribution of, 100, 101, 122n1, 122n3, 245
Global economy, future of: overview, 112; in China, 118–22; in the European Union, 116–17; and globalization debate, 121–22; in the United States, 112–16

Global financial crisis (GFC), 6, 101–102, 104–105, 117, 245
Globalization: and American skepticism of, 113–14; and China, 142–45; and compartmentalization of global economy, 100; and economy trends, 121–22; and European Union, 167–68; future of, 232–33; impact on war and conflict, 53; and interconnectedness in today's world, 5, 15, 225; and Latin America, 174–75, 184–87; and terrorism, 49. *See also* Anti-globalization; *entries beginning with* Global; NAFTA (North American Free Trade Agreement)
Global warming, 31, 142, 143, 232. *See also* Kyoto Accord
Global War on Terror, humanitarian intervention issue, 85–86, 245
Goldberg, Philip, 181
Gold standard for U.S. currency, 109
Great Depression, 12, 104, 245
Great Leap Forward, 135, 138–39, 245
Great Proletarian Cultural Revolution (China), 135–38, 139, 245
Greece: debt crisis of, 117, 152, 166–67, 169, 171n23; and Eurozone, 165; as member of EU, 155, 156
Green Revolution (Iran), 15, 30, 219, 235, 246
Guantanamo Bay, 27, 80, 246
Gül, Abdullah, 213, 214–15
Guzmán, Gustavo, 181

Haiti: coups in 1991 and 2004, 274; as failed state, 230; humanitarian interventions in, 78, 82, 89–90; and remittances, 176; and social blight, 190, 191–92. *See also* Latin America
Hamas, 203–205, 246
Haniyya, Isma'il, 203
Hariri, Rafik, 219
Harmonious society in China, 127–28, 247
Health epidemics, global, 55–57
Herzl, Theodore, 197
H1N1 (swine) flu, 3, 56

HIV/AIDS, 3, 55, 65, 229, 235
Hizballah (Hezbollah), 201, 218, 219
Holocaust, 133–35, 198, 209, 235
Homicide rate in Latin America, 190
Hua Guofeng, 139
Humanitarian aid, 74
Humanitarian intervention, 66–99;
    overview, 66–67; concept of,
    67–72; conclusion, 86–87; ethics
    and politics of, 74–81; and Global
    War on Terror, 85–86; Select Cases
    Relevant to debate on (ppendix A:
    The Post-Cold-War Era), 87–93;
    Select Cases Relevant to debate
    on (Appendix B: The Cold War
    Era), 93–96; what it is NOT, 72–74.
    See also *entries beginning with*
    Humanitarian intervention
Humanitarian intervention cases
    in post-cold-war era (Appendix
    A): Afghanistan invasion (2001),
    91; Bosnia (1993–1995), 88–89;
    Darfur conflict and subsequent
    peacekeeping (2003–), 80, 92, 143;
    East Timor (1999–2000), 90–91;
    Haiti (1994), 89–90; Iraq invasion
    (2003), 91–92; Kosovo (1999), 90;
    Liberia (1990) and Sierra Leone
    (1997–1998), 87; Libyan Civil
    War intervention (2011), 92–93;
    Rwandan genocide (1994), 89;
    Somalia (1992–1993), 88; U.S.- led
    Enforcement of No-Fly Zones in
    Iraq (1991–2003), 87–88
Humanitarian intervention cases
    in cold-war era (Appendix B):
    Congo Belgian interventions (1960
    and 1964), 93–94; East Pakistan/
    Bangladesh Indian intervention
    (1971), 94; Grenada intervention
    by U.S. (1983), 95; Kampuchea/
    Cambodia intervention by
    Vietnam (1978–1979), 95; Panama
    intervention by U.S. (1989–1990),
    95–96; Uganda intervention
    by Israel (1976), 94; Uganda
    intervention by Tarzania (1978–
    1979), 94–95

Humanitarian intervention in
    international law: overview, 81–82;
    customary international law, 83–85;
    UN Charter paradigm, 82–83
Humanitarian intervention issues:
    criteria for severity and scale
    of abuse, 75–77; customary
    international law, 83–85;
    Global War on Terror, 85–86;
    humanitarian aid, 74; human rights
    vs. human security, 70–72; motives
    of intervening parties, 69–70;
    nationals' rescue, 72; peacekeeping,
    72–74, 257; responsibility to protect,
    68–69; selectivity of intervention,
    78–82; UN Charter paradigm,
    82–83
Human rights: and Afghanistan,
    91; and China, 81, 143; defined,
    247; and the EU, 157, 167; and
    humanitarian interventions, 67–68,
    95; vs. human security, 70–72; and
    Iran, 209; and neo-cons of Bush
    era, 14; and NGOs, 46, 60; in post-
    Cold War period, 67; and President
    Carter, 14, 17; and President
    Obama, 27–28, 31; and problem
    of motive, 69–70; and signs of
    progress, 188–89; and Turkey,
    214; and Universal Declaration
    of Human Rights (1948), 66; and
    World Social Forum, 174
Human trafficking, 3, 41, 247
Hussein, Saddam: identification of,
    247; repressive regime of, 86, 91;
    takeover as Iraq president (1968),
    207; and U.S invasion of Iraq, 91;
    and WMD, 21, 22, 210

Idealism, defined, 12, 15, 247
Idealism and realism in American
    foreign policy: analysis of foreign
    policy tradition, 11–12; and Cold
    War, 13–14; and contradictory
    philosophies of two parties, 15;
    and foreign policy realists, 12–13;
    idealism defined, 247; and idealists,
    13; and neo-cons of Bush era, 14;

and Obama as "practical idealist,"
15, 16; and power of presidency,
15–16; realism, defined, 259; and
Soviet Union's fall, 14–15; three
great eras of foreign policy prior to
WWII, 12; and Vietnam War, 14
IMF (International Monetary Fund).
See International Monetary Fund
Immigration and remittances in Latin
America, 176–77
Imperialism, 12, 81, 138, 145–46, 248
Import-Substitution-Industrialization
(ISI) schemes, 184–85
Inter-American Democracy Charter,
188
Inter-American Development Bank,
176, 194, 248
Inter-American system in Latin
America, 188
International (governmental)
organizations (IGOs), 59, 248
International anarchy, 42, 44–46, 248
International law, humanitarian
intervention issue, 81–85
International Monetary Fund (IMF):
and Argentina, 179; and China, 115;
core purpose of, 109; creation of,
106, 108; and currency unification,
110; and floating currencies, 109,
244; and global currency proposal,
108–109, 110; and gold standard
abandoned, 109; and loss of power
in Latin America, 180–82; power
of, 110; and reinvention in 1970s,
109–10; and World Bank, 111
International security, 39–65;
overview, 39; background of,
39–41; concepts and approaches
to, 41–47; contemporary issues,
47–58; solutions and conclusions
for, 58–61. *See also* International
security issues
International security issues:
economic structuralism, 44–45;
environmental degradation, 57–58;
global health epidemics, 55–57;
international terrorism, 47–50,
263; liberal international relations

theory, 43–44, 251; poverty and
economics, 52–55; realist theory,
42–43; social constructivism,
45–47; theoretical debates on, 47.
See also WMD
International security issues,
contemporary. *See* Contemporary
international security issues
Internet use: and Arab Spring, 220,
231; and China censorship, 121, 127,
140; and cybernationalists, 241; and
instantaneous communication,
5; in Latin America, 185; and
terrorism, 49; and transnational
networks, 60; and Zhao Wei affair,
136–37
Iran and Iraq, 205–11; Ahmadinejad
as Rafsanjani's successor, 208; and
Iran hostage crisis, 207; Iranian
history from 1502–1921, 205;
Iranian Qajar dynasty overthrown
in 1921, 205; Iran in 1950s, 205–206;
and Iran-Iraq war, 207; Iran's White
Revolution, 206, 266; Iraq's first
elections, 210–11; and Khomeini,
206–208; Obama administration
and Iran, 208; post-Saddam era,
210–11; and Saddam Hussein,
207–208. *See also* Iraq War
Iran-Iraq war, 207, 249
Iran's White Revolution, 206
Iraq War: and Abu Ghraib photos,
23, 80, 235; buildup to, 21; cost
to U.S. since 2003 invasion, 211;
justification for, 20–21, 80–81,
86; lack of support for, 33n3; and
Obamas opposition to, 25; and
Powell's "Pottery Barn Rule," 21–22;
and voter concerns, 23, 34n5. *See
also* Iran and Iraq
ISI schemes. *See* Import-Substitution-
Industrialization (ISI) schemes
Islam, radical. *See* Radical Islam
Israeli Defense Forces (IDF), 198, 249
'Izz al-Din al-Qassam brigades, 216

Al-Ja'afari, Ibrahim, 210
Jerusalem, 199, 204, 231

Jiang Wen, 137
Johnson, Lyndon, 17, 29, 250
Al-Jumayyil, Bashir, 200
Justice and Development Party (AKP),
    213–15

Kant, Immanuel, 43
Karzai, Hamid, 32, 250
Kellogg-Briand pact, 13, 250
Kemal, Mustafa, 211–12
Kennedy, John F., 17, 33nn1–2, 250
Kerry, John, 23, 33n4
Keynes, John Maynard, 108
Khomeini, Rohallah, 206–207, 208,
    217, 250
Kirchner, Cristina Fernández de,
    179
Kirchner, Néstor, 179
Kirkpatrick, Jeane, 14, 250
Kosovo intervention, 67–68, 80, 90
Kyoto Accord, 20, 58, 250. *See also*
    Global warming

Lake, Anthony, 14
Latin America, 173–195; overview,
    7, 173–74; Brazil: new leader of,
    182–83; and crime across borders,
    189–190; global foreign policy
    trends of, 184–87; and immigration
    and remittances, 176–77; and
    integrating for strength, 183–84;
    and Monroe Doctrine, 179–182;
    and neoliberalism, 176–79;
    outliers: Cuba and Haiti, 190–92;
    poverty and inequality in, 174–76;
    and pragmatism, 192; and signs of
    progress, 188–89. See also *names of
    specific countries*
League of Nations, 12, 13, 16, 198, 250,
    251
Levant, the, 196, 251
Liberal international relations theory,
    43–44, 251
Libyan intervention by NATO/
    coalition, 15, 30–31, 66, 70, 81,
    92–93
Lin Zexu, 132
Lin Zexu (film), 134

Lisbon Strategy. *See* Open method of
    coordination
Liu Shaoqi, 138–39
"The Lost Decade." *See* Ten Years of
    Chaos in China
Lugar, Richard, 25
Lula. *See* Silva, Luiz Inácio Lula da

Maastricht Treaty (1991), 164–65
Al-Maliki, Nuri, 210–11
Maoism, 138, 252
Mao Zedong: as both nationalist
    and communist leader, 138;
    and Great Leap Forward, 135,
    138–39, 245; and Great Proletarian
    Cultural Revolution, 135–38, 139,
    245; identification of, 252; major
    political movements under, 138–39;
    and Red Guards, 139; and victor
    narrative, 133–34
Mara Salvatrucha (MS-13) gang, 190
Marxism, 138
Mazen, Abu. *See* Abbas, Mahmud
McCain, John, 24, 26, 34, 34n6, 252
McCrystal, Stanley, 29, 252
Mello, Sérgio Vieira de, 183
Menderes, Adnan, 212
Merkel, Angela, 117, 128
Mexico: and drugs, 3, 186, 190; and
    economic shocks, 175; and global
    exports, 185; and immigration and
    remittances, 176; and NAFTA, 116,
    177, 181, 186; U.S.-Mexican relations,
    180–81, 186, 190. *See also* Latin
    America
Middle East, 196–224; overview,
    196–97; Arab-Israeli conflict,
    197–205, 221; Arab Spring, 218–21,
    228; conclusion, 221; geographical
    region of, 196; Iran and Iraq,
    205–15; Radical Islam, 215–18;
    Turkey, 211–15
Monnet, Jean, 153, 165
Monroe, James, 179, 253
Monroe Doctrine, 12–13, 179, 184, 253
Morales, Evo, 177–78, 181, 189
Mossadegh, Muhammad, 205–206,
    253

Motives of intervening parties, humanitarian intervention issue, 69–70
Mubarak, Hosni, 217, 219–20, 253
Mughniyyah, Imad, 201
Mújica, José, 189
Muslim Brotherhood (MB) of Egypt, 196, 215–16, 223, 253
Al-Mussawi, Abbas, 201

NAFTA (North American Free Trade Agreement), 113, 116, 177, 181, 186, 255
Nanjing Massacre, 134, 138, 142, 253
Nasrallah, Hasan, 201
Al-Nasser, Gamal 'Abd, 199, 216, 254
Nationalism of China: American understanding of, 128–29; and anti-Japanese sentiment, 142; and Century of Humiliation, 132–33; and Chinese identity, 129–30, 230; and founding of the PRC, 138; and the fourth generation, 135–36; and Japanese militarism, 137; as key to transition from communist to capitalist ideologies, 141; as party propaganda, 129; and pride in Chinese superiority over U.S., 131; and pride in "pasts" as central to, 130; and Sinocentric cultural nationalism, 132, 141; understanding nature of, 137–38; and victimization narratives, 134–35; and Zhao Wei affair, 136–37
Nationals' rescue as nonhumanitarian intervention, 72
NATO (North Atlantic Treaty Organization): and the Arab Spring, 15, 30–31; Article V invoked after 9/11, 19; creation of, 15–16; defined, 255; and international security, 44, 59; intervention in Libyan Civil War (2011), 30–31, 66, 70, 81, 92–93; and Kosovo intervention, 67–68, 90
Negroponte, John, 21, 254
Neoconservatives ("neo-cons") of Bush era, 14, 254

Neoliberalism: defined, 254; and EU, 7, 162; and international security, 43, 45; and Latin America, 176–79
Neorealism (structural realism), 42–44, 254
Netanyahu, Benjamin, 202, 204, 254
NGOs (nongovernmental organizations): and the global economy, 102; and humanitarian aid, 74; and human rights, 46, 60; and international security, 45, 46
9/11 attacks. *See* September 11, 2001
Nixon, Richard, 17, 109, 114, 255
Nongovernmental organizations (NGOs). *See* NGOs
Noriega, Manuel, 18, 95, 255
North American Free Trade Agreement. *See* NAFTA
Northern Triangle, 190
North-South divide, 45, 255
NPT (Nuclear Nonproliferation Treaty), 52
Nuclear Nonproliferation Treaty (NPT), 52
Nuclear proliferation, 143, 226

OAS. *See* Organization of American States
Obama, Barack: agenda faced after 2008 election, 26–27; anti-Iraq War speech, 25; background of, 24–25; and bin Laden's killing, 29–30; and Copenhagen summit, 31, 240; and Cuba, 191; "Energy and Climate Partnership for the Americas," 187; failure to close Guantanamo Bay, 27; first major policy decision of, 29; foreign policy of, 16; goals of, 31–32; and Iran, 208; and Kennedy comparison, 17, 33nn1–2; and Latin America, 173, 192; and Nobel Peace Prize, 27–28; popularity in Latin America, 187; as "practical idealist," 15; as presidential candidate (2008), 26; on Reagan, 17–18; "Renewing U.S. Leadership in the Americas," 182; and response to Arab Spring, 30–31; on U.S. exceptionalism, 32;

Obama, Barack (*continued*)
as U.S. senator, 25–26; worldwide
support for, 23–24
Occidentalism, 131
Olmert, Ehud, 203, 204, 256
OPEC (Organization of Petroleum
Exporting Countries), 154–55,
169n6, 169n7
Open method of coordination (EU),
162–63, 256
Opium Wars of 1840–1842 and
1856–1860, 132, 134, 138, 256
Organization of American States
(OAS), 59, 183, 256
Organization of Petroleum Exporting
Countries. *See* OPEC
Oslo Accords, 201, 257
Osman I, 211, 257
Overview of book, 6–7

Palestine Liberation Organization
(PLO), 200–203, 244
Palestinian Authority (PA), 202–203,
218, 257
Palin, Sarah, 26, 257
Peacekeeping, 72–74, 257
People's Liberation Army (PLA), 140,
143
People's Republic of China (PRC), 138,
140, 146, 239
Perpetual Peace (Kant), 43
Petraeus, David, 29, 258
Pinochet, Augusto, 188–89
Pinsker, Leo, 197
PLO. *See* Palestine Liberation
Organization
Post–Cold War period: and Chinese
preconceptions persist, 129; and
debate on new world order, 14–15;
and decline in terrorism, 48; effects
of changed global economics,
113; and emergence of China as
competitor, 114; floodgates opened
for finding "disappeared," 188;
foreign policies have fared well
during, 192; human intervention
problematic, 229; and human
rights issues emerged, 67; in

Latin America, 173; and nuclear
ambitions, 51; and structural shift
internationally, 41; and upheavals
in Haiti, 191–92; U.S. favorability in
decline in Latin America, 180. *See
also* Cold War period
Poverty and economics, 52–55
Poverty and inequality in Latin
America: and Chile as success
story, 175–76; countries affected by
inequality, 176; and decline in faith
in government, 174; and erosion
of middle class, 175, 176; and
globalization, 174–75; and rise in
civil society groups, 174
Powell, Colin, 21, 22, 258
Pragmatism and Latin America,
191–92
PRC. *See* People's Republic of China
Presidential leadership in world
affairs, 16–19. See also *names of
specific presidents*
"Problems without passports," 3, 7, 58
Putin, Vladimir, 26, 27, 258

Qajar dynasty, 205, 258
Qutb, Sayyid, 216–17, 259

Rabin, Yitzhak, 202, 259
Radical Islam: founding of, 216;
Hizballah (Hezbollah) as success
story, 218; and Islamic Revolution
in Iran, 217–18; and Muslim
Brotherhood of Egypt, 215–16; and
al-Qaeda in Pakistan, 216–17; and
Sayyid Qutb, 216; and the Taliban,
217; Yassin as founder of Hamas,
216
Rafsanjani, Hashemi, 208, 259
Rape of Nanking, The (Chang), 134
Reagan, Ronald, 17–18, 114, 259
Realism, defined, 259
Realist theory, and international
security, 42–43, 259
Red Guards (China), 135, 136, 137, 139,
259
"Reform and Opening" (China),
139–41

Remittances, 176–77, 186, 194, 259
Responsibility to protect, humanitarian intervention issue, 68–69
Rice, Condoleeza, 25, 260
Rio Group, 183–84
Rogue states, 33, 229
Romney, Mitt, 32, 260
Roosevelt, Franklin, 16, 31, 260
Roosevelt, Theodore, 12–13, 16, 260
Rothschild, Edmund de, 197
Roussef, Dilma, 182
Rumsfeld, Donald, 21, 260
Rwandan genocide (1994), 72–73, 77–78, 80, 82, 89, 229, 230

Al-Sadat, Anwar, 199, 216, 260
Saleh, Ali Abdullah, 219
Sarkozy, Nicolas, 128
Saving Strangers (Wheeler), 69
Schuman, Robert, 153–54
Scowcroft, Brent, 21, 37, 261
Second Lebanon War, 203, 250, 261
Security, international. *See* International security
Selectivity of humanitarian intervention: and effectiveness as issue, 80; and inconsistency of interventions, 78; and justification for Iraq War questioned, 80–81; and legitimacy of interventions, 79; and multilateral intervention preferable, 79–80; and realist international relations theory, 78–79; and regional organizations, 81; U.S. role minimized in Libya operation, 81; and weakness of emerging norm, 79
September 11, 2001: aftermath of, 14, 21; and bin Laden's killing, 30, 32; and Bush's reelection, 23; and changes in American policy, 20; defined, 261; and humanitarian interventions, 85–86; and images of terrorism, 47–48; and international equation, 19–20; as wake-up call, 4–5. *See also* Afghanistan; Al-Qaeda

Sezer, Ahmet Necdet, 214
Shalit, Gilad, 203
Sharon, Ariel, 202–203, 261
Silva, Luiz Inácio Lula da, 173, 178, 182–83, 186
Sino-Japanese "Jiawu" War of 1894–1895, 132, 142, 145, 262
Six Day War, 199, 262
Smith, Adam, 5
Smoot-Hawley tariff, 12
Social constructivism, and international security, 45–47
Somoza, Anastasio, 14, 262
South American Defense Council, 183
Stalin, Joseph, 16, 263

Talabani, Jalal, 210
Taliban: allied support for attacks on, 20; defined, 263; formation of, 217; and neutralizing of a necessity, 29, 91, 209; remote drone attacks on, 15
Tenet, George, 21, 263
Ten years of Chaos in China, 135–36, 147nn2–3. *See also* Jiang Wen; Red Guards; Zhao Wei affair
Terrorism, and international security, 47–50, 241, 263
Tiananmen Square in Beijing, 18, 138, 140, 264. *See also* Beijing Spring
Tindemans, Leo, 159
Transnational crime, 189
Treaty of Lausanne, 212, 264
Treaty of Lisbon, 168
Treaty of Rome, 154, 163, 170n16, 264
Treaty of Versailles, 12, 264
Treaty on European Union, 159–160
Truman, Harry, 16, 31, 264
Tuberculosis, 3, 55, 264
Turkey: and AKP, 213–15; Erdoğan's resolution of financial crisis, 214; as EU potential member, 156, 170n12–13, 221; and foreign policy changes, 215, 221; founding of, 211; and Gül's election, 214–15; and Kemal, 211–12; and Menderes, 212; and military coup in 1960, 212–13; questions on future of, 228; reforms instituted by Kemal (Atatürk), 212;

and resurgence of Islamists, 213;
and Treaty of Lausanne, 212,
264; and Welfare Party (Islamist)
1991, 213, 266
Twitter, 5, 219, 222, 223, 231

Uganda intervention by Israel (1976),
72, 84, 94, 96
UNASUR. *See* Union of South
American Nations
UN Charter paradigm, 82–83
Unilateralism doctrine of U.S., 27,
115–16
Union of South American Nations
(UNASUR), 181, 184
United Nations (UN): charter of,
82–83; and China, 143; defined,
265; establishment of, 59, 227; and
nationalism, 230; and no-fly zone
over Libya, 66; paying U.S. dues
to, 4; and ratification of NPT, 52;
and UNSCOP, 198, 265. *See also*
Humanitarian intervention cases;
NATO
United Nations Special Committee on
Palestine (UNSCOP), 198, 265
U.S.-China relations in 21st century:
and balance of power, 144, 236;
Chinese nationalism limits
friendship with U.S., 145–46;
crisis management needed to
avoid conflict, 146–47; and distrust
of China by Americans, 146; and
energy and natural resources in
demand, 145; evolution of, 144;
and geography as mitigating
factor, 144–45; and hedging of
policies, 147; and probability of
conflict, 143–44; and U.S.-China
energy insecurity spiral, 145;
and U.S. security environment,
144
U.S.-Mexican relations. *See under*
Mexico

Venezuela. *See* Chávez, Hugo
Vietnam War, 14, 40, 266
Vilayet-e Faqih (Khomeini), 217

Village in August (Xiao Jun), 134
Virtue Party (VP), 213, 266

Walzer, Michael, 75
"War of Resistance against Japan" of
1931/1937–1945, 132, 147n1
Warriors of Heaven and Earth (film),
137. *See also* Nationalism of China
Washington, George, 11–12
Weapons of mass destruction. *See*
WMD
Wheeler, Nicholas, 69
White Revolution (Iran), 206, 266
Wilson, Woodrow, 13, 14, 27, 266
WMD (Weapons of mass destruction):
and Cold War, 40; defined, 266;
failure to find in Iraq, 86; and
Saddam Hussein, 21, 22, 91; spread
of, 50–52, 227
Wolfowitz, Paul, 112
Women: and "comfort women" in
Asia, 233n4; enhancing human
rights in Afghanistan for, 91;
improved representation in Latin
America by, 177; in protest in Iran,
24; slaughter of in Darfur, 229; and
suppression of family planning in
Iran, 208; and White Revolution
(Iran), 206
World Bank, 110–12, 115, 266
World Social Forums, 174–75
World Trade Organization (WTO):
and China, 115; creation of, 106;
and demise of multilateral trade
negotiations, 108; as dispute
settlement forum, 107; and Doha
Round (2002), 107–108, 242; GATT
replaced by, 107, 113
WTO (World Trade Organization).
See World Trade Organization

Yassin, Ahmad, 216
Yasukuni Shrine, 137
Yom Kippur War, 199, 267

Al-Zawahiri, Ayman, 216–17
Zhao Wei affair, 136–37
Zionism, 197, 267